A Tale of Two Factions

SUNY series in the Social and Economic History of the Middle East

Donald Quataert, editor

A Tale of Two Factions

Myth, Memory, and Identity in Ottoman Egypt and Yemen

Jane Hathaway

State University of New York Press

Published by
State University of New York Press, Albany

Printed in the United States of America

For information, address State University of New York Press,
90 State Street, Suite 700, Albany, NY 12207

Production by Kelli Williams
Marketing by Anne M. Valentine

Library of Congress Cataloging-in-Publication Data

Hathaway, Jane.
A tale of two factions : myth, memory, and identity in Ottoman Egypt and Yemen / Jane Hathaway.
p. cm. — (SUNY series in the social and economic history of the Middle East)
Includes bibliographical references (p.) and index.
ISBN 0-7914-5883-0 (alk. paper) — ISBN 0-7914-5884-9 (alk. paper)
1. Egypt—History—1517–1882. 2. Egypt—Economic conditions—1517–1882. 3. Egypt—Social conditions. 4. Yemen—History. 5. Yemen—Economic conditions. 6. Yemen—Social conditions. I. Title. II. Series.

DT97.H38 2003
962′.03—dc22 2003055622

10 9 8 7 6 5 4 3 2 1

In Memoriam

Ulrich Haarmann
Cem Taylan
Jeanette Wakin
Marilyn Waldman

Contents

Abbreviations

BSOAS	*Bulletin of the School of Oriental and African Studies*
EI[1]	*Encyclopaedia of Islam*, 1st edition
EI[2]	*Encyclopaedia of Islam*, 2nd edition

Note on Transliteration

I have omitted diacritical markings, except for *ʿayn* and *hamza*, in Arabic and Turkish proper nouns and in Turkish common nouns not derived from Arabic, as well as in personal names, such as Ismail and Osman, commonly written without diacriticals.

Otherwise, the transliteration system used for both Arabic and Ottoman Turkish is that employed by the *International Journal of Middle East Studies*. Names and titles of Ottoman officials and provincial grandees, as well as titles of literary works in Ottoman Turkish and the names of their authors, are rendered in Turkish; Egyptian and Yemeni place names, literary titles in Arabic, and the names of their authors are rendered in Arabic. Provincial offices, with the exception of *defterdar*, are rendered in Arabic. Terms that can be found in English dictionaries, such as "mamluk," "reaya," "Sufi," and "ulema," retain the spellings found there.

Illustrations

Acknowledgments

I love historical mysteries, and this book is the product of my obstinate desire to solve one of the more perplexing ones within my own specialty, the study of Ottoman Egypt. Egyptian society in the seventeenth century was riven by the rivalry between two factions, the Faqaris and Qasimis, whose origins no one could explain. This book results from my search for their origins and the unexpected things I found along the way. The search has been marked by epiphanies that I would not have found credible had I not experienced them myself. Twice I was led to major revelations by happening to open books lying on conference exhibit tables. I learned about a major primary source, the *Sīrat al-Ẓāhir Baybars*, while listening to a conference paper by Professor Linda Northrup, an expert on the Mamluk sultanate.

The sources on which I have drawn in writing this book have been wildly eclectic, and the people who have contributed to its gestation have been similarly numerous, diverse, and far-flung. I have tried to acknowledge most of them in the endnotes. Here, I will limit myself to mentioning only major debts of gratitude; if I have omitted anyone, it is through absentmindedness alone. Research for this book was facilitated by a grant from the American Research Institute in Turkey, whose pleasant Istanbul facilities I enjoyed during the summers of 1997 and 1999 and whose library I used extensively during revisions in the summer of 2002. I am particularly grateful to ARIT-Istanbul's director, Dr. Anthony Greenwood, for locating a fairly obscure source after I had left Istanbul. I must also thank the Turkish Ministry of Culture for granting me research permission; the staff of the Topkapı Palace Library and the director of the Topkapı Palace Museum, Dr. Filiz Çağman; and the directors and staff of the Süleymaniye Library and the Başbakanlık Archives. Ohio State's College of Humanities awarded me two one-quarter Special Research Assignments that gave me time to pursue this research. For research assistance during the early stages of the project, I thank Boğaç Ergene,

Ayşe Koçoğlu, and Vincent Wilhite. I accomplished much of the writing at the Institute for Advanced Study in Princeton during the first part of 2000, when I was supposed to be working on a different project. For providing extremely congenial environments in which to undertake final revisions, I am grateful to the staff of the Atatürk Institute at Bosphorus University, and to its director, Şevket Pamuk, and Associate Director, Asım Karaömerlioğlu, as well as to the Institut Français d'Archéologie Orientale in Cairo, above all Christian Velud, Hoda Khouzam, and Richard McGregor. Thanks to Martha Mundy for moral support and guidance on Yemeni place names, to Leslie Peirce for useful advice on practical matters connected with preparation of the manuscript, and to Amalia Levanoni for providing some last minute Mamluk sources. Thanks to Donald Quataert for his encouragement and for accepting this book as part of the series he edits. My colleagues Stephen Dale, Barbara Hanawalt, and Geoffrey Parker read an earlier version of the manuscript and offered valuable comments, as did Gabriel Piterberg and an anonymous reader for the State University of New York Press. Thanks to John Tully of the Goldberg Center in Ohio State's Department of History and to Cord Camera for their help in producing the illustrations for this book.

When I started research for this book, I decided that I would dedicate the final product to the memory of my late colleague Marilyn Waldman, who died in 1996. In the intervening years, three more friends and colleagues have died, all prematurely. Although they lived in widely separated places and worked in different fields, all enriched my professional and personal life. All four, as well, were strikingly similar in their empathy, generosity, and profound humanism and humanity.

Finally, special thanks to Beshir and Stella, and above all to my husband, Robert "Mimar Bob" Simkins. May we never be the subject of similar origin myths.

Introduction

Centuries ago, in the land of Egypt, there were two factions: the Faqaris and the Qasimis. They had always been enemies; anything one faction got, the other had to acquire. Hence, they divided all the subprovinces of Egypt, along with all the wealth that the subprovinces produced, between them. In those days, Egypt was the largest province of the Ottoman Empire; the Ottoman governor would arrive in Cairo from Istanbul and divide up all the provincial offices between the two factions. This started sometime around 1640 and continued until about 1730, when the Faqaris finally vanquished the Qasimis. But some claimed that the factions really originated with the Ottoman conquest of Egypt in 1517.

The paragraph you have just read is a précis of the conventional scholarly wisdom regarding the Faqaris and Qasimis, two large, rather diffuse military and political factions whose rivalry divided Egyptian society during the seventeenth and early eighteenth centuries of the Common Era. With a few contextual changes, however, it could just as easily describe the Blues and Greens of the late Roman Empire, the Guelphs and Ghibellines of medieval Tuscany, or even the Hatfields and McCoys of the postbellum United States. The bilateral character of this instance of factionalism differentiates it from earlier and later forms of multilateral rivalry in Egypt and elsewhere, leading one to suspect that the same sorts of factors that led to the emergence of better-studied two-faction systems also contributed to the appearance of the Faqaris and Qasimis.

This consideration is of some significance because historically, bilateral factionalism has shaped the political culture of numerous premodern societies. Neither late Roman nor medieval Tuscan politics and customs would be explicable without reference to the two-faction political scheme that divided these societies.[1] In early Islamic history, the Qays (northern Arab) and Yemen (southern Arab) factions, under a variety of synonymous appellations, utterly dominated the politics of the Umayyad caliphate (661–750 C.E.).[2] Thus, when a similar phenomenon appears in seventeenth-century Egypt, it seems only reasonable to examine it through the same lens as that through which we typically view the just noted systems. In other words, no matter how many permutations the two factions undergo, their salient feature is their insistent bilateralism, and that feature should remain in the foreground of our analysis.

Yet this turns out to be an almost insurmountable challenge where Egypt's factions are concerned. For the Faqaris and Qasimis took shape in a society whose political culture had been dominated by households, that is, conglomerations of patron-client ties that culminated in the household head.[3] Such a household culture had likewise been a feature of the Mamluk sultanate, which ruled Egypt from 1250 until the Ottoman conquest in 1517. These households are frequently called "factions" in secondary scholarship,[4] hence the temptation to treat the Faqaris and Qasimis as simply two factions among many such. More generally, a pervasive tendency exists in secondary scholarship on Ottoman Egypt to assume that the political culture that emerged during the Ottoman era was fundamentally similar to that of the Mamluk sultanate, even if it were not a continuation or revival of Mamluk usages but contained undeniably Ottoman elements.[5] By this logic, the template of Mamluk sultanate-era political culture as constructed in secondary scholarship—featuring powerful emirs, multiple factions, and a foreign elite alienated from the "indigenous" population—should suffice to explain Ottoman-era political culture. This tendency is compounded by the influence of nationalism, specifically Egyptian nationalism, and the hegemony of the Egyptian nation-state's current territorial boundaries in secondary scholarship on both Mamluk and Ottoman Egypt.[6] As a result, the distinctive bilateralism of the Faqaris and Qasimis is overlooked or explained away as yet another example of "the old pattern of Mamluk factionalism."[7]

But these two factions are different from the multiple factions of the Mamluk sultanate. Their essential character and the manner in which they operated are inextricably linked to the period in which they emerged. Indeed, if we look outside the boundaries of present-day Egypt, we see other Ottoman provinces and regions just outside Ottoman territory where bilateral factionalism emerged during the same general period. In Ottoman Lebanon and Palestine, the ancient Northern and Southern, or Qays and Yemen, Arab factions were the focus of Ottoman administration; Ottoman governors by and large tended to favor the Qaysis, although this was by no means a strict policy.[8] In Damascus, localized Janissaries competed for positions and revenues with Janissaries newly arrived from the imperial capital;[9] Aleppo's imperial Janissaries, meanwhile, competed with the descendants of the Prophet Muhammad.[10] East of the Ottoman border, in Iran, the Safavid Shah ᶜAbbas (r.1588–1629) went so far as to encourage the inveterate rivalry of two factions, ostensibly Sufi in origin, known as Haydaris and Niᶜmatullahis.[11] Never have the Faqaris and Qasimis been compared to any of these other regional bilateral factional systems, yet the very suggestion of doing so immediately broadens our frame of reference while, at the same time, linking it to the chronological context in which the factions emerged. The Faqari and Qasimi factions may have been unique to Ottoman Egypt, but the broader phenomenon of bilateral factionalism was not. On the contrary, Egypt's two factions and those of other Ottoman provinces, to say nothing of contemporary non-Ottoman territories and bilateral factional systems in other eras, were symptomatic of decentralized empires with populations of disparate backgrounds.

Egypt's Place in the Ottoman Empire

By the same token, Egypt's place in the Ottoman Empire was distinctive but not entirely different from that of other provinces. During its first century as an Ottoman province, Egypt was instrumental in the Ottoman conquest of and subsequent administration and defense of Yemen; together, Egypt and Yemen shouldered the Ottoman defense against the Portuguese in the Red Sea and Indian Ocean. In the middle years of the following century, troops from Egypt played a key role in the Ottoman struggle for and ultimate conquest of Crete (1669), along with numerous Anatolian mercenaries and North African naval forces.[12] In keeping with these extraordinary duties, Egypt's provincial administration was distinctive. Egypt's territorial integrity was preserved when other territories conquered by the Ottomans were subdivided. The *timar* system was never imposed in Egypt; instead, by the end of the seventeenth century, the governor held the province as an enormous tax farm. Subprovincial governors were likewise salaried tax farmers, while the regiments of Ottoman soldiery stationed in the province received cash salaries from the imperial treasury. Large contingents of soldiery stationed in Egypt participated routinely in Ottoman campaigns against the Hapsburg Empire in central and southeastern Europe, and against the Shiᶜite Safavid empire in Iran. And every year, Egypt sent a pilgrimage caravan to the Holy Cities of

Mecca and Medina, providing grain for the inhabitants of those cities and protection for the pilgrims.[13]

In these duties, Egypt was distinctive among Ottoman provinces. It was not, however, unique. The North African provinces and Yemen were also *timar*-free, and by the late seventeenth century, in any case, the *timar* had been largely displaced by tax farming throughout the empire.[14] Damascus sent its own pilgrim caravan to the Holy Cities every year.[15] Meanwhile, Baghdad served as the Ottoman "forward" province against the Safavids while Hungary and Belgrade fulfilled the same role against the Hapsburgs.[16] In short, Egypt played its distinctive fiscal, military, and ceremonial roles in combination with these and other provinces. Members of Egypt's households accordingly cultivated patron-client ties not only with officials in Istanbul, but also with households in other Ottoman provinces.[17] Thus, to view Egypt as hermetically sealed within its current political boundaries, sufficient unto itself, is to deny its importance as an integral part of the Ottoman Empire. Moreover, the picture of Ottoman Egypt's political culture that results from such an approach will inevitably be distorted.

Egypt and the Crisis of the Seventeenth Century

This distinctively Ottoman context is critical to our purposes, for it holds the clues to the factions' origins. The Faqari and Qasimi factions were forged in the encounter between Egypt and other provinces, on the one hand, and between Egypt and Ottoman imperial institutions, on the other. These encounters were colored in turn by the political, social, demographic, and economic changes that swept the entire empire—and indeed, much of the world—in the course of the seventeenth century.

So far as the factions' origins are concerned, the demographic dislocations are arguably the most critical feature of the crises, which began at the close of the sixteenth century. The wave of peasant upheavals and migrations collectively known as the Jalali (Celali) rebellions brought peasant mercenaries into the Anatolian countryside and also into the hinterlands of other Ottoman provinces, including Egypt.[18] Transformations in neighboring polities also resonated in Ottoman territories. As the Russian Empire grew more aggressively expansionist, certain of its regional populations moved closer to or even into Ottoman lands. Meanwhile, as Georgian slaves began to displace the Turcoman Kızılbash tribal elite in the Safavid Empire, these tribal elements became available for Ottoman exploitation. Safavid manipulation of other populations under their rule, as well as the erratic exchanges of territory between the Ottomans and Safavids during these years, added to this demographic flux.[19] Balkan and Anatolian mercenaries begin to appear in the entourages of provincial grandees, along with mercenaries from among the peasant and tribal populations of the Arab provinces themselves and elite military slaves (mamluks) from the Caucasus. Egypt confronted these same sorts of profound demographic change among its military and administrative echelons, as well as among its tribal and peasant populations. Balkan and Anatolian mercenaries entered the same households as Circassian and Georgian mamluks; both might find themselves elbow to elbow with bedouin or Turcoman tribesmen.[20] In such circumstances, myriad new regional influences came to bear on Egypt's household political culture. At the same time, group cohesion, particularly for men and women of disparate ethnic and regional backgrounds within a single household, inevitably became a vital concern. This was the atmosphere in which the Faqari and Qasimi factions emerged, and I will argue in later chapters that they emerged at least in part as a result of these changes.

These crises contributed to a process of decentralization that affected all of the Ottoman provinces in the course of the seventeenth century. Decentralization is, however, as problematic a concept in its own way as the outmoded paradigm of a three hundred-year Ottoman decline beginning in the late sixteenth century and running straight through to the westernizing reforms of the nineteenth century. Historians of the Ottoman Empire have by and large accepted a revisionist interpretation whereby the empire suffers a series of wrenching economic and demographic crises in the late sixteenth and early seventeenth centuries, resulting in a slow but steady adaptation of its fiscal and administrative structures and practices to a changed reality.[21] Notwithstanding, they acknowledge that Ottoman provincial administration during the seventeenth century became increasingly decentralized, at least until the reforms of the Köprülü family of grand viziers late in the century. The "decentralization" paradigm, however, as it is deployed in secondary scholarship, can become a convenient substitute for the "decline" paradigm inasmuch as decentralization is often portrayed as inherently "bad" while a highly centralized state is portrayed as inherently "good."[22] In the historiography of Ottoman Egypt, furthermore, decentralization is depicted as a zero-sum game: under a decentralized administration, Egypt's grandees and local notables assume predominant authority whereas a centralized administration suppresses these grandees.[23] That is to say, "central" and "provincial," and by the same token "centralized" and "decentralized," become mutually exclusive categories. Such a scheme ignores the subtle interplays among different ranks of personnel firmly rooted in Egypt, temporarily based in Egypt, transplanted from the capital, and operating from the capital, to say nothing of contacts and exchanges independent of the imperial government between Egypt and other Ottoman provinces.

As misguided as the false dichotomy between center and province is that between an alien (read: Turkish) ruling elite and a static "indigenous" (read: Arab) population, a notion that is particularly tenacious where Egypt is concerned.[24] Egypt's factionalism was not simply a game of the elite, to which the "common people" were oblivious. Rather, as the chronicles themselves point out, this brand of bilateral factionalism was society-wide: "soldiers, bedouin, and peasants" participated in it. At no time, furthermore, was Egypt's population of all economic strata in greater flux than in the seventeenth century, when, in addition to the inflow from outside the province, migration of peasants, Muslim scholars (ulema), and tribespeople from the countryside to Cairo and other urban centers was rampant.[25] As in other Ottoman provinces and in the imperial capital, the Janissary corps in particular was by the seventeenth century thoroughly integrated with the artisanate; meanwhile, artisans, peasants, and tribesmen had the opportunity to participate in the military-administrative cadres as mercenaries or as paid proxies for those whose names appeared in the salary registers.[26] Although a wide gap undeniably existed between, say, the pilgrimage commander and a humble peasant in the Nile Delta, in-between their two stations lay a fluid, constantly changing welter of commercial, military, and administrative positions open to a broad range of people of various ethnic, geographical, and occupational backgrounds. In this milieu, as I will argue in the next chapter, bilateral factionalism served as a unifying force.

If Egypt's two-faction system is indeed typical of decentralized empires with diverse populations, then the Faqari and Qasimi factions can offer a key to how decentralized provincial administration worked. In their formation, we can discover a key mechanism by which participants in the political culture of an Ottoman province manipulated decentralization to make it a viable environment within which to inhabit, administer, and extract a living from that province.

The Narrative of the Factions' History

Scholarship on the Faqaris and Qasimis dates back to the late 1950s and early 1960s, when Peter M. Holt laid out the basic narrative of the factions' political history. With a few modifications to Holt's conclusions, based on my own earlier research, this narrative runs as follows. The factions probably emerged in the early decades of the seventeenth century. Beginning in the 1630s, the Faqari faction was dominated by the great Ridvan Bey, who monopolized the post of pilgrimage commander (*amīr al-ḥājj*) for an extraordinary twenty-five years, from 1631 until his death in 1656. Ridvan Bey's political ally was ʿAli Bey, governor of the huge, grain-rich subprovince of Jirja in Upper Egypt. During the 1640s, Ridvan's and ʿAli's hegemony was unsuccessfully challenged by two presumed Qasimis, Qansuh and Memi, or Mamay, Beys. Following ʿAli's death in 1653 and Ridvan's in 1656, Mehmed Bey al-Faqari assumed the governorship of Jirja and rebelled against the Ottoman governor, forcing a military expedition against him. Perhaps in response to this rebellion, a strain of Bosnian beys, evidently trained in Istanbul, was injected into the Qasimi faction; their leader, Ahmed Bey Bushnaq ("the Bosniak"), was appointed pilgrimage commander and seems to have given the Qasimis the hegemony that the Faqaris had previously held. Ultimately, however, the Ottoman central authority withdrew its support from him, as well. In the final years of the seventeenth century, Egypt's administration was dominated by a Faqari triumvirate consisting of two regimental officers, Hasan Agha Bilifya of the Gönüllüyan regiment and Mustafa Kâhya al-Qazdağlı of the Janissary (Mustahfizan) regiment, along with Hasan Agha's son-in-law, the financial administrator (*defterdar*) Ismail Bey; they were briefly challenged in the 1690s by a rival Faqari chieftain, Ibrahim Bey b. Dhu'l-Faqar, and by the militant Janissary barracks boss Küçük Mehmed Başodabaşı. In the opening years of the eighteenth century, the conflict between the two factions became more graphic; the upheavals fomented by another militant Janissary boss, Ifranj Ahmed, resulted in a civil war pitting the Faqaris, allied with the Janissaries, against the Qasimis, allied with the rival ʿAzeban regiment. Despite the assassination of the Qasimi chieftain ʿIvaz Bey in the course of the conflict, the Qasimis emerged strengthened under the leadership of the superannuated Ibrahim Bey Abu Shanab, a purported nephew of Ahmed Bey Bushnaq. During the 1720s, however, the Qasimi faction was ripped asunder by the insoluble conflict between ʿIvaz Bey's son Ismail Bey and Abu Shanab's mamluk Çerkes ("Circassian") Mehmed Bey. Çerkes Mehmed went so far as to ally with the Faqari chieftain Dhu'l-Faqar Bey against Ibn ʿIvaz, whom Dhu'l-Faqar ultimately assassinated. With Ibn ʿIvaz out of the way, however, the Faqari-Qasimi struggle reignited, culminating in the death of Çerkes Mehmed and the virtual annihilation of the Qasimis in 1730. Dhu'l-Faqar Bey, meanwhile, had been assassinated, and the Faqaris were now dominated by the household founded by Mustafa Kâhya al-Qazdağlı. The Qazdağlı household would ultimately supersede the politics of bilateral factionalism, effectively running Egypt until the French invasion of 1798.[27]

The Origin Myths

Existing alongside this historical reality, nonetheless, is a body of lore that explains the origins of the factions within the context of three rather formulaic origin myths. In a seminal article published in the *Bulletin of the School of Oriental and African Studies* in 1962, Holt carefully dissected the various strands of origin mythology[28] and concluded that there are three basic origin myths: (1) The myth presented in the four early eighteenth-century chronicles known collectively as the Damurdashi group and repeated, in edited form, in the chronicle of ᶜAbd al-Rahman al-Jabarti (1754–1825) notes the pervasiveness in the late 1600s of two factions called Saᶜd and Haram; these appellations usually denote the two bedouin blocs allied with the Faqaris and Qasimis, respectively. A stream of parallel binary oppositions precedes the introduction of Saᶜd and Haram; thus, in the chronicle of al-Qinali, "Tubbaᶜi and . . . Kulaybi, Zughbi and Hilali, Qalaʾuni and Baybarsi."[29] (2) A myth presented by al-Jabarti suggests that the eponymous founders of the factions, Dhu'l-Faqar and Qasim, were the sons of an aged Mamluk emir who quarreled while displaying their equestrian skills before the victorious Ottoman sultan Selim I. (A more elaborate version of this myth appears in the early eighteenth-century chronicle of Ahmed Çelebi b. ᶜAbd al-Ghani.)[30] (3) An alternative myth presented by both the Damurdashi chronicles and al-Jabarti focuses on the rivalry between Dhu'l-Faqar Bey the pilgrimage commander and Qasim Bey the *defterdar*. The rivalry is "resolved" after each bey invites the other to a feast at his home, and Dhu'l-Faqar demonstrates that the numerous mamluks in attendance at his feast far outstrip Qasim's splendid banquet hall.[31]

Since the appearance of Holt's article, those few historians who have addressed the problem of reconciling these quite disparate myths with the apparent historical reality have attempted to identify two eponymous seventeenth-century faction-founders, that is, two beys named Dhu'l-Faqar and Qasim who flourished during the seventeenth century. Michael Winter, in his 1992 book *Egyptian Society under Ottoman Rule, 1517–1798*, seems more or less content with Holt's findings in a slightly earlier article.[32] Doris Behrens-Abouseif goes considerably farther in *Egypt's Adjustment to Ottoman Rule.* After a careful consideration of early Ottoman-era sources, particularly the too seldom-consulted chronicle of Ahmad b. Zunbul, she concludes that the Qasimi and Faqari factions did indeed stem from two seventeenth-century grandees named Qasim Bey and Dhu'l-Faqar Bey, although the latter was not the better-documented late seventeenth-century Dhu'l-Faqar, the father of Ibrahim Bey b. Dhu'l-Faqar, but an earlier grandee of the same name.[33] Moreover, the story of jousting before Sultan Selim drew on reality, for Selim, she claimed, based on Ibn Zunbul, had sponsored a series of equestrian contests between Ottoman and Mamluk champions.[34] Holt himself, in his earlier article, had identified a powerful and long-lived Qasim Bey who seemed a viable candidate for founder of the Qasimis.[35] Rejecting both of the seventeenth-century Dhu'l-Faqar Beys as insufficiently visible, Holt hazarded the guess that Ridvan Bey al-Faqari, the highly visible and influential grandee who monopolized the pilgrimage command from 1631–56, might have been given the honorific title Dhu'l-Faqar by some of his admirers.[36]

Notwithstanding the insights gained from these scholarly efforts, this approach is fundamentally unsound. Most obviously, by looking for two eponymous founders, we are allowing the myths to shape our inquiry. Outside of the origin myths themselves, who said the founders have to be eponymous, and who said there have to be two of them? This assumption itself reflects a tenacious positivist approach to narrative sources whereby a chronicle is first and foremost a mine of facts rather than a coherent narrative in its own right, with a coherent internal structure.[37] Only by abandoning this approach can we restore the cogency of the origin myths and reevaluate them as something more than facts masquerading as fiction.

In addition to the basic disparity between the myths and the reality of seventeenth-century Egypt, we must confront the fact that the two factions and their origin myths are all adduced in eighteenth-century chronicles whose descriptions were later spliced together and edited by al-Jabarti in the early nineteenth century. Seventeenth-century narratives, however, with the intriguing exceptions of Yusuf b. Muhammad al-Shirbini's *Hazz al-quḥūf* and Evliya Çelebi's *Book of Travels* (*Seyahatname*), do not mention the factions. Nor do the factions appear in central Ottoman archival documents until the 1720s.[38] Indeed, historians of Ottoman Egypt are in a position strikingly similar to that of our colleagues who investigate the origins of the Ottoman Empire: the latter must rely on a crystallized narrative presented in fifteenth-century chronicles to recapture the reality of the late thirteenth and early fourteenth centuries. And much of this narrative consists, in fact, of strands of myth, filtered through collective memory, codified, and reified at more than a century's distance.[39] The Faqari and Qasimi origin myths would seem to be the end results of a similar process.

Rather than ignoring this intertextuality, we need to address it directly. In other words, we need to ask why grandees in the early seventeenth century would deploy these particular origin myths, or why eighteenth-century chroniclers would deploy them to explain seventeenth-century phenomena. Turning to the myths themselves, why do they take the eccentric forms that they do? Why do the Damurdashi chronicles spin out strings of paired opposites? Why do al-Jabarti and Ahmed Çelebi dredge up the tale of the aged emir and his two restless sons? Where does the tale of Dhu'l-Faqar and Qasim Beys exchanging dinner invitations come from? Are these simply eighteenth-century inventions imposed on a vaguely remembered sixteenth- and seventeenth-century reality?

In point of fact, some of the allusions to be found in the origin myths are definitely not eighteenth-century inventions but derive from much longer established bodies of popular lore. In particular, al-Qinali's strings of opposites—Tubbaʿi and Kulaybi, Hilali and Zughbi, Qalaʾuni and Baybarsi—allude to characters in well-known Arabic popular epics that were recited orally, although they were also written down by at least the eighteenth and nineteenth centuries.[40] The allusions are to pre- and early-Islamic history and to the history of the Mamluk sultanate, but as portrayed in popular stories. This realization points toward the conclusion that the factions' origins were placed within the framework of widely recited popular narratives.

The logical next question is, why bother imposing these folkloric templates on the factions? And why do so in the eighteenth century if chroniclers in the seventeenth century, when the factions ostensibly appeared and were most active, had not seen fit to do so? Perhaps the eighteenth-century chroniclers could not remember when or how the factions had actually emerged but were forced to resort to stock "origin myth" devices, often drawn from well-known bodies of popular lore. This does not necessarily mean that the origin myths presented by the eighteenth-century chroniclers are devoid of evidentiary value; on the contrary, they illustrate the eighteenth-century administrative cadre's conception of their predecessors a century earlier. And it makes sense that these origin myths should be codified in the early decades of the eighteenth century, just as the factions themselves were nearing desuetude: the Qasimi faction split in two and was devastated in 1730 by the Faqaris, who were themselves shortly eclipsed by a single household, the Qazdağlıs, that arose from within their midst.[41]

And what of the factions during their purported heyday in the seventeenth century? Why are they so seldom mentioned in the available contemporary sources? Perhaps precisely because they were emerging, crystallizing, shaping their own identities. Predictably, what references we have to the factions during this early period are tentative and imprecise, rather than formulaic and pat. And, as we shall see in a later chapter, they don't necessarily occur in chronicles limited to Egypt. It took decades for a coherent picture of the factions to "gel"—that is, for them to assume "from time immemorial" status and to come to seem eternal and inevitable.

In the history of Ottoman Egypt in general, there seems to be a consistent "lag time" of at least several decades, and sometimes as much as a century, between the introduction of a new social and/or political phenomenon and its reification as a permanent fixture. Elsewhere, I have used the chronicle of Ottoman Egypt that the poet Ismail al-Khashshab (d. 1815) wrote for the French occupying force as a sort of whipping boy because of the obvious errors the author makes in representing fairly recent Egyptian history; he bungles even events that occurred less than a century before he was writing.[42] Still, his account is telling because it reflects the collective memory of a relatively high echelon of bureaucrats and intellectuals. Al-Khashshab admits that his history derives not from consulting previous authoritative histories nor from keeping a written record of events, still less from the sort of "field work" of deciphering tombstone inscriptions to which his contemporary and friend, the historian al-Jabarti, had recourse;[43] instead, al-Khashshab relied on the stories or narrated events (*akhbār*) told him by his father and by other members of the ulema.[44] Inevitably, his *Tadhkira li-ahl al-baṣāʾir* (*Memoir for the Discerning*) transmits some of these popularly conceived narratives. Thus, we find that the early nineteenth-century intelligentsia remembered the Faqari and Qasimi factions, but in rather broad strokes; they were confused as to the intra-factional divisions that ultimately tore the two factions asunder in the 1720s and 1730s. Al-Khashshab portrays the Qasimi chieftain Çerkes Mehmed Bey as a Faqari, of all things, simply because Çerkes was the mortal enemy of Ismail Bey b. ʿIvaz Bey, who was undeniably a Qasimi.[45] The enemy of a Qasimi, al-Khashshab must have reasoned, had to be a Faqari. He could not grasp that Çerkes Mehmed and Ismail b. ʿIvaz were two Qasimi leaders whose enmity divided that faction. For already, popular perception of these two obsolete factions had ossified, so that it was no longer possible to regard them as dynamic entities that changed over time. Each faction had crystallized in popular memory as monolithic in itself, and as irrevocably opposed to the other faction. In fact, the defining characteristic of each faction was its opposition to the other; a single faction that divided against itself had no place in this scheme of things.

If we go back a century farther, however, we see the chroniclers of the early to mid-eighteenth century doing essentially the same thing: presenting a crystallized memory of the previous century as objective fact. Where al-Khashshab—and presumably a whole generation of intelligentsia—saw two entrenched factions devoid of internal divisions, chroniclers such as Ahmed Çelebi and the Damurdashi chroniclers saw two factions that were forged in the crucible of the Ottoman conquest of Egypt, and that were already fully formed by the early seventeenth century. The idea of two gradually and fitfully coalescing blocs whose development was neither parallel nor symmetrical did not occur to these chroniclers who, after all, had barely known a time when the factions did not dominate Egypt's political life. In the latter decades of the sixteenth century and into the seventeenth century, meanwhile, the Ottoman conquest and the early decades of Ottoman rule in Egypt had similarly blurred, becoming an era when valorous Circassian chivalry lost out to the sheer destructive might of gun and cannon power, and when the noble sultans Selim and Süleyman saved Circassian chivalry from utter obliteration.[46]

Collective Memory and Invented Tradition

What we are witnessing in these eighteenth-century chronicles, then, is the deployment or modification of tropes and motifs from older bodies of lore to describe seventeenth-century developments in Egypt's political culture. I believe, however, that this textual strategy was not limited to the chroniclers but was adopted by the faction members themselves. Specifically, the faction members used the frameworks and tropes of popular epics to explain their own reality and to foster group cohesion within each faction.

As a result of the long shadow cast by the Mamluk sultanate and its institutions, secondary scholarship on Egypt during the Ottoman period has stressed the efficacy of a nebulous "Mamluk institution" whereby slave status and service to a common master acted as the chief sources of group cohesion among recruits to Egypt's military and administrative cadres.[47] Meanwhile, the convenient rubrics of "inveterate factionalism" and a "Turkish-speaking elite" minimize the challenge of socializing a raw young recruit, far from his (or sometimes her) native land, language, and traditions, to an entirely new life-style and career, to say nothing of instilling loyalty to a patron, household, and faction of whom the recruit had no prior knowledge. This was a time, furthermore, when this cadre consisted of ever more disparate elements: recruits of the *devshirme*—the practice of "collecting" boys from among the Christian subjects of the Ottoman Balkans and Anatolia—Caucasian mamluks, Balkan and Anatolian mercenaries, local elements from the Arab provinces, deserters from various enemy armies. The so-called military-administrative elite was itself riven by wealth and status disparities: while the beys and the higher officers competed in ostentation and political leverage with the Ottoman governor, the rank and file, as well as the lower officer echelons, were soldiers and shopkeepers of decidedly humble substance. In the light of these considerations, the fact that two factions endured for roughly a century and that tenacious factional loyalties were still visible decades thereafter seems extraordinary.

In such circumstances, the factions themselves had to serve as sources of cohesion and community feeling. Factionalism in and of itself is a socially divisive phenomenon. Notwithstanding, each individual faction can incorporate members from disparate backgrounds by imbuing them with a sense of group cohesion; this is particularly noticeable in a society in which two factions predominate since few things foster unity like hostility toward a common foe. Even so, how to encourage raw recruits to identify with one faction of two, with which they had no prior connection, of which they had presumably never heard before coming to Cairo? I believe that the answer may have lain in popular stories of the sort described above. But it was not as if some calculating mastermind cynically plied the new recruits with seductive stories of swashbuckling heroes and swooning maidens. The process had to have been far more subtle and perhaps even unconscious. As the factions took shape and became a fixture of Egypt's political culture, various origin traditions of a fairly predictable type no doubt began to attach to them and were orally transmitted from one region to another and down the generations. The origins of two implacably opposed factions are typically attributed to two historical figures, often brothers or relatives of some other kind, who quarreled, creating an irreparable rift. Thus, preexisting origin myths containing these tropes could be fairly readily applied to the two factions. The fact that there are several origin traditions suggests that none of them is "true." In fact, each of them—the quarreling brothers, the builder-bey *versus* the mamluk-acquiring-bey, the string of opposing pairs—suggests an attempt to frame the peculiar case of the factions within existing origin myths. By repeating these stories and occasionally adding details from the lore of their home cultures, such as magic swords and larger than life heroes, the recruits themselves contributed to the origin myths, making them a living, evolving, and reciprocal tradition. Recruits also told stories about their higher-ups, past and present: the narrator of Ahmed Kâhya ᶜAzeban al-Damurdashi's chronicle justifies the work's existence by explaining that members of his regiment had asked him to recount the deeds of Cairo's grandees and regimental officers (see chapter two). In this respect, story-telling helped to cut across rank and class boundaries. This was, in short, a continuous process by which recruits absorbed popular origin myths as part of their acclimation to a new society, while at the same time contributing to these myths by injecting elements from their home cultures.[48]

In this respect, the origin myths that contribute to factional cohesion are invented traditions in the manner of Eric Hobsbawm's and Terrence Ranger's by now classic edited volume.[49] In most, if not all, of the cases in Hobsbawm's and Ranger's volume, the traditions in question served a nationalistic purpose: to strengthen or even to create nationalist sentiment by fostering a sense of group cohesion. In the case of our factions, no nationalist purpose is served although the tales are unquestionably used to foster group cohesion. Even a seemingly "neutral" origin tradition, such as that offered by the Damurdashi chronicles, reinforces a sense of factional identity by the simple act of laying out, in an authoritative tone, the oppositions that divide Saᶜd from Haram and Faqari from Qasimi. Merely hearing the oppositions repeated would reinforce a faction member's identification with one or the other member of each pair. In daily life, when he or she was not sitting listening to stories but practicing equestrian exercises, learning how to shoot a rifle, selling goods in the bazaar, or negotiating with coffee merchants, the faction member might not feel his or her factional identity so strongly. But the stories themselves created their own space, a sort of narrative reality, in which factional identity was all-important and in which one or the other faction might take the rhetorical role of hero while the other took the rhetorical role of villain. The acts of telling and listening to stories, by reintroducing this rhetorical reality, themselves contributed to factional identity.

These invented traditions, in their turn, create collective memory of the sort on which group cohesion depends. Every American schoolchild learns the story of George Washington chopping down the cherry tree, then refusing to lie about it. The story is so familiar to Americans that it has become part of our collective memory of our first president, even though we acknowledge that it is probably spurious. George

Washington himself is a cornerstone of American nationalism; he and the other Founding Fathers, as they have come to be known—even though they, of course, never referred to themselves in this fashion—have become part of our national myth, exemplifying what most Americans regard as great about the United States. As an example of a particular moral quality, and in a particular educational setting, this story has unquestionable staying power, no matter how many uncomfortable revelations, such as that of Thomas Jefferson's affair with one of his slaves, may be dredged up by revisionist historians. Such stories exist on a different narrative plane from the "revelations," and their rhetorical force is not appreciably diminished by tawdry reality.

Nor was it a coincidence that popular lore should be deployed to explain the seventeenth-century upheavals specifically, albeit this deployment was part of an ongoing process. Premodern societies not uncommonly digested and assimilated wrenching social changes, and above all migrations and similar demographic convulsions of just the sort that the Ottoman Empire suffered in the seventeenth century, by means of popular epics. In such cases, the motifs and tropes of earlier migration narratives could serve to frame the new developments.[50] Indeed, one of the most popular premodern Arabic epics—and one evoked by the Damurdashi chronicles to frame the enmity of Sa^cd and Haram—that of the Banu Hilal, describes the migration of this bedouin tribe from the Arabian peninsula into Egypt and ultimately across North Africa.[51] In evoking such well-known tales, the Damurdashi stories and the other origin myths reflect not so much "what really happened" as they do an attempt to frame what happened according to established topoi and motifs.

Likewise, the setting in which the tales of the advent of the two factions may have been told—in the barracks, in the coffeehouses, in the governor's council chamber, in the harem of a grandee household—also played its part in the cultural function of these stories. This was a society, like many pretwentieth-century societies, in which storytelling was a major group social activity. The household of a grandee, the harem of his wife, or the barracks—the very place to which a new recruit would have been introduced on first arriving in Cairo—would have been the natural setting for such storytelling. Many famous cycles of tales are framed by the device of the storyteller spinning his or her yarns in a ruler's court or in the house of some great lord. *The Thousand and One Nights*, to take the most famous example from the Middle East, is supposed to consist of tales told by Shahrazad to the sultan Shahriar in the harem of his palace.[52] King Arthur is said to have had the custom of asking to hear edifying stories on feast days, when he held court and presided over the famed Round Table.[53] Even the chronicles that relate the origin myths of the factions are rife with transitional phrases that hint at their oral lineage: from "And the narrator said" (*Wa-qāla al-rāwi*) and "We shall speak of him later" (*Lahū maᶜnā kilām*) to "Now look, my brother, at . . ." (*Fa-anḍara yā akhi ilā . . .*).[54] And in the same sense that the story of George Washington and the cherry tree serves a certain acculturative purpose at a certain stage of a child's education and in the space of the classroom, so these heroic tales served a similar purpose for new recruits in the space where they learned the ropes of Egypt's military-administrative culture. There were other times and spaces for the mundane realities of collecting one's salary, paying bribes, bidding for tax farms, and forming business partnerships—as there are for the mundane realities of paying taxes and taking out a mortgage.

By the same token, the heroic stories of the early Islamic caliph-hero ᶜAli b. Abi Talib and his magical sword Dhu'l-Faqar became part of the collective memory of the Janissary corps—a story with which virtually every Janissary, regardless of background, could identify on some level. And we can only imagine that the tales of Dhu'l-Faqar and Qasim Beys likewise became part of the collective memory of the factions. Most faction members, particularly by the late seventeenth and early eighteenth centuries, were so far removed from any possible "founding father" of the factions that they were in a position to believe these tales, or at least to suspend disbelief, and even to believe that the factions began with Selim I's conquest of Egypt. When faction members did remember some great leader, it tended to be one of the two great seventeenth-century Ridvan Beys: Ridvan Bey al-Faqari, the longtime pilgrimage commander, or Ridvan Bey Abu'l-Shawarib the Qasimi. The two Ridvans represented two "real-life" poles of the two factions, whereas Dhu'l-Faqar and Qasim Beys of the origin myth represented a different, archetypal reality: as Holt, recognizing the sheer mythic quality of the origin narratives, pointed out, "Qasim and Dhu'l-Faqar are almost allegorical figures of Avarice and Ambition, struggling for domination over Egypt."[55]

In these stories and traditions the factions and, indeed, the Ottoman conquest "lived" for large numbers of recruits to Egypt's military and administrative cadres. The accretions and allusions contained in these various tales can help us to understand how these recruits made sense of what was, for many of them, an entirely new and strange world with a history all its own that had to be assimilated. To this new world the recruits brought the baggage of their former worlds, itself often only vaguely remembered and half-digested. Consequently, we find in certain traditions bits of incompletely transmitted Islamic lore, regional folk mythology, and perhaps a dash of imperfectly understood Ottoman history, all mingled in a single story or character. All these ingredients together formed the collective memory of the military-administrative class, and it was through the agency of this collective memory that traditions of the factions and their origins were transmitted down through the generations.

Structure and Sources of this Book

In sum, this book is an attempt to understand how the Faqari and Qasimi factions worked within the political culture of Ottoman Egypt. By this, I do not mean a retelling or even an analysis of the political events in which the factions participated during the seventeenth and eighteenth centuries; these have already been laid out by Holt and others, including the present author. I mean the reasons why a two-faction system arose in Egypt, the peculiar character of this factional culture, the nature of the legends that attached to the origin of these two factions, and why these particular legends persisted. This undertaking requires a different approach from those hitherto employed in studying Ottoman Egypt. While I will be using some of the same types of sources employed in such studies, I will also be looking closely at the factional origin myths themselves and at the themes and motifs that tend to recur within them, and analyzing each of these themes and motifs. Each chapter of the book takes on a different theme or motif, or a different genre of origin myth. After this obligatory introductory explanation of the factions, their history, and the unanswered questions that I shall attempt to answer, I start with an exploration of the nature of Ottoman Egypt's peculiarly bilateral factionalism (chapter 1), followed by an analysis of the role of popular narratives in the construction of the factions' origin myths (chapter 2). Chapter 3 takes on the essential dichotomy of the Saᶜd and Haram tribal groupings while chapter 4 addresses the place of Yemen in the origins of the Faqari and Qasimi factions. Though never mentioned in the origin myths, Yemen is a shadowy presence lurking behind the factions and playing a real role, I am convinced, in their genesis. And no wonder: Yemen was symbiotically linked to Egypt both throughout its brief tenure as an Ottoman province and after the Ottoman expulsion from Yemen in the 1620s and 1630s. Subsequent chapters proceed more or less in accordance with the motifs introduced by the three principal origin myths. Thus, chapter 5 explores the ramifications of the red-white color dichotomy and chapter 6 those of the dichotomous heraldic emblems, epitomized by the knob atop the Faqaris' spears and the "disk" (more properly a metal plate) atop the Qasimis.' My study next turns to the origin myth involving Sultan Selim's visit to the Mamluk emir Sudun. Chapter 7 examines the figure of Selim himself in the origin myth while chapter 8 lingers on the symbolic possibilities of the mulberry tree under which Sudun supposedly chained his two sons. Chapter 9 focuses on the "alternative" origin myth of Qasim Bey inviting Dhu'l-Faqar Bey to a feast, and the ensuing argument over whether monuments or mamluks are of greater value. The remaining chapters take a slightly different tack by taking a hard look at the candidates whom other historians have favored for eponymous founders of the Qasimi and Faqari factions. Chapter 10 unveils an unsuspected twist to the career of the aforementioned Qasim Bey and his mamluk Qansuh, then ponders the implications of the Qasimi chieftain Ridvan Bey Abu'l-Shawarib's assertions of Circassian superiority and Arab lineage. Chapter 11 disputes the notion that the other Ridvan Bey was the "first Faqari," then presents what I believe is the true namesake of the Faqari faction: ᶜAli b. Abi Talib's quasi-miraculous sword Dhu'l-Faqar, which takes on a life of its own in Ottoman legend.

As you might expect, the sources on which I draw are eclectic. I start, naturally enough, with the Arabic chronicles in which the origin myths appear. These include the four early eighteenth-century chronicles known collectively as the Damurdashi group of chronicles. All are structured around the same basic set of events, and all have some connection to the ᶜAzeban regiment, a corps of Ottoman infantry stationed in Egypt following the conquest. Al-Qinali, author of the earliest chronicle, entitled *Majmūᶜ laṭīf* (*Pleasant Compendium*), claims to be in the service of one Hasan Agha al-Damurdashi of the ᶜAzeban corps, while the latest and most detailed of the chronicles, *Al-durra al-muṣāna* (*The Protected Pearl*), was supposedly composed by one Ahmed Kâhya ᶜAzeban al-Damurdashi.[56] Also among these chronicles is Ahmed Çelebi b. ᶜAbd al-Ghani's *Awḍaḥ al-ishārāt* (*The Clearest Signs*), apparently composed in the late 1730s, and finally al-Jabarti's comparatively well-known *ᶜAjāʾib al-āthār* (*The Most Wondrous Remains*), compiled in the early nineteenth century. I make more limited use of the *Book of Travels* (*Seyahatname*) of the late seventeenth-century Ottoman traveler Evliya Çelebi and the early seventeenth-century Arabic chronicle of Muhammad ᶜAbd al-Muᶜti al-Ishaqi. In the chapter on Yemen, I exploit a number of Arabic chronicles of Yemen dating from the tenth to the eighteenth centuries C.E. But in addition to these more or less conventional narrative sources, I employ several that have never before been brought to bear on Ottoman Egyptian history: namely, the heroic epic revolving around Baybars, founder of the Mamluk sultanate (*Sīrat al-Ẓāhir Baybars*); *The Adventures of Sayf ben Dhi Yazan*, an epic of a mythical king of pre-Islamic Yemen; and even *The Book of Dede Korkut*, a classic of medieval Turkic folklore. Adding folkloric sources to the more or less canonical narrative histories is an innovation that is, I believe, long overdue. Likewise, my study at various points, but above all in the chapter exploring representations of the sword Dhu'l-Faqar, exploits an eclectic array of visual evidence: post-Timurid and Ottoman miniatures, Ottoman battle flags, paintings and sketches by European visitors to the Ottoman Empire, tombstones of Ottoman soldiers. I also chose to search far beyond the borders of Egypt, and even beyond the spatial and temporal borders of the Ottoman Empire, for analogs to the symbols and patterns that I encountered in Egypt's factionalism. Factions in Byzantine Constantinople, medieval Florence, and Safavid Iran; mulberry trees in East Asian folk tradition; Verdian and Wagnerian operas; even the Virgin Mary as portrayed on votive candles in my native San Antonio find their way into this book. The goal of these varied references is to make Egypt's factions and their accoutrements potentially comprehensible to a wide audience, but at the same time to stress that these factions need not be studied or understood solely within an Egyptian context. On the contrary, I am convinced that they cannot be understood within this narrow context, and that such a narrow approach has been the primary cause of our failure to understand them properly thus far.

Appendix

Origin Myths of the Factions

Below are translations of two of the three origin myths of the Faqari and Qasimi/Sa^cd and Haram factions. The first myth appears in the chronicle of Ahmed Çelebi while the second occurs in different versions in three of the chronicles of the Damurdashi group. A third myth, in which Dhu'l-Faqar and Qasim Beys exchange banquet invitations, will be introduced in chapter 9.

(1) Ahmed Çelebi b. ᶜAbd al Ghani, *Awḍaḥ al ishārāt fī man tawalla Miṣr al-Qāhira min al-wuzarāʾ wa'l-bāshāt* (*The Clearest Signs: The Ministers and Pashas Who Governed Cairo*) (c. 1737):

> When Sultan Selim came to Cairo, after he had conquered it, . . . a group of grandees came and greeted him. He asked, "Is anyone left who has not met us?" [i.e., surrendered]; they told him, "Sudun al-ᶜAjami." "And why hasn't he come to us?" They told him, "He is very old and can't ride or walk; and besides, when Qansuh al-Ghuri [the Mamluk sultan whom Selim defeated in Syria, r. 1501–16] went up to fight you, he built two enclosures [s. *bāb*, literally door or gate] in his house, fearing that his sons would make a fool of him and ride out with al-Ghuri. He has two sons, the greatest horsemen of their time; one is called Qasim and the other Dhu'l-Faqar. He put both of them in chains and built the enclosures." Sultan Selim said, "It is our duty to go to him." Then he rode immediately . . . to Sudun al-ᶜAjami's mansion. He saw the two built enclosures, as [the grandees] had described them, and ordered [the grandees] to destroy them. Then he entered and found the platform [*masṭaba*: a raised platform for receptions and the

like] shaded by the mulberry tree, and he dismounted under the tree and sent for the emir. [The grandees] told [Sudun] that Sultan Selim had come to his mansion, and he quickly came out; the servants carried him until he was standing before the sultan. When [Selim] saw him, he rose and greeted him, and granted him security for himself, his property, and his sons. He then asked for his sons, and they were brought in irons. The sultan ordered that their chains be broken, and gave them security for their persons. Then he asked to see a demonstration of the chivalric exercises [*furūsiyya*] that the emirs had told him about. . . .

The next day, [Sudun] notified the sultan, who rode with his retinue to Qasr al-ᶜAyni [the locale in Cairo dominated by the palace of the Mamluk emir al-ᶜAyni, today a major thoroughfare] and found it spread with the most sumptuous carpets. Then Qasim said to his brother, "I'll be on the sultan's side, and you be on Egypt's side." His brother agreed. [Qasim] went over to the sultan's group [*jamāᶜa*] and selected about 100 horsemen, while Dhu'l Faqar took about 100 from his own group. Then they stood before each other, Qasim facing the palace [of al-ᶜAyni], Dhu'l-Faqar facing the canal [at the other end of the street]. Then horseman came out against horseman [i.e., they jousted two-by-two] until finally Qasim came out against his brother Dhu'l-Faqar. They went out and engaged in warlike fighting, and Dhu'l-Faqar saw treachery in his brother's eye once, then again, and saw that he was bearing down on him to kill him.

When he saw this, he said, "Brother, what is this?" [Qasim] replied, "This is combat"; then he took advantage of him and was about to cut off his head, but [Dhu'l-Faqar] shielded himself from him, and the sword fell on his thigh so that he was lightly wounded. When he felt the steel, he raised his sword and said to [his brother], "This is war!" He tried to cut off [Qasim's] head, but [Qasim] fled toward the palace. When the sultan's group, who were [Qasim's] party, saw him fleeing toward them, with his brother Dhu'l-Faqar [pursuing him] like an eagle, they confronted Dhu'l-Faqar and attacked him with the intent of killing him. . . . He responded with parry and thrust, and his group followed him while Qasim's fled. Then the sultan came down from the pavilion to his group and to the emirs of Egypt, and separated them from each other. . . .

> Then the sultan sent for [Qasim and Dhu'l-Faqar] and bestowed robes of honor on them, and gave each of them three districts [to administer] and assigned them salaries. And from that day, there appeared in Egypt the Faqariyya and the Qasimiyya; the Faqariyya turn to the people of Egypt, and the Qasimiyya turn to the side of the sultanate. . . .[1]

(2a) Mustafa b. Ibrahim al-Maddah al-Qinali, *Majmūʿ laṭīf* (*Pleasant Compendium*) (c. 1739):

> The people of Egypt from ancient times were in two factions (*farqatayn*), soldiers and bedouin and peasants (*raʿāya*): white flag and red flag. The white was Tubbaʿi and the red Kulaybi, Zughbi and Hilali, Qalaʾuni and Baybarsi until the administration (*dawla*) of the House of Osman . . . [when they became] Faqari-Saʿd and Qasimi-Haram. The Faqari loves protégés [*jirāqāt*, Arabicized plural of Turkish *çırak*, "apprentice"], and the Qasimi loves building. The people of Cairo used to recognize the Faqari and the Qasimi in processions, whether the procession of the noble *maḥfil* [the symbolic litter that accompanies the pilgrimage to Mecca] or the procession of the [new] governor, by the javelins that went in front of the beys (*sanājiq*) and aghas and higher officers (*ikhtiyāriyya*) and the regiments [*ujāqāt*, Arabicized plural of Turkish *ocak*, "regiment"]: the Faqari's javelins had a pomegranate (*rummāna*) and the Qasimi's javelins had a metal plate (*jalba*); this was a matter known between them.[2]

(2b) Anonymous, *Kitāb al-durra al-munṣāna fī waqāʿ [sic] al-Kināna* (*The Book of the Precious Pearl: Events in Egypt [land of the Kinana tribe]*):

> The people of Egypt, beys, aghas, and the seven regiments, were two factions (*farqatayn*): White Flag from the Yemeni Tubbaʿ and Red Flag from Kulayb brother of al-Zir, Saʿd and Haram, Faqari and Qasimi. . . . The Faqaris had numbers and generosity, and the Qasimis had property and stinginess. We used to recognize the Faqari and the Qasimi in the procession of the governor or the procession of the *maḥfil*: the Faqari's javelins with a pomegranate, and the Qasimi's javelins with a metal plate.[3]

(2c) Ahmed Kâhya ᶜAzeban al-Damurdashi, *Al-durra al-muṣāna fī akhbār al-Kināna* (*The Protected Pearl: History of Egypt [land of the Kināna tribe]*) (c. 1755):

> In his [Baltacı Hasan Pasha, governor of Egypt 1687–88] days, the administration (*dawla*) of Egypt was in two factions (*farqatayn*): Saᶜd and Haram, Tubbaᶜi and Kulaybi, [Husayni] and Yazidi. The Husayni's banner was white, and the Yazidi's banner was red. And Akri [?] and Qaysi. We used to recognize Saᶜd and Haram from processions: the Saᶜd's knob had a circular metal plate, and the Nisf Haram's javelins had a metal plate without a knob. . . .[4]

1

Bilateral Factionalism in Ottoman Egypt

What makes a faction more than a group, a sect, or a household? In the case of the Faqaris and Qasimis, to say nothing of competing pairs of factions in numerous earlier, later, and contemporaneous societies, the defining characteristics of these factions were that there were only two of them; they opposed each other; and they divided most, if not all, of society between them. Accordingly, their identifying markers—names, colors, symbols—and the rituals in which they participated took on this same bilateral character: they were diametrically opposed, offered clear alternatives to each other, or were glaringly incompatible. This chapter illustrates this point by presenting definitive features of Egypt's factional political cultural in comparison to similar features in other bilateral factional cultures.

Breaking Out of the Mamluk Paradigm

Before we undertake this task, however, it is worth asking why the bilateralism of the Faqaris and Qasimis has received so little attention. Our understanding of the origins and functions of these two factions has, I believe, been hampered by the Mamluk historiographical framework within which historians of premodern Ottoman Egypt have habitually placed them. I contend that if we are to understand these factions on their own terms and in their own historical and social context, we must adopt a framework that gives due weight to the fact that these two factions utterly polarized Egyptian society, forcing virtually every member of the military-administrative population, as well as merchants, artisans, and bedouin tribes, to choose one side or the other side while not allowing for any alternative.

We know very well that factions were an integral and unavoidable feature of the history of the Mamluk sultanate (1250–1517), which ruled Egypt, Syria, the Hijaz (the western Arabian peninsula), and southeastern Anatolia before the Ottoman conquest in 1516–17. Each Mamluk grandee, or emir, following his manumission, purchased large numbers of his own mamluks, or military slaves, whose education and military training he oversaw. These mamluks, whose paramount loyalty was to the patron who had nurtured them, formed the basis of the emir's faction. With the support of his faction, the emir might attain the sultanate. In that event, his faction attempted to protect his interests from the mamluks of his predecessor, who formed a separate faction. The new sultan would typically keep the mamluks of his faction near him in Cairo, while giving the mamluks of his predecessor governorships and other administrative offices in the provinces, notably Syria.[1] In this fashion, the sultan could keep his potential rivals at a reasonably comfortable distance, although he could not prevent them from building up their own power bases in the provinces. By the same token, the sultan's own mamluks, once manumitted, could establish power bases in the capital; the sultan might promote one of them to succeed him. In short, each faction was closely associated with a particular Mamluk sultan. The names of these factions derive from the regnal titles of the sultans: thus, the faction of the founder of the Mamluk sultanate, al-Zahir Baybars al-Bunduqdari (r. 1260–77), came to be known as "Zahiris" while the faction of al-Muʾayyad Shaykh (r. 1412–21) were known as "Muʾayyadis."[2]

Parallels to the factionalism of the Mamluk sultanate certainly existed in Ottoman-era Egypt, most notably in the great households and families of the Ottoman period. An enterprising Ottoman-era grandee established a household, either within a regimental barracks or within an elite residence, by purchasing mamluks, attracting mercenaries, and otherwise nurturing patron-client ties.[3] In numerous cases, these households and followings came to be known by the names or sobriquets (*laqab*s) of their founders. This was true of the powerful households founded in the late seventeenth and early eighteenth centuries by regimental commanders, above all the long-lived Qazdağlı (a.k.a. Qazdughli) household, founded by Mustafa Kâhya al-Qazdağlı, which came to dominate Egypt for most of the eighteenth century.[4] Two households of the early eighteenth century, founded by the rival beys Çerkes Mehmed and Ismail b. ʿIvaz, are memorialized in Arabic chronicles by the names of illustrious predecessors: Çerkes Mehmed's household is designated the "Shanabiyya," after his patron, Ibrahim Bey Abu Shanab; Ismail Bey's household, meanwhile, is called "Shawariba," after his father's patron's patron's father, Ridvan Bey Abu'l-Shawarib. (Coincidentally or not, then, these two competing households took sobriquets meaning "moustachioed.")[5] In all these cases, the name of the founding father endured over several generations. Toward the end of the eighteenth century, in contrast, competing members of the Qazdağlı household formed their own followings, each of which was designated by the name of its immediate patron. Thus, the chronicler al-Jabarti refers to the followers of Mehmed (Muhammad) Bey Abu'l-Dhahab as *Muḥammadiyya*.[6]

Notwithstanding, each of the above-mentioned households and subhouseholds belonged to either the Faqari or Qasimi faction. The Qazdağlıs were offshoots of the Faqaris; meanwhile, both Çerkes Mehmed Bey and Ismail Bey b. ᶜIvaz were Qasimis. Clearly, the Faqari and Qasimi factions transcended these individual households. Moreover, while the process of household formation in Ottoman Egypt resembled the formation of factions under the Mamluk sultanate, the emergence of the Faqari and Qasimi factions, to the extent it can be ascertained, was far more complex and mysterious—in a word, mythic.

The terminology employed in contemporary sources for the Faqaris and Qasimis, as opposed to that employed for single households and for the factions of the Mamluk sultanate, sheds light on the varying perceptions of these groups. A grandee's household during the Ottoman period, if centered in an actual residence, was termed *bayt* (house) in Arabic or *kapı* (door, gate) in Ottoman Turkish.[7] A household based in the regimental barracks in Cairo's citadel, drawing much of its strength and structure from the regimental hierarchy, was typically referred to as *ṭaraf* (side), *ṭāʾifa* (guild, party, sect), or *jamāᶜa* (group).[8] In the former case, the terminology stresses the physical setting of the household in a residence, or, to take the literal meaning of *kapı*, inside an imposing doorway, in keeping with the classical Ottoman—and, indeed, ancient Middle Eastern—structuring of power according to "inner" and "outer" spaces separated by a doorway or threshold.[9] In the latter case, the fact of the group's coalescing is stressed. By the same token, Mamluk-era chroniclers refer to an individual faction as *ṭāʾifa*, emphasizing its coherence as a collectivity of mamluks of the same sultan.[10]

The terminology that contemporary observers employ for the Faqaris or Qasimis, in contrast, is *farīq* or *farqa* and, to designate the two of them, the dual forms *farīqayn* and *farqatayn*.[11] These words derive from the Arabic root *f-r-q*, signifying "to separate" or "to differentiate." Thus, these terms at least implicitly emphasize not belonging and coherence, but separation and distinction. Premodern Arabic chronicles of different regions, as well as premodern Arabic literary genres, employ the word *farīq* to designate one of two sides in a contest or conflict. Today, in fact, the term *farīq* is used to denote rival sports teams, particularly in football. More to the point, *farīqayn* in premodern usage not infrequently designates two implacably opposed sides in a military and ideological conflict, such as that between the Muslims and the Crusaders or, later, the Ottomans and the Catholic Hapsburgs; that between the Mamluk sultanate, as defender of the Muslim community, and the invading Mongol hordes; or, to take an intra-Islamic example, that between the Hanafi and Shafiᶜi legal rites of Sunni Islam.[12] In short, the use of *farīq* and *farīqayn*, or derivations thereof, seems to indicate two opposing sides, as opposed to the coalescing of members or a residential headquarters. Nor does *farīq* typically designate a single household or even a single faction of the Mamluk sultanate.[13] If terminology is any guide, then, the Faqaris and Qasimis are fundamentally different from both the households of the Ottoman era and the factions of the Mamluk era.

To be sure, the Mamluk-era factions operated in much the same fashion as the Ottoman-era households in the sense that each functioned largely as an interest group attached to a particular patron, with all the internal squabbles, splits, and offshoots that one would expect within such a structure. The Faqaris and Qasimis suffered internal divisions and ruptures, as well, as the deadly rivalry between Çerkes Mehmed Bey and Ismail Bey b. ᶜIvaz most graphically illustrates. Yet these two blocs differed in character from Mamluk factions and from Ottoman-era households. They were, in the first place, much longer lived. Leaving aside for the moment the myths of their origins, their presence in Egyptian society ostensibly dates to the 1640s.[14] Their collapse came nearly a century later, when a decisive confrontation in 1730 virtually wiped out the Qasimis; the Faqaris, meanwhile, were largely superseded by a powerful household, the Qazdağlıs, that arose from within their midst.[15] Even so, factional sentiment, or at least suspicion of continuing factional loyalties, survived well into the 1760s, when the late Qazdağlı grandee ᶜAli Bey al-Kabir established his hegemony. Part of his strategy for consolidating power consisted of eradicating all lingering members of the defunct Qasimi faction—even those firmly allied with previous generations of Qazdağlıs.[16] Meanwhile, the Faqaris' and Qasimis' influence was not limited to the narrow ruling elite that presided in Cairo. The two blocs divided virtually all of society throughout the province: bedouin tribes in different Egyptian subprovinces were affiliated with one bloc or another; subprovincial and district governors were obliged to choose sides, as were artisans in Cairo and most other towns. As we shall see, furthermore, the factional rivalry extended, to some degree, beyond the borders of Egypt.

Clearly, we are dealing with a phenomenon quite different from the relatively narrow, short-lived factions of the Mamluk sultanate. Yet secondary scholarship on pre-nineteenth-century Ottoman Egypt has persisted in interpreting these two groups as if they were part and parcel of inveterate Mamluk factionalism.[17] Such an approach necessarily assumes that the forces that gave rise to the Faqaris and Qasimis were identical to those that shaped the political culture of the Mamluk sultanate and that, in fact, Mamluk paradigms are all that we need to understand these two enormous, extraordinarily long-lived groups. Yet a vital point that secondary scholarship has thus far seemed to overlook is that the Faqaris and Qasimis divided Egyptian society into two; there was no question of an independent third alternative. Perhaps the most graphic example of this reality is the case of the early eighteenth-century grandee ᶜAbdurrahman Bey, the governor of the enormous Upper Egyptian subprovince of Jirja, who was assassinated because he would not remain loyal to either bloc but claimed variously to be a Faqari and a Qasimi.[18] The insistent bilateralism of these two blocs, along with their social inclusiveness, is the feature that most clearly distinguishes them from the factions of the Mamluk sultanate. In this bilateralism, they resemble less the Mamluk-era factions than they do other well-known historical examples of two rival blocs that divided their respective societies, notably the Guelphs and Ghibellines of medieval Tuscany, whose enmity pervades Canto X of Dante's *Inferno*;[19] the Blues and Greens of the Byzantine Empire; and the northern and southern, or Qaysi and Yemeni, Arabs whose rivalry emerged in the early centuries of Islam. A particularly sharp and intriguing comparison can be drawn, meanwhile, with the contemporary Haydari and Niᶜmatullahi, or Niᶜmati, factions of Iran, which originated in the followings of two rival fifteenth-century Sufi leaders but which came to polarize the cities of Iran from the sixteenth through the nineteenth centuries.[20] As we shall see, historical connections may, in fact, exist between the Blues and Greens and, on the one hand, the Qays and Yemen, and, on the other, the blocs of Ottoman Egypt.

Indeed, the political culture, as well as the surrounding mythology, of the Faqaris and Qasimis exhibits some of the same characteristics as these earlier and contemporary episodes of bilateral factionalism. Like the Guelphs and Ghibellines, Blues and Greens, Haydaris and Niᶜmatis, and above all the Qays and Yemen, the Faqari-Qasimi conflict was society wide, encompassing not simply the military-administrative cadre but large segments of the urban and even rural populations. In the case of Ottoman Egyptian factionalism, the rural element was particularly visible because of the participation of bedouin tribes in factional struggles through their allegiance to the Saᶜd and Haram, two bedouin blocs allied respectively with the Faqaris and Qasimis. In remarkably similar fashion, the Haydaris and Niᶜmatis enjoyed alliances with two specific (although genealogically related) Turcoman tribes in the rural hinterland.[21] In this regard, both the Faqari-Qasimi rivalry and that of the Haydaris and Niᶜmatis strongly resemble the Qays-Yemen rivalry. We can identify other key features of the Faqari-Qasimi political culture as typical of bilateral factional rivalry—and, not incidentally, uncharacteristic of Mamluk sultanate political culture. In the remainder of the chapter, I will consider five such features—color dichotomy, fictive genealogy, origin myths centering on two brothers, competing symbols, and public ritual—before passing to a consideration of the functions that a two-faction system fulfilled.

Color Dichotomy

Color dichotomy is perhaps the most visible symptom of bilateral factionalism: that is, the phenomenon whereby each faction is identified by a distinguishing color, displayed in its members' clothing and/or in its banners and other identifying insignia. While color distinctions may certainly figure in societies with more than two factions, a large number of factions, as in the Mamluk sultanate, tends to make color distinctions less effective as markers of factional allegiance.

The colors in question are typically quite basic, if not primary, colors. In the Byzantine Empire, for a notable example, the two dominant factions were known by the names of the colors with which they were associated: blue and green. These factions consisted of the professional performers and their fans who participated in the chariot races staged by the Roman emperors beginning roughly in the second century B.C.E. The colors were those that the rival competitors displayed on their chariots and on the banners that accompanied them into the arena, as well as in their clothing. Initially, there had been four factions that derived their colors from either the four seasons or the four elements believed in classical Greek science to comprise the universe: earth (green), air (white), fire (red), and water (blue). Yet quite early on, factional rivalries took the form of competition between *pairs* of colors (Blue and either Red or White *vs.* Green and either Red or White), rather than among all four; in other words, Roman/Byzantine factionalism was inherently bilateral.[22] Nor were the factions and factional rivalries restricted to Rome; arenas and factional competition spread to Constantinople and Alexandria and, by the late fifth century, throughout Byzantium's Asian territories.[23]

Indeed, during the last millennium of Byzantine history, chariot racing, along with theatricals, displaced gladiatorial spectacles as the public entertainment of choice and remained a fixture well into the Middle Ages.[24] The factions played a prominent role in these public exhibitions. By this period in Byzantine history, the Blues and Greens had come to overshadow the other two factions while still maintaining the paired alliances, although these were now fixed as Blue and White *vs.* Green and Red.[25] The Byzantine emperor himself belonged to one of the four factions and supported the interests of either the Blues or the Greens. Like the urban brotherhoods, known to scholars as *futuwwa* organizations, of medieval Islam, the factions were dominated by young men, who were responsible for most of the violence for which the factions were blamed.[26]

As Speros Vryonis has noted, the Blue-Green rivalry contributed to the conditions that underlay the rise of Islam and the early Muslim conquests. Factional enmities were exploited by the Sasanian Persian Empire in its conflicts with the Byzantines during the century preceding Islam's advent. The "young men" of Antioch unsuccessfully defended the city against the invading Sasanian emperor Khusrau I Anushirvan in 540 C.E., while those of Jerusalem massacred the Persian garrison after the city's conquest by Khusrau II Parviz in 614 C.E.[27] After conquering Antioch, however, Anushirvan transported a number of faction members to the heartland of the Persian Empire, where he built a "new Antioch" for them near his capital of Ctesiphon on the Tigris River. Here, he erected a hippodrome where the young men could carry on their chariot contests. Anushirvan supported the Greens in deliberate contrast to his enemy, the Byzantine emperor Justinian (r. 527–65 C.E.), who favored the Blues.[28] The factions may even have facilitated the Muslim conquest of Egypt in 640 C.E. According to John of Nikiu, the Blue and Green leaders "assieged the city of Misr [future site of Cairo] and harassed the Romans during the days of the Moslem"[29]—meaning, presumably, that they diverted the Byzantines' attention from the invading Muslim armies. How or whether the Blues and Greens in the conquered eastern Byzantine provinces were incorporated into the fledgling Muslim society has yet to be investigated. Certainly it strains credulity to imagine that a rivalry that had permeated societies in widely scattered Byzantine provinces for over half a millennium could disappear overnight, especially when it continued until at least the twelfth century C.E. in Byzantine territories not conquered by the early Muslims.[30]

Of more profound consequence among the Arabs themselves was the pervasive and still inadequately understood enmity between northern, or Qaysi, and southern, or Yemeni, Arabs. Ultimately, this division is rooted in geography. Qaysi Arabs were those living in the region extending from the northernmost borders of Yemen to the deserts of what are now Jordan, southern Syria, and southwestern Iraq. Yemeni Arabs, as the name implies, inhabited Yemen and, more generally, the southern regions of the Arabian peninsula. They spoke a southern Arabian language that, while Semitic, was written in a different script from the northern dialects that would form the basis for classical and modern Arabic, and contained a number of other distinctive features.[31] The ancient kingdom of Yemen cultivated a distinctive southern Arabian civilization that enjoyed important links to Ethiopia and, as attested in the Hebrew Bible, to the kingdoms of the Hebrews in Palestine.[32]

Migrations of southern Arabs northward into the peninsula occurred periodically in connection with political upheavals and trade, particularly trade in frankincense and myrrh, produced from the resin of two species of tree that grow in what are now eastern Yemen and western Oman.[33] In the sixth century C.E., however, a series of disasters led to a wave of northward migrations of Yemeni Arabs. The late rulers of the ancient Himyarite kingdom of northern Yemen converted to Judaism in the early centuries of the Common Era and began persecuting their Christian subjects, many of whom had converted under Ethiopian influence. In retaliation, the ruler of Ethiopia, a client of the Byzantine Empire, invaded Yemen in 525 C.E.[34] The upheaval caused by the Ethiopian occupation was compounded by natural disaster in 550 C.E., when the ancient Maʾrib Dam collapsed, destroying the basis of Yemen's prosperous agricultural economy.[35] Finally, in 570 C.E., the Sasanians invaded Yemen and ousted the Ethiopians.[36] Cumulatively, these disasters put an end to Yemen's preeminence as the Arabian peninsula's center of commerce and high culture. The initiative now passed to the bedouin tribes farther north in the peninsula. At the same time, waves of Yemeni tribes, fleeing the turmoil in Yemen, migrated northward into the interior of the peninsula. It was perhaps during this period that the differences between northern and southern tribes became a serious source of division in the tribal politics of the peninsula.

The advent of Islam did much to sharpen and ritualize the division between northern and southern Arabs. The Prophet Muhammad was himself a northern, or Qaysi, Arab, as were most of his early converts in Mecca. His migration, or *hijra*, to Medina in 622 C.E. brought him into the midst of a largely Yemeni, and partially Jewish, agricultural community. The initial dispute over the leadership of the Muslim community following the Prophet's death in 632 C.E. pitted the Qaysi Meccan immigrants (*muhājirūn*) against the Yemeni Medinese "helpers" (*anṣār*); the choice of the Prophet's father-in-law, Abu Bakr, as first caliph, or community leader, sanctioned a Qaysi monopoly of the caliphate. Later ᶜAlid and Shiᶜite groups, who insisted that the caliph be a descendant of the Prophet—while taking a fundamentally different approach to the selection of the caliph—retained this Qaysi exclusivism.

This emerging division between northern and southern Arabs was exacerbated by the tribal migrations that resulted from the civil wars triggered by the apostasy of bedouin tribes on the Prophet's death, and by the early Muslim conquests. The early Muslim armies included large numbers of both Qaysi and Yemeni tribesmen, and both groups were appointed to high offices in the early caliphal administrations. As a result, the garrison towns that the early caliphs established throughout their expanding empire came to include a bewildering mixture of northern and southern Arabs; by this point, in consequence, the literal geographical significance of the "northern" and "southern" labels had become virtually meaningless.

If we accept Patricia Crone's argument, however, it was the civil war that disrupted the Umayyad dynasty in the late seventh century C.E. that gave definitive shape to Qays and Yemen as distinct factions. On the death of the second Umayyad caliph in 683, the Qays, along with certain Yemeni tribes, supported a Meccan opponent of ᶜAli for caliph; the leader of a collateral branch of the Umayyads ultimately crushed this opponent with the support of the Kalb, a branch of the Yemeni grouping, and their allies. Following the civil war, Yemen and Qays, or "Mudar," as they were typically called under the Umayyads (Mudar being an ancestor of Qays), solidified into blocs and acquired the unrelenting bilateral character for which they are so well-known.[37] After the collapse of the Umayyad caliphate in 750 C.E. and the rise of the assimilationist ᶜAbbasid dynasty, the Qays-Yemen rivalry became somewhat more muted, yet it continued unabated in certain regions, notably Egypt and Greater Syria. In Egypt, the civil war between the ᶜAbbasid brothers al-Amin and al-Maʾmun from 809–13 occasioned fierce fighting between Yemeni (pro-Amin) and Qaysi (pro-Maʾmun) bedouin in the Nile Delta, exacerbated by both factions' frustration with ᶜAbbasid taxation policies.[38] Under the Ottomans, Lebanon above all was riven by Qaysi-Yemeni rivalry; the Ottoman central government followed a loose pattern of backing Qaysi families.[39] In some Syrian and Palestinian villages, the Qays-Yemen rivalry was still visible in the nineteenth and even the early twentieth century,[40] although it had acquired the character of an entrenched small-town feud.

The Qaysi-Yemeni struggle, like that of the Blues and Greens, is characterized by a pronounced color dichotomy: the Qaysi color is red, the Yemeni color white. Indeed, the tribespeople and other partisans of Qays and Yemen appear to have attached as much importance to the visual display of their colors as the Byzantine Blues and Greens. Qaysis and Yemenis wore red and white, respectively; in twentieth-century Syrian and Palestinian villages, as more than one observer has noted, a bride dressed in red would be obliged to change into white clothing if her wedding procession passed through a Yemeni village.[41] Geographical Yemen even boasts place names containing the Arabic words *aḥmar* (red) and *abyaḍ* (white).[42] Likewise, Qaysi and Yemeni tribes flew their respective colors on their tribal banners.

We do not know the source, or even the purported source, of the red and white dichotomy. In contrast to the Byzantine case, there is no tradition of colors representing primordial elements. It would, moreover, be foolhardy to speculate that Qays and Yemen drew any color traditions from the Byzantine Red and White subfactions; after all, the adoption of an identifying color is a basic strategy of group solidarity and differentiation, and red and white appear as identifying colors in a number of cultures.

Is it merely coincidental that the Faqari-Qasimi color dichotomy mirrors that of Qays and Yemen? Like the Yemeni Arabs, the Faqaris carried white banners and, if we are to believe al-Jabarti's account, not only wore white clothing but preferred to eat white food with white utensils. A similar preference for red, the Qaysi color, prevailed among the Qasimis.[43] I believe that a connection existed and was bound up with the two factions' alliances with the Saᶜd and Haram bedouin blocs, even though, as I point out in chapter 3, both groups may have originated in geographical Yemen and both seem to have been Yemeni, or southern Arab, populations.

Fictive Genealogies

Qays and Yemen do, however, exhibit a symptom of factional conflict that we do not find among the Byzantine factions: the practice of constructing genealogies linking the faction to a mythic ancestor. Given the extraordinary weight attached to genealogy within tribal societies in general and within pre-Islamic and early-Islamic Arabian society in particular, it may perhaps seem natural that the distinction between Qays and Yemen would be predicated on descent. The two factions are believed to descend from two mythic Arab ancestors: the Qaysi, or northern, Arabs from ʿAdnan and the Yemeni, or southern, Arabs from Qahtan.[44] Identification with one or the other of these two mythic Arab figures was quite strong well into the twentieth century.[45] Ultimately, these two Arab ancestors could be traced back to Ishmael, son of the biblical and Qurʾanic patriarch Abraham, thence to Shem, one of the three sons of Noah, thence to Adam, the first man. Thus, this Arab genealogical tradition built on the ancient tradition, well-represented in medieval Islamic letters, of tracing divergent populations to the three sons of Noah—Shem, Ham, and Japheth—who were thought to have given rise to the three principal groups of peoples—what Enlightenment European science would call the "Semitic, Hamitic, and Indo-European."[46]

The Faqaris and Qasimis exploited the fictive genealogy, as well, although not in so consistent or deliberate a fashion as Qays and Yemen. In the version of the factional origin myth reported by Ahmed Çelebi and by al-Jabarti and cited in the introduction, the factions stem from the quarrel between two brothers, Dhu'l-Faqar and Qasim. We also have evidence that faction leaders were aware of traditional Arab genealogies and willing to exploit them for their own purposes. In the most famous, although long misconstrued, example, the Qasimi leader Abu'l-Shawarib Ridvan Bey commissioned a genealogy demonstrating his descent from the Mamluk sultan Barquq (r. 1382–99), the first of the Circassian sultans who would dominate the sultanate until its demise. Barquq, the genealogy goes on to demonstrate, can trace his descent to the Prophet's tribe of Quraysh, thence to ʿAdnan, Ishmael son of Abraham, Shem son of Noah, and ultimately Adam.[47] This genealogy, then, takes the traditional Qaysi Arab genealogy and grafts it onto the tradition of Circassian descent from the Arabs. In so doing, Ridvan Bey's genealogist transforms the latter tradition, which depends on an equally pervasive genealogical tradition that many populations of the Caucasus region descended from the family of the last ruler of the Yemeni Arab kingdom of Ghassan (on this, see chapter 10). This Qasimi insistence on Qaysi descent is rather striking and corresponds, in fact, to a far more muted Faqari connection to the Yemeni Arabs. The very lack of a concocted Faqari genealogy analogous to that of Abu'l-Shawarib Ridvan Bey arguably attests to the Faqaris' awareness that they could not possibly claim a connection to the Quraysh. For this reason, perhaps, Abu'l-Shawarib's near contemporary Ridvan Bey al-Faqari, a Georgian mamluk whom P.M. Holt erroneously identified as the source of the genealogy cited above,[48] never emphasized his ethnicity but built his reputation solely on his lengthy service as pilgrimage commander.[49] Nonetheless, the Faqaris' link to the Yemeni Saᶜd bedouin indicates that the Qaysi-Yemeni genealogical dichotomy played a by no means negligible part in the contrasting identities forged by the Qasimis and Faqaris.

The Qaysi-Yemeni conflict was arguably the touchstone of bilateral factionalism in Muslim societies generally. Even if they enjoyed no direct lineal connection to Arab tribes themselves, competing political and social groups within these societies retained the tribal divisions as part of their collective memory and sought legitimacy by fabricating historical links to these tribes. In their own historical imaginations, then, if not in actual fact, the Qasimis were Qaysi and the Faqaris Yemeni. This self-conceptualization must therefore account for the color dichotomy: Qaysi red for the Qasimis, Yemeni white for the Faqaris.

The "Two Brothers" Origin Myth

Fictive genealogies exploited by factions such as the Faqaris and Qasimis typically terminate in mythic factional ancestors; ᶜAdnan and Qahtan, the putative sires of Qays and Yemen, respectively, are prime examples of such mythic ancestors. Yet a typical feature of factional origin mythology that even ᶜAdnan and Qahtan do not exhibit is the tradition that the opposing factions derive from two brothers who unexpectedly quarreled, leading to an irreparable split. The trope of two quarreling brothers in folk mythology is, of course, virtually as old as human history. It is well-represented in the biblical stories of Cain and Abel and Jacob and Esau, as well as the Greek myth of Proetus and Acrisius, the sons of King Abas of Argolis, who were supposed to rule alternately after their father's death but, predictably, refused to follow this prescription.[50] Closer to the Faqaris and Qasimis in both time and place, the Haydari and Niᶜmatullahi/Niᶜmati factions in Safavid and Qajar Iran were the subject of several different origin myths, in addition to the "factual" attribution of the factions to two divergent Sufi orders; these included a myth identifying Haydar and Niᶜmatullah as the overlords of two adjacent villages occupying the site of present-day Isfahan, and one insisting that they were two rival Iranian princes.[51]

By far the most famous fractious brothers in Islamic history, however, were not mythical figures at all but very real historical personages: al-Amin and al-Maʾmun, the two eldest sons of the caliph Harun al-Rashid (r. 786-809 C.E.), who is familiar to western readers from the *Thousand and One Nights*. Harun elected to divide his vast empire between his two sons on his death. Al-Amin was to succeed his father as caliph and rule the western half of the empire; al-Maʾmun was to rule the eastern half and succeed al-Amin as caliph. In the end, this scheme worked about as well as King Abas' throne-sharing plan in the Greek myth. Ignoring his late father's wishes, al-Amin named his own son to succeed him as caliph, whereupon al-Maʾmun raised a large army and attacked his brother's domain. The ensuing civil war, which lasted from 809 through 813 C.E., resulted in al-Maʾmun's seizure of the caliphate and the execution of al-Amin by his brother's general. These harrowing events scarred the Muslim community deeply and gave rise to a body of lore concerning portents of the civil war that Harun al-Rashid supposedly encountered before his death but ignored.[52] This fraternal struggle arguably served as a point of reference for parallel fraternal struggles anywhere in the Islamic realm.

For its part, the origin myth transmitted by Ahmed Çelebi and al-Jabarti exhibits a pattern that, on the surface, bears greater similarity to the circumstances of the ʿAbbasid civil war. In this myth, Dhu'l-Faqar and Qasim are two sons of a Mamluk emir named Sudun. (Ahmed Çelebi asserts, implausibly, that this is Sudun al-ʿAjami, the commander in chief of the Mamluk sultan Qaytbay, who ruled from 1468–96.)[53] Following his conquest of Egypt in 1517, the Ottoman sultan Selim I (r. 1512–20) learns that Sudun has sequestered himself from the fighting and prevented his sons from participating by chaining them up in two specially built enclosures. Hearing that the two sons are champions at the equestrian exercises known as *furūsiyya*, which were widely practiced not only in the Mamluk sultanate but, with variations, in most Turco-Iranian military societies, Selim orders them to display their talents by jousting before him. In the course of the joust, the brothers fall out, thus giving rise to the two factions that bear their names.[54] This origin myth, then, combines the familiar motif of two quarreling brothers with a pattern, common to Arabic epics, of two champions confronting one another in single combat. At the same time, the myth draws on the dislocations caused by foreign conquest and occupation of a society. Several Arabic chroniclers, even those who do not transmit this particular origin myth, insist that the factions date to the Ottoman conquest of Egypt.[55] The centrality of Sultan Selim

I to the myth is not unlike the defining roles played by Alexander the Great and Khusrau I Anushirvan in accounts of the origins of many ancient customs and edifices in the Middle East and Central Asia.[56]

What makes the "two brothers" motif so natural to myths of the origins of bilateral factionalism is the implication that until conflict erupted between the two brothers, a unified whole existed. Key to this motif, then, is not simply the presence of two brothers but the struggle between them. Two factions that cooperated with each other would neither lend themselves to an explanation centered on disruption and conflict, nor would they give rise to a society that was truly split in two. Likewise, a variety of volatile, short-lived factions on the model of the Mamluk sultanate would not find a satisfactory explication in a "brothers" myth. The motif itself, rooted in the most primal blood relationships—that between a father and his sons and that between brothers—bespeaks a division that is likewise primal and long-lasting, if not permanent. Such a fundamental split, the myth implies, cannot be healed by virtue of political expediency. It is a deep, enduring rift brought about by wrenching political and/or social change, such as the death of a powerful ruler or the conquest of a kingdom. The pervasiveness of this division encourages popular memory to cast it in either-or terms, or to adopt myths that cast the division in this way, and to assign each side basic, easily recognizable characteristics and symbols.

Competing Symbols

Second only to color as a marker of factional identity is the identifying symbol, which can take the form of an emblem depicted on a banner or a coat of arms. Competing family and factional coats of arms, bearing recognizable symbols and motifs, were integral to the internal divisions that plagued the city-states of medieval and Renaissance Italy, and may still be seen in that country.[57] This competing symbolism can be likened to the contrasting emblems that identify enemy armies; thus, for example, the Crusader forces emblazoned some version of the cross of Christ on their shields, banners, and tunics, while certain of their Muslim opponents deployed the crescent.[58] The Faqaris' and Qasimis' competing symbols were the so-called knob and disk that they carried as standards on the ends of their spears. In chapter 6, I will demonstrate that the knob and the disk were, in fact, the Ottoman *tuğ*, typically a knob from which horsetails are suspended, and the *ʿalem* of the Mamluk sultanate, typically a spade-shaped metal plate, often with inscriptions worked into the metal. The fact that the

Faqaris and Qasimis carried these emblems did not, however, mean that they identified or sympathized with the Ottoman Empire and the Mamluk sultanate, respectively. By the early eighteenth century, if not before, these standards had lost their original political meanings—and thus their symbolic force—and served solely to identify the two factions and to distinguish one from the other.

Notwithstanding the diminution of the standards' symbolic force in Ottoman Egypt, the very fact that they were visible markers of the two factions' competition distinguishes this bilateral factional conflict from the multilateral rivalries of the Mamluk sultanate. In a society in which numerous parties compete for influence, the power of any single party's symbol is unavoidably diluted. For six or ten different factions to have deployed different standards would have rendered the standards far less memorable; likewise, it is easier to remember the offices designated by the blazons embossed on Mamluk glass and metalwork than which sultans or emirs deployed them.[59] In such a case, standards would become little more than logos, not unlike the stars, animals, rockets, and other designs on football jersies. But when deployed by only two competing factions, the standards become markers of identity.

Public Rituals

The factions' identities were embedded in public consciousness and, ultimately, in collective memory through public visibility, which was in turn enhanced by the factions' participation in public rituals. Equestrian exercises are one example of such public rituals, although they took place in a relatively circumscribed space—the hippodrome—and if they were for practice, rather than in celebration of a holiday or military victory, there was no guarantee that the identifying markers of the factions would be on display. Even storytelling could be a public ritual if it took place in, say, a coffeehouse, but in this case, the space was even more circumscribed, and identifying symbols were even less likely to be visible. Official public processions, however, were another matter. These were occasions when the public could count on the factions' identifying symbols being intensely visible. Not for nothing does the Damurdashi chronicler al-Qinali point out that: "The people of Cairo recognized the Faqari and the Qasimi in processions, whether the procession of the holy *maḥfil* [more properly *maḥmil*, the symbolic litter that accompanied the pilgrimage to Mecca] or the procession of the [new] pasha":[60] at no other time were the factions so easily recognizable.

Much the same could be said of public rituals in other societies marked by bilateral factionalism. Publicly visible, ritualized factionalism also characterized the contemporary Haydari-Niᶜmati factionalism of Safavid Iran, which originated in two fifteenth-century Sufi brotherhoods with divergent philosophies: one Shiᶜite-leaning, the other staunchly Sunni.[61] By the seventeenth century, nonetheless, popular memory had forgotten these historical figures and come to regard the two blocs as simply inveterate and generic rivals, much as Saᶜd and Haram appear in Shirbini's *Hazz al-quḥūf* (see chapter 3). The two groups seem to have fed on a form of bilateral factionalism ingrained in Iranian urban society since as early as the tenth century, when ostensibly religious competition between Shiᶜite and Sunni Muslims, and between the Hanafi and Shafiᶜi legal rites, devastated entire cities.[62] The two factions divided up every urban center in the Safavid domains between themselves: a certain number of neighborhoods would be Haydari strongholds, the rest Niᶜmati. Haydaris and Niᶜmatis periodically staged ritualized public battles, employing fists, sticks, and stones, similar to the melées that broke out on the Rialto in Renaissance Venice.[63] Like the Venetian "wars of the fists," the Haydari-Niᶜmati battles were particularly visible on holidays—above all during the Islamic lunar month of Muharram, when the two factions held competing processions to commemorate the martyrdom of ᶜAli's son Husayn.[64] The equivalent occasion in the late Roman and Byzantine Empires was the processions of the Blue and Green factions and their respective fans into the arena to kick off chariot races, whether on holidays or not.[65] The wedding processions of Qaysi and Yemeni villagers in early twentieth-century Palestine, in which the bride wore a red or white veil according to her family's factional allegiance, performed a similar function, if on a humbler scale.[66] All such processions ostensibly served higher, or at least different, political, social, and religious purposes, but at some level, they functioned as vehicles for public factional display. A distinctive feature of the processions in which the Faqaris and Qasimis marched, however, was that they were not competing but common processions in which members of both factions marched, although presumably not together. In these circumstances, distinguishing emblems were more important than ever.

Moreover, as the "wars of the fists" and the Haydari-Niᶜmati brawls suggest, those processing were not a closed elite, rigidly separated from the viewing public. In the same way that the military-administrative population included multiple social and economic strata, the processions incorporated members of these different strata, either as direct participants or as "camp followers" who caught up the end of the procession or shouted encouragement from the sidelines. The procession thus fixed factional identity in the minds of those watching and those processing alike. Between these two groups, in any case, there was considerable fluidity. Likewise, factional identity itself was fluid and transient. The "we" of the Damurdashi chronicles who struggled to tell the factions apart could also belong to the factions, if only for the space of a morning or afternoon. Even those who only stood and watched participated in the event of the procession and gave the factions legitimacy by bearing witness to their existence.

Processions and other public ceremonies could themselves play critical roles in framing certain social institutions, factions included. When Evliya Çelebi describes Istanbul's craft guilds in the early seventeenth century, what he is, in fact, describing is a procession of guilds (he does the same for Cairo in a later volume);[67] that is, he does not break down the institutional structure of the Ottoman Empire's artisanal classes. One is tempted to assume that Evliya uses the procession as a convenient framework within which to present the existing guilds in some sort of logical order. Yet on closer inspection, we discover that the procession itself determines the composition of the guilds. The guilds of prostitutes and thieves, we suspect, do not exist outside of processions. This does not mean that these guilds are not "real" for the purposes of the procession; however, their reality is circumscribed by the procession. Likewise, the procession presents a certain social structure that, again, is "real" within the confines of the procession. On the other hand, other primary sources dealing with guilds, notably manuals for craft associations and market supervisors (both exploited by Evliya elsewhere in his *Book of Travels*),[68] present their own version of the guild reality: the guild as ritualized confraternity, the guild as a regulatory mechanism with responsibilities to the state. The point is not to dismiss the procession description as an "unreliable" source on the guilds but to recognize that the procession presents one facet of the institution's multifaceted reality.

In the same fashion, the procession presents one facet of the factions' reality. In everyday life, when one was absorbed in the myriad daily realities of living in Cairo, factional identity arguably receded into the background.[69] But the processions themselves, like publicly recited stories, created a space in which factional identity was paramount. Indeed, those members of Cairo's population who did not belong to the military-administrative echelons may have identified with one or the other faction only during processions. The act of processing, with its color-coded flags and identifying symbols, thus contributed to factional identity.

The Functions of Bilateral Factions

Having established that the Faqaris and Qasimis were an example of bilateral factionalism and, therefore, exploited terminology, symbols, and myths in ways distinct from multifactional societies, we may ask what distinguished the *functions* of these two factions within the society of seventeenth-century Ottoman Egypt. In this regard, it is worth pointing out that while each faction strove to distinguish itself from the opposing faction, internally, each faction fostered a strongly cohesive identity. After all, how could a soldier or an artisan be inspired to stake everything on battling the enemy faction unless he had a strong sense of himself as a Faqari or Qasimi? This shared identity was no small achievement in a society that was receiving large numbers of new arrivals from many different walks of life and from a vast array of regions and countries. Egypt's military society during the early decades of the seventeenth century absorbed troops dispatched from the imperial capital, consisting largely of *devshirme* recruits from the Balkans and western Anatolia; mercenaries from central and eastern Anatolia; and mamluks from the Caucasus, purchased by already established beys and officers of diverse ethnic origins. In addition, members of the local population had begun to enroll in the Janissary regiment in particular, hoping to gain protection and relief from taxes; meanwhile, bedouin tribes were increasingly recruited for battlefield duty.

A remarkable feature of Egypt's factions during this period is that *each* incorporated members from widely divergent and often traditionally hostile ethnicities. Of particular note is the domination of the Qasimi faction during these years by a combination of Circassians and Bosnians. Assertions of Circassian identity by Abu'l-Shawarib Ridvan Bey in the 1630s gave way to the brief hegemony of Ahmed Bey Bushnaq ("the Bosniak") in the late 1650s; in the later part of the seventeenth century and well into the eighteenth, Ahmed Bey's ostensible nephew, Ibrahim Bey Abu Shanab, assumed leadership of the faction in conjunction with the Circassian ᶜIvaz Bey. As Metin Kunt has pointed out, hostility between "western" populations, such as Bosnians, Albanians, and other Balkan peoples, and "eastern" populations from the Caucasus and neighboring regions, was common among the Ottoman military-administrative elite in the imperial center during the seventeenth century.[70] Indeed, Ahmed Bey Bushnaq's appointment as commander of the pilgrimage to Mecca in 1656 was greeted with suspicion by the Faqaris, who deplored the assumption of authority by an "outsider" (*ajnabī*).[71] That Bosnians were fully incorporated into the Qasimi faction by the following generation testifies to the power of the faction as a unifying force: Ibrahim Bey Abu Shanab's Qasimi identity clearly overrode his Bosnian identity, and any traditional enmity toward Circassians such as his fellow Qasimi ᶜIvaz Bey, in the context of Egypt's military-administrative elite. By the same token, the Faqari faction brought together Anatolian Turks and Greeks, Bosnians, Circassians, Georgians, Abkhazians, Laz, Armenians, and other ethnicities. In general terms, factional identity smoothed over the glaring differences that might otherwise have separated the motley crew that participated in Ottoman Egypt's political culture: differences of ethnicity, geographical origin, native language, occupation, wealth, age, even gender. Thus, factional identity served the role that national identity would serve in the nineteenth and twentieth centuries, although the faction's capacity for absorbing dissimilar groups was much greater than that of most nations, based as they were and are on considerations of ethnicity, language, and territorial origin.[72] In that respect, it may make more sense to liken factional cohesion to that of an army, a club, a British public school, a secret society, or even a Mafia household.

We must stress the fact that, although established locals clearly joined their ranks, the Faqari and Qasimi factions were in the business of assimilating large numbers of young men and women who were more or less uprooted from their places of origin and who were utterly unfamiliar with Egypt or, at least, with Cairo. In the case of *devshirme* recruits and mamluks, they might only recently have converted to Islam and begun to learn Turkish, to say nothing of Arabic. Naturally, a new arrival's most immediate attachment was to the head of the household that he (or she) joined. But the faction of which this household was a part provided a more deeply rooted, even corporate identity, reinforced by the distinctive colors, symbols, and rituals of that faction. We might make an analogy to loyalty to a particular political candidate *versus* loyalty to that candidate's party. The latter provides the framework, the larger context, for the former. Not surprisingly, when the Faqari and Qasimi factions began to disintegrate early in the eighteenth century, key members turned to alternative sources of corporate identity; thus, for example, the Janissary officer ᶜOsman Çavuş al-Qazdağlı, a Faqari, crossed factional lines to aid a fellow Janissary from the Qasimi faction.[73]

A final point about this form of bilateral factionalism is its ability to incorporate diverse households headed by grandees with potentially incompatible interests. Each of our two factions consisted of numerous households; it was not possible to belong to one or the other faction without belonging to a household within that faction.

Yet the Faqari and Qasimi factions were somehow greater than the sum of their parts. Collective factional identity overrode the ethnic compositions of specific households, as well as their particular interests. Thus, a largely Bosnian household, such as that of Ibrahim Bey Abu Shanab, was able not only to coexist but to cooperate with a heavily Circassian household, such as that of ᶜIvaz Bey; by the same token, a Janissary household, such as that of the Gediks, cooperated with a beylical household such as that of Ismail Bey b. ᶜIvaz.[74]

This ability to override household concerns is, I think, peculiar to bilateral factionalism. In the Mamluk sultanate, each of the numerous factions was roughly equivalent to the household of a particular sultan—and, indeed, took its name from that sultan's regnal title.[75] There was no transcendent source of identity, as there was in seventeenth-century Ottoman Egypt. The use of a common term—"faction"—to describe two societies that exhibited this fundamental difference is therefore misleading and has contributed to historiographical confusion. Bilateral factionalism, though inherently divisive, was not fragmentary but assimilative; in Ottoman Egypt, it lent cohesion to a society in demographic flux. Thus, it served the same purpose as the Blues and Greens or the Qays and Yemen, and should be regarded in the same light as those factional systems.

2

Bir Varmış, Bir Yokmuş

Folklore and Binary Oppositions in the Factional Origin Myths

A key indicator of the bilateral character of the Faqari and Qasimi factions is the origin myths associated with them, all of which stress the mutual enmity of two individuals or parties. The most insistent on this point is the origin myth presented, with numerous variations, in the Damurdashi group of chronicles. These chronicles list diametrically opposed pairs in order to stress, by analogy, the enmity of the Faqaris and Qasimis—or at least of their associated bedouin blocs, Sa^{c}d and Haram. Not coincidentally, most of these pairs can be identified as antagonistic characters in Arab popular lore. This finding underlines the bilateralism of the Faqaris' and Qasimis' struggle. Beyond this, however, it suggests that popular tales, particularly epic adventures, were used as vehicles by which to introduce factional differences to new members of Egypt's military and administrative population, and to inculcate factional loyalty among them. This chapter examines these binary oppositions and explores the manner in which allusions to popular epics could be used as a means of acculturation.

Binary oppositions are arguably implicit in Middle Eastern folktales from the opening lines. The typical Turkish tale begins, *Bir varmış, bir yokmuş*: "There was and there was not." The same basic formula exists in Arabic, *Kān mā-kān*, although one also encounters the variant *kān yā mā-kān*, which can translate to "Oh, how very long ago it was." Both the Turkish and the Arabic phrases probably derive from the Persian equivalent, *Yeki būd, yeki nā-būd*.[1] The formula has an amulet-like quality, as if it would ward off evil by refusing to insist on the absolute truth of the story.[2] At the same time, this formula establishes a polarity, a pairing of opposites, and creates the potential for a series of polar opposites throughout the narrative—not unlike the famous opening lines of Dickens' *A Tale of Two Cities*: "It was the best of times, it was the worst of times, it was the age of wisdom, it was the age of foolishness, it was the epoch of belief, it was the epoch of incredulity. . . ."

The chronicles of Ottoman Egypt do not begin with *Bir varmış, bir yokmuş*, *Kān mā-kān*, or *Yeki būd, yeki nā-būd*. Conventionally, they start with the *bismillah*, an invocation of God, who has created all things and made it possible for the chronicler to record the deeds of the Ottoman dynasty, or the governors of Egypt, or Egypt's beys and aghas. In a chronicle, the *bismillah*, rather than the more folk-magical amulet-formula, gives the author entrée into the story he has decided, or been commissioned, to tell.

For he is, make no mistake, telling a story. And following the *bismillah*, he must provide the justification for his story. The Damurdashi group of chronicles, composed during the first half of the eighteenth century, constitute the most folkloric[3] of the currently available corpus of chronicles, in Arabic or Turkish, of Ottoman Egypt. Ahmed Kâhya ᶜAzeban al-Damurdashi, ostensibly the author of the latest and most inclusive of these chronicles, gives a suitably folkloric reason for its existence: "Some of the brothers (*ikhwān*) had asked me about events in Cairo among the *sancak beys* (*sanājiq*) and the aghas and the officers (*ikhtiyāriyya*) of the seven regiments since the deposition of Sultan Mehmed [IV, r. 1648–1687]."[4] The author, whether Ahmed the deputy commander (*kâhya*) of the ᶜAzeban regiment or merely an associate, proceeds to tell them, beginning in 1100 A.H./1688 C.E. (His *terminus a quo* conveniently combines a new reign with the beginning of a new Islamic century.) "In those days," he explains, "the administration (*dawla*) of Egypt was divided into two factions (*farqatayn*)." Here, his narrative obligingly assumes the binary opposition that he is describing: "Saᶜd and Haram, Tubbaᶜi and Kulaybi, Husayni and Yazidi, Akri [?] and Qaysi." He lets loose, as it were, a string of *bir varmış, bir yokmuş*es, paired in such a way as immediately to evoke, to those familiar with regional folklore, two irremediably opposed poles. Each of these pairs of opposites following Saᶜd and Haram would have been well-known to his listeners from basic Islamic tradition and from Arab, and perhaps Turkish, folktales; his evocation of them would have served to emphasize the depth of Saᶜd's and Haram's enmity.

One can even imagine his audience—of soldiers, Sufis, or both[5]—making appropriate exclamations after each evocation, in the same manner that, for example, one spins a noisemaker at every mention of the evil counselor Haman during the reading of the Book of Esther on the Jewish holiday of Purim. To make a slightly different analogy, the scene must have resembled act 1, scene 1 of Verdi's *Il Trovatore,* when Ferrando, captain of the Aragonese palace guard, recounts the dreadful story of the gypsy woman who threw the Count di Luna's baby brother into a fire to avenge her own mother's burning at the stake.[6] I introduce these analogies not to trivialize the presentation of the two factions but to emphasize the point that this presentation takes the form of a story and, as such, evokes other stories from the vast corpus of Middle Eastern folklore. However the Damurdashi chronicles came to be written down, they must certainly have originated in oral narrative—perhaps, indeed, stories told to soldiers in the barracks. I shall return to this point presently.

The Binary Oppositions

The specific pairs of opposites evoked in the versions of the origin myth recounted in the various Damurdashi chronicles themselves draw on much earlier Islamic oral tradition and popular oral lore. "Husayni and Yazidi" refer to the martyrdom of Husayn, the younger son of the Prophet's cousin and son-in-law ᶜAli, by the army of the Umayyad ruler Yazid b. Muᶜawiya at Karbala in southern Iraq in 680 C.E. Husayn's martyrdom, which dealt a decisive blow to ᶜAlid opposition to the Umayyad caliphate, became a touchstone for Shiᶜites and, as early as the tenth century C.E., was commemorated in an annual reenactment of the incident. This "Passion play," known as *taᶜziyeh,* is still performed in Iran and among Shiᶜite populations throughout the world, including eastern Turkey, northern India, and, in a striking twist to the traditional reenactment, Trinidad.[7] Yazid, in Shiᶜite eyes—and in not a few Sunni eyes, as well—occupies much the same place as Haman in the Book of Esther; that is to say, he becomes the veritable personification of evil.

"Tubbaᶜi and Kulaybi" are more purely folkloric, although like most folkloric characters, they have their origin in historical realities. *Tubbaᶜ* was the title assumed by the rulers of the Himyarite dynasty, which controlled the northern portion of Yemen in the early centuries of the Common Era.[8] Their evocation in connection with Egypt's factions seems paradoxical in view of the earlier Damurdashi chronicler al-Qinali's insistence that the Tubbaᶜi carried a white flag: the dynasty was supposedly called "Himyarite" as a consequence of its leaders' preference for red (*ḥamrāʾ* in Arabic) robes.[9] Nonetheless, Islamic tradition gives the Himyarites a critical connection with the Kaᶜba in

Mecca, for one of their rulers in the third century is supposed to have been the first person to drape the Kaᶜba with a *kiswa*--a precursor to the elaborately embroidered coverings that, under Muslim rule, would be woven each year in Egypt and transported to Mecca with the pilgrimage caravan.[10] In this respect, then, the Tubbaᶜs were servants of the Holy Places during the pre-Islamic era.

The other member of this opposed pair, Kulaybi, probably refers to the pre-Islamic Qaysi, or northern Arab, tyrant Kulayb (literally, little dog) b. Rabiᶜa al-Taghlibi, who earned his name from the small dog that accompanied him wherever he went. Wherever the dog barked, Kulayb claimed that territory as his private property. His tyranny, according to legend, triggered the Battle of Basus in the late fifth century C.E. between his own tribe of Taghlib b. Waʾil and the brother tribe of Bakr b. Waʾil.[11] Kulayb was the subject of much popular lore and appears even in the famous pre-Islamic poems known as *muᶜallaqāt*.[12]

More germane to the Damurdashi origin myths, however, is the fact that Hasan al-Tubbaᶜi and Kulayb b. Rabiᶜa are the protagonist and antagonist of the *Qiṣṣat al-Zīr*.[13] Whatever their bases in historical reality, they would have been known to the soldiers who heard this origin myth as characters in an ancient tale whose enmity served as an analog for the enmity of Saᶜd and Haram. The two Damurdashi chronicles for which no author is adduced, seemingly composed during the 1730s, reinforce Kulayb's folkloric identity by pointing out that he is the brother of al-Zir. In the tale summarized by M. C. Lyons, Kulayb's brother Salim is known as al-Zir.[14]

The last of al-Damurdashi's binary oppositions, "Akri and Qaysi," almost certainly evokes the ancient division of the Arabs of the Arabian peninsula into northern, or Qaysi, and southern, or Yemeni, populations. This division, as noted in the previous chapter and in chapter 3, goes back to the basic cultural and linguistic differences between the Arab tribes of the interior of the peninsula and those native to Yemen and the Hadramawt.[15] Many later tribal and political rivalries partook of this most basic division, which appears to have crystallized following the early Islamic conquests and the spread of Arab tribes outside the Arabian peninsula. Indeed, the Qaysi-Yemeni division bears on two of the other binary oppositions in al-Damurdashi's list: namely, "Tubbaᶜi and Kulaybi" and "Husayni and Yazidi." The Himyarite *Tubba*ᶜs, as noted above, were the supreme example of the achievements of south Arabian civilization, while Kulaybi evidently alludes to a pre-Islamic Qaysi leader—a leader who supposedly proclaimed himself king after a victory over the united

Yemeni tribes.[16] Meanwhile, "Husayni," and ᶜAlids in general, are sometimes associated with those Yemeni Arabs who settled in Iraq and came to feel disenfranchised by the Umayyad state,[17] whereas "Yazidi" refers unmistakably to the Umayyad establishment.

What makes this particular binary opposition problematic is the mysterious "Akri." A relatively straightforward hypothesis is that it is a misrendering of Bakri, referring to the tribe of Bakr b. Waʾil. Although the Bakr were themselves a tribe of the northern, or Qaysi, subdivision of Rabiᶜa, Rabiᶜa allied with the Yemeni ᶜAzd population in the eastern Iranian province of Khurasan against a northern bloc known as Qays/Tamim. Indeed, the basic tribal rivalry took on a different coloring in each major province of the Umayyad empire.[18]

The chronicle of the Damurdashi group author known as al-Qinali gives a more elaborate list of binary oppositions, including, in addition to Tubbaᶜi and Kulaybi, Zughbi and Hilali, and Qalaʾuni and Baybarsi. These pairings, too, evoke both historical and mythologized characters and events. As P. M. Holt points out, Zughbi and Hilali are tribes in the great epic of the migration of the Banu Hilal bedouin from the central portion of the Arabian peninsula known as al-Najd westward into Egypt and, ultimately, as far as Morocco and Spain. Their peregrinations are memorialized in three epic cycles.[19] In the early nineteenth century, according to Edward W. Lane, these stories were widely recited, always to the accompaniment of a two-stringed instrument (*rabāb*) known as the "poet's fiddle."[20] The Hilalis' historical migration to Egypt occurred during the eighth century C.E., and their sweep through North Africa during the eleventh, at the instigation of the Fatimid caliph al-Mustansir (r. 1036–94);[21] nonetheless, the legends that sprang up around them place them in the service of the ᶜAbbasid caliph Harun al-Rashid (r. 786–809) and his sons al-Maʾmun (r. 813–33) and al-Muᶜtasim (r. 833–42). Although the Hilalis were followed in their westward migrations by the confederation of the Banu Sulaym, the Sulaym barely figure in the Hilali epics. In a different epic, however, they appear as the perennial enemies of the Banu Kilab.[22] The Zughba, meanwhile, were one of three chief subdivisions of the Banu Hilal; the notion of a rivalry between them and the "Hilalis" may stem from the historical infighting among the Zughba and the other two Hilali subdivisions, in the course of which each group allied sporadically with other Arab and Berber tribes.[23] In the principal Banu Hilal epic, however, the Zughba are not related to the Banu Hilal but instead are resident in the Najd when the Banu Hilal first arrive there, fleeing a famine. The Hilali hero Abu Zayd must subdue the Zughbi chieftain Dhiʾab. In a second epic, Dhiʾab betrays and kills Abu Zayd in a struggle for control of the "seven thrones and fourteen strong castles" of the Maghrib and Spain.[24]

Al-Qinali presents a further dichotomy between Qalaʾuni and Baybarsi. In contrast to all the other pairings, this one quite plainly refers to the history of the Mamluk sultanate—or at least, to that history as reconstructed for popular consumption during the Ottoman era. Baybars al-Bunduqdari was the founder of the Mamluk sultanate. A Kıpchak Turk, probably from the territory of what is now Ukraine, he was purchased as a mamluk by the Ayyubid sultan al-Salih Najm al-Din Ayyub (r. 1240–49). Ten years of bloody coups and countercoups followed al-Salih's death in 1249, as the late sultan's mamluks struggled for supremacy. After scoring a critical victory over a Mongol army at ʿAyn Jalut in Syria in 1260, Baybars participated in the assassination of the mamluk general Qutuz, who had seized the throne, and ascended the throne himself.[25]

Qalaʾun was, like Baybars, a Kıpchak mamluk of al-Salih Ayyub. Following the death of Baybars' son in 1280, Qalaʾun was chosen by the powerful circle of former mamluks of al-Salih to assume the office of sultan.[26] Qalaʾun has the distinction of founding the Mamluk sultanate's only viable dynasty; his descendants dominated the Mamluk regime for 120 years following Baybars' death.[27]

That said, the folkloric personae of Baybars and Qalaʾun bear only the most tenuous resemblance to the historical reality, hazy as the latter is. Baybars is the hero of a narrative known as the *Sīrat al-Ẓāhir Baybars,* which may have originated in heroic legends that began to circulate within a generation of Baybars' death but which, by the later part of the Ottoman era, had burgeoned into an immense and varied epic cycle. The earliest extant manuscript of this epic was composed in the sixteenth century; most surviving manuscripts date from the nineteenth century.[28] Like other tales from the Arabic oral tradition, all are chock-full of accretions from the Ottoman era, so that the Baybars of the epic routinely fires off cannon and drinks coffee. Moreover, Ottoman titles and institutions abound in the tales; provincial governors are termed pashas, for a notable example.[29] Notwithstanding, much of the story line centers on continual struggles against the Crusaders, on the one hand, and the Mongols, on the other. We can conclude only that these tales reflect Ottoman-era popular memory of the events of the early Mamluk sultanate, embellished with stock elements of shape-changing wizards and damsels in distress.

As depicted in these tales, Baybars is not really a Turkish mamluk at all but the "Persian" (*ʿAjam*) prince Mahmud, son of the last Khwarazm-shah, "Alqan Shah Jamak," whose Central Asian kingdom has been overrun by "Hulaʾun" (Hulagu) and the Mongols.[30] This fanciful lineage may ultimately derive from a claim to Khwarazmian descent on the part of Baybars' predecessor Qutuz; the historical Baybars, for his part, married the daughter of the historical last Khwarazm-shah, who, after his defeat by Genghis Khan, was invited to Egypt by al-Salih Najm al-Din Ayyub. Baybars' son was named for his Khwarazm-shah grandfather.[31] Moreover, the Kıpchak tribe from which Baybars came had been driven into the Crimea by the Mongol incursions. In the epic, Baybars' comrades-in-arms are the Ismaili Shiʿite guerrillas who inhabit the mountains of Lebanon. Improbable though such an alliance might seem, the historical Baybars did conquer the Syrian strongholds of the Ismaili Assassins and subsequently exploited the Assassins' unique skills for his own ends.[32] Different manuscripts present different versions of the rivalries between Baybars and other mamluks. In a late-nineteenth-century Egyptian manuscript, Aybak is Baybars' chief rival,[33] while in the most extensive manuscript, copied in nineteenth-century Aleppo, his nemesis is Qalaʾun. In this latter manuscript, Baybars and Qalaʾun are purchased from the same slave market and transported to Egypt jointly. Qalaʾun is contemptuous of Baybars' degraded physical state, which is only exacerbated by a bout of diarrhea during the journey to Egypt.[34] Qalaʾun himself is portrayed as an arrogant Turk who speaks a broken Arabic replete with Turkicisms. (This feature may have some basis in historical fact, since Qalaʾun was enslaved at a relatively late age and never achieved fluency in Arabic.)[35] When Baybars dies, Qalaʾun attempts to promote his own son for the succession. It is almost surely this rivalry that al-Qinali evokes by opposing "Baybarsi" to "Qalaʾuni."

In sum, the storytellers of the Damurdashi group of chronicles situate their versions of the Saʿd-Haram origin myth within the familiar genre of popular oral epics by making direct reference to characters from these epics. By this means, the Saʿd-Haram origin myth is shaped by these preceding myths, just as those myths must have been shaped by still earlier tales, such as those of the giant hero ʿAntar and those included in the Iranian epic *Shahname*.[36] The binary oppositions so familiar from these earlier stories—such essential framing devices in many folkloric epics—shaped the popular perception of the political realities that had prevailed in Egypt a century earlier. Saʿd and Haram really existed, just as Baybars and the Banu Hilal really existed. But the reality of the early seventeenth century was not the reality of the early eighteenth, when al-Qinali and Ahmed Kâhya ʿAzeban al-Damurdashi presumably narrated their tales. These chroniclers created a reality that worked in their particular political and social context by using the accommodating framework of the popular epic.

If, then, the narrators of the Damurdashi chronicles present the factions in terms of a series of binary oppositions, does it follow that the two factions themselves identified with these pairs of opposites? That is to say, did members of the Faqari faction, allied with the Nisf Saᶜd, identify with the white flag, Tubbaᶜ, Husayn, the Zughba, Qalaᵓun, and Yemen (or Bakr)? Did the Qasimis likewise identify with the red flag, Kulayb, Yazid, the Hilalis, Baybars, and Qays? Although Holt seems to think that the pairings line up pretty convincingly,[37] I am inclined to believe that al-Qinali got his pairings backward, and that the affiliation should be Faqari/Saᶜd-Tubbaᶜ-Husayn-Hilali-Baybars-Yemen *vs.* Qasimi/Haram-Kulayb-Yazid-Zughba-Qalaᵓun-Qays. (If anything, the rearranged order suggests how mechanical the narration had become.) In this case, the Qasimis/Haram are consistently portrayed as the "bad guys": Kulayb b. Rabiᶜa and Yazid b. Muᶜawiya were, according to the stories, tyrants; even Qalaᵓun and the Banu Zughba plotted the downfall of heroes. This does not mean, however, that the Damurdashi chroniclers are somehow anti-Qasimi; on the contrary, the Damurdashi group's connection to the ᶜAzab regiment implies Qasimi sympathies, as at least one prominent scholar has noted,[38] and Ahmed Kâhya ᶜAzeban al-Damurdashi treats certain Qasimi leaders downright reverentially.[39] Instead, these negative attributes, I believe, have nothing to do with the Qasimis' everyday political and economic activities but everything to do with the context of the origin myths in which they appear. The Qasimis, I would argue, occupy the position of the rhetorical "villain" in these myths, in the same way that perfectly decent members of the Shiᶜite community take the roles of the evil men in red in the Passion play. This may, in fact, be part of the rhetorical purpose of the string of binary oppositions; it may be part of the story even if it has no connection to historical reality. Since so little is known about the genesis and purpose of the Damurdashi chronicles, however, these must remain speculations. It is worth noting, however, that the rather different version of the factional origin myth transmitted by Ahmed Çelebi, about whom we are equally ill-informed, is blatantly pro-Faqari, even though nothing in the rest of his chronicle hints at such a stance.[40]

Why Folklore?

But why include these folkloric allusions in a chronicle? Were they simply a concession to age-old ritual, much like the processions in which the factions marched? Did they serve any practical purpose at the time when the chronicles were compiled—even as a prompt for collective memory? Again, the chronicle's connection to the ᶜAzeban corps provides a clue. Ahmed Kâhya ᶜAzeban's assertion that "the brethren" asked him to recount the deeds of past heroes makes sense if we consider the circumstances of soldiers in the ᶜAzeban or any other regiment. We know from archival evidence that Egypt's regiments in the early eighteenth century contained young men—mamluks, mercenaries, members of the palace soldiery—from a disparate array of locales: Abkhazia, Albania, Anatolia, Armenia, Bosnia, Bulgaria, Circassia, Georgia, Greece, Hungary, Macedonia, Romania, Russia, Serbia, as well as Egypt itself and other Arab provinces.[41] These young men suddenly found themselves in a strange regiment in a strange land (or at least a strange city or neighborhood), attached to a household and a faction for no self-evident reason, although some may well have shared ethnicity, language, or even blood ties with the head of that household.[42] In any event, they needed to be socialized and to make sense of their new environment. More than that, they needed to internalize their new identities as members of a particular household and faction.

Here, the analogy of the child at Purim or, even better, Passover makes perfect sense. At the Passover seder, the youngest child makes sense of the unfamiliar holiday rituals by asking "why": Why is this night different from all others? Why on this night do we eat unleavened bread? and so on. By the same token, we can imagine a young recruit from Bosnia or Georgia or eastern Anatolia—or even Upper Egypt—asking his commanding officer, Why do we hate the Qasimis? How did these two factions come to be, and why? Why do we carry a white banner while the Qasimis carry a red one? Why do our standards have a knob, while theirs have a disk? And in both cases, the authority figure can truthfully answer, "We were bondsmen in the land of Egypt."

Just as the youngest child, over years of seders, internalizes the story of the Exodus of the Hebrews, so the young recruit internalized a body of lore repeated by successive household heads and barracks commanders—although to be sure, a highly ritualized annual holiday is rather different from the presumably more casual, ad hoc atmosphere of barracks or coffeehouse storytelling.[43] Until the Damurdashi chronicles were written down, however, the story undoubtedly changed as the years passed and eyewitnesses to the events described became ever rarer. By the early eighteenth century, memory of the factions' origins had blurred; they had begun to assume "from time immemorial" status even while drawing ever closer to the brink of obsolescence. This combination created the ideal conditions for the crystallization of an origin tradition.

I want to stress, though, that the form this tradition took, that of a story or series of stories, is not coincidental. Children are taught the Passover tradition, as well as a host of other basic religious, historical, and cultural traditions, by hearing stories about the origins of these traditions. The frame of the story triggers memory and retention. By the same token, the rhetoric of the storyteller—in this case, the binary oppositions—serves to fix the nature of the subject being explained, and to personalize it, so that the raw recruit hearing the story feels an automatic sympathy with and connection to the protagonists, and a corresponding automatic antipathy toward the antagonists. In the case of a recruit listening to al-Damurdashi's tale, the binary oppositions undoubtedly helped him to internalize the factional lore, for he could easily connect them to binary oppositions with which he was familiar from his home culture: quarreling village factions, family feuds, rival religions or sects of a single religion, various Christian or animist traditions, various bits of regional mythology.

In this regard, the memoirs of Konstantin Mihalowicz prove instructive. Mihalowicz was, so far as we can tell, a Serbian soldier serving in the Hapsburg army in the Balkans late in the fifteenth century; he was captured by the forces of Sultan Mehmed II and served as a Janissary auxiliary until he was able to escape and rejoin the Hapsburgs. This sort of experience cannot have been so very uncommon; what is uncommon, however, is the fact that Mihalowicz later prepared a memoir of his experiences that provides a useful window onto Janissary culture of the period. In the absence of a formal orientation to Ottoman, and more specifically Janissary, history, traditions, and folkways, Mihalowicz evidently gleaned what information he could from his own observations of Ottoman military life and, most intriguingly, from the stories told by his comrades-in-arms. Some of the stories that he reproduces reflect the filtering of Islamic tradition through the mental frameworks of recruits from myriad backgrounds. The Janissaries had, for a notable example, a special reverence for ᶜAli b. Abi Talib and for his double-bladed sword Dhu'l-Faqar—a reverence strengthened by the mystical traditions of the Bektashi Sufi order, to which the Janissaries had a particular attachment. Mihalowicz's account of the sword, however, reads like the Arthurian legends of the sword in the stone and of Excalibur: on the Prophet Muhammad's death, ᶜAli supposedly struck Dhu'l-Faqar against a rock until it became embedded in the rock; when his own time drew nigh, ᶜAli threw the sword into the sea, which "bubbled and seethed" for three days in mourning for ᶜAli.[44] If such stories, so different from the "canonical" traditions of the sword found in the *ḥadīth* and the Prophetic biographical (*sīra*) literature,[45] were current among late fifteenth-century Janissaries, they must certainly have drawn on the native folklore of the diverse recruits who entered the regiment over the years. Indeed, the Dhu'l-Faqar traditions must have resonated with these recruits, because they shared telling features with the various "magic sword" legends with which these recruits would surely have been familiar from childhood. It seems only natural that the recruits would mold the Dhu'l-Faqar tales to fit their own familiar mythologies; by this means, they could participate in—in fact, contribute to—and thus, more easily identify with, Janissary culture.

At the same time, these motifs can only have been reinforced by the tales themselves, which teem with magic swords (occasionally even thrown into the sea) and the like.[46] Furthermore, they contained universal elements—heroic warriors, suffering maidens, evil enchanters, miraculous victories, poignant self-sacrifices—familiar to listeners from many different cultures and reminiscent, no doubt, of the stories on which these recruits had been raised. This was true even of the tales of the Prophet Muhammad and his companions, which at first blush might seem the most "alien" to the cultures from which many of the new recruits had been removed. The figure of ᶜAli b. Abi Talib seems to have struck a chord with Mihalowicz, as it must have with most recruits: the virtuous hero of almost superhuman strength.[47] His son Husayn's martyrdom must have resonated with recruits of various Christian backgrounds as reminiscent of Jesus' Passion; the larger theme of an heroic champion of justice betrayed by the uncaring masses and slaughtered by tyrants would have elicited even wider sympathy.

Many recruits, furthermore, were drawn into the spiritual life of their regiments through the Sufi orders with which these regiments were affiliated and through whose influence their sympathy for ᶜAli may have been reinforced. The Janissaries' connection to the Bektashi order is well-known. Yet other Sufi orders—notably, two offshoots of the Khalwati (Turkish, Halveti) order—likewise held an attraction for certain regiments in certain locations. The branch of that order founded by Ibrahim Gülsheni, who came to Egypt from northwestern Iran around the end of the fifteenth century, was popular among Ottoman soldiers, regardless of regiment, stationed in Egypt during the sixteenth century. Even two Ottoman governors reportedly became disciples of the shaykh, while the widow of the last Mamluk sultan, Tumanbay, executed after the Ottoman conquest, reportedly married Gülsheni's son.[48] By the late seventeenth century, according to Evliya Çelebi, the ranks of the Khalwatis, and Gülsheni's disciples more specifically, included not only soldiers but government officials.[49] The name by which the chronicler al-Damurdashi is known, meanwhile, refers to the Khalwati suborder founded in Egypt by Shams al-Din Muhammad Demirdash, who accompanied Gülsheni; *Al-Durra al-muṣāna* mentions two Sufi *baba*s, or shaykhs, one of them clearly Demirdashi/Gülsheni, who seem to have been attached to the ᶜAzeban regiment.[50] The story of Husayn's martyrdom at Karbala by Yazid b. Muᶜawiya was thus probably as well-known among Egypt's soldiers as the lore of the sword Dhu'l-Faqar—which Husayn had inherited from his father.

The Damurdashi chronicles take this process one step farther by using the tales that the soldiers have presumably already learned to impart history. In effect, the tales provide narrative frameworks within which to organize fairly recent historical events for the specific purpose of reciting them. The use of such frameworks is a tried and true technique of storytellers throughout history. Folklorists have repeatedly demonstrated that a basic story framework serves as a sort of a set piece on which the storyteller can improvise as the occasion demands.[51] The Damurdashi chronicles certainly adhere to this principle. Whenever a new Ottoman governor docks at Alexandria, for example, the narrative proceeds with a stock account of his journey to Cairo and the processions and feasts staged by Egypt's grandees to welcome him. The same turns of phrase appear; only the names of the governors and the grandees change, along with select details.[52] This is not to suggest that these governors' accession ceremonies were not real events that occurred in real time; they were. But as relayed by the Damurdashi chronicles, they adhere to a set framework. Through such narrative strategies, events become stories; in fact, the term *akhbār* refers to these sorts of event-narratives, which we should be careful to distinguish from unnarrated events.

So it was a matter of the soldiers' using the structures and motifs of their native folklore to assimilate the heroic tales they encountered in Cairo, then using the structures and motifs of these heroic tales to assimilate historical events of the last century or so. But cultural encounters, and narrative encounters, are two-way streets. As much as Egyptian folklore must have affected these soldiers' perceptions of history, their vaguely remembered native folklore and, to an even greater extent, their daily routine in Ottoman Cairo left a mark on the corpus of Egyptian folklore. Thus, the folktales that have come down to us today are replete with Ottoman-era anachronisms. Nowhere are these more evident than in the *Sīrat al-Ẓāhir Baybars*. Surviving manuscripts of this epic reflect the preoccupations of the Ottoman-era soldiery, particularly during the seventeenth and early eighteenth centuries: pashas, aghas, cannon, firearms, coffee, and exposure to a bewildering variety of peoples from all corners of the world.

It would seem natural for soldiers in the barracks of Ottoman Cairo to evoke the exploits of the legendary Baybars, who, like Alexander, had by now acquired a mythical persona that bore only a scant resemblance to his historical identity. We can conjecture that these tales were part of the cultural baggage that recruits to the Ottoman regiments, and to the households of grandees, acquired as part of their acculturation to Egypt. As in the case of Mihalowicz, the Baybars tales probably "took" so effectively because they dovetailed with traditions with which the recruits were familiar from their native lands. Virtually every culture has myths of great warrior-heroes, such as Alexander or St. George. It is even conceivable that newcomers from Iran and certain regions of the Caucasus and Transcaucasus, to say nothing of other parts of the Ottoman Empire, may already have been familiar with some version or other of the Baybars stories or the tales of the *Shahname.*

We may gauge the pervasiveness of these tales within Egyptian society by the chroniclers' remarkably casual allusions to their protagonists and antagonists. No explanation is given; familiarity is assumed. If the binary oppositions of the Damurdashi chronicles themselves point to such widespread familiarity, other narrative sources from throughout the Ottoman period reinforce this impression. In his descriptions of the Egyptian countryside, the seventeenth-century traveler Evliya Çelebi reports numerous local traditions attributing the founding of towns and the establishment of practices to Noah and his sons; to Joseph; to Moses, Pharaoh, and Haman; to King Solomon and his vizier Asaf; but also to the Hilalis; and to the culture heroes Sayf ben Dhi Yazan, a mythical ruler of Yemen, and the black-skinned giant ᶜAntar.[53] In Ibn Zunbul's sixteenth-century account of the Ottoman conquest of Egypt, the superhuman prowess of the mythical Mamluk emir Sharbak is compared to that of ᶜAntar; indeed, Sharbak is supposed to have composed a poem lamenting the Mamluk defeat in which he invokes the tales of ᶜAntar and al-Zir.[54] Writing in the early eighteenth century, Ahmed Çelebi claims that a Delta bedouin population is descended from the Hilali hero Abu Zayd.[55] Meanwhile, the Danish naturalist Carsten Niebuhr, describing Yemen in the latter half of the eighteenth century, reports that the most popular stories are those of ᶜAntar, the *Shahname* hero Rustam son of Zal, and Baybars.[56] Given Yemen's sustained links to Egypt, to be examined in detail in chapter 4, we can probably conclude that similar, if not identical, preferences prevailed in Egypt.

These stories, as much as any other feature of the recruits' acculturation—*furūsiyya* exercises, Sufi indoctrination, fluency in Turkish or Cairene Arabic, even the physical setting of the barracks—contributed to group solidarity within the specific regiment or household. Over and above identification with the household or regiment, of course, the Saᶜd-Haram origin myth reinforced factional identification. The Damurdashi chronicles' presentation of this myth seems to represent a process of factional allegiance-building—and, more broadly, military acculturation—that was accomplished in part by means of folklore. Even the binary oppositions played a role in the process by accustoming a recruit to identifying with the rhetorical "good guy" or "bad guy" role his faction occupied in this dichotomy. By framing the seventeenth-century reality in terms of heroes past, moreover, the storytellers bestowed legitimacy upon the factions by rhetorically linking them to these cultural icons and portraying their struggles as reenactments of those recounted in the myths.[57] In more mundane terms, this was part of a healthful socializing exercise, similar to the way in which, in the children's game of cowboys and Indians, one group plays the cowboys, the other the Indians (in the old days, the Indians were typically the "bad guys," but in today's more enlightened society, they are just as likely to be the "good guys"). Indeed, Qasim Bey's words, as relayed by Ahmed Çelebi, are curiously reminiscent of those of a child proposing such a game: "I'll be on the sultan's side, and you be on Egypt's side."[58] In a modern-day parallel to this scenario, the Egyptian Nobel Laureate Naguib Mahfouz, in a collection of oral reminiscences, recalls hearing folk poetry chanted in the neighborhood coffeehouse during his childhood, ". . . and if the folk poet told the story of Abu Zayd al-Hilali, the crowd would divide into two factions (*farīqayn*), the first supporters of Abu Zayd, the second supporters of Dhiʾab, like football fans today. . . ."[59]

As Mahfouz's account implies, there was a distinctly performative element to these tales. Whether or not the accounts of the two factions specifically were told in public settings, older, better-established tales, such as those of the Hilalis and Baybars, were unquestionably recited in public arenas,[60] where faction members, at work in their shops or on guard at the city gates, would have heard them. As noted above, the written texts of the Damurdashi chronicles, Ahmed Çelebi, and even al-Jabarti contain what amount to narrative prompts, indicating that at least some of the material they contain may once have been orally recounted. In that case, the recitation may have been accompanied by the accoutrements of public performance: the "poet's fiddle," a handdrum, perhaps a hanging bearing paintings of the action, as in modern-day recitations of the *Shahname* in Iran.[61] It may not be too far-fetched to suggest that on occasion, listeners acted out some of the events described in these tales, much as Shiᶜites acted out the events of Husayn's martyrdom, if more informally.

On close consideration, this sort of acculturation through storytelling seems more natural than surprising, particularly if we invoke the biblical exhortation that is echoed in the Passover Haggadah: "Thou shalt tell thy son" (Exod. 13:8). Here, of course, we are dealing with a society in which fictive kinship was arguably more important than blood kinship. Yet in such an environment, a fictionalized past could serve to build fictive bonds. In effect, then, these origin myths exploited folklore in order to teach and to acculturate a new generation.

3

Saᶜd and Haram

The Factions' Bedouin Equivalents

In the origin myths transmitted in the Damurdashi group of chronicles and in al-Jabarti's *ᶜAjāʾib al-āthār*, the division between Saᶜd and Haram predates and even seems to take precedence over the division between Faqari and Qasimi. Although none of the chroniclers in question explicitly states that the Saᶜd and Haram are bedouin tribal groupings, this becomes apparent from the manner in which the chronicles present the two blocs and from the activities in which they engage. In the narrative of the chronicles, furthermore, the Saᶜd, without exception, identify with the Faqaris while the Haram identify with the Qasimis; indeed, one of the Damurdashi myths emphasizes this circumstance by referring to the factions as Faqari-Saᶜd and Qasimi-Haram.[1] These two bedouin blocs carried the factional rivalry from the cities and major towns into the countryside, both in Egypt and beyond. Their participation and, on occasion, preeminence in Egypt's factional rivalry thus contributed to the pervasive, society wide character of this distinctive brand of factionalism. This chapter, therefore, explores the identities and functions of the Saᶜd and Haram: from the implications of their names and their representation in the chronicles to their probable origins, components, and arenas of operations. The object of this exploration is to ascertain the role that Saᶜd and Haram played in determining the dynamics of factional political culture.

The Connotations of *Niṣf*

Toward the end of his account of the origin of the names Faqari and Qasimi, Ahmed Kâhya ᶜAzeban al-Damurdashi begins to refer to the two factions to which these names attached as *Niṣf* Saᶜd and *Niṣf* Haram.[2] Indeed, that is how they appear later in his chronicle, as well as in those of al-Jabarti and Ahmed Çelebi. The prefix *niṣf*, literally, "half," marks the two blocs as bedouin tribal groups. Such fractions were a feature of Arab tribal settlement and dispersal patterns. Even in the early centuries of the Common Era, the bedouin confederations of Yemen were typically divided into various fractional subdivisions, notably thirds (s. *thulth*), fourths (s. *rub*ᶜ), fifths (s. *khums*), or ninths (s. *tsī*ᶜ).[3]

For a parallel of even greater antiquity and broader geographical scope, we may cite the biblical account of the settlement of the Twelve Tribes of Israel, purportedly descended from Joseph and his brothers, in the land of Canaan. Joseph's own tribe was so large that it was divided into two tribes named after his two sons, Ephraim and Manasseh. Once the tribes had reached the Promised Land, Manasseh in turn split into two, half the tribe remaining east of the Jordan River, along with the tribes of Reuben and Gad, the other settling west of the Jordan in association with Ephraim. The Bible repeatedly refers to this eastern tribe as "the half-tribe of Manasseh."[4] Rare mentions are also made of the remaining (western) half, both halves, and even "all of Manasseh."[5] What concerns us, in any case, is that in this context, when a recognized tribe split into two or more parts and each part went its own way, the fraction prefix remained as a reminder of the unity that had been. Half of Manasseh's descendants settled east of the Jordan; the other half settled to the west.[6] The implication, then, is that if half of Saᶜd and half of Haram had settled in Egypt, the other halves must have migrated—or remained—somewhere else.

In point of fact, the most likely place for them to have remained was Yemen. This conclusion results both from sources placing the two tribal blocs in Yemen before and after the Ottoman conquest, and from chance remarks in Ottoman-era Egyptian chronicles that link the two blocs to Yemen. Because the body of evidence for the two blocs varies in both quantity and conclusiveness, however, we must examine each bloc separately.

The Haram in Yemen

The name *Ḥarām* arouses our suspicions at once. It derives from the Arabic root *ḥ-r-m*, connoting "to forbid" or "to restrict." A *ḥaram*, minus the long *a*, is a restricted place or even a sacred precinct, keeping in mind that what is sacred is often ritually taboo, as well. Thus, the

Muslim Holy Cities of Mecca and Medina are commonly known, even today, as *Al-Ḥaramayn al-sharīfayn* (the two noble sanctuaries). The same word, anglicized to "harem," denotes a restricted quarter reserved for the women of a household.[7] The adjectival form, *ḥarām*, can have the same double-barreled meaning of "sacred" and "forbidden." Thus, the Kaᶜba, situated in the *ḥaram* of Mecca, is known as the *bayt al-ḥarām*: the sacred house that is, at the same time, off limits to non-Muslims and which even Muslims may enter only at specified times of year.[8] The mosque surrounding it is known as *al-masjid al-ḥarām*, or "the sacred mosque."

Ḥarām can also carry what at first seems an unequivocally negative meaning. In Islamic law, the worst possible human actions are those labeled *ḥarām*, or absolutely forbidden, as opposed to "objectionable but not forbidden."[9] Analogous usages in the Bible, however, point to the ambivalence of this term in this context, as well. In Deuteronomy and Joshua, *herem* and various verbs derived from the same root recur repeatedly to denote the Israelites' total annihilation of indigenous settlements in the land of Canaan: men, women, and children are killed, no booty is taken except precious metals for the tabernacle, and the site is abandoned. Such measures were supposed to prevent the Israelites' being seduced by the idolatry of these populations.[10] English translations typically render *herem* as "proscription" or "doom,"[11] yet there is also a connotation of rendering the sites off limits, that is, ritually taboo. For these sites are not only to be utterly destroyed; nothing is to be removed from them, and no one is to touch anything that has been in them. In common parlance, in both Arabic and modern Turkish, the word *ḥarām* connotes "unthinkable," "absolutely forbidden," while *ḥarāmī* is used for a thief.[12] *Ibn ḥarām*, literally "son of the forbidden," refers to an illegitimate child and is no small insult.[13]

A bedouin tribe called *Ḥarām* could, in light of the foregoing, be a tribe with extraordinary, sacred characteristics or roles; or, on the other hand, it could be considered an anathema. Yet neither quality is readily apparent from pre-Ottoman accounts of this tribe. The tribe evidently had a lengthy presence in Yemen. Even pre-Islamic inscriptions in the distinctive south Arabian language refer to a Ḥ-R-MM.[14] This was evidently a clan belonging to the tribal group known as Daᶜa, who invaded the mountainous central inland region of Yemen in the late antique period.[15] By the thirteenth century, at least parts of the tribe would appear to have migrated north. The seventeenth-century Zaydi chronicler Yahya b. al-Husayn notes that the Jabal Haram, or

"Mountains of the Haram," submitted to the Zaydi imam in the late thirteenth century; these were evidently located in the northern highlands of Yemen.[16] The colorful Moroccan traveler Ibn Battuta (1304–77) reports a population of "Banu Haram" living in Hali, the northernmost city in Yemen, right on the border of the Hijaz, a century later.[17] In Ottoman times, the *sharīf* of Mecca kept a garrison there.[18] Ibn Battuta further describes the Banu Haram sharing Hali with the Banu Kinana, a well-known population of Qaysi, or "northern," Arabs to whom, in fact, the Quraysh confederation belongs.[19] The Kinana figure in the title of al-Damurdashi's chronicle: *Al-Durra al-muṣāna fī akhbār al-Kināna*, literally, *The Protected Pearl: History of the Kināna.*

When Ibn Battuta remarks on the Banu Haram in Hali, he apparently intends no offense in employing this name. But could his description of Hali contain a coded double-entendre? Certain negative associations attach to the Banu Kinana, who joined the Qurayshi elite of Mecca in opposing the Prophet Muhammad in the early years of Islam. In Ibn Ishaq's biography of the Prophet, the devil, Iblis, is said to have appeared in the form of a leader of the Banu Kinana to the Quraysh, and encouraged them to ride out to fight the Muslims at the wells of Badr, north of Mecca, in 624 C.E.[20] The result was a resounding defeat for the Meccans. By the fourteenth century, to be sure, Kinana was not necessarily associated with the Qaysi tribe of that name but had become a byword for Egypt, where the Kinana's descendants had settled after the Muslim conquest. But if a fourteenth-century audience *would* have recognized the Kinana as enemies of Islam, then Ibn Battuta could have used their cohabitation with the "Banu Haram," or bastards, to make the point that Hali was in bad hands.

Tentative though this suggestion is, it gains more credibility when we examine the use of "Banu Haram" by a chronicler who witnessed the Ottoman "reconquest" of Yemen in the 1560s, following the revolt of the Zaydi imam al-Mutahhar b. Sharaf al-Din. The author, known as Rumuzi,[21] composed an unabashedly partisan *Fethname-i Yemen*, part of a larger history that included a general history of Yemen and accounts of the Ottoman conquest of Tunisia. By his own account (fo. 2v), the author composed the work during the reign of Selim II (1566–74), not long after the revolt had been quashed. A *fethname*, or saga of a conquest, is by its very nature a self-aggrandizing product of the victorious side, designed to glorify its own might and to instill dread in its enemies and potential enemies.[22] The vanquished foe, understandably, does not come off terribly well in such a context.

In this *fethname*, the target of Rumuzi's opprobrium is the Zaydi imam al-Mutahhar, whom the author prefers to call Shuwayᶜ (the [wretched] little Shi^c^ite)[23] or Lenk (lame), for he was lame in one leg. Al-Mutahhar and his followers engaged the Ottoman admiral Sinan Pasha, fighting what amounted to a guerrilla war in Yemen's rugged mountains and inhospitable plains. Small wonder that Rumuzi describes the struggle as more difficult than the Ottoman campaigns in the Balkans (fo. 34v). Rumuzi first employs the Persianate epithet *Haramzade* (son of Haram) to refer to al-Mutahhar himself; his aim is specifically to mock al-Mutahhar's lineage. The Zaydi imams were *sharīfs*, or descendants of the Prophet; on the basis of his Prophetic descent, al-Mutahhar claimed the caliphate. In fact, Rumuzi insists with a striking lack of subtlety, al-Mutahhar is an illegitimate bastard who has forged his lineage in the belief that "every *sharīf* must have a caliphate" (fo. 53r). Rumuzi is consistent in his use of Haramzade to refer specifially to the illegitimate lineage of al-Mutahhar and his descendants; on the imam's death, the author points out that he left two *Haramzadeler* (fo. 90v). For the Zaydi forces in general, Rumuzi uses the less insinuating, if equally pejorative, *Haramiler* (fos. 75r, 75v, 79v)—the same word used by the polymath Kâtib Çelebi some seventy years later to refer to the Hapsburg navy.[24] Here, his implication is perhaps not that the Zaydis as a whole are illegitimate, but rather that their practices include that which is forbidden to true Muslims—perhaps, as in the modern usage of this word, theft. His near contemporary, the better-known Arabophone chronicler al-Nahrawali al-Makki, points out that al-Mutahhar had radicalized Yemeni Zaydism by introducing rituals typically associated with Ismaili and Twelver Shi^c^ites, such as cursing the first three caliphs recognized by Sunnis—Abu Bakr, ^c^Umar, and ^c^Uthman—and including the line "Come to the best of works" in the call to prayer.[25] These public rites, furthermore, underscored al-Mutahhar's opposition to the Sunni Ottomans.

At several points (fos. 55r, 64v, 80v), Rumuzi indulges in a bit of wordplay, rearranging the letters of "Zaydi" to yield "Yazid," a clear reference to the Umayyad caliph Yazid b. Mu^c^awiya, whose army massacred ^c^Ali's younger son Husayn and his followers at Karbala. To render his point unmistakable, the author makes a direct analogy between the campaign against the Zaydis and Karbala (fo. 37v).[26]

Interestingly, these allusions to the struggle over the caliphate within the original Muslim community find echoes in the equally unsubtle rhetoric that the Zaydis employed against the Tahirids, Shafi^c^i Arabs who ruled the coastal region of Yemen during the fifteenth and early sixteenth centuries. To be sure, the Tahirids could be accused of inviting this slander by claiming descent from the Umayyads, albeit via the pious caliph ^c^Umar b. ^c^Abd al-^c^Aziz (r. 717–20 C.E.). The seventeenth-century Zaydi chronicler Yahya b. al-Husayn b. al-Qasim, a grandson of the founder of the Qasimi imamate, takes full advantage: recounting the surrender of the then Zaydi imam to the last Tahirid ruler in 1506, he accuses the Tahirid forces of "inflict[ing] on him the tortures [suffered by] the family of Husayn at Karbala." Ultimately, God got even with the Tahirids by wiping them out just as he had wiped out the Umayyads. As if to show that he is equally opposed to the Tahirids' Mamluk conquerors, Yahya compares the Mamluk emir Husayn al-Kurdi's sack of Mecca to Yazid's invasion of Medina.[27] Yet, astonishingly, Yahya does not apply these Umayyad analogies to the Ottomans, despite the fact that the Zaydi forces had expelled the Ottomans from Yemen during his lifetime. The reason may be that Yahya, like the Qasimis in general, was antagonistic toward the line of al-Mutahhar, the anti-Ottoman zealot whom Rumuzi pillories.[28] Nevertheless, each side—Zaydi and Ottoman—in some fashion claimed the rhetorical stance of the martyred line of ᶜAli and Husayn, as against the illegitimate oppressors Muᶜawiya and Yazid. Generally speaking, such a confrontation between two Muslim forces representing two alternative approaches to political and religious leadership, as well as two opposing geopolitical agendas, called forth such rhetoric, whose touchstones were the defining struggles of Islam's early history.

The question with which this line of inquiry leaves us is, Are the Haram of the south Arabian inscriptions and Ibn Battuta's Haram the same general population as Rumuzi's Haram? This question is complicated, of course, by the sometimes rhetorically charged, partisan use of the epithet Haram. Moreover, we cannot always tell when the term is being employed in the service of partisan name-calling. Nonetheless, as diffuse as our evidence for the Haram in Yemen is, an examination of the Haram in Egypt will, I think, point to connections linking the Haram in all these sources.

The Haram in Egypt

Already in the early tenth century, the Yemeni tribal genealogist al-Hamdani (ca. 893–945?) notes that the Banu Haram are in Egypt, "and among them are judges, legists, justices, and rural shaykhs."[29] Evidently, they were well-integrated in Egypt even at this early date. These Banu Haram are, moreover, a key component of the Khazraj confederation, one of the two blocs that dominated Medina at the time of the Prophet's *hijra* in 622 C.E. As such, they are Yemeni, or southern, Arabs, as opposed to Qaysis, or northerners.

A group called Haram was evidently still well-established in Egypt during the late Mamluk sultanate. They appear several times in the chronicles of Ibn Iyas, whose *History of the Circassian Mamluks* gives us the distinct impression that the Mamluk sultanate had to deal not only with Saᶜd and Haram, but with a third tribal conglomerate known as the Banu Waᵓil. In fact, it seems that the Haram's chief rivalry in the late fifteenth century was with not the Saᶜd but the Waᵓil. If we consider Ibn Iyas' reports collectively, we can discern the development of relations among these three groups. In Dhu'l-Hijja 875/May-June 1471, the chronicler reports, "the sultan gave a robe of honor to Baqar ibn Baqar, who was invested with the command of the bedouin of Sharqiyya," a subprovince of Egypt situated in the eastern Nile Delta. "He replaced one of his ancestors, ᶜIsa ibn Baqar. . . ."[30] We know from chronicles based on Ibn Iyas' contemporary Ahmad b. Zunbul that the Banu Baqar or Baqara were a tribe belonging to the Haram.[31] A few lines later, Ibn Iyas notes that two Mamluk emirs were dispatched to Sharqiyya "to halt the depredations of the bedouin" and to arrest every member of the Banu Saᶜd and Banu Waᵓil.[32] We might therefore conclude that the Mamluk sultan had chosen to promote the Banu Haram in Sharqiyya and, ultimately, to give them absolute supremacy over their rivals. The Banu Saᶜd do not reappear in either of Ibn Iyas' chronicles, leading one to suspect that they migrated out of Sharqiyya, or possibly out of Egypt, although they may simply have adopted a low profile. The Banu Waᵓil now became the Haram's chief enemies in Sharqiyya. From the 1470s through the 1490s, their constant fighting and brigandage rendered travel to or within the subprovince well-nigh impossible, and a steady stream of Mamluk emirs was dispatched from Cairo to bring the chaotic situation under control.[33] In Dhu'l-Hijja 876/June 1472, the Banu Haram and Banu Waᵓil went so far as to march all the way to the northernmost quarter of Cairo, where they pillaged the shops and stole the clothing of the residents.[34]

Quite strikingly, the Banu Waᵓil cease to appear in Ibn Iyas' annals after 1500. Of the three Sharqiyya tribal blocs with whom we began, only the Haram are left. Finally, as the Ottomans were advancing through Syria in 1516, the son of the Harami shaykh Ahmad b. Baqar rebelled against the last Mamluk sultan, Tumanbay, and offered his services to the Ottomans.[35] Thus, after being at least loose Mamluk clients, the Haram had betrayed the sultanate. Selim I and, later, Khayrbay, the first governor of Ottoman Egypt, confirmed the Banu Baqara as chiefs of the Arabs of Sharqiyya.[36] Although the Banu Baqara were driven out of Sharqiyya in the 1530s and 1540s by an enterprising Ottoman governor,[37] they evidently remained a presence in the

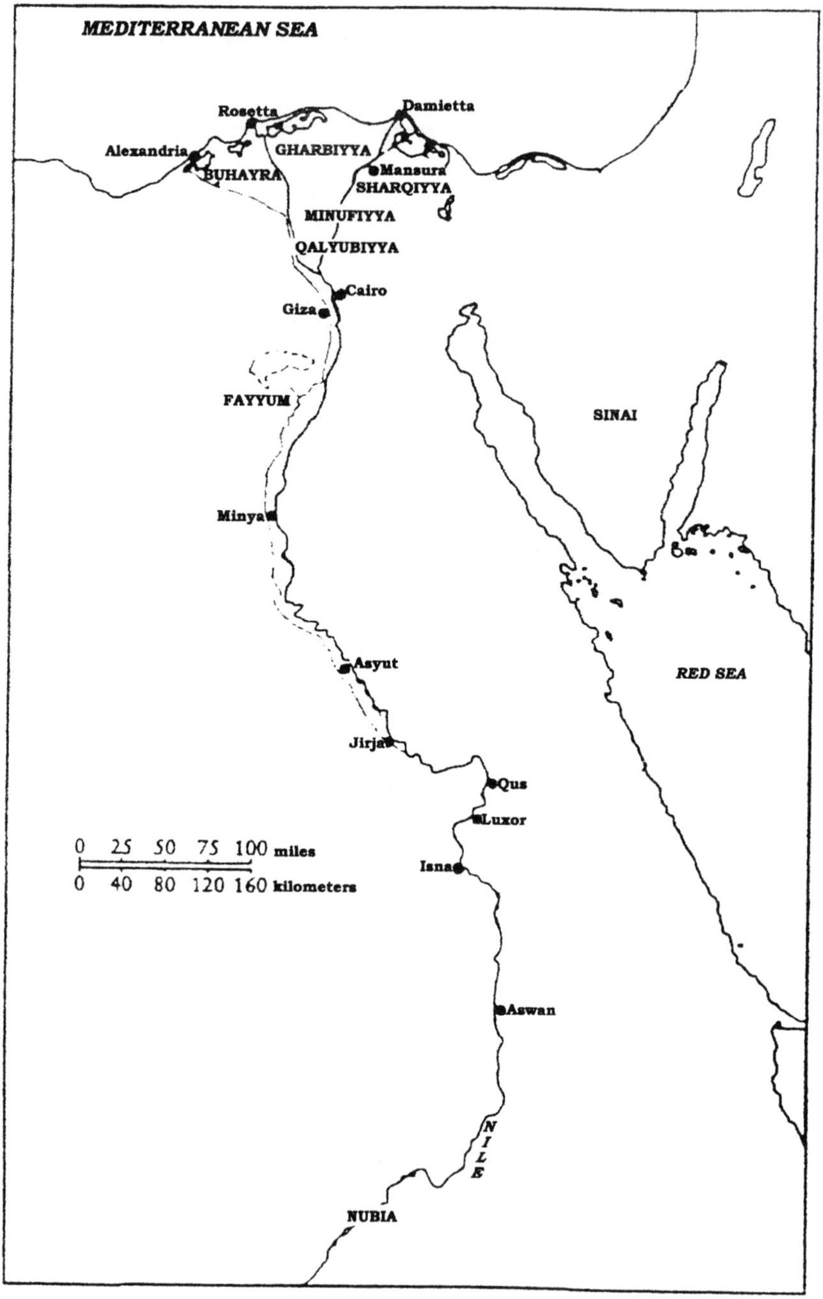

Fig. 3.1. Egypt, showing major towns and provinces

Delta. They appear in Mansura subprovince in the 1720s; their leader at the time was another Shaykh Ahmad al-Baqri, whom Ahmed Çelebi calls *shaykh Niṣf Ḥarām*.[38] By this time, furthermore, the Haram had taken over the western Delta subprovince of Buhayra; al-Damurdashi tells us that all the bedouin of that region belonged to the Nisf Haram.[39]

The early seventeenth century, when the Faqari and Qasimi factions are reported first to have emerged, was also a period of significant migration from the Egyptian countryside to Cairo. A work credited with reflecting this population shift is Shirbini's *Hazz al-quḥūf*; the author, a religious scholar who had moved to Cairo from the countryside, satirizes the behavior and customs of peasants by way of distancing ulema of rural origin from the mass of the rural population.[40] The Haram and Saᶜd appear in Shirbini's work, but only in the most negative light. According to Shirbini, the Saᶜd and Haram oppress the populace with exactions; meanwhile, ruinous feuds erupt between them. Their behavior is due principally to ignorance, which leads them to adopt barbarous customs (*sunna jāhiliyya*).[41] Shirbini mentions Saᶜd and Haram in tandem, as if one is unthinkable without the other. To him, they seem to be little more than generic oppressors of the countryside. This may indeed have been the image that popular opinion in the capital, of which Shirbini's work is thought to be representative,[42] had of them. By the nineteenth century, Edward W. Lane can report that "their names are commonly applied to any two persons or parties at enmity with each other."[43] In other words, Saᶜd and Haram functioned as a template for bilateral factionalism, not unlike the Haydaris and Niᶜmatis in Iran at this same time.[44]

Writing late in the seventeenth century, the traveler Evliya Çelebi, who spent much of the last decade of his life in Egypt, remarks scathingly on the *Ḥarām ḳavmı* (Haram people, or Haram tribe) who inhabit the Nile Delta subprovinces of Minufiyya and Gharbiyya, as well as the region around Bilbays northeast of Cairo. He claims, in one of his typical attempts to link contemporary phenomena to biblical and Qurᵓanic narratives, that the Haram descend from the Pharaoh who antagonized Moses. Moreover, he asserts that the Haram's perennial enemy is not the Saᶜd or even the Waᵓil but the Cüzam, or Juzzam, a tribal name not encountered elsewhere.[45]

It is not until the early eighteenth century, however, that we encounter any sort of significant link between the Haram bedouin of Egypt, and Yemen. Al-Damurdashi's chronicle notes the presence of "Zayidiyya" in the Egyptian countryside on two separate occasions, each of which is instructive. In 1124 A.H./1712 C.E., the Faqari chieftain Qaytas Bey attempted to trick the Qasimi grandee Ibrahim Bey Abu

Shanab by sending him to the district of Giza, just west of Cairo, while Qaytas secretly returned to Cairo, where he intended to rout the remaining Qasimi leadership. Before riding out, al-Damurdashi informs us, Abu Shanab received the services of the Zayidiyya "from among the descendants of the Circassians" (*min dhuriyyat Jarākisa*).[46] Some fifteen years later, Abu Shanab's mamluk Çerkes Mehmed Bey was locked in a struggle for provincial supremacy with his Faqari rival Dhu'l-Faqar Bey. According to the chronicler, the "Zayidiyya of the Nisf Haram" cast their lot with Çerkes Mehmed and attempted to seize Giza from the pro-Dhu'l-Faqar *kāshif*, or governor. Dhu'l-Faqar Bey received an official order from the Ottoman governor of Egypt to annihilate the Zayidiyya: men, women, and children over five years of age. When he and his followers launched an artillery assault on Giza, destroying part of the Temple of Karnak, the Zayidiyya retreated and rejoined Çerkes Mehmed in Jirja.[47] Recounting this same incident, the contemporary chronicler Ahmed Çelebi gives the group's name as *Zayda* and claims that they are descended from Abu Zayd al-Hilali, hero of the epics of the migratory Banu Hilal bedouin described in chapter 2.[48] Although it attests to the identification of real life populations with legendary characters, noted in the previous chapter, this assertion does not seem terribly convincing, given that Abu Zayd was a quasi-mythical figure and that the Hilalis ultimately dispersed across North Africa.[49] Had this group been descendants of someone named Abu Zayd, moreover, they are more likely to have been called Banu Zayd or simply Zayd.

It seems more likely that "Zayidiyya" in both these contexts means "Zaydis," even if this particular group of bedouin had abandoned any Zaydi confession they may have had; it appears with this sense in a number of chronicles dealing with Yemen.[50] The name remains a reminder of a perhaps long-departed Zaydi past in the same way that, for example, the sobriquet al-Musulmani, al-Ashkenazi, or even the derogatory Çıfıt attached to mamluks who were converts to Islam from Judaism[51] or even in the way that sobriquets linger down the generations long after they have lost their relevance, as in the case of the Egyptian households known as Qazdağlı, Shawarabi, and Shanabi.[52]

These Zayidiyya seem to be a well-known quantity to the characters in al-Damurdashi's chronicle. Although the chronicler never specifically calls them bedouin, circumstantial evidence, particularly in the second account of their appearance, indicates that they were exactly that. The Nisf Haram were themselves a bedouin bloc; logically, "Zayidiyya of the Nisf Haram" would be a subgroup of this bloc: a member tribe or even a client tribe, in the same way that the "Arabs of Quraysh" during the Prophet Muhammad's lifetime were clients of the Quraysh.[53] In al-Damurdashi's pages, they behave suspiciously like what we commonly think of as a tribe. They inhabit the countryside around the town of Wasim in the subprovince of Giza, just west of Cairo.[54] When Dhu'l-Faqar Bey attacks them, they deposit their embroidered stuffs (*muwāshāhum*) and old women with the peasants (*fallāḥīn*) and ride off with their women and children to join Çerkes Mehmed in Jirja. They are clearly a nomadic, or at least seminomadic, population, engaged in the sort of native handicrafts that are the stuff of touristic stereotypes. Moreover, al-Damurdashi's description of their actions gives the impression that they were trying to expand the Banu Haram's base of operations by adding Giza to their bases in Buhayra, Mansura, and possibly Sharqiyya.

What are we to make of al-Damurdashi's designation of these Zayidiyya as "descendants of the Circassians?" It is, of course, possible that the Jarakisa or Çerakise to whom the chronicler refers are not the ethnic group at all but simply Egypt's Çerakise cavalry regiment, the smallest and most poorly paid of the seven regiments stationed in Egypt.[55] The regimental rolls, as reproduced in pay registers of the seventeenth and eighteenth centuries, included many sons of beys and other provincial grandees,[56] although the fates of sons of Çerakise corps members are unknown. *Zaydi* identity, however, would make sense only in the context of a fictive genealogy, such as that commissioned by the Qasimi chieftain Ridvan Bey Abu'l-Shawarib (see chapter 10). If Ridvan Bey could pose as the scion of Arab-descended Circassians who had "returned" to Egypt following the Ottoman conquest, then perhaps these Zayidiyya could likewise claim descent from returned Circassians. Perhaps, in fact, they were recognized as "Circassian" because of the circulation of genealogical legends such as Ridvan Bey's. It is certainly worth noting, in any event, that Ridvan Bey claimed to be of Qurayshi descent, just like the Zaydi imams of Yemen, even if not a direct descendant of the Prophet. A fictive link between the Quraysh and Circassians was evidently available for exploitation in Ottoman Egypt.

In sum, the Nisf Haram evidently included a not insubstantial group of Yemeni Zaydis, or at least their descendants or perceived descendants, who at some point had settled in the Nile Delta. They could well have been settled in Egypt by grandees following the Ottoman defeat in Yemen (on which more in the following chapter). Indeed, the last Ottoman governor of Yemen, Qansuh Pasha, was a former Circassian bey of Egypt who, before being dispatched to Yemen, had been an opponent of Ridvan Bey al-Faqari.[57] When the Zaydis were besieging Mocha, Qansuh Pasha fled the province with the Zaydi imam's permission and passed through Mecca before returning to Egypt. In Mecca, he encountered none other than Ridvan Bey al-Faqari rebuilding the Kaᶜba. It would be tempting to assert that Qansuh brought along a group of Zaydi tribesmen who subsequently settled in the Egyptian countryside. We do know that he took an extremely unruly force of largely Rumi soldiers to Yemen.[58] Unfortunately, however, we simply do not know who, if anyone, accompanied him back.

The Saᶜd in the Arabian Peninsula

As difficult as the Haram are to trace, the Saᶜd are even more elusive. The search begins promisingly enough. A population called Banu Saᶜd was an important presence in Mecca during the Prophet Muhammad's lifetime. According to the Prophetic biographical literature, the Prophet was nursed by Halima bint Abu Dhuʾayb of the Banu Saᶜd b. Bakr;[59] thus, the Banu Saᶜd to whom Halima belonged, even if not of the Quraysh, had an enviable pedigree, coupled with a tradition of close service to the Prophet. Unfortunately for our purposes, Saᶜd was a relatively common male first name in the pre- and early Islamic Arabian peninsula. There appear to have been numerous lines of Banu Saᶜd, including the line founded by the ancestor of the Prophet's milk-mother. An arguably even more prestigious Saᶜd in early Islamic history was Saᶜd b. Abi'l-Waqqas, one of the first to follow the Prophet from Mecca to Medina, one of the earliest converts to Islam who, moreover, played a key role in the Prophet's military victories and in the early conquests of the early caliphs. Because he was skilled in the use of the bow and arrow, and, in fact, shot the first arrow in defense of Islam, he came to be regarded as the patron saint of archers.[60] Saᶜd b. Muᶜadh and Saᶜd b. ᶜUbada, meanwhile, were the respective chiefs of the two major clans in Medina, Aws and Khazraj, who invited the Prophet to immigrate to their city from Mecca. On the Prophet's death, Saᶜd b. ᶜUbada was the initial choice of the Medinese to succeed him as leader of the Muslim community.[61]

As in the case of the Haram, there is evidence that the Saᶜd enjoyed a presence in southern Arabia at some point in their history. To be sure, the name Saᶜd does not appear in the south Arabian inscriptions, nor does Ibn Battuta mention a tribal population by that name. However, the Saᶜd are noticeable in genealogies of tribes in the Hadramawt, the southernmost part of today's Yemen, extending into western Oman and bordering the Arabian Sea. The Saᶜd of Hadramawt are unquestionably Yemeni Arabs—that is, descendants of Qahtan, as opposed to Qaysi descendants of ᶜAdnan.[62] (Interestingly, the Waʾil also belong to these Qahtani lineages.)[63] Meanwhile, in the Zaydi stronghold of northern Yemen, Saᶜd and the Qaysi tribe of Rabiᶜa jockeyed for dominance in Saᶜda, capital of the first Zaydi imam al-Hadi (d. 911 C.E.), who won the Saᶜd's support.[64] The seventeenth-century Zaydi chronicler Yahya b. al-Husayn, furthermore, mentions a place called Bani Saᶜd, no doubt after the tribal population who either lives or used to live there.[65] It is difficult to determine this site's location within Yemen, but we get the vague impression that it lies near the then Zaydi imam's stronghold of Sanᶜa. Of course, it is equally difficult to tell whether the Banu Saᶜd who apparently inhabited this site belong to the same lineage as the Saᶜd of far northern Yemen, to say nothing of the Saᶜd of the Hadramawt.

The word *saᶜd,* unlike the word *ḥarām,* has an unequivocally positive meaning, namely, "good fortune." The related noun *saᶜāda* (happiness) was frequently applied to the Ottoman imperial palace and, more specifically, to the threshold in front of the sultan's audience chamber, known to historians and tourists alike as the *Bāb al-Saᶜāda/Babüssaade,* or "Gate of Felicity." In a rather ironic twist on the ambivalent meanings of *ḥarām,* the harem of the imperial palace was known as *Dār al-Saᶜāda/Darüssaade,* or "Abode of Felicity." Of greater significance for our purposes, *saᶜd* is applied to the Ottoman sultans by the decidedly pro-Ottoman chronicler al-Nahrawali al-Makki, who refers to Sultan Selim II (r. 1566–74) as *ṣāḥib al-saᶜd,* or "the possessor of good fortune," "the fortunate."[66] For rhetorical purposes, *saᶜd* connoted the exact opposite of *ḥarām,* and at least one chronicler of Yemen and vicinity took advantage of this connotation.

The Saᶜd in Egypt

Nor do the Saᶜd appear to occupy as prominent a place as the Haram in late Mamluk history. As noted above, Ibn Iyas mentions their presence in Sharqiyya subprovince in the early 1470s, before Sultan Qaytbay (r. 1468–96) ordered their arrest, along with that of the Banu Waʾil, giving the Haram supremacy in Sharqiyya. Although the Waʾil evidently recovered from this misfortune and continued to antagonize the Haram, the Saᶜd do not reappear in either of Ibn Iyas' chronicles. In fact, there is no further mention of them in Egypt before Shirbini's chronicle of the late seventeenth century. We might imagine a scenario in which the Saᶜd fled Egypt for the Yemeni highlands and/or the Hadramawt, then returned in the wake of the Ottoman expulsion from Yemen, but it would be impossible to verify it. In any event, Shirbini's scathing characterization of Saᶜd and Haram gives the distinct impression that both groups were well-known quantities in the Egyptian countryside by the later seventeenth century. In that case, the Saᶜd could hardly have been recent returnees.

What we can affirm is that in the pages of al-Damurdashi and Ahmed Çelebi, the Saᶜd appear time and again as bedouin supporters of the Faqari faction and, more broadly, of Ottoman government-sponsored initiatives. The late seventeenth-century Faqari chieftain Hasan Agha Bilifya, who, I have argued elsewhere, was almost certainly a product of the imperial palace,[67] is labeled *shaykh Niṣf Saᶜd* by al-Damurdashi in much the same fashion as his Qasimi counterpart ᶜIvaz Bey is labeled *shaykh Niṣf Ḥarām*.[68]

Regional Breakdown in Egypt

Within Ottoman Egypt, at least after the sixteenth century, the Saᶜd and Haram evidently operated as the rural tribal counterparts to the Faqari and Qasimi grandees, who were ostensibly concentrated in Cairo, the riverain port of Jirja, and other sizable cities and towns. The strength and character of the two factions outside of Cairo, particularly vis-à-vis bedouin groups not affiliated with either faction, have yet to be fully ascertained. It appears, nonetheless, that Saᶜd and Haram competed for fiscal and military dominance in a number of Egypt's subprovinces in the same fashion that the Haram and Waʾil had done under the late Mamluk sultanate. By the late seventeenth century, tax-farming, or *iltizām*, had replaced the old Mamluk system of *iqṭāᶜ*, or "military fiefs," as well as the system of Istanbul-appointed tax collectors (*amīns*) that the Ottomans had attempted to impose on Egypt during the sixteenth century. The tax farms of villages and, indeed, entire subprovinces were auctioned off to individual grandees, who tended to reside in the large towns and delegate tax collecting and maintenance duties to various agents.[69] These agents in turn were obliged to cultivate amicable relations with the tribes of the countryside—or, alternatively, to bludgeon them into submission—if they wished to perform their assigned tasks with any degree of efficacy. In practice, this meant that the bedouin bloc aligned with a particular grandee would predominate in the territory covered by the grandee's tax farm, and could, in fact, become fiscally formidable by administering the tax farm on behalf of the grandee or his agent. Just as the subprovincial governorships of Egypt, in the form of tax farms, were (at least ostensibly) divided between the Faqaris and Qasimis, so parts of the countryside came to be correspondingly divided between Saᶜd and Haram. The Faqari leader Hasan Agha Bilifya and the household that he founded, for a notable example, drew their wealth in the first instance from a cluster of village tax farms in the Upper Egyptian subprovince of al-Bahnasa; the household name, in fact, comes from one of these villages, Bilifya.[70] Given Hasan Agha's close connection to the Saᶜd, one would naturally expect the Saᶜd to be dominant in that region.

Indeed, what emerges from a perusal of the chronicles is that much of the Egyptian countryside was a veritable checkerboard of Saᶜd and Haram holdings. The Haram had at various times monopolized the Delta provinces of Sharqiyya, Buhayra, and Mansura; they seem also to have had a presence in Minufiyya, strategically located in-between Sharqiyya and Buhayra.[71] The Saᶜd, meanwhile, controlled the subprovince of Qalyubiyya, just south of all these Haram holdings and just north of Cairo. And in association with Hasan Agha Bilifya and his tenacious household, al-Bahnasa was "theirs."

Other subprovinces, however, were bones of contention between the two rival blocs and, correspondingly, between the Faqari and Qasimi factions with whom they were allied. The writings of Ibn Iyas and, later, of Shirbini make it plain, as we have seen, that violent clashes between bedouin blocs competing for the same provincial revenues were not uncommon. By the same token, a struggle over a tax farm between two grandees typically involved a broader struggle between the tribal blocs with whom each grandee was affiliated. We have already observed the "Zayidiyya of the Nisf Haram" trying to establish themselves in Giza with the help of Çerkes Mehmed Bey; they were then chased away by Dhu'l-Faqar Bey and the Saᶜd, with the consent of the Ottoman governor.[72]

In many cases, fiscal and military strategies were pursued not by the two huge bedouin blocs as coherent wholes but by particular subgroups who might dominate the blocs at a given point or represent them in a particular place. By the last years of the Mamluk sultanate, as noted above, the Banu Baqara had established themselves as the most influential element within the Nisf Haram. In 1538, notwithstanding, they faced competition from the clan of Sulayman b. Qartam, who had himself rebelled against the Mamluk sultanate and had finally been executed in 1503.[73] In the early part of the eighteenth century, a family of agrarian bedouin associated with the Nisf Saᶜd make several troublesome appearances in the pages of al-Damurdashi's and Ahmed Çelebi's chronicles. These are the bedouin chieftain Habib and his sons. Based in Dijwa in the Saʿd stronghold of Qalyubiyya subprovince, the Ḥabāʾiba, as the Arabophone chroniclers call them, antagonized various Qasimi leaders, particularly Ismail Bey b. ʿIvaz, and brought down upon themselves numerous raids of varying degrees of effectiveness.[74] Finally, in 1745, Ibrahim Çavuş al-Qazdağlı destroyed the Ḥabāʾiba's military power and plundered Dijwa; the surviving Ḥabāʾiba chieftains settled elsewhere in the countryside and became ordinary taxpaying peasants.[75]

Conclusion: Saʿd-Haram and the Problem of the Hawwara

During the latter half of the eighteenth century, the Saʿd-Haram struggle, which for over a century had constituted a rural counterpart to the Faqari-Qasimi rivalry, was displaced in Upper Egypt by the hegemony of the powerful Hawwara confederation, which did not adhere to either of the two blocs. Even before the Hawwara emerged as a potent political force, not all of Egypt's bedouin had belonged to either the Nisf Saʿd or the Nisf Haram. On the contrary, there were always autonomous "floating" bedouin groups who might never ally with either bloc, or who might ally temporarily with one or the other before spinning off again. This seems to have been particularly true of the tribes who had migrated to Egypt from North Africa (the Maghrib). A bloc known simply as the Maghariba (North Africans), and particularly the clan of the Banu Wafi, was a force in portions of Upper Egypt and the Delta during the seventeenth and early eighteenth centuries;[76] they had no lasting allegiance to either the Saʿd or Haram. Nonetheless, they do not seem to have had any decisive effect on the regional rivalries of the two major blocs.

In the eighteenth century, however, another North African tribal grouping, the Hawwara, did become a major player in Egypt's regional fiscal and political struggles. This huge Berber group migrated, over the course of roughly a millennium, from Algeria to what is now Libya, then into Lower Egypt and finally Upper Egypt, where they were entrenched by the late fourteenth century.[77] The Hawwara did not fit easily into the binary opposition that had been established between the Saʿd and Haram or, earlier, between the Haram and Waʾil. The fact that they appeared sympathetic to Faqari or Qasimi grandees at different times did not mean that they allied with or were absorbed by the Saʿd or Haram bedouin. Nor did they participate in the scramble for subprovinces in which the Saʿd and Haram constantly engaged. Ensconced in Jirja by the fifteenth century, they seem not to have attempted to claim holdings in Lower Egypt. In the early eighteenth century, Ottoman attempts to incorporate Jirja more directly into the fiscal administration of Egypt had the effect of giving the Hawwara unprecedented leverage in Egyptian politics, for they could now alter the balance of factional power by supporting a governor of Jirja from one or the other faction.[78] A certain analogy can be drawn between the Hawwara's efflorescence and that of the Qazdağlı household. Although the Qazdağlıs originated within the Faqari faction, they ultimately outgrew—or eclipsed—the old binary opposition between the two factions. The Hawwara's experience is, of course, not so clear-cut; they never eclipsed the Saᶜd and Haram. Rather ironically, by harboring the last remaining beys of the Qasimi faction, the Hawwara ultimately laid themselves open to the revenge of ᶜAli Bey and the later Qazdağlı grandees.[79] More broadly, however, in a critical region of Egypt, they arguably transcended the bilateralism of the two rival bedouin blocs, thus transforming the political culture of Upper Egypt.

Similarly, leadership of the Hawwara was concentrated in one dominant chieftain, who by the mid-eighteenth century ruled as a veritable prince of Upper Egypt.[80] By contrast, no single bedouin chieftain was able to assume control of either the Saᶜd or Haram in its entirety. To be sure, certain shaykhs of the Banu Baqara are labelled *shaykh Niṣf Ḥarām*, yet they impress us more as chiefs of particular tribes that have managed to monopolize the leadership stratum of a huge, dispersed conglomerate. A chief such as Habib, meanwhile, was essentially a patriarch whose family was affiliated with the Nisf Saᶜd. Given these circumstances, perhaps individual grandees of the Ottoman administration, such as Hasan Agha Bilifya or ᶜIvaz Bey, brought an elusive unity to these rather diffuse bedouin groups while themselves benefiting from the tribal affiliation. A sort of codependency may have functioned. In this respect, too, the Hawwara defied the existing political culture by upsetting the balance between grandees and bedouin, for the Hawwara chief functioned as the equal of any of Egypt's grandees.

In sum, the Saᶜd and Haram were a part of the Egyptian scene well before the Faqari and Qasimi factions, with whom they came to be associated, emerged; however, the Haram would seem to have been a forceful presence long before the Saᶜd. This lack of symmetry and parallelism likewise characterized the emergence of the Faqaris and Qasimis, as I have hinted in the introduction and will attempt to substantiate in later chapters. Yet by the late seventeenth century, the status of the Saᶜd and Haram seems to change in the popular consciousness, so that they are no longer discrete, identifiable tribal groupings in particular locations, but simply a Punch-and-Judy or Heckel-and-Jeckel sort of byword for disorder in the countryside. We might say that the Haram, who seem to have been a permanent fixture in the Egyptian countryside from at least the fifteenth century (and possibly long before that), always needed an opposing tribal conglomerate against whom to position themselves, and in the seventeenth century, this role was filled by the Saᶜd, just as it had been filled by the Waᵓil in earlier centuries. But the Hawwara, and in particular their increasing implication in the affairs of Egypt's grandees, arguably upset this balance, bringing an end to the two tribal-bloc system as surely as the Qazdağlı household brought an end to the two-faction system.

4

The Yemeni Connection to Egypt's Factions

The last chapter demonstrated that Sa ͨd and Haram supply an unmistakable Yemeni connection to Egypt's factionalism, not least because the two tribal blocs may have originated in Yemen. The unquestioned hegemony of the boundaries of the modern Egyptian nation-state in the historiography of Ottoman Egypt, however, has meant that Yemen has received virtually no attention in studies of Ottoman Egypt, despite the fact that Yemen was almost symbiotically linked to Egypt for the century (1538–1636) during which the Ottomans first ruled it. More broadly, Yemen has been a partner, silent or otherwise, in Egypt's history from remote antiquity until the recent past. This chapter breaks out of the nation-state straitjacket to explore Yemen's links with Egypt during the Ottoman period, culminating in the exposition of an unexpected Yemeni angle to the inception of bilateral factionalism in Egypt.

Yemen's Pre-Ottoman History and Character

Yemen's distance from any Islamic central authority has made it historically an attractive haven for militant offshoots of normative Sunni Islam, particularly the two smaller branches of Shi ͨism: Ismaili, or "Sevener," Shi ͨism, and Zaydi, or "Fiver," Shi ͨism. Zaydism was established in Yemen by the imam Yahya al-Hadi (d. 911), a descendant of ͨAli's son Hasan who migrated from Medina to Yemen late in the ninth century and established his capital at the northern highland city of Sa ͨda.[1] Unlike Ismaili or Twelver Shi ͨite doctrine, Zaydi theology posits an active, visible imam, or leader of the Muslim community, descended from either Hasan or his brother Husayn, who is learned

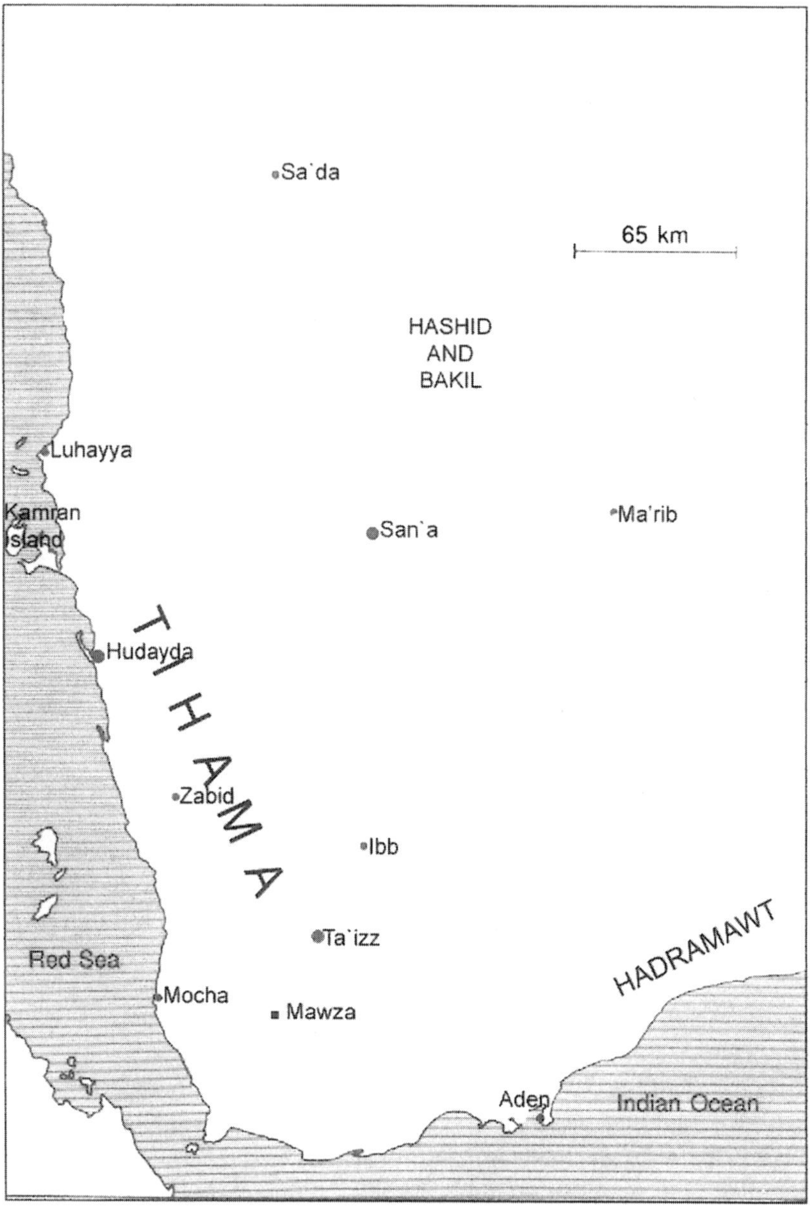

Fig. 4.1. Yemen in the sixteenth and seventeenth centuries

in the religious sciences and who publicly proves himself worthy of leading the Muslim community, in battle if necessary.[2] What this has meant in Yemeni history is that scions of numerous lines of Hasanid and, less frequently, Husaynid descendants have proclaimed their *daᶜwas*, or "calls"—occasionally simultaneously, so that the supporters of one line were obliged to fight it out with supporters of another.

From Saᶜda, Imam al-Hadi attacked the Ismaili proselytes known as Carmatians, who had established themselves in Yemen several decades before, and defeated them shortly before his death in 911.[3] He is said, in fact, to have wielded ᶜAli's sword Dhu'l-Faqar against them.[4] Beginning in the following century, however, Yemen entered a lengthy period during which it was continuously an ally, if not a virtual dependency, of Egypt under Ismaili Sulayhid rule (1038–1138),[5] then under the staunchly Sunni regimes of the Ayyubids (1173–1227), Rasulids (1227–1454), and Tahirids (1454–1507).[6]

The Tahirids were ruling the southern coastal region from their capital at Zabid when the Portuguese appeared in the Indian Ocean at the close of the fifteenth century. In 1513, the Portuguese, after a string of unsuccessful attacks on the Yemeni coast, took Kamran island in the Red Sea; this prompted the Mamluk sultan of Egypt to intervene for fear the Portuguese would soon have unbridled access to the Hijaz.[7] A Mamluk naval force proceeded to attack the Tahirids on the western and southern coasts in 1514, earning the opprobrium of Yemeni chroniclers.[8] This was just the period when the Mamluk sultanate, itself never a formidable naval power, was accepting the aid of its more powerful Ottoman neighbor against the Portuguese. These joint operations led to a very curious interlude in Yemeni history, during which Ottoman naval commanders were, in actual fact, administering the Yemeni port cities. Al-Nahrawali refers to this period as the "era of the *levends*," *levend* being a common Ottoman term for a naval mercenary.[9]

In fact, Yemen must certainly have loomed large in the Ottoman decision to conquer Egypt from the Mamluks. Mamluk ineffectiveness against the Portuguese in the Red Sea clearly alarmed the Ottomans. Yemen, after all, served as the gateway to Mecca and Medina for pilgrims coming from India, the Far East, and eastern Africa; as such, it was also the first line of defense against any threat to Egypt from those regions. Once they had conquered Egypt, the Ottomans used it as a base of operations against the Portuguese.[10] Some of the greatest naval commanders in Ottoman history contributed to the anti-Portuguese effort, notably Salman Reis, whom al-Nahrawali counts as one of the *levend* rulers of Yemen,[11] and Koca Sinan Pasha (fl. 1568–71).

Yemen became a formal addition to the Ottoman Empire only under the Hungarian eunuch Süleyman Pasha in 1538. Originally appointed governor of Egypt, Süleyman Pasha was ordered to the Indian Ocean to protect the empire's southern extremity from the Portuguese, who had just killed the sultan of Gujarat; along the way, he took effective control of Yemen in its entirety, then pursued the Portuguese admiral, Albuquerque, to India. Al-Nahrawali and Yahya b. al-Husayn paint a decidedly unattractive picture of Süleyman Pasha. Still, nothing can compare to the description offered by the British India Office functionary Robert Playfair, writing in the 1850s: "He was about eighty years of age, and he is represented as having been short and stout, and so hideous, and of so savage a disposition, as to have resembled a beast rather than a man."[12] Playfair's comments are no doubt a partial reference to Süleyman's eunuchhood. Notwithstanding, he comes across as gratuitously violent and brutal; landing at Aden, he distributed robes of honor to the last Tahirid ruler and his entourage, then ordered them hanged. After hearing of this, the Indian princes were, rather understandably, reluctant to aid Süleyman's campaign, which ended inconclusively.[13] Süleyman returned to Yemen, where he executed the last *levend* governor of Zabid and all his slaves,[14] then proceeded to Egypt, then finally back to Istanbul.[15]

One Long Struggle Against the Zaydis?

During the ensuing years, Yemen existed in a virtual symbiosis with Ottoman Egypt. In fact, it is an unspoken presence throughout much of the history of Ottoman Egypt, particularly the first century or so of that history, when Yemen was a fellow Ottoman province. Unspoken or not, Yemen was inextricably linked to Egypt strategically, commercially, intellectually, and perhaps even culturally during this period. Governors of Egypt were often posted to Yemen at the completion of their terms, and vice versa. One particularly resilient governor, Hasan Pasha b. Hüseyin, governed Yemen for an astonishing twenty-five years (1580–1604) before being transferred to Egypt; while in Yemen, he amassed an enormous fortune.[16] Meanwhile, the Ottoman garrisons at Sanᶜa, Aden, Mocha, and Zabid consisted of troops from the seven Egyptian regiments, commanded by a bey of Egypt.[17] It was probably no accident that the land tenure system in Ottoman Yemen was identical to the system in Egypt: retaining Mamluk-era terminology, it was based on grants of taxation rights over specific cities and districts, each headed by a bey or agha with the title of *ᶜāmil* or *kāshif*.[18] This made it all the easier for officials based in Egypt to make a smooth transition to Yemen and vice versa. The third Ottoman governor of Yemen, in fact, was the former Circassian Mamluk emir Özdemir Bey, who had accompanied Süleyman Pasha to Yemen and remained to combat the rebellious *levend* remnant and the equally rebellious Zaydi and other Arab tribes until he was appointed governor in 1549. Following his deposition seven years later, he conquered Abyssinia for Sultan Süleyman I.[19]

The fact remained, however, that it was virtually impossible for a single imperial power to control all of Yemen. Like the Rasulids, Tahirids, and Mamluks before them, the Ottoman governors held sway mainly in the southern coastal region, particularly around the administrative capital of Zabid and the ports of Aden and Mocha. In the latter part of the sixteenth century, the Porte experimented with dividing Yemen into two administrative units, each governed by a Beylerbeyi: one, known as "Yemen," consisting of twelve *sancak*s, or districts, the other, known as "Sanᶜa," consisting of seventeen *sancak*s.[20] Al-Nahrawali confirms the impression, conveyed by imperial orders, that "Sanᶜa," which included the interior highlands, was typically assigned to a pasha from Istanbul, while "Yemen" or "Tihāʾim" (plural of Tihama), which comprised the central and southern coastal regions, was more readily assigned to localized beys of Egypt and their sons, who were promoted to the rank of pasha.[21] Al-Nahrawali claims that the division was the brainchild of the deposed governor Mahmud Pasha (1561–65), who wanted to torment his successor, Ridvan Pasha, by saddling him with the turbulent highlands.[22] Notwithstanding, the strategic rationale behind these decisions may have been the difficulty of controlling the highlands, on the one hand, and the Egyptian grandees' experience with the Red Sea trade and the port customs, on the other. Control of the ports was critical to the effort against the Portuguese, while control of both ports and highlands was critical to the flourishing coffee trade.

Coffee had been introduced into Yemen from Ethiopia, where it grew wild, sometime in the fifteenth century.[23] It first achieved popularity among Yemen's Sufi orders, who allegedly used it to stay awake during their mystical rituals. The passing of the porcelain coffee cup among the Sufi "brothers" became an important rite of communal solidarity. In short order, the drink became a staple among the Ottoman soldiery in Yemen.[24] Coffee invaded Egypt via the Hijaz in the early to mid-sixteenth century, then spread quickly to Syria and Istanbul and from there to Italy and the rest of Europe.[25] Haci ᶜAli, the Turcophone continuator of al-Nahrawali, mentions a man from Harput in eastern Anatolia, whom he calls a Yemeni merchant, living in Egypt in 1623 while Evliya Çelebi, some fifty years later, reports merchants from Sammanud in the Nile Delta trading directly with Yemen and India;[26] by this time, Anatolia, Egypt, and Yemen were linked in an international coffee network. Coffeehouses (Turkish s. *kahvehane*) were already ubiquitous in the Egyptian countryside by the late seventeenth century.[27] The widespread popularity of Yemeni coffee allowed the Ottomans to compensate for the Portuguese inroads into the Indian spice trade that resulted from Vasco da Gama's discovery of the Cape Route around Africa.[28] By the eighteenth century, coffee was so pervasive that it had turned Yemen into a forerunner of Washington state today: coffee was everywhere. The growing regions had evidently expanded as far south as the Hadramawt. The Danish naturalist Carsten Niebuhr repeatedly recounts spending the night in one of the "coffee huts" that dotted the countryside of the Tihama.[29]

One problem with the coffee trade, however, was that the coffee trees themselves grew not on the coast but in Yemen's central highlands, which were largely the domain of Ismaili tribes.[30] The Ismailis were, so to speak, the wildcard in the politics of Ottoman Yemen, existing geographically and politically in-between the Zaydis, who were loyal to their imam, and the Ottoman authorities, along with the mostly Shafiᶜi coastal population who tended to support them. To get the coffee beans from the mountains to the coast for processing and shipment therefore required the Ottomans to reach some sort of agreement, or at least modus vivendi, with these tribes. Any tribal unrest would, naturally, threaten tax and customs revenues, to say nothing of the coffee supply itself. About such agreements we have distressingly little direct information. During the late sixteenth century, however, they would have been the purview of the pasha who governed Sanᶜa. We also know from archival sources that the Ottomans levied taxes on the tribal regions of the interior, and that the garrison forces' salaries were drawn from customs levies on *bāharāt*, literally "spices," which came to be virtually synonymous with coffee.[31] Small wonder, then, that Ridvan Pasha, the first governor of "Sanᶜa," resolved to complete the pacification of the Ismaili territories under his control. Oppressive taxation and ruthless pacification attempts, however, could easily push the Ismailis into the arms of the Zaydi imam, who might use their support to launch a revolt against the Ottomans. To balance things out, therefore, the Ottoman administration rewarded those Ismaili leaders who were quietist, rather than militant, and content to live under Ottoman rule; thus, Ridvan Pasha bestowed tax farms on the chief Ismaili missionary, his two sons, and his grandson.[32] Subsequently, two missionaries of the Hamdani family fought for the Ottomans.[33] We must remember, however, that the Ismailis, like the Zaydis, seldom if ever acted as a monolithic entity. As a result of Ridvan Pasha's measures, combined with the activities of the Zaydi imam al-Mutahhar (of whom more below), al-Nahrawali tells us, the Ismailis were split into five groups: those quietists who continued to follow their chief missionary, those allied with Ridvan Pasha, those who did not take sides, those who supported al-Mutahhar, and those who fled Yemen for India.[34]

Arguably, the Zaydi imam al-Mutahhar b. Sharaf al-Din (r. 1558–68) took advantage of the administrative division of Yemen and the antagonism between the two Ottoman governors to launch the first major Zaydi rebellion against Ottoman rule in Yemen. Given the inherently fractious nature of the Zaydi imamate, any attempt at rebellion perhaps required a correspondingly fractious Ottoman administration. In 1566, al-Mutahhar declared full-scale *jihād* against the Ottoman administration. His militant, ideologically couched opposition to the Ottomans was a departure from previous Zaydi practice. Al-Nahrawali points out that unlike previous Zaydi imams, including his own father, al-Mutahhar introduced fanatical, unabashedly Shiᶜite practices. In particular, he inserted the line "Come to the best of works" (*Hayyā li khayr al ᶜamal*) into the call to prayer, even in predominantly Shafiᶜi cities, and began to curse the first three Sunni caliphs in his Friday sermons.[35] These practices were unequivocal markers of Shiᶜite identity and, in a Sunni context, could hardly be taken as anything other than revolutionary.

The struggle for Yemen between the Ottomans and al-Mutahhar was particularly hard fought and brutal. Wave after wave of Ottoman soldiers was dispatched to the administrative unit of "Sanᶜa" from Egypt and from the administrative unit of "Yemen," each troop commanded by a *sancak beyi*, or district governor.[36] Service in the highlands was often a convenient way of getting rid of potentially troublesome elements who might otherwise have tried to establish a local power base in Egypt. As al-Ishaqi grimly points out, beys sent there were seldom heard from again.[37] Soldiers posted to "Sanᶜa" are known to have fled to "Yemen" to escape this duty.[38] Others left southern Arabia altogether, relocating to Mecca, Egypt, or Istanbul.[39] Still others deserted to al-Mutahhar.[40] Those who stayed and fought for the Ottoman side—ordinary Ottoman soldiers, bedouin from Egypt, Ismailis—died in large numbers, either in battle or of disease.[41] The Ottomans enjoyed no technological advantage of the sort that had made Egypt a relatively easy conquest decades earlier. The Zaydis had acquired firearms and cannon during the occupation of the Mamluks and the *levends*; moreover, they could always retreat into the mountains.[42] Yet firearms were apparently not always effective against the Zaydis, anyhow: one imperial order requests archers from Syria for Yemen.[43] By the time Hasan Pasha (not to be confused with Hasan b. Hüseyin, the twenty-five-year governor) arrived to govern "Yemen" in late 1567, the Zaydis controlled the entire interior region and were advancing on Mocha.[44]

In a sense, Egypt saved Yemen for the Ottomans. After al-Mutahhar rejected an offer of amnesty, the Porte sent a joint invasion force: Özdemiroğlu Osman Pasha, son of the famous Özdemir Pasha, led the naval force from Egypt, consisting of three thousand soldiers from Egypt's regiments; the grand vizier Koca Sinan Pasha, despite being a legendary admiral, led the land force, consisting of large numbers of Egyptian troops and bedouin reinforcements, along with soldiers from several other Ottoman provinces.[45] In the end, Sinan Pasha was the real hero of this "second conquest of Yemen." It was he who accepted al-Mutahhar's surrender, then gallantly appointed him administrator (*ᶜāmil*) of the northern highland stronghold of Saᶜda under Ottoman rule. (By some twist of fate, the future chronicler Rumuzi was dispatched to receive al-Mutahhar's vow of peace in person.)[46] Following this ordeal, Ottoman Yemen was restored to its original status as an undivided administrative unit.

Al-Mutahhar's defeat and subsequent death, of illness, in 1572 put an end, for all practical purposes, to the efficacy of his line of Zaydi imams, despite the fact that he left behind two *Haramzadeler*, as Rumuzi so piquantly calls them. Some two decades of inconclusive infighting among rival lines of imams and the twenty-five-year Ottoman governor Hasan Pasha b. Hüseyin ensued.[47] In the closing years of the sixteenth century, however, a new line of Zaydi imams, originating with al-Qasim (r. 1598–1620), proclaimed a new *daᶜwa* in their home district in the mountainous central part of the province. From the very beginning of his *daᶜwa*, al-Qasim was in conflict with a series of Ottoman governors until his death of a stomach ailment in 1620.[48] It was left to his son and successor, al-Muʾayyad Muhammad, to force the Ottomans out of Yemen.

Our principal account of this last, unsuccessful Ottoman struggle to hold Yemen occurs in an Ottoman Turkish continuation to al-Nahrawali's history by one Haci ᶜAli.[49] This time, the Ottoman effort seems far more halfhearted than the effort against al-Mutahhar. Upheaval in the imperial capital prevented the Porte from focusing on Yemen in the early years of al-Muʾayyad's imamate.[50] By 1630, it was evident that the Ottomans intended to let Yemen go—perhaps because it represented too great an investment in manpower and materiel. Moreover, the Portuguese were yielding pride of place to the British and Dutch, with whom the Ottomans were on considerably better terms.[51] Although the last Ottoman governor of Yemen, Qansuh Pasha, a former bey of Egypt, landed with a force of some eight thousand soldiers and Arab tribesmen from Egypt, their numbers were quickly depleted by desertion and disease, as well as warfare.[52] Meanwhile, the imam's armies were enlarged by seemingly inexhaustible waves of Arab tribesmen.[53] Finally, Qansuh Pasha, in desperation, appealed to the imam for safe passage to Mecca—where he found Ridvan Bey al-Faqari rebuilding the Ka^cba, which had been swept away in a flood, as if no war were going on in Yemen.[54] Arnavud (Albanian) Mustafa Bey, another grandee of Egypt, remained in Mocha with one thousand Ottoman soldiers while the imam's forces laid siege to the city. He sent a desperate message to the governor of Egypt, pleading for reinforcements, but never received a reply. By this time, his men were utterly demoralized. Three hundred died in the course of the siege. Finally, in 1636, Mustafa Bey and the remnant of his army evacuated Mocha on an Indian merchant ship and sailed back to Egypt.[55] With that, the first period of Ottoman rule in Yemen ended.

Haydar Agha and the Red Flag

Before the debacle of Qansuh Pasha's tenure, however, there was a stretch of several years in which it seemed that the Ottomans might be gaining the upper hand over the Zaydis. Sultan Murad IV had taken the throne in 1623 and inaugurated a policy of aggressive militarism that would culminate in the Ottoman reconquest of Baghdad from the Safavids in 1638. The man whom Murad appointed governor of Yemen was Haydar Agha, the commander of the imperial cavalry, or *sipahi*s, who, as governor, was promoted to the rank of pasha. To Haci ᶜAli, Haydar Pasha is a genuine hero whose administration marks a turning point in the Ottoman effort in Yemen. Haydar cracked down on the corrupt Ottoman beys, often the sons of prominent pashas, who had split the Ottoman soldiery into quarreling factions (s. *tefrīḳe*) and plundered the province to make their fortunes. Under Haydar, the Ottoman forces in Yemen achieved a unity and effectiveness they had rarely had before. As Haci ᶜAli tells it, the Zaydi imam al-Muʾayyad was terrified of Haydar Pasha and sued for peace, resuming his rebellion only when Haydar was deposed.[56] There is no doubt a measure of hero-worshiping exaggeration in Haci ᶜAli's account. Quite a different picture is painted by the Zaydi chronicler Yahya b. al-Husayn, who depicts Haydar as ruthless and immoral, if militarily effective; in Yahya's version, Haydar always asks the imam for peace.[57] Indeed, Haci ᶜAli more or less reinvents Haydar Pasha as a sort of Ottoman Baybars—or, indeed, a provincial Murad IV. In the same way that Murad briefly reinvigorated an empire weary of palace intrigue combined with territorial losses in both east and west, Haydar Pasha briefly reinvigorated a province weary of Zaydi advances and the Yemeni quagmire in general. He probably seemed heroic enough to Ottoman subjects in Yemen, Egypt, and the Hijaz.

This hero carried a red flag. Haci ᶜAli refers to him as *kızıl bayrak ağası*, or "red flag agha." His red flag was the emblem of the *sipahi*, or cavalry, forces whom he had commanded. The *sipahi*s had been the backbone of the Ottoman army almost since the empire's inception, and their distinguishing color was evidently always red. In the fourteenth century, according to legend, Hajji Bektash Veli instructed Sultan Orhan to assign the Janissaries white headgear, to distinguish them from the provincial cavalry, whose headgear was red.[58]

All this is worth mentioning because Haydar Agha has a curious resonance in the origin myths of the Faqari and Qasimi factions in Egypt. Intriguingly, the Ottoman governor appointed to Egypt in 1640, a few years after the Ottoman expulsion from Yemen, was none other than the son of Haydar Agha, the hero of Yemen. It was the son's fate always to be known by the name of his more illustrious father: Haydar Aghazade Mehmed Pasha.[59] And even more intriguingly, in a sort of "alternative" origin myth invoked by al-Jabarti and al-Hallaq, the two factions appear either during Haydar Aghazade Mehmed Pasha's governorship or shortly before. After noting the appearance of Saᶜd and Haram, then relaying the myth of the aged Mamluk emir and his two sons, al-Jabarti almost laconically adds that the first appearance of the Faqaris and Qasimis was in 1050 A.H., or 1640 C.E., "but God alone knows the truth."[60] Al-Hallaq, meanwhile, claims that "the event that occurred during [Haydar Aghazade's] time was the greatest of events."[61] The event in question was the showdown between Qansuh and Memi, or Mamay, Beys, on the one hand, and Ridvan and ᶜAli Beys, on the other. Qansuh, a follower of Qasim Bey the *defterdar*, or financial administrator, supposed founder of the Qasimi faction, was *qāʾim maqām*, or deputy governor, when Haydar Aghazade Mehmed arrived in Egypt. According to al-Hallaq, the new governor allowed Qansuh Bey to control all administrative appointments within the province, so that Qansuh and his sidekick, Memi,[62] came to dominate

Egypt's grandees and soldiery. With the new governor's backing, Qansuh and Memi attempted to usurp the positions of the longtime pilgrimage commander Ridvan Bey (later known as al-Faqari) and his ally ᶜAli Bey, the governor of Jirja. This culminated in an armed confrontation between ᶜAli and Ridvan, with their troops, and Qansuh and Memi, with theirs. Mehmed Pasha, impressed by the nearly four thousand-strong rifle-toting army that ᶜAli had brought down from Jirja, had meanwhile turned against Qansuh and Memi, who gave themselves up after Memi refused to fight the governor. Qansuh, Memi, and a number of their followers were executed and their posts redistributed to followers of Ridvan and ᶜAli. Haydar Aghazade Mehmed Pasha might have come out of this affair relatively unscathed had he not attempted to seize Ridvan's and ᶜAli's properties; according to al-Hallaq, he felt cheated after having salvaged nothing from Qansuh's and Memi's estates. But at this, Ridvan and ᶜAli persuaded the Porte to depose him.[63] Several years later, in 1649–50, he turns up at the head of the then-floundering Ottoman attempt to subdue Crete, where he was equally unsuccessful and was similarly deposed.[64]

In the eighteenth-century Arabic chronicles that cover the seventeenth century, this episode is the first overt rivalry between the Qasimis and Faqaris as established factions, since Qansuh and Memi were supposely Qasimis, Ridvan and ᶜAli Faqaris.[65] Al Hallaq, however, never mentions the two factions. In any case, Haydar Aghazade Mehmed Pasha is linked, if not to the factions' emergence, then to what was, at least in the eyes of later chroniclers, their earliest observable political action.

Even this would not be particularly remarkable were it not for the baggage that Haydar Aghazade Mehmed Pasha carries. His very name, by incorporating that of his father, calls Yemen to mind and invites comparison between his actions in Egypt and his father's achievements in Yemen. While his father had been the hero of Yemen, the son was appointed governor of Egypt after Yemen had been lost, and proceeded to let himself be manipulated by local grandees. His tenure also witnessed a disturbance within Egypt's Janissary corps by a gang of "rebels" (*zorbalar*) headed by one Yemenli Fazli, presumably a soldier either from Yemen or who had served in Yemen. These "rebels" seem to belong to the mercenaries employed by Ridvan and ᶜAli.[66]

Then there are the eerie parallels between the story of Haydar Agha's adventures in Yemen and that of Haydar Aghazade's misadventure in Egypt. When Haydar Aghazade Mehmed arrived in Egypt, Qansuh Bey, the follower of Qasim Bey, was *qāʾim maqām*. A decade earlier, his father had been deposed from the governorship of Yemen when an Egyptian bey, also named Qansuh and also a follower of Qasim Bey,[67] was appointed to replace him. This earlier Qansuh effectively "lost" Yemen for the Ottomans when he was run out by the imam al-Muʾayyad. The same story seems to unfold in Egypt over ten years later, with a slightly twisted plot and slightly different characters: Haydar Aghazade Mehmed instead of Haydar Agha, a different Qansuh Bey, and Ridvan and ʿAli instead of the Zaydi imam. The parallels between the two episodes, combined with the timing of the Egyptian strife, lead us to suspect that, once again, Yemen is an unspoken presence in Egypt's history—this time, in the early public assertion of the Faqari and Qasimi factions.

I do not want to overstress this connection between the respective experiences of the father and son governors, however. The similarities between the accounts of their governorships may indeed be little more than coincidence. Haydar Agha was certainly not the first or only Ottoman governor whose son followed in his footsteps; an earlier and a better-known specimen was Özdemiroğlu Osman Pasha, son of Özdemir Pasha, the conqueror of Abyssinia. Both father and son served as governor of Yemen, and the son went on to become grand vizier.[68]

Post-expulsion Exchanges

What these episodes illustrate, in any case, is the continuous exchange between Egypt and Yemen during the century of Ottoman rule over the latter province. Governors relocating from Egypt to Yemen and vice versa must surely have taken along personnel from their previous posting. Undoubtedly Hasan Pasha b. Hüseyin, who governed Yemen for twenty-five years before being assigned to Egypt, served as an unprecedented conduit for Yemeni influence in Egypt. He had made his fortune in Yemen; it is difficult to believe that he would have given up his connections there once posted to Cairo. Ongoing warfare in Yemen, lamentably, provided the most reliable conduit of exchange. Egyptian beys, soldiers, and bedouin tribesmen routinely served in Yemen; the soldiers, at least, occasionally deserted to the Zaydi imam, who used them either as auxiliary troops or as agricultural workers.[69] Even decades after Yemen had been lost, Evliya tells of a group of Ethiopian rebels who fled from the Ottoman governor of Abyssinia to the Zaydi imam; in the late eighteenth century, meanwhile, Niebuhr reports occasional "vagabond Turks" who served the imam as gunners.[70] If some Ottoman soldiers stayed in Yemen, then Yemeni soldiers, most of whom were tribesmen, must occasionally have returned to Egypt with the Ottoman detachments. In the face of the Ottoman expulsion, tribesmen who had supported the Ottomans must have been tempted to join them in flight. Indeed, plausible ancestors for the Zayidiyya of the Nile Delta may be not the Zaydis who supported the Qasimi imams but the family of al-Mutahhar and their followers. For ironically, in view of the hostility al-Mutahhar elicited in Rumuzi, his sons were taken onto the Ottoman payroll and given tax farms. One of them evidently served as a spy for the Ottomans.[71]

Naturally, Egypt's connections with Yemen did not come to a screeching halt once the Ottomans had been driven from the province. Sultan Mehmed IV (r. 1648–87) seriously contemplated a Yemeni campaign in 1672, and even called up troops from Egypt before abandoning the plan.[72] All the while, the coffee trade from Aden, and later Mocha, continued briskly, peaking only two or three decades after the Ottoman ouster. Indeed, the great coffee fortunes of some of Egypt's grandee households, such as the Qazdağlıs, the Gediks, and the Sharaybis, were made well after the Ottomans had left Yemen.[73] So far as transport of the coffee within Yemen was concerned, the Ottomans for the rest of the seventeenth century were at the virtual mercy of the Qasimi imam, who derived a healthy profit from the coffee trade.[74] Yet the grandees of Egypt must have continued to cultivate a working relationship with the tribes of the Yemeni interior, above all the Ismailis, particularly during the eighteenth century, when the Qasimi dynasty's grip had weakened outside their northern stronghold. The eighteenth-century chronicler al-Bahkali mentions a dispute between two "Turkish merchants" and two *sharīfs*, or descendants of the Prophet, who were in the Qasimi imam's entourage.[75] On the other hand, as in Egypt and the Mediterranean, the Ottomans faced competition from the French, who were trading their own coffee directly with the imam.[76] We can assume only that the commercial relationship was one of mutual dependence: the grandees depended on the tribes for the coffee itself; the tribes depended on the grandees for ships and control of the port customs in Egypt. The exact nature of these alliances is well-nigh impossible to fathom, however. They must certainly have been fairly complex, involving a whole web of tribes and grandees in various locations, rather than a simple one-to-one correspondence. Yet both chronicles and archival documents are remarkably silent on what must have been a dynamic, volatile, and highly influential connection.

In short, Yemen is indeed a (virtually) "silent partner" in much of Egypt's history, certainly during the Islamic period and above all during the Ottoman period. The archival documents only fleetingly give voice to this partnership, the chronicles hardly at all. We are not helped by the fact that during the sixteenth century, when this symbiosis was strongest, few chronicles were composed in either Egypt or Yemen. The richest source on the ties that bound Egypt to Yemen and both provinces to the Hijaz during this period is al-Nahrawali's chronicle, which seems to be unique in its interprovincial view.

As difficult as economic and political ties are to verify, intellectual ties are even harder to trace, at least before the late eighteenth-century cross-fertilization between ᶜAbd al-Rahman al-Jabarti and Murtada al-Zabidi (d. 1791), a scholar of Indian origin who lived in Zabid for some years while receiving religious instruction.[77] Perhaps the most famous of Yemeni ulema of the Ottoman period was the Hadrami Shaykh Muhyi al-Din ᶜAbd al-Qadir al-ᶜAydarus (1570–1627), author of a contemporary history, whose wide travels took him to Cairo and Damascus.[78] Still, the chronicles of Ibn al-Daybaᶜ reveal that Zabid in particular during the sixteenth century boasted several prominent Shafiᶜi ulema surnamed al-Jabarti, who may or may not have been direct ancestors of the Egyptian historian.[79] Although Zabid was the hub of Shafiᶜi (and Hanafi) scholarly activity in Yemen, the modest southern town of Mawzaᶜ, just inland from Mocha, produced the judge and historian Shams al-Din ᶜAbd al-Samad al-Mawzaᶜi, author of a history of the Ottoman conquest of Yemen.[80] Collectively, these scholars represent an active and productive population of Shafiᶜi (and, to a lesser extent, Hanafi) ulema in Yemen's coastal towns who must, like Murtada al-Zabidi, have had contact with their Egyptian counterparts through the pilgrimage to Mecca, and through visits to Egypt itself. The existence at Cairo's venerable al-Azhar University of a *rīwāq*, or dormitory, for Yemeni students attests to the consistency of this contact.[81] In fact, as John O. Voll's work on the Mizjaji family has suggested, Yemen was a critical link in an intellectual chain connecting Egypt with the Hijaz, the Hadramawt, eastern Africa, India, and even China.[82]

All this obliges us to conclude that the lack of graphic evidence unequivocally linking our two factions to Yemen does not necessarily mean that no such links existed. The circumstantial evidence, mysterious as it sometimes is, is nothing if not compelling. It is also the case, furthermore, that Ottoman narrative sources in general are fairly reticent about the connections between and among different Ottoman provinces. This characteristic arguably encourages present-day historians to persist in treating Egypt and Yemen, to say nothing of other Ottoman provinces, as protonation states, sufficient unto themselves or interacting solely with the Ottoman center while ignoring fellow provinces. This, however, would be a mistake, for reticence is not the same thing as total silence. That there was movement between Egypt and Yemen before, during, and after the first period of Ottoman rule is clear; only the specific features of this movement remain obscure. The Qasimi faction, in a sense, owed its very existence to the Ottoman campaign in Yemen. The chronicles' reticence in describing contacts between Egypt and Yemen—their very lack of fascination—could be taken as an indication that these contacts not only occurred but were commonplace enough to seem literally unremarkable. We would not want to make the mistake of assuming that connections did not exist when, in fact, they may have been so pervasive and natural as hardly to have warranted mention.

5

Red and White

The Colors of the Factions' Banners

Absolutely critical to the contrasting identities of the Faqaris and Qasimis are the different-colored banners that the two factions carried. The various origin myths, in fact, give the impression that the factions were initially differentiated above all else by the colors of their flags—and furthermore, in at least one version of the myth, by the colors of their clothing, food, and utensils, as well. Two chroniclers of the Damurdashi group, al-Qinali and an anonymous author, present the divergent banner colors as, initially, at least, the overriding identifying feature of the two factions:

Al-Qinali:

> The people of Egypt from ancient times were in two factions (*farqatayn*): soldiers and bedouin and peasants, white flag and red flag. The white was Tubbaʿi, and the red was Kulaybi. . . .

Anonymous:

> The people of Egypt, beys, aghas and the seven regiments, were two factions: White Flag from the Yemeni Tubbaʿ and Red Flag from Kulayb brother of al-Zir. . . .[1]

On the face of it, the fact that each faction carried a flag of its preferred color may not seem such a startling revelation. After all, color is one of the most common, most easily deployable, and most easily recognizable markers of any political or ideological group, as we have already seen with great clarity in our considerations of Byzantine and pre-Islamic Arab factionalism. And what better way to rally a sizable political grouping—or any grouping, for that matter—than by waving a brightly colored pennant above their heads? This simple observation makes it all the more surprising that there has been no serious consideration of the banners of the Faqari and Qasimi factions, and of the colors of those banners. This chapter examines the factions' use of colored banners against the backdrop of the role of colored banners in Islamic, and more particularly Ottoman, history. It then contextualizes the factions' more general color preferences by probing the connections between distinctly Ottoman identifying colors and color dichotomies in early Islamic and pre-Islamic history. Finally, it returns to the framework of the origin myths by inquiring into the significance of deploying red and white banners in public processions.

Colored Banners in Islamic History

The colors of banners seem to have carried particular weight in the Byzantine Empire and among the tribal armies of the early Islamic empires. As we have already seen, the Roman and Byzantine circus factions carried banners in their distinctive elemental colors: blue, green, white, and red. The early Muslim armies could hardly have helped encountering these banners in the course of their conquests; we know for a fact that they encountered them in Egypt, whether or not they were influenced by them.[2] In Islamic annals, a tradition persists that the banner of the Prophet Muhammad's tribe of Quraysh was white and that of Amr b. al-ᶜAs, the conqueror of Egypt, red.[3] Notwithstanding, the banners of the tribes who made up the early Muslim armies evidently displayed a variety of colors, singly and in combination, with no consistent regard even for the fundamental red-white distinction between Qaysi and Yemeni tribes.[4]

No doubt the most famous, or at least notorious, reference to banner colors in early-Islamic history is the saying ascribed to the Prophet mentioning "a people coming from the East with black banners" who would presage the appearance of the messianic figure known as the Mahdi.[5] The proselytes of the ᶜAbbasid revolution took full advantage of the eschatological expectations raised by black banners in their campaign to undermine the Umayyad dynasty from within. Even after the ᶜAbbasids had triumphed over the Umayyads in 750, they continued to deploy black as their dynastic color; not only the banners but the headdresses and garments of the ᶜAbbasid caliphs were black. Their highest military officers and administrative officials were likewise obliged to wear black, whereas functionaries below the rank of judge were forbidden to do so.[6] The ubiquitous black created a striking contrast with the banners and dynastic color of the Umayyads, which had been white, after the personal flag of the dynasty's founder.[7] Yet the caliphal banner that the commander of the ʿAbbasid armies carried was made of white silk, inscribed with Qurʾanic verses and paeans to the caliph; it was paired with a "gilded" banner usually carried by the crown prince.[8]

The Ismaili Shiʿite counter-caliphate founded by the Fatimids took white as its dynastic color, creating a visual contrast to the ʿAbbasid enemy.[9] It seems to have been under the influence of the Fatimid proselytizing mission, or *daʿwa*—and the Ismaili *daʿwa* more generally—that white became the Shiʿite color, in deliberate opposition to the black of the ʿAbbasid "establishment."[10] Nonetheless, red and yellow were associated with the Fatimid caliph's person; the caliph seems to have worn red and to have been flanked by red and yellow banners on certain important occasions.[11] On conquering Egypt, in fact, Sultan Selim I is said to have handled a red flag emblazoned with a lion, on which was written *Naṣr min Allāh* (Victory is from God), a phrase attested on Fatimid ceremonial banners.[12]

The Ayyubids and Mamluks, who succeeded the Fatimids in Egypt and Syria, retained the association of yellow with the ruler. Salah al-Din (Saladin), the founder of the Ayyubid dynasty, carried a yellow flag emblazoned with an eagle, supposedly inherited from the Zangid dynasty, whose protégé he had been.[13] Yellow was likewise the Mamluk sultan's official color, and Mamluk sultanic banners were yellow.[14] In a concession to the elaborate hierarchy of blazons peculiar to the Mamluk sultanate, a Mamluk emir would emblazon his personal banners with the blazon of his office, and would retain this blazon when and if he became sultan.[15] Nonetheless, the Mamluks evidently used red banners, as well; the late Mamluk chronicler Ibn Taghri Birdi reports that Sultan al-Muʾayyad Shaykh (r. 1412–21) sent a red banner to a Turkic vassal dynasty in southeastern Anatolia.[16] As custodians of the Holy Cities and commanders of the pilgrimage, moreover, the Mamluks had the prerogative of deploying the Prophet's banner. This banner was believed to be a genuine relic of the Prophet, unlikely as that may seem. On conquering Egypt or shortly thereafter, the Ottomans took possession of this banner. Known as the *sancak-i şerif* (noble banner), it was unfurled before the Ottoman armies as they set off on campaign. There is to this day in the second court of the Topkapı Palace, just before the Gate of Felicity (Bāb al-Saʿāda, or Babüssaade), a mount built into the flagstones for the Prophet's banner. The Ottoman historian Silahdar Mehmed Agha, whose title bespeaks a solid military background, relates that the banner was made of black wool. We may surmise, therefore, that the banner was black in color. Unfortunately, this is as much as any narrative source tells us about the banner's appearance; about its shape, inscriptions, or embellishments we remain ignorant.[17]

Farther east, medieval Turco-Iranian military patronage states, such as those of the Ghaznavids, Seljuks, Timurids, and early Ottomans, appear to have been more directly affected by the banner traditions of the nomadic Turkic and Mongol populations of the Central Asian steppes, who in turn were influenced by the traditions of the various empires and kingdoms that ruled China, Japan, and Korea. The banners of these Asian polities tended, in contrast to the Arab tribal banners, to consist of substantial sheets of cloth mounted horizontally, so that they acquired added visual force by fluttering in the wind; their color schemes were influenced by Chinese cosmology, which assigned a different color to each geographical quadrant. Chinese cloth flags and color schemes were adopted by the Mongols and other Central Asian nomadic populations.[18] The nomads themselves, meanwhile, pioneered the use of the *tuğ*, a staff topped with yak- or horsetails. Originally carrying considerable totemic significance, the *tuğ* ultimately came to represent supreme military authority.[19]

Mongol and Turkic dynasties in medieval Iran and Central Asia seem to have preferred white banners,[20] a choice that may possibly have been influenced by the Chinese association of white with the West; all these empires were, of course, situated west of China and the Mongol Great Khan. The Mongol Ilkhanid dynasty, which ruled Iran and Iraq after Hulagu Khan sacked Baghdad in 1258, used a white flag. White was also the color of the flag borne by the Oghuz Turks, the huge confederation that crossed the Oxus River in the eleventh century, giving rise to both the Seljuk and Ottoman dynasties.[21] Continuing the Oghuz tradition, the sultans of the Rum Seljuk offshoot, who ruled central and eastern Anatolia from their capital at Konya between c. 1071 and 1243, carried a white flag. According to one version of the story, the Seljuk sultan ʿAlaʾeddin Keykubad sent one of these white flags to Osman Bey, founder of the Ottoman dynasty, in recognition of Ottoman autonomy.[22] Not surprisingly, competing origin myths exist for the Ottomans' flags, just as they do for the Janissary headdress. *Menakibname*s, or collections of elegiac miracle stories, of the legendary thirteenth-century warrior-Sufi Sarı Saltuk claim that Osman adopted Sarı Saltuk's white battle flag after the saint, foreseeing the Ottomans' greatness, had bestowed his sash, turban, and staff on Osman in a gesture reminiscent of Hajji Bektash's intervention in the founding of the Janissaries, noted below.[23] On the other hand, M. Fuad Köprülü notes that the Anatolian Seljuk and early Ottoman armies included followers of the eleventh-century Iranian mystic Abu Ishaq Kazaruni. These devotees carried Ishaqi banners, which were embroidered in gold with verses from the Qurʾan.[24]

Certain Oghuz—and, by extension, Seljuk and early Ottoman—attitudes toward red and white can be gleaned from the *Book of Dede Korkut*, a cycle of twelve heroic tales dating back before the Oghuz migration across the Oxus but still popular among the Anatolian Seljuks and the early Ottomans. The tales evoke colors continuously, often in contrast to one another; the most frequently occurring are white, red, and black. The Oghuz armies are depicted as carrying white banners; in the Tale of Bamsi Beyrek, the hero's white banner is implicitly linked with that of the Prophet.[25] Otherwise, white seems to connote virility, but also virtue and innocence. The tents of the Oghuz heroes tend to be white, yet white is also the color of healthy, untouched skin, particularly the skin of virginal young girls, who are frequently likened to white geese.[26] Red, on the other hand, seems to have feminine overtones, perhaps in part because it is associated with menstrual blood. Hence, when Bayindir Khan gives a feast, he erects a white tent for all guests with male children and a red tent for all guests with female children. At least one warrior-heroine pitches a red tent, and brides tend to dress in red—as they still did in Anatolia in recent times.[27] In the tale of Bamsi Beyrek, the young hero offends his companions, who are dressed in white, by donning a red robe sent him as part of her trousseau by his bride-to-be.[28] Black and blue are unlucky colors: the colors in which infidels dress, the colors of death and mourning. When a hero dies or is thought to have died, his household immediately "changes white [clothing] for black."[29]

Ottoman Banner Colors

Apart from the *sancak-i şerif*, the Ottomans followed other eastern Turkic dynasties in employing white banners, as the various stories of white flags bestowed by the Seljuk sultan and Sarı Saltuk attest. However, unlike the Rum Seljuks and the Ilkhanids, they also made frequent use of red banners. In fact, red and white, and more particularly red and white banners, figure rather prominently in Ottoman political culture. This bichromatic scheme is reflected already in the origin myths of the Janissaries. When Orhan assumed the beylik, according to the accounts of the fifteenth-century chroniclers Aşıkpaşazade and Uruc, his brother advised him to make a sartorial distinction between the provincial cavalry, free Muslims who held land grants known as *timar*s, and the new corps of slave soldiers. The provincial cavalry, or beys, wore red caps; Orhan therefore dressed himself and his Janissaries in white caps. In Uruc's account, Orhan obtained the appropriate white cap from "Hajji Bektash of Khurasan" (who died in the thirteenth century, but never mind).[30] The somewhat earlier compilation of Bektashi legends known as the *Vilayetname of Hajji Bektash* takes the Bektashi connection farther by asserting that the Seljuk sultan sent Osman, the founder of the Ottoman dynasty, to Hajji Bektash for judgment after Osman violated a truce with the Byzantines. The dervish bestowed the distinctive white headdress on Osman, along with a candle and a sword. On hearing of this, the Seljuk sultan awarded Osman a land grant (*sancak*) and sent him a white flag.[31] In the first origin myth, then, the red-white dichotomy serves primarily to distinguish two different corps of soldiery. The use of red caps for provincial troops probably did not originate with the Ottomans; red caps are attested for the free Turcoman troops of the bey of Karaman in Central Anatolia in the late thirteenth century.[32] In the myth, notwithstanding, both colors are portrayed as unmistakably "Ottoman," although white is somehow more closely identified with the sultan, as well as with the Janissary corps itself. The *Vilayetname* myth goes so far as to relate the white headdress and, implicitly, the white banner to Osman's prowess and legitimacy. As in the *Book of Dede Korkut*, the color white seems to indicate the virtuous masculine virility on which legitimate military authority is founded. In a startling adaptation of this color logic, Bektashi lore relates that Hajji Bektash once levitated into the air, allowing an astonished disciple to glimpse, beneath his robe, his testicles, which took the form of a red and a white rose.[33] This tale may intend to demonstrate Hajji Bektash's transcendence of fleshly desires or, alternatively, his assumption of both purely spiritual (white) and mundane (red) qualities. Read in connection with the saint's link to the Ottomans, it could also ratify both red and white as Ottoman colors (on which see below).

This red-white distinction between the Janissaries and the free cavalry seems to be borne out in later Ottoman history. On campaign, according to Riza Nour, Selim I's (r. 1512–20) personal flag was white while "the army's" flag was red.[34] In his account of Selim's conquest of Egypt, Şiri ᶜAli describes the red banners (s. *kızıl bayrak*) of the Ottoman cavalry under the grand vizier Khadim Sinan Pasha as so numerous that their reflection turned the waters of the Nile red.[35] Likewise, during Süleyman I's reign (1520–66), the Janissaries reportedly marched under a white flag while the timariot cavalry marched under a red one.[36] Yet although a white banner may have represented the Janissaries as a whole, the subdivisions of the corps adopted a wide array of banners. Each division, or *orta*, had its own distinguishing banner; the colors of these banners and the symbols emblazoned on them were, furthermore, quite varied.[37] Still, the Janissaries also had a special attachment to the image of the caliph ᶜAli's sword Dhu'l-Faqar, and habitually carried a large banner displaying the distinctive Ottoman version of that image; several of the *ortas*' identifying emblems also incorporated Dhu'l-Faqar. The ground of the Dhu'l-Faqar banner could be either red or white, and Sultan Selim seems to have carried both red and white Dhu'l-Faqar banners to Egypt (see chapter 11).

It is certainly worth noting that these basic colors were employed as markers not only by military entities, but also by groupings within "civilian" society. The major Sufi orders often carried banners and wore turbans of specific colors; we have already noted the Bektashi connection with white. In nineteenth-century Cairo, Edward W. Lane reports that the banner of the Qadiri order was white, that of the order of the beloved Egyptian saint Ahmad al-Badawi red, that of the Rifaᶜis black, that of the order of Ibrahim al-Dasuqi (the Burhaniyya or Barāhima) green.[38] In the mid-eighteenth century, indeed, the former grand vizier Hekimoğlu ᶜAli Pasha, encamped below Banja Luka in Bosnia, supposedly had a dream in which the founders of these very four Sufi orders appeared, each carrying the appropriately colored banner. (The shaykhs told him that if he vowed to go to Egypt—which he did—he would succeed in taking Banja Luka from the Hapsburgs—which he did.)[39] Colored flags were also carried by the population at large during major celebrations, such as the annual inundation of the Nile in Cairo.[40]

In sum, both red and white seem to have enjoyed precedence as "Ottoman" colors. A certain shade of deep red, known in Turkish as *al*, came to be regarded as the Ottoman dynastic color, much as the royal purple (porphyry) was the special preserve of Roman and later Byzantine emperors.[41] It is, indeed, conceivable that the Ottomans adopted this general color preference from the Byzantines. Most specimens of Ottoman battle and processional flags preserved in museums, whether in Turkey or elsewhere, are of this color (sometimes called simply *kızıl*, a generic term for red). Indeed, the red ground of the flag of republican Turkey clearly derives from this earlier Ottoman prototype.

Red and White Banners in the Ottoman Provinces

There is, then, a lengthy and highly visible tradition of red and white flags at the Ottoman center, yet in this context, the red and white flags are not antagonistic but complementary. Both symbolize and reinforce the authority of the Ottoman dynasty. In the provinces, however, we occasionally find a red or a white flag being used as a symbol of opposition, at least implicitly against a rival color deployed by the enemy side.

The hero of Ottoman Yemen, Haydar Agha, who briefly turned the tide against the Qasimi imam in the 1620s (see chapter 4), is described in Haci ᶜAli's chronicle as marching into Yemen with "the red flag" (*kızıl bayrak*).[42] Haydar Agha was the *kâhya*, or lieutenant, of Caᶜfer Pasha, governor of Yemen from 1607–17, as well as commander of the imperial *sipahi* corps, based in Istanbul;[43] as such, like the timariot cavalry of Orhan's day, his "official color," and hence the color of the flag he carried, was red. At first blush, this seems appropriate in the context of the Ottoman struggle for Yemen, for white is not only a generic color for Shiᶜite rebellion against Sunni rule,[44] but also, at least according to A. S. Tritton, specifically "the Zaydi color."[45] On the other hand, Robert Playfair, who personally observed the Qasimi imams, albeit some two centuries after their victory over the Ottomans, has the imam carrying a red flag emblazoned with an image of Dhu'l-Faqar.[46] While they were certainly Shiᶜites struggling to throw off Sunni rule, the Qasimi imams were also descendants of the Prophet and, as such, would have been northern, Qaysi Arabs even though they resided in Yemen. As Qaysis, they would have been inclined toward a red flag; as Shiᶜites, toward a white. Haydar Agha, to be sure, did not choose the color of his flag so as to contrast with that of the Zaydi enemy; the red *sipahi* flag, as we have seen, goes back to the reign of Orhan, over three hundred years before. Whatever the color of the Qasimi imam's flag in this conflict, that of Haydar Agha's flag has more to do with the *sipahi*s as representatives of Ottoman authority than it does with the Zaydi-Sunni or the Qaysi-Yemeni rivalry.

If Haydar Agha does not provide us with an unequivocal example of competing flag colors, we do have a much more clear-cut case in Ottoman Palestine. In the mid-sixteenth century, Sultan Süleyman I received complaints about the *alaybeği*, or officer in charge of mustering troops, of the town of Nablus on the west bank of the Jordan river. This officer, one Toklu (lustful, or mumpsy)[47] Mehmed, was, according to the imperial orders responding to the complaints, fomenting discord with the aid of "the White Flag Group" (*akbayraklu taife*).[48] Significantly, the *sipahi*s seem to be the chief source of the complaints, so that we may speculate that Toklu Mehmed was deploying the white flag in opposition to the red *sipahi* flag. Indeed, the *alaybeği* would probably have been a Janissary.[49] Since this was Palestine, however, where the Qays-Yemen rivalry was still going strong in the early twentieth century, it may be that elements of the Qays-Yemen antagonism had bonded with elements of a *sipahi*-Janissary rivalry. This is an intriguing idea, since the same sort of dynamic may have played into Egypt's factional conflicts, albeit in subtler fashion. But if the Qays-Yemen color dichotomy mirrored a dichotomy within Ottoman political culture, then it would be all the easier for elements, such as Janissaries and mamluks, approaching the Qays-Yemen conflict from outside to be absorbed into it. Particularly in a procession, I might add. For the *alaybeği* was responsible not only for mustering troops, but also for leading them as they marched in procession. In few other situations would the conflict between white flag and red flag have been so visually graphic or seemed so dichotomous; the rarified atmosphere of the occasion would have encouraged all participants—even all observers—to choose one side or the other and to behave accordingly. (This subject is discussed in more detail in chapter 6.)

Red and White/Qays and Yemen

The exploits of Haydar Agha and Toklu Mehmed illustrate, to varying degrees, an Ottoman red-white tradition meshing with a provincial Qays-Yemen color tradition. In the case of Haydar Agha, the Ottoman tradition predominates; the Qaysi-Yemeni color dichotomy is only vaguely implicit in the provincial context. Toklu Mehmed's disturbances, on the other hand, point to a genuine meshing of the two color traditions within a Syrian provincial setting.

Indeed, the most visible markers of Qaysi-Yemeni difference were the contrasting colors that the two parties preferred. Red was the Qaysi color, white the Yemeni color. How and when these color associations originated is not clear. A story from the *Thousand and One Nights* claims that red is associated with Mudaris, hence Qaysis, because of the red leather tent in which Mudar himself had lived in the desert.[50] Such an elemental split, however, most likely has roots as deep as those of the Byzantine circus faction colors, which allegedly derived from the colors of the four natural elements (see chapter 1). Whatever the case, the persistence of this color dichotomy in certain regions of the Middle East, notably Syria and Palestine, is remarkable. In fact, the Qays-Yemen rivalry, with its attendant color dichotomy, was a constant feature of political culture in Ottoman Greater Syria, which included Lebanon and Palestine. The Ottoman central authority was aware of this conflict in the region as early as the mid-sixteenth century. An order from the sultan to the governor (*beylerbeyi*) of the province of Damascus (Sham) in 1565 notes that "the people of Halilürrahman are divided into two tribes (*ḳabīle*) named Qaysi and Yemeni," whose continuous conflicts scare people away from Friday prayers at the tomb.[51] Halilürrahman is the Palestinian town of Hebron, site of the tomb of the patriarch Abraham, who in Muslim tradition is often called the "friend" (*khalīl*) of God (*al-Raḥmān*, the Merciful); Hebron lies some one hundred kilometers south of Nablus. Chroniclers and diplomats reported Qays-Yemen strife in the same general region in the eighteenth and nineteenth centuries.[52] In Lebanon during the seventeenth and eighteenth centuries, political culture centered on competing families associated with Qays and Yemen; the Ottoman central authority more frequently supported the Qaysi families.[53] Color competition, with occasional modifications, naturally accompanied this factionalism; a nineteenth-century British consul in Jerusalem reported that the Qaysis wore dark red turbans with yellow stripes while the Yemenis preferred lighter colors.[54]

Did such a struggle, complete with clash of colors, exist in Ottoman Egypt? The origin myths transmitted by the Damurdashi chronicles at least implicitly evoke the Qaysi-Yemeni dichotomy. Al-Qinali is the least direct, asserting merely that "the white was Tubbaʿi, and the red was Kulaybi." We must supply the association between Tubbaʿi and Yemeni, as well as that between Kulaybi and Qaysi. Neither is terribly hard to do, since the Tubbaʿs of Himyar were clearly southern, or Yemeni Arabs, while Kulayb was almost certainly the pre-Islamic Qaysi leader Kulayb b. Rabiʿa. The anonymous *Majmūʿ al-durra al-munṣāna* is a bit more explicit: "White Flag from the Yemeni Tubbaʿ and Red Flag from Kulayb brother of al-Zir. . . ." Here, at least, the link between Tubbaʿ and Yemen is plain. Kulayb, on the other hand, is identified as the anti-hero of the *Qiṣṣat al-Zīr*, yet in that tale, al-Zir and Kulayb are supposedly sons of Rabiʿa, eponymous founder of one of the main Qaysi divisions.[55] Moreover, Hasan al-Tubbaʿi in the *Qiṣṣat al-Zīr* is a Yemeni ruler and the archenemy of the family of Rabiʿa; he is ultimately killed by Kulayb.[56] This squares with semilegendary accounts of pre-Islamic history in which Kulayb b. Rabiʿa declares himself king after defeating the united Yemeni tribes.[57] In short, these two Damurdashi chronicles link the factional split fairly convincingly, if indirectly, to the Qays-Yemen conflict.

Ahmed Kâhya al-Damurdashi, finally, is the most explicit of all:

> And in his [Baltacı Hasan Pasha, governor 1098–99/1687] days, the administration of Egypt was in two factions (*farqatayn*): Saᶜd and Haram, Tubbaᶜi and Kulaybi, [Husayni] and Yazidi. The Husayni's flag was white, and the Yazidi's flag was red. And Akri [?] and Qaysi. . . .

He explicitly mentions Qays, if not Yemen. Through his stream of binary oppositions, furthermore, he more or less unequivocally links Kulayb to Qays and Tubbaᶜ to Yemen, and, by extension, to the red flag and the white flag, respectively.

On purely historical grounds, there is a problem with ascribing a white flag to a party called "Tubbaᶜi," for the rulers of Yemen's ancient Himyarite kingdom, who took the title *tubbaᶜ*, were associated with the color red. Indeed, the appellation "Himyari" is said to have come from their affinity for red (*ḥamrāʾ*) in Arabic) robes.[58] On the other hand, Islamic tradition maintains that the greatest *tubbaᶜ*, the third-century conqueror Asᶜad al-Himyari, was the first person to drape a *kiswa*, or covering, over the Kaᶜba, centuries before the advent of Islam.[59] This very act of reverence for what would become Islam's holiest shrine arguably links Asᶜad al-Himyari, and thus the "Tubbaᶜi" party, to Husayn and the family of the Prophet, and thus, in the context of the Damurdashi origin myths, to white, as opposed to Yazid and red.

On the basis of these accounts, we can only conclude, in any event, that the ancient Qaysi-Yemeni rivalry, with its corresponding color dichotomy, survived in seventeenth-century Egypt, or at least was remembered by eighteenth-century chroniclers as having been alive and well in those days. Outside the Damurdashi chronicles, however, we have little evidence to corroborate this finding. Other Ottoman-era sources do not, to my knowledge, mention a Qaysi-Yemeni rivalry in Egypt. To be sure, the struggle may have been present in Egypt during the early centuries of Islam. A red-white color division informs the Muslim conquest of Egypt, for while the Quraysh's flag, and therefore the flag of the caliph, was white, the flag of the Arabs who conquered Egypt under the general Amr b. al-ᶜAs was red.[60] Amr, himself a Qurayshi, was, at least by later definitions, a Qaysi; as a member of the Banu Waʾil, furthermore, he was arguably a Kulaybi.[61] The connotations of his genealogy at the time of the conquest, however, remain unclear, nor does his genealogy suffice to explain the red flag. The Qays-Yemen split is attested two centuries later; as we saw in chapter 1, the ᶜAbbasid tax regime of the early ninth century triggered conflicts between Qaysi and Yemeni bedouin in the Nile Delta. By the sixteenth century, however, the Qays-Yemen rivalry is far more frequently associated with Ottoman Syria, Lebanon, and Palestine than it is with Ottoman Egypt.

The Husayni-Yazidi Dichotomy in Procession

If we reexamine the passage from Ahmed Kâhya al-Damurdashi's *Al-Durra al-muṣāna*, quoted above, we notice that while it certainly signals a connection between Qays and Yemen, on the one hand, and red and white banners, on the other, what al-Damurdashi actually describes is the banner colors of the "Husaynis" and "Yazidis." His text alludes to yet another color tradition that meshed with both the Turco-Ottoman tradition and that of the Qays-Yemen rivalry. This tradition springs from the civil wars of early Islamic history, and more specifically from the revolt of Husayn b. ᶜAli against Yazid b. Muᶜawiya, who had succeeded to the caliphate on his father's death in 680. Husayn was encouraged to rebel by both the partisans of his father, ᶜAli, and by Muslims who opposed Yazid's hereditary succession, which marked the beginning of a true Umayyad dynasty. Husayn led a band from Medina to Kufa, his father's old base of support in Iraq, but was trapped by Yazid's forces at Karbala, in the desert near the Euphrates river, and massacred along with his followers on the tenth of Muharram, the first month of the Islamic lunar year 61 (680 C.E.); the date is known in Arabic as ᶜĀshūrāᵓ, or "the tenth." Twelver Shiᶜite communities today stage reenactments of this incident during Muharram and the succeeding month of Safar each year; these reenactments have been described by Western observers as veritable Passion plays.

These Passion plays may supply the link between the Husayni-Yazidi dichotomy and the red and white banners, for the actors portraying members of the opposing sides wear these colors. To be sure, the family of the Prophet, whom Husayn represents, are typically associated with green banners and clothing. And indeed, this is the color worn at their entrance by the actors portraying Husayn and his doomed party in the Passion plays. Before their confrontation with Yazid's men, however, the actors playing the members of Husayn's party don white garments, meant to represent their burial shrouds, for Husayn is thought to have worn his shroud into battle, knowing that he would be killed. White, in this context, is the color of martyrdom. Red, on the other hand, is the color typically worn by the forces of Yazid in the Passion plays.[62]

The Passion Plays of Husayn seem to have evolved during the first two or three centuries after the events they commemorate; they were first officially sanctioned by the Persian Buyid dynasty, which took over military and political authority from the ʿAbbasid caliphs in 945 C.E.[63] News of the commemorations would have reached Egypt via scholars and merchants traveling from Baghdad and the Buyid domains in Iran; during the Ottoman era, soldiers who had deserted from the Safavid armies or who had served in Ottoman territories bordering the Safavid domains would likewise have transmitted reports of the strange customs, much as Konstantin Mihalowicz transmitted the lore of the Janissaries. Under official Safavid encouragement, Passion plays and related Muharram commemorative festivities flourished; by the time the Safavid dynasty collapsed in 1722—around the time when the first Damurdashi chronicles were compiled—they had reached their fully developed form as *taʿziyeh*, a series of reenactments of the martyrdoms of Husayn and other Shiʿite heroes with dramatic narrative recitations.[64] It is interesting to note, in this regard, that the Safavid shahs, and particularly ʿAbbas I (r. 1588–1629), encouraged the participation in these spectacles of the two rival Iranian factions called Haydari and Niʿmati, whose antagonism mirrored that of the Faqaris and Qasimis (see chapter 1).[65]

Although Passion plays were not performed in Egypt, even under the Ismaili Shiʿite Fatimid dynasty (969–1171 C.E.), who founded Cairo, Egypt was arguably receptive to the sympathy for Husayn that these plays evoked. Husayn was revered as an early Islamic hero by Egypt's overwhelmingly Sunni Muslim population—as, indeed, he is by most Muslims, regardless of sect. The Ottomans themselves sponsored an upbeat ʿĀshūrāʾ celebration designed to counter the doleful message of the Passion plays; it featured the mass distribution of sweets.[66] Following Husayn's martyrdom, his head was, according to legend, miraculously transported to Egypt; the ʿAbbasids built a mosque-cum-shrine at the site in Cairo where the head was thought to have been buried.[67] Until well into the seventeenth century, when the mosque-university of al-Azhar emerged as Egypt's preeminent educational institution, the Husayniyya shrine was a significant site of Sunni juridical education.[68] As late as the closing years of the eighteenth century, it served as a center for the influential Khalwati mystical order.[69] Given the Damurdashi chroniclers' association with the Khalwati order, it is quite possible that the chronicles absorbed both a sympathy for Husayn and a vague familiarity with the colors associated with the Passion plays through the order, which had originated in northwestern Iran and the southern Caucasus.[70] It is, in any case, far more likely that the Damurdashi chronicles' association of white and red with the "Husayni" and "Yazidi" groups, respectively, stems from this more popular, even folkloric source than from a consideration of the sartorial habits of ancient dynasties.

Red and White Food and Utensils

In one of the versions of the origin myth transmitted by al-Jabarti (to be discussed in detail in chapter 9), each member of the Faqari and Qasimi factions "loved the color in which he appeared and hated the other color in everything he used, even dishes and food and drink."[71] The overall connotation is that the color dichotomy extended to the minutest details of the faction members' daily lives. Although the account is clearly a tall tale that fails to reflect actual conditions in Ottoman Egypt, the existence of such a myth points to the presence in Egyptian popular lore of a "package" of markers of factional identity that may derive from older traditions.

The story of pervasive, all-consuming opposing color preferences has undeniable resonances in the folklore of other cultures. The infamous rivalry of the Blues and Greens in the Roman and Byzantine Empires, discussed in chapter 1, provides one possible analog. Alan Cameron cites the example of "Metrodotus the Blue who had a green table," memorialized in an anonymous Greek epigram. This Metrodotus, Cameron deduces, was a factional leader in Roman Salonica (today a city in eastern Greece). He so despised the rival Green faction that, so far from eschewing green furnishings and utensils, he kept a green table in his home "as a perpetual reminder" of the hated foe.[72] Although this is the opposite of the Faqaris' and Qasimis' alleged practice, Metrodotus' example shows how color rivalries can, in extreme cases, make the leap from clothing and heraldic emblems, where they normally manifest themselves, to furnishings and other household accoutrements. If nothing else, this analogy points to the conclusion that the Faqari-Qasimi rivalry had the same general character and intensity as that of the Blues and Greens.

Are we really to believe, though, that Qasimis ate only lentil soup and lamb while Faqaris ate yogurt, white cheese, perhaps the occasional chicken? Perhaps not, but here again, the *Book of Dede Korkut* may hold a clue to culinary attitudes that at first seem fantastic. In these Turkic legends, as noted above, white is the color of virtue and purity; *koumiss*—fermented mare's milk—and yogurt are singled out as white, virtuous foods—as are, interestingly enough, white sheep (evidently, the external color trumps the internal).[73] If, leaving the sheep aside, we think of white foods as constituting, above all, milk products, we can easily see their association with virtue, purity, and innocence, to say nothing of maternal nurturing—the well springs of male virility, also symbolized by white in Dede Korkut's tales. Red, in contrast, is the color of blood: both the blood of animals, which renders their meat *ḥarām*, and female menstrual blood, which pollutes the pure whiteness of "gooselike maidens" and symbolizes the feminine weakness that, in Dede Korkut's universe, compromises male virtue.[74] In this context, white and red foods, like white and red clothing and tents, comprise a veritable Turkic *yang* and *yin* of male and female, virtuous and tainted, virile and weak.

Associations of primal colors with primal food groups can be traced back as far as the Hebrew Bible. As Jaroslav Stetkevych notes, Esau, the elder brother of Jacob, is a "red" man who sells his birthright for a "red pottage" of lentils.[75] Here, too, red is a decidedly negative color, much like the "red death" evoked in *Dede Korkut*; moreover, it highlights the rivalry of two brothers born, like Qasim and Dhu'l-Faqar, of an antiquated, isolated father. The color association is, furthermore, thoroughgoing: red food is the sustenance of the red man, forebear of the Edomites, traditionally associated with the Romans. The Romans would, of course, become a perennial threat to the Jews, and their Byzantine successors the perennial enemies of the Muslims; their imperial color, moreover, was a form of red. In the light of such a venerable and resonant precedent, the extension of the Faqari-Qasimi rivalry to food and cutlery does not seem so far-fetched, after all.

Red Flag *versus* White Flag?

Did the authors of the Damurdashi chronicles even know what these colors evoked? Probably not entirely. The vague, heavily folkloric connections they adduce for the colors probably reflect the state of knowledge or memory in the early eighteenth century. In fact, the folkloric elements themselves no doubt heavily colored the chroniclers' apprehension of what the colors represented. In these accounts, white and red are paired as binary oppositions, part of a series including Saʿd and Haram, Tubbaʿi and Kulaybi, Husayni and Yazidi, Hilali and Zughbi, Baybarsi and Qalaʾuni. The color dichotomy, however, evokes and partakes of several overlapping color traditions, notably those associated with the Qays-Yemen rivalry, the entrenched Turkic color sensibility reflected in both flags and folklore, and the Shiʿite staging of Husayn's martyrdom. These color associations combine with the binary oppositions to produce polarized, color-coded factional identities: "white" are the good guys—the men in the white hats, so to speak—along with Husayn, Baybars, the Hilalis, and the Tubbaʿs/Yemenis, while red are the bad guys, along with Yazid, Qalaʾun, the Zughba, and the Kulaybis/Qaysis.

So the chroniclers' presentation of the factional colors seems heavily biased in favor of white/Faqari, and all the associations we have adduced seem to buttress the case for this bias. It is important, however, not to overlook a curious put perhaps telling feature of the Damurdashi accounts of the factions: while they all associate white and red flags with Saᶜd and Haram, they never claim that the Faqari and Qasimi factions carried color-coded flags in processions. What they say is, with slight variations: "We used to recognize them in processions because the Faqaris' standard had a knob and the Qasimis' standard had a disk."[76] This is a neutral comment; there is nothing inherently positive about a knob or negative about a disk. Colors are not mentioned here. To be sure, al-Jabarti asserts that "What distinguished one faction from the other was that if they rode in processions, the Faqaris' flag was white, and their standards had a knob, while the Qasimis' flag was red, and their standards had a disk."[77] (On the so-called knobs and disks specifically, see chapter 6.) But al-Jabarti not infrequently edits his sources to suit his own sense of logic; given all this talk of red and white flags, he must have reasoned, it is only logical to assume that the factions carried flags of those colors in procession. The fact that he changes "We used to recognize" to "What distinguished one faction from the other"—implies that he never actually saw the factions in procession himself; by the time he was born, moreover, the two factions had largely been eclipsed by the Qazdağlı household. But if the factions did carry red and white flags, why don't the Damurdashi chroniclers, who presumably did see the processions, mention that fact, especially after they have gone to the trouble of pointing out the contrasting colors? It seems unlikely that the factions would have given up carrying banners entirely; paintings by European visitors later in the eighteenth century show no shortage of flags.[78] But perhaps these flags were of many colors; perhaps, in addition, both factions carried both red and white flags, so that the color dichotomy was rendered meaningless in processions, where the factions presented their identities to the public. The Ottomans may, from the moment they set foot in Egypt, have confused the issue: we recall that Selim I carried both red and white flags, and that both red and white could signify Ottoman authority. Older folkloric associations of red and white may have faded before the public reality of a multicolored Ottoman procession. That is, the red-*vs.*-white dichotomy was remembered as a factional distinguisher, but in the factions' public appearances, at least by the eighteenth century, it did not necessarily serve that purpose.

6

The Knob and the Disk—The Factions' Standards

In addition to different-colored flags, the Faqari and Qasimi factions carried different sorts of javelins (Arabic s. *mizrāq*). The origin myths transmitted by the Damurdashi group of chronicles, in fact, assert that these javelins, as opposed to the red and white flags, were the chief identifying characteristic of the two factions; it was from their javelins, the chroniclers tell us, that they recognized the factions in processions, such as the procession that accompanied a new Ottoman governor from the riverain port of Bulaq, where new governors typically disembarked after sailing up the Nile from Alexandria, up to Cairo's citadel; and the procession that accompanied the pilgrimage caravan, with the Prophet's symbolic litter, to the point of departure at Birkat al-Hajj.[1] In other words, these javelins were the factions' chief distinguishing features. It therefore makes sense to ask just what they were and what was distinctive about them. This chapter takes on this task while also extending the inquiry to the role of heraldic insignia in processions and the importance of processions themselves in shaping the factions' identities.

Why would anyone carry a javelin in a procession, unless he were going to participate in a javelin-throwing contest? Perhaps the grandees of Egypt did carry their javelins when riding out to the hippodrome for a hearty game of *jirit*, an equestrian contest that the Ottomans seem to have introduced to Egypt and that resembled a form of polo played with javelins in place of mallets and balls.[2] But would they carry them out to meet the governor or see off the pilgrims? One rather suspects not. What they would carry were not javelins but long wooden staves that performed much the same function as flagstaffs, bearing symbols that were of particular importance to the group carrying them and thereby identifying that group. A javelin or lance could indeed serve this purpose if it were used not as a sporting implement but as a ceremonial object. In any case, it was the standards attached to these lances or javelins that enabled the chroniclers to distinguish Faqaris from Qasimis.

Standards in History

Like flags, standards mounted on poles have a lengthy history as markers of particular military groupings. As in the case of flags, notwithstanding, the standards of medieval Central Asian nomads, above all the Mongols, and the polities they influenced are of most help in deciphering the Faqaris' and Qasimis' "javelins." The Mongols carried a highly distinctive standard known as the *tuğ*, whose chief element was the "tails" of horse or, especially, yak hair that hung from it—symbols of the animals on which these nomads' livelihoods and military prowess depended. Following Genghis Khan's invasion of China in the twelfth century, the Mongols introduced the *tuğ*, featuring yak tails, to the Middle Kingdom while adopting the large, horizontal silk banners of previous Chinese dynasties. The *tuğ* subsequently passed to Korea and Japan, which were both subject to Chinese cultural and political influences of varying intensity, depending on the period. Japanese *tuğ*s featured "tails" made of oiled paper.[3]

Among the Turco-Persian military patronage states that succeeded the Mongols in Iran, Central Asia, northern India, and Anatolia, the Ottomans are most notable for adopting and elaborating the *tuğ*. Ottoman *tuğ*s typically feature black or brown horsetails, as opposed to the Mongol yaktails, which were either left white or dyed a variety of colors. The number of Ottoman horsetails varied from one to three, depending on the rank of the commander whom the *tuğ* preceded. Even more striking, however, is the Ottoman elaboration of the tip, or finial, of the staff from which the *tuğ* hung. Whereas the Mongol finial takes the form of a trident—or, as Zdzislaw Zygulski terms it, a "horn-shaped and spiked motif"[4]—the typical Ottoman finial is a golden ball that truly "crowns" the horsetails and arguably competes with them for visual dominance (figure 6.1). And whereas the Mongol *tuğ* was occasionally used as a staff for a banner, most famously in the case of Genghis Khan's standard,[5] the Ottoman *tuğ* was seldom used in this manner but was instead carried alongside Ottoman banners.

Other Turco-Persian polities appear to have chosen finials over horsetails or vice versa. The Ilkhanid rulers of Iran in the fourteenth century appear to have used black horsetail *tuğ*s at the top of flag-

Fig. 6.1. An Ottoman *tuğ* (eighteenth century). Topkapı Palace Museum 1/1000. (By permission of the Topkapı Palace Museum.)

poles; these, at any rate, are depicted in their miniatures of Mahmud of Ghazna, who lived some three hundred years earlier.[6] A fifteenth-century Akkoyunlu (White Sheep) Turcoman painted scroll showing porcelain being transported westward from China includes several plain black horsetail *tuğ*s.[7] Roughly a century later, Babur (1483–1530), a Central Asian chieftain who traced his descent from both Genghis Khan and Tamerlane, founded the Mughal Empire, which would rule northern India from 1526 through 1858, all told. In his memoirs, Babur describes participating in "the Mongol yaktail ceremony," which consisted of erecting nine standards, wrapping them with cloth, and showering them with fermented mare's milk, or *koumiss*.[8] This peculiar ritual features Central Asian steppe elements, notably the reverence for *koumiss* evident in the *Book of Dede Korkut* (see chapter 5), along with overtones of "the ancient Iranic rite of worshipping the deity represented as a sword stuck into the ground;"[9] yet it also calls to mind Hindu and Jain *puja* ceremonies in which the statue of a god is ritually bathed in milk, spices, and/or clarified butter (*ghee*).[10] Babur's grandson Akbar (r. 1556–1605) favored a modified yaktail flagstaff with a Safavid-style metal finial (described below).[11]

In contrast, the standards of the Safavids and Mamluks consist of metal ornaments with no animal tails whatsoever. The quintessential Safavid finial, usually at the top of a flagstaff, took the form of two curving metal serpents on either side of a metal plate, usually ovoid, inscribed with calligraphy glorifying God and the Shiᶜite imams, particularly ᶜAli. A more modest version with a metal disk surmounted by a spike is also represented in Safavid miniatures.[12] Illuminated manuscripts of three different Ottoman accounts of Husayn's martyrdom at Karbala show a metal disk topped with three spikes, always atop a staff around which the martyr's shroud is wrapped.[13] The inscribed ovoid metal plate seems to have come to be associated specifically with Shiᶜism. Large, highly elaborate versions, often topped with white, green, and red plumes, can be seen in modern-day Iranian "Passion plays" and processions marking ᶜĀshūrāᵓ, the commemoration of Husayn's martyrdom.[14] The later Qasimi imams of Yemen, according to Carsten Niebuhr, carried "a standard, having upon it a small silver box filled with amulets,"[15] not unlike the amulet-boxes and miniature Qurᵓans in cases hung from flagstaffs in the armies of many premodern Muslim polities, including the Ottoman Empire.[16]

A metal plate such as the Safavids used is known as an "*ᶜalem*" (literally sign, or flag). The Ottomans had their own *ᶜalem*s at the tops of their flagstaffs, typically in the shape of a spade such as one finds in a modern deck of playing cards, or a sort of lozenge; the *tuğ*s, carried separately, arguably dominated these *ᶜalem*s visually.[17] The standard of the Mamluk sultanate was a different sort of *ᶜalem*: a flat plate of metal in the shape of a long spade or knife blade, often with Qurᵓanic calligraphy worked into the plate (fig. 6.2). In point of fact,

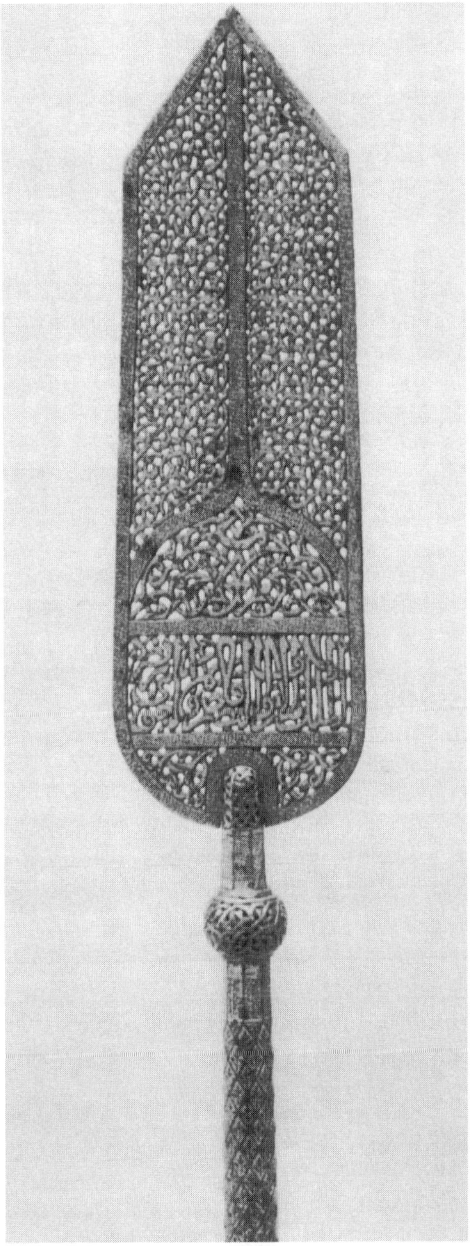

Fig. 6.2. A Mamluk ᶜ*alem* (sixteenth century). Topkapı Palace Museum 1/617. (By permission of the Topkapı Palace Museum.)

the bulbous minarets on Mamluk mosques look more like *tuğ*s than these *ᶜalem*s do.

This comparison leads to a further point: the *tuğ* was rather like a mobile version of the *manjak*, the metal ornament atop the dome of a typical mosque, as well as minarets and even *minbar*s, the "pulpits" from the steps of which mosque preachers give their Friday sermons. *Manjak*s, like *tuğ*s, varied along with the polities that employed them. The typical Mamluk *manjak* is an undulating metal rod ending in a ring. Ottoman versions take the same form, although some boast crescents or even crescent-star combinations. Mosques built in Yemen under the most recent Zaydi dynasty, which reigned from 1890–1962, tend not to have minarets, although they do display *manjak*s on their roofs. These, as well as the *manjak*s on older Zaydi minarets, were originally topped with crescents, which ultimately gave way to metal doves.[18] The *manjak*, in any case, had an amuletic purpose; it was supposed to protect the mosque from evil.[19] The word is related to the Turkish *boncuk*, "bead," most frequently associated with the blue beads (s. *mavi boncuk*) or "eye" beads (s. *nazar boncuğu*) that are worn or hung on walls to ward off the evil eye. In English slang, the same word becomes *mojo*, a sort of good luck charm.

The standard, then, was the army's mobile amulet; in the case of the Yemeni standard described by Niebuhr, this was literally true, for the amulets hung from the standard were supposed "to render [the imam] invincible."[20] The "amulet boxes" that adorned the standards of the Zaydi imam and the miniature Qurʾans that graced those of the Ottomans must have had the same purpose. Far more than an ordinary good luck charm, the standard had almost totemic significance. If the enemy captured it, he dealt a severe blow to the army's morale, indeed, to its aura of invincibility. And, of course, the enemy was fully aware of this significance. That is why Mamluk *ᶜalem*s from the Ottoman conquest of Egypt are proudly displayed in the Topkapı Palace and Istanbul's military museum today, while Ottoman *tuğ*s from the rout at Vienna are displayed in that city's City Museum.

The Knob and the Disk

Al-Qinali's *Majmūᶜ laṭīf* and the anonymous *Majmūᶜ al-durra al-munṣāna* agree that what distinguished the Faqaris' standards from the Qasimis' was that the Faqaris' standards had a *rummāna* while the Qasimis' standards had a *jalba*. These appear to be technical terms for the specific heraldic devices that topped these standards. *Rummāna* must derive from the Arabic *rummān* (pomegranate). In armorial terms, we may infer that the *rummāna* was a spherical or egg-shaped attachment, resembling what else but a pomegranate. *Jalba* as used in armory evidently derives from the Persian *chalap*, referring to "broad plates of brass used as cymbals";[21] Reinhart Dozy defines the *jalba* as a "large, flat plate of metal."[22] So the Faqaris' standard evidently bore a spherical or egg-shaped attachment while the Qasimis' standard bore a large, flat piece of metal. Or, if we take into account Ahmed Kâhya al-Damurdashi's slightly different rendering, the Saᶜd/Faqaris' standard had a spherical attachment with a circular plate of metal, while the Haram/Qasimis' standard had a plate of metal with no spherical attachment.

The preceding discussion of standards allows us to make the educated guess that the Faqaris' standard was actually an Ottoman *tuğ*, with or without horsetails. This would make sense, given the Faqaris' association with the Janissaries and, as we shall see in chapter 11, the Ottoman Dhu'l-Faqar flag. Certain varieties of Ottoman *tuğ*, above all those dating from the reign of Süleyman I, moreover, bore a series of metal plates, usually in a circular or heart shape, below a series of horse tails; one of these *tuğ*s would fit even Ahmed Kâhya ᶜAzeban's description.[23]

A French merchant named Jean de Thévenot, who traveled through North Africa, the Levant, and India in the mid-seventeenth century, states in no uncertain terms that the Faqari chieftain Mehmed Bey, who inherited the governorship of Jirja from his patron, ᶜAli Bey, carried a *tuğ*—or, more precisely, had it carried for him. In September 1658, according to Thévenot, Mehmed Bey descended on Cairo with an army of over three thousand so as to intimidate the Ottoman governor, who had summoned him to the capital to settle his accounts. As part of the bey's grandiose procession to the citadel came "the bey's *tuğ* (*toug*), which is a horse tail at the end of a pike," along with a large flag.[24] Thévenot mentions a horsetail but not a knob, whereas the Arabophone chroniclers mention a knob but not a horsetail. Nonetheless, Thévenot's use of the word *tuğ* leaves little doubt that the device, like almost all Ottoman *tuğ*s, was topped by a knob.

The Qasimis, meanwhile, must have carried a Mamluk *ᶜalem*. It is less likely that they carried a Safavid *ᶜalem* given the relative unavailability of such objects in Egypt, to say nothing of the implacable ideological opposition that had existed between the Ottomans and the Safavids. If their standards had borne Safavid-style snakes, furthermore, the chronicles would surely have mentioned it, as laconic as they are about the details of the factions' standards. On the other hand, the wording of al-Damurdashi's account makes us suspect that the Mamluk *ᶜalem* is intended: the chronicler notes that the Faqaris' standard had a *rummāna* with a circular *jalba* while the Qasimis' had a *jalba* with no *rummāna*; he does not specify that the Qasimis' *jalba* was circular like the Faqaris.' If we infer that it was not circular, then the likely candidate is the spade-shaped Mamluk *ᶜalem.*

Zygulski supplies some corroborative evidence for the Mamluk *ᶜalem* hypothesis, together with support for the *tuğ* theory. He describes standards captured by Napoleon Bonaparte's forces at the Battle of the Pyramids in 1798, and now housed in the Army Museum in Paris. Most of these "terminate in balls, not differing from the classic Ottoman type, but there are also examples with flat metal shields, a kind of Mameluke *ᶜalam.*"[25] These may well be the old Faqari and Qasimi standards, still in use decades after the two factions they represented had dwindled into obsolescence, in a classic illustration of the truism that old customs linger in everyday material culture long after they have been abandoned in official circles.

The Processional Gaze

By the time of the French invasion and even by the early eighteenth century, when the Damurdashi chronicles were composed, these heraldic devices had probably lost their political and ideological associations in the minds of those who observed them. This seems evident from the chroniclers' descriptions of them: no political or ideological connection is mentioned; instead, these standards serve solely to identify the factions. The wording is telling: "We knew Saᶜd and Haram in processions from their standards." One gets the feeling that the chroniclers are groping for ways of telling the two apart, and the standards seem to be the only distinguishing mark they can come up with. Their descriptions imply, furthermore, that since the factions carried their standards only when participating in official processions, this was the only time they could be distinguished. By the early eighteenth century, in fact, this may have been one of the few occasions on which the differences between the two factions were publicly visible.

And they had to be publicly visible. That is, it was not enough for the knob and disk to be present in these processions; to serve as identifying markers that would be preserved in collective memory, they had to be visible to the public at large. This meant that they had to be identifiable from some distance away, and this in turn probably meant that they had to be elevated, carried above the heads of those processing. Some readers will perhaps have seen the Macy's Thanksgiving

Day parade in New York. Viewing the parade on television, with the advantage of multiple camera angles, is one thing, but viewing it in person is often quite a challenge, unless one has staked out an office window several stories high along the parade route. We might find ourselves crammed shoulder to shoulder, having to peer through several rows of backs to glimpse the marchers. The only elements clearly visible to us are the balloons, which float high overhead. By the same token, a tradesman, even a low-ranking Janissary, in Ottoman Cairo might stand on tiptoe and squint, trying to catch a glimpse of the governor's procession as it passed by on its way up to the citadel. What he would see most clearly would be, indeed, the standards, which would be held aloft by bearers on horseback.

Our hypothetical tradesman in this instance is not unlike someone looking at Ottoman or Safavid miniature paintings of military conflicts. Standards of the sort discussed above are carefully placed in such paintings. They identify real, often contemporary polities; painters do not generally introduce them into battle scenes from the *Shahname* or other bodies of quasi-legendary lore. When looking at a contemporary battle scene, then, how does the viewer sort out two clumps of soldiery on the painted page? How does he or she tell which army is which? Often, the most direct tack is to look up at the top of the painting, where the standards are often depicted, sometimes even outside the picture frame. An Ottoman painting of the battle of Chaldiran, where Selim I defeated the Safavid Shah Ismail in 1514, is a perfect example of this kind of miniature (fig. 6.3). The Ottoman and Safavid troops are dressed differently and carry different gear—the Janissaries and their pikes are literally foregrounded—but what stands out, literally and figuratively, is the opposing armies' standards, thrusting up above the picture frame. No distinguishing symbols can be discerned on the armies' flags, but above the flag on the left is the characteristic Safavid serpent finial, while above the flag on the right are two Ottoman *ᶜalem*s or two Ottoman *tuğ*s, minus the horsetails.[26]

Could the Damurdashi chroniclers' remarks derive, at least in part, from looking at paintings of processions, rather than actually viewing them? On the one hand, miniatures produced in Ottoman Egypt are evidently scarce;[27] what representations we have of processions are either the work of European visitors, who painted what they saw, or Ottoman paintings from the imperial capital. But otherwise, we have to wonder at the wording of the Damurdashi chronicles' description of these heraldic devices. Surely a chronicler connected with a military regiment, if describing a *tuğ* or an *ᶜalem*, would use those terms, as opposed to *rummāna* and *jalba*—unless *rummāna* and

Fig. 6.3. The Battle of Chaldiran, 1514. From Şükrü Bitlisi, *Selimname*, Topkapı Palace Library, MS Hazine 1597–98, fo. 113a. (By permission of the Topkapı Palace Museum.)

jalba are *not* technical terms but common words employed for the benefit of someone unfamiliar with *tuğ*s and ᶜ*alem*s, such as a very raw recruit to Egypt's military regiments. In that case, it is at least conceivable that illuminated manuscripts, presumably of mediocre or low quality, were occasionally used to tutor such recruits, just as illustrated *furūsiyya* manuals were produced for the benefit of soldiers of the Mamluk sultanate.[28] Indeed, the Damurdashi chronicles seem to describe not so much actual *tuğ*s and *ᶜalem*s as the rather schematic depictions of these emblems in miniatures or in city views. In the miniature of Chaldiran mentioned above, the Ottoman flag is indeed mounted on a pole topped by what might be described as a pomegranate, which could portray the actual flagstaff or a schematized *tuğ* without horsetails. The Armenian chronicler Eremya Çelebi prepared a map for Armenian pilgrims in which he depicted the administrative hierarchy of Ottoman cities by sketching *tuğ*s beside each one; in his scheme, the number of *tuğ*s corresponded to the number of horsetails that would hang from the governor's *tuğ*. Eremya's *tuğ*s are even more schematic than the ones in the miniature of Chaldiran: a pomegranate on a stick, we might say.[29] The visual evidence, while far from conclusive, at least hints at the possibility that "knob" and "disk" could refer to a two-dimensional, pictorial reality in addition to, or even as opposed to, the three-dimensional reality of a public performance.

A further implication of the Damurdashi descriptions is that by the time the Damurdashi chroniclers were writing, the standards had displaced the colors as identifying features. All three of these chronicles give the clear impression that the only way to tell the factions apart during processions was by their standards. This must mean that they no longer paid strict attention to the red-white color distinction, or, on the other hand, that they no longer carried distinguishing banners, or perhaps any banners. Al-Jabarti splices together these various accounts and smoothes out their differences and inconsistencies, so that he emerges with a more articulate description that asserts that "the flag of the Faqaris was white, and their standards had a *rummāna*, while the flag of the Qasimis was red, and their standards had a *jalba*." But here, as elsewhere, he may be guilty of overediting his colloquial sources; the Damurdashi chroniclers never give the impression that they had seen red and white flags in processions.

There is no indication, furthermore, that the chroniclers recognize the ideological implications of these divergent standards: that, for example, the *jalba* of the Qasimis might evoke the Mamluks or the Safavids while the Faqaris' *tuğ* evoked the Ottomans. Instead, the *jalba*, or *ᶜalem*, and the *tuğ* have degenerated into mere factional signatures—the last such remaining, apparently. We might make an analogy to the manner in which logos of sports teams lose their original associations and come to be associated solely with the teams that adopt them, at least in the eyes of their fans, or, even more damningly, with the manner in which ancient names and symbols come to be associated solely with products whose advertising teams have adopted them. How many American teenagers today, for example, are aware that Nike is the goddess of victory in Greek mythology? By the same token, the Faqaris and Qasimis, whether or not they intended to do so, had evidently achieved one hundred percent association of *ᶜalem* and *tuğ* with their factions.

And yet the irony of this use of standards to distinguish between the two factions is that they would not retain even this purpose. If the spoils of the French invasion are any indication, both knobs and disks were employed in the Egyptian armies of the late eighteenth century, which consisted almost entirely of the household troops of the grandees of that time, who in turn were largely Georgian beys of the greater Qazdağlı household. The Qazdağlıs had originated within the Faqari faction; several decades earlier, they would probably never have carried Mamluk *ᶜalem*s, as opposed to Ottoman *tuğ*s, in processions. But once they had transcended the factional divisions and come to dominate Egypt's political culture, they evidently used both, although on exactly what occasions and in what combinations we do not know. They may not have used them indiscriminately. Certain households within the Qazdağlı bloc may have deployed the *tuğ* or the *ᶜalem*, or neither, or some other emblem entirely. As Zygulski points out, more study is needed.

7

Selim and Sudun in the Origin Myths

Almost without exception, the various origin myths of the Faqari and Qasimi factions assign a pivotal role to the Ottoman conquest of Egypt in 1517. "Faqari and Qasimi appeared among the soldiers and bedouin and villages of Egypt only under the administration of the House of Osman," says al-Damurdashi, while al-Qinali asserts that "the people of Egypt from ancient times were in two factions (*farqatayn*) . . . until the administration of the House of Osman . . . [when they became] Faqari-Saᶜd and Qasimi-Haram. . . ."[1] The implication is that the Ottoman conquest somehow triggered the emergence of the two factions. Ahmed Çelebi and al-Jabarti, however, present two different versions of a tradition that not only links the Ottoman conquest to the appearance of the factions circumstantially, but also gives the conqueror of Egypt, Sultan Selim I (r. 1512–20), an active role in their founding.

According to this myth, Selim, on arriving in Cairo in January 1517, following the decisive defeat of the last Mamluk sultan, Tumanbay, is taken to the residence of an aged emir named Sudun who has stayed out of the fighting, preferring to sequester himself on his estate with his two sons, Qasim and Dhu'l-Faqar. On hearing that the sons are experts at the equestrian exercises known as *furūsiyya*, Selim orders them to demonstrate their skills to him in a joust the next day. In Ahmed Çelebi's version, the Ottoman soldiers fall in on Qasim's side while the "Egyptians" (usually taken to mean defeated Mamluks) join Dhu'l-Faqar; in al-Jabarti's account, the pairings are reversed. Although the two chroniclers' narratives differ in key details, the gist of the story is that a permanent rift opens between the forces of Dhu'l-Faqar and those of Qasim. From that day forward, the factions named after the two brothers have persisted, with their distinguishing colors and heraldic devices.[2] This chapter considers the functions that Selim and Sudun serve as protagonists of this explanatory story, against the background of Selim's place in canonical Ottoman historical memory, and the elements of late Mamluk sultanate history that probably contributed to the making of Sudun.

Selim as Messianic Figure

In this particular myth, Selim bears direct responsibility for pitting Dhu'l-Faqar and Qasim against each other. The rather vague awareness that the factions did not exist before the Ottoman conquest becomes focused on the character of Selim, who sets the fateful events in motion. Indeed, he appears as a virtual deus ex machina, bursting onto the Egyptian scene and stirring the pot, so that Egyptian society is irrevocably altered. He is unmistakably a transformer. Yet despite the fact that he brought to an end the Mamluk society that Egypt had known for some 250 years, Selim never appears in a negative light in any of these chronicles. If anything, he comes across as an archetypal, truly larger than life figure, one of those Great Men whose deeds arguably change history.

This portrayal is remarkably consistent with the image of Selim in "canonical," central Ottoman history and literature. Here, Selim is the second of three larger than life sultan-heroes, the first being Sultan Mehmed the Conqueror (Mehmed II, r. 1451–81), the last Selim's own son, Sultan Süleyman "the Magnificent" (Süleyman I, r. 1520–66). By virtue of never having been defeated on the battlefield, all three achieved the status of "succored by God" (*muʾayyad min ʿind Allāh* in Arabic).[3] Collectively, these three emperors serve an almost eschatological function in Ottoman history, and certainly in Ottoman collective memory.

Mehmed the Conqueror (Fatih Mehmed in Turkish) conquered Constantinople in 1453, fulfilling numerous Prophetic sayings concerning that city and its conquest,[4] and bringing to an end the Byzantine Empire, against which successive Muslim polities had struggled for centuries. This conquest, which was viewed by European Christians even more than by Muslims in eschatological terms,[5] transformed the Ottomans from a border principality into the heirs of the Roman Empire. Recent scholarship has introduced the notion that Mehmed already contemplated the Ottoman conquest of Egypt and the Hijaz, and entertained a vision of the Ottoman Empire as guardian of the Holy Cities of Mecca and Medina. Indeed, the unwilling Janissary Konstantin Mihalowicz has him declaring, "I would march to attack the Zoldan [i.e., the Mamluk sultan of Cairo], but I fear God, lest I besmirch the holy cities."[6]

Within this framework, Selim becomes the ruler who fulfilled the Conqueror's vision. With his conquests, the Ottoman sultan became custodian of the two Holy Cities (*khādim al-Ḥaramayn al-Sharīfayn*); this expansion, combined with Selim's militancy toward the Shiᶜite Safavid empire, which had consolidated its rule in Iran at the beginning of the sixteenth century, and its adherents in eastern Anatolia, solidified the Ottoman Empire's status as the bastion of Sunni Islam.[7] Indeed, the statesman and man of letters Celalzade Mustafa Çelebi, author of one of the *Selimname*s discussed below, makes special mention of Selim's reverence for the tombs of the prophets that he passed en route to Egypt.[8]

Ottoman historical writing has not accorded Selim the eschatological weight it has bestowed upon his son and successor, Süleyman I, who consolidated his father's territorial gains with impressive advances against both the Hapsburgs in the west and the Safavids in the east, while extending Ottoman rule to Yemen and Abyssinia in the south. During Süleyman's four-decade reign, the Ottoman Empire reached its greatest territorial extent; legal and administrative institutions came to fruition, earning Süleyman the sobriquet Kanuni, or "the lawgiver."[9] In Egypt, in fact, Süleyman's first grand vizier, Ibrahim Pasha, in 1525 promulgated the law code, or *Kanunname*, that would serve as the basis for the province's administration until 1798.[10] The length of Süleyman's reign and the empire's achievements during it encouraged a number of Ottoman intellectuals to regard him as a *mujaddid*, or "renewer"—that is, the quasi-eschatological figure who appears in each Islamic century to "renew" the Islamic community. Rising apocalyptic expectations throughout much of the Muslim world during the sixteenth century, as the Muslim year 1000 (1592 C.E.) approached, only heightened this tendency.[11]

Selim, who ruled for a scant eight years, despite his extraordinary military achievements, was not so widely acclaimed as *mujaddid*. Among prominent Ottoman men of letters, only the former grand vizier Lütfi Pasha (1488–1563?), in his history of the Ottomans, describes Selim as the "renewer" of the tenth Islamic century.[12] Selim was, however, accorded the title *ṣāḥib-i kıran*, or world conqueror, by a larger number of Ottoman historians. According to the sixteenth-century man of letters Gelibolulu Mustafa ᶜAli, Selim would surely have been a *ṣāḥib-i kıran* had he only lived long enough. As it was, only three historical figures had achieved this status: Alexander the Great, Genghis Khan, and Tamerlane.[13]

These three legendary conquerors make heady company for Selim. Each is credited with well-nigh superhuman feats of military prowess. Alexander, or, in the Turco-Persian form, Iskender, would have been best-known to Ottoman readers and listeners from three medieval Persian poetic epics in which he reshapes the culture and even the topography of the Middle East and Central Asia. Profiting from the lessons of his tutor Aristotle, he introduces the benefits of Hellenistic civilization to the region. In the course of his peregrinations in search of the water of life, he builds a wall at the northernmost limit of civilized territory to keep out the hordes of Gog and Magog. (According to a tradition reported by al-Ishaqi, Iskender walled up twenty-one of the twenty-two tribes of Gog and Magog but let the last—the Turks—go free.)[14] He also founds key cities in the Caucasus.[15] Like Iskender, Genghis Khan and Timur founded world empires that brought large swatches of Asia into a common civilizational orbit. The Mongol Ilkhanid and Timurid achievements in architecture, poetry, and the sciences profoundly influenced the great Asian empires of the early modern era, notably the Ottoman, Safavid, and Mughal. Indeed, miniature painting produced under the Ilkhanids and the various Timurid principalities, to say nothing of the later empires, is replete with representations of Alexander and Timur, and even occasionally Genghis.[16] Moreover, the cachet of descent from Genghis and Timur endured well into the early modern era, serving as an important component of self-definition for Turco-Persian dynasties such as the Mughals and the Shaybanid Uzbeks.[17] So far as the extent of his territorial conquests is concerned, Selim I certainly bears comparison to Genghis and Timur, if not to Alexander. Unlike those of Genghis and Timur, furthermore, his conquests succeeded in bringing the Holy Cities of Mecca, Medina, and Jerusalem under his enlightened rule. In a purely Ottoman context, his prestige as a conqueror is surpassed only by that of Mehmed the Conqueror.

So far as Egypt was concerned, moreover, Selim did approach *mujaddid* status, at least in the pages of a genre known as the *Selimname*. These are not historical chronicles in the conventional sense but hagiographies, glorifying Selim's personality and recounting his military exploits—not only against the Mamluks in the Arab lands, but against the Safavids and their adherents in Azerbaijan and eastern Anatolia, as well. A large number of *Selimname*s exists from the decades following the conquest of Egypt. Those *Selimname*s prepared by statesmen and bureaucrats in the imperial capital are, inevitably, the most blatantly partisan and the most likely to portray Selim in eschatological terms. Celalzade Salih Çelebi, the brother of Celalzade

Mustafa, claims in his *Tārīḫ-i Mıṣr-ı cedīd* (New History of Egypt) that after defeating the Mamluks, Selim was hailed as "renewer of the laws" (*mücedded-i kanunlar*), presumably referring to the imposition of sultanic law in Egypt.[18] Abdullah Çelebi Ridvan Paşazade's *Tārīḫ-i Mıṣır* (History of Egypt), which covers Egypt from the Creation to 1056–1646 and is thus, strictly speaking, not a *Selimname*, employs the more customary "succored by God" (*müʾeyyed fī* [sic] *ʿind Allāh*), while Şiri ʿAli's *Tārīḫ-i fetḥ-i Mıṣır* (History of the Conquest of Egypt), a more conventional example of the genre, offers "shadow of God" (*ẓill Allāh*).[19] Evliya Çelebi's late seventeenth-century travel account depicts Selim as being protected from physical harm during his occupation of Cairo by the Prophet himself, who regards Selim's conquest of Egypt as a service to him. This motif is reinforced by the image, a few pages later, of Selim reverently handling the Prophetic relics stored in the Mamluk treasury.[20] Even al-Ishaqi, whose chronicle purports to be a general history of Egypt, reports the apocryphal tale in which Selim's father, Bayezid II (r. 1488–1512), hears a prophecy that he will be undone by a male son and plots to kill Selim at birth; the child is saved, however, by being hidden in the harem with his sisters.[21] Evliya Çelebi repeats a tradition that a Spanish and a Portuguese monk came to Sultan Bayezid II and predicted that his son Selim would rule Mecca and Medina, while his grandson Süleyman would conquer the *Kızıl Elma* (Red [or Golden] Apple).[22] In these and other centrally produced panegyric works, the Mamluks are typically disparaged as "nasty Circassians" (*Çerākise-i nākise*); Celalzade Mustafa goes so far as to call them "Circassian devils" (*şeytan Çerkesler*).[23] Here, Selim is unquestionably a *mujaddid*-like figure of mythical stature.

But *Selimname*s were also produced in Egypt by Arabophone chroniclers or by Turcophone chroniclers who based their accounts on earlier Arabic sources, above all the chronicle of Ahmad b. Zunbul (d. 1553). These "local" chronicles are far more likely to be sympathetic toward the defeated Mamluks. Even so, they do not treat Selim as a tyrant or usurper of any kind; on the contrary, they portray him in quite a favorable light. He treats the defeated Mamluks well, offering amnesty to any who agrees to join the Ottoman administration and even, in a famous episode, ordering the execution of his vizier Yunus Pasha, who accuses him of allowing the Mamluks to reestablish their hegemony.[24] Of course, they also present the defeated party's viewpoint: the Mamluk emir Kurtbay, then the last Mamluk sultan, Tumanbay (the personages and order differ in various versions), lecture Selim on his dishonorable use of cannon and firearms.[25] Even Evliya Çelebi's travelogue contains an abbreviated account of Selim's encounters with Tumanbay and Kurtbay, inspired in part, no doubt, by this same tradition.[26] Notwithstanding, many *Selimname*s and later Egyptian chronicles credit Selim with "saving" the Circassian chivalry that had been endangered by the Mamluks' defeat. To subsequent Egyptian chroniclers, he becomes a sort of latter-day Baybars, coming from a distant land to (re-)establish just rule in Egypt.[27] In this fashion, he does act as a renewer of sorts—although not in the simplistic sense of resuscitating the Mamluk sultanate, which he had no intention of doing.

Single Combat

A consistent theme running throughout most of the sources discussed above, whether "centrist" or "local," is the Mamluks' ineffectiveness against Ottoman firepower, which the chroniclers, again inspired by Ibn Zunbul, condemn as dishonorable and unfair. Notwithstanding, these narratives present an old-fashioned, swashbuckling account of the final struggle for Cairo. Once again, this tradition is exemplified by the chronicle of Ibn Zunbul, who would have been a young man in Cairo at the time of the conquest. In Ibn Zunbul's version, the confrontation between Ottomans and Mamluks takes the form of a series of single-combat *furūsiyya* confrontations between Ottoman and Mamluk heroes; Ibn Zunbul is clearly on the side of the Mamluks.[28] Doris Behrens-Abouseif has adduced these episodes as evidence that the origin myth of Dhu'l-Faqar and Qasim Beys dueling before Selim has some basis in historical fact.[29] What I wish to stress here, however, is the relevance of the *trope* of single combat to the origin *myth*.

In many, if not most, cultural contexts, there is something undeniably heroic about two vigorous champions deciding a conflict in single combat. A highlight of medieval European courtly chivalry was the joust between two champions, usually with the honor and the favor of a lady fair at stake.[30] Likewise, in pre- and early-Islamic Arabia, a battle typically opened with a preliminary stage in which the contending armies stood (on horseback) in two facing lines while noted champions from each side faced off two by two in the space in-between.[31] Medieval Muslim chivalry, which the *furūsiyya* exercises embodied, placed a similar value on single combat. To be sure, *furūsiyya* was not identical to European chivalry, or even to the pre- and early-Islamic knightly culture that is supposed to have influenced European chivalry. *Furūsiyya* was above all a body of equestrian exercises designed to prepare a young man for cavalry-based warfare; conventions of courtly love played little, if any, part in it. Likewise, the literature that *furūsiyya* generated had little in common with the love poems of the troubadours, with the knightly poetry of pre-Islamic Arabia, or with the court poetry of Golden Age Islamic Spain.[32] The numerous *furūsiyya* manuals that have come down to us are exactly that: training manuals, describing in considerable detail, often with illustrations, the various exercises that comprise the art.[33] Under the Mamluks, polo, which originated in Central Asia, and various forms of target practice formed the core of these exercises. Indeed, despite the Mamluk-era chroniclers' complaints that *furūsiyya* was neglected under the later Circassian sultans,[34] the Mamluks refined *furūsiyya* to a high art, producing a vast literature on the subject. Mamluk biographical dictionaries are full of legendary *furūsiyya* champions (of whom more below). In fact, the conventional historiography asserts that the Mamluks' attachment to the knightly ideal represented by cavalry-based *furūsiyya* explains their humiliating defeat by the Ottomans, who had adopted cannon and firearms manned by infantry.[35] Sultan Qansuh al-Ghuri's efforts to introduce a very primitive form of cannon met with open contempt on the part of the high-ranking Mamluk emirs.[36] Even after traditional cavalry warfare had proven ineffective against firepower, nonetheless, the Ottomans nurtured the *furūsiyya* exercises in Egypt, and even introduced a new equestrian exercise, *jirit*, a cousin of polo in which the participants threw javelins from horseback.[37]

Heroic single combat is certainly described in these *furūsiyya* manuals, but in a technical fashion. Romantic epics that illustrate the ideals and practices of *furūsiyya* are not, however, far to seek. The *Sīrat al-Ẓāhir Baybars*, that Mamluk-Ottoman cultural hybrid, as well as other popular tales, such as the Hilali epics and *Sīrat al-amīra dhāt al-himma*, abound with episodes of champions (both male and female!) nobly struggling one-on-one.[38] In addition, Mamluk-era chronicles include examples of single combats staged before the sultan, as when Sultan al-Muʾayyad Shaykh (r. 1412–21) hosted a series of lance fights performed by noted champions.[39] In a cultural context that valued stories of such exploits, it would be natural for Selim to stage single combats during his occupation of Cairo—or at least for later narrators of his conquest to assert that he did. For Selim's process to Cairo, rather like the process of the Ottoman governor in later years, was in some sense a ritual, a bit of playacting on a grand stage set. Such combats would have resembled the entertainments for the ruler's pleasure staged in countless nineteenth-century operas and ballets. It is no surprise, by the same token, that the eighteenth-century chroniclers' framing of the origins of the two factions, which they attribute in any case to Selim's occupation of Cairo, should adopt this same trope. Regardless of its basis in historical reality, this schema of two champions fighting in single combat before a ruler would have rung true from a narrative standpoint. It not only accords with the *furūsiyya* ideal, but also fits the general framework of two unalterably opposed sides. Ironically, it would go quite nicely with the binary oppositions of the Damurdashi chronicles, which, however, do not transmit this particular origin myth.

It is worth noting that within the culture of *furūsiyya*, the Ottoman tradition of red and white banners, and more particularly the red and white Dhu'l-Faqar banners that Selim brought to Egypt (see chapters 5 and 11), would have loomed especially large. In *furūsiyya* manuals, the opposing teams are, rather like modern-day football teams, identified by the colors of their clothing and banners, as well as the symbols that might be emblazoned on these. If Selim did oversee jousts between individual *furūsiyya* champions, then it is not unlikely that one champion would have carried a red Ottoman flag, while his opponent would have carried a white one. Both flags may even have borne the image of the sword Dhu'l-Faqar. Even if these jousts existed only in collective memory of the conquest, the image of Selim's banners must have been linked to them along with the image of the sultan himself. These considerations would lead us to suspect that both the Faqaris' and the Qasimis' banners may have been, or at least may have derived from, old Ottoman Dhu'l-Faqar flags. As in the case of the standards, unfortunately, material evidence is lacking.

Sudun

In the versions of the origin myth in which Selim I plays a part, he encounters a superannuated Mamluk emir named Sudun. Ahmed Çelebi asserts, in fact, that this aged emir is the famous Sudun al-ᶜAjami (the Persian, or the foreigner), who served as army commander, or *atabek*, to the Mamluk sultan Qaytbay (r. 1468–96). In purely historical terms, this identification is untenable. Sudun al-ᶜAjami did continue in administrative service after Qaytbay's death, serving as *atabek* to Qansuh al-Ghuri. In this capacity, he led the Mamluk army in the decisive confrontation with the Ottomans at Marj Dabiq in northern Syria in late 1516. In the course of the Mamluks' rout by Selim, Sudun al-ᶜAjami was mortally wounded and died. Thus, he cannot have been present when Selim entered Cairo a few months later. Moreover, so far from having two sons named Dhu'l-Faqar and Qasim, Sudun al-ᶜAjami appears to have had only one son, Sharaf al-Din Yunus.[40]

I suspect, however, that the emir Sudun of the origin myth need not be an historical figure whose presence in Cairo in 1517 is verifiable. The function that Sudun serves in this origin myth is that of an embodiment of the old, defeated Mamluk order. To a chronicler such as Ahmed Çelebi, writing over two hundred years after the event he describes is supposed to have taken place, Sudun al-ᶜAjami would no doubt have been the most prominent Mamluk emir named Sudun with whom he would have been familiar; he was unquestionably one of the best-documented Mamluk emirs of that name.

This leads to the question, Were there other Mamluk emirs named Sudun whom we might identify with the aged father of the origin myth? Indeed, there were quite a number of emirs named Sudun under the early Circassian Mamluk sultans, leading one to suspect that this highly popular name was typically Circassian. Ibn Taghri Birdi mentions no fewer than forty-two emirs known as Sudun or al-Suduni between 1382 and 1438.[41] Highly intriguing, nonetheless, is the fact that several Suduns appear in late Mamluk chronicles and biographical dictionaries who happen to be great champions at various *furūsiyya* exercises. Ibn Taghri Birdi notes that Sudun Taz, stable master (*amīr aḫūr kabīr*) under Sultan Faraj b. Barquq (r. 1399–1412), was an accomplished lancer, while a few years later, one of the greatest *furūsiyya* masters was Kızıl (Red) al Suduni; the adjectival form Suduni may indicate that he was the client or mamluk of an emir named Sudun.[42] It is certainly worth entertaining the notion that in an origin myth as archetypal as this one, Sudun may be a stock character: the archetypal *furūsiyya* champion. We can certainly call to mind a number of other myths and legends in which stock characters of this sort appear, with stock names: Haman, for example, the evil advisor in the biblical book of Esther, becomes the archetypal evil vizier in popular Muslim accounts of the story of Moses.[43]

But an intriguing twist to the search for Sudun is provided by Ibn Taghri Birdi in the opening pages of his *History of Egypt*. In describing the origins of the first Circassian Mamluk sultan, Barquq (r. 1382–99), Ibn Taghri Birdi rejects the tradition that Barquq's real name was Sudun.[44] Unfortunately, he does not tell us why this tradition persisted or where it came from, aside from citing two judges and two merchants who allegedly transmitted it. Given the legendary associations of Barquq with the descendants of the Arab chieftain Kisa who "returned" to Egypt after centuries in Circassia (see chapter 10), we may speculate that the name Sudun somehow evokes the Circassian pedigree, to say nothing of the glory of Circassian chivalry. Given the ubiquity of the name among Circassian Mamluk emirs, furthermore, the name may evoke a generic Circassian Mamluk, much as the name Paddy, for example, once evoked a generic Irishman—or as "Mehmetçik" in modern Turkey evokes a young conscript. Arguably, then, the character in the origin myth could hardly be named anything other than Sudun.

What else does the origin myth tell us about this Sudun? He was quite old; he refused to participate in the Mamluk defense against the Ottomans. These qualities make him sound almost like a throwback to the "glory days" of Mamluk chivalry, before Qansuh al-Ghuri began experimenting with cannon and special corps of cannoneers. From this standpoint, too, his name makes sense; "Sudun" would have evoked the high point of Qaytbay's reign, when Sudun al-ᶜAjami was one of the greatest cavalry commanders, or even an earlier period when great *furūsiyya* champions graced the sultan's court. The name may have been as evocative, in its own way, as Iskender or Rustam (who will appear in chapter 10).

Selim as Agent of Continuity and Change

The meeting between the victorious Sultan Selim and the aged Sudun, then, represents the confrontation of the old, *furūsiyya*-based Mamluk order with the new, gunpowder-powered Ottoman order. Selim achieves heroic stature by patronizing the old culture, as it were assuming the role of the Mamluk sultans of old who routinely patronized *furūsiyya* displays. In so doing, Selim integrates the old culture with the new, thus bridging the Mamluk and Ottoman eras in Egypt. He thus combines successorship to the Mamluk throne with his exalted status as *ṣāḥib-i kıran*. It is no accident that Ibn Iyas includes Selim in the Mamluk line when he describes him as "the forty-eighth of the kings of Egypt and their descendants (*awlādihim*), and the third of the kings of Rum in Egypt," after Khushqadam (r. 1461–67) and Timurbugha (r. 1467).[45] For, in this context, Selim was an extraordinary world conqueror who preserved the culture that he conquered and, furthermore, brought it to fruition.

The point that the origin myth makes regarding Selim I is that he introduces an entirely new order while reshaping the old one. His role in the myth, then, is that of catalyst, someone whose appearance on the scene radically changes the status quo. In this, he is indeed representative of history's *ṣāḥib-i kıran*s, yet at the same time, he bears comparison to legendary rulers—*ṣāḥib-i kıran*s and otherwise—who changed the order of things and introduced radically new institutions. He is thus comparable not only to Alexander the Great but also to rulers legendary for reshaping their own societies without necessarily conquering huge swatches of territory, notably the Sasanian emperor Khusrau I Anushirvan (r. 531–79 C.E.). Although he did extend the territorial limits of the Sasanian empire to their greatest extent, Khusrau I Anushirvan was better-known to audiences of the Ottoman era as the paradigm of the just ruler. As such, he was the subject of numerous exemplary tales, many of which were adapted to later rulers.[46] Evliya Çelebi, meanwhile, makes special mention of monumental buildings and cities that were founded by Anushirvan, and even claims that two of his viziers became Muslims after meeting the Prophet.[47]

What differentiates Selim's role from those of Alexander, Genghis Khan, Timur, and even Anushirvan is that he bears responsibility for creating a fundamental division—something that *ṣāḥib-i kırans*, let alone perfectly just rulers, do not typically do. In this, he more closely resembles the legendary ʿAbbasid caliph Harun al-Rashid (r. 786–809 C.E.), whose decision to divide his empire between his two sons, al-Amin and al-Maʾmun, led to civil war and fratricide and, in the process, created a pan-Islamic paradigm for fraternal strife. In the origin myths of the Faqaris and Qasimis, of course, Selim is not himself the father figure; that role is taken by Sudun. At the risk of seeming too psychologically deterministic, I might suggest that Selim usurps the role of father from Sudun—and, of course, such a scenario is highly charged from not only a psychological, but also an historical perspective. By displacing Sudun as father within his own household, Selim symbolically displaces the Mamluk sultanate as supreme political authority within Egypt. Here, the suggestion that Sultan Barquq's name was originally Sudun adds a piquant touch since Barquq inaugurated the line of Circassian sultans that dominated the later Mamluk sultanate and that was overthrown by Selim.

In the world of myth and legend, this schema makes sense, whatever may have happened in "reality." In both fact and legend, Selim fundamentally changed the Ottoman Empire, and certainly Egypt. Any institution that he founded, therefore, would possess a certain aura of legitimacy and authority. His conquest of Egypt clearly remains a watershed in the chronicles of Egypt composed two centuries later. The chronicles of the early eighteenth century, if they retain very little trace of the details of the early Ottoman administration in Egypt, nonetheless recognize Selim's conquest as the source of cataclysmic change in Egyptian society. In this context, it makes perfect sense for them to claim that the two factions had not existed before Selim arrived on the scene. For in the context of the origin myths, Selim is a deus ex machina.

8

The Mulberry Tree in the Origin Myths

Ahmed Çelebi's account of the origin of the Faqari and Qasimi factions, wherein Sultan Selim plays such a pivotal role, is both the fullest version of the origin myth and the most perplexing. As I have noted elsewhere,[1] this origin myth abruptly interpolates itself into the chronicler's account of the end of the eighteenth-century Faqari grandee Qaytas Bey. The bey, a client of Ibrahim Bey b. Dhu'l-Faqar (d. 1691), was blamed, in large measure, for the excesses of the civil war that followed the revolt of the lower Janissary officer Ifranj Ahmed Başodabaşı in 1711. ᶜAbdi Pasha, appointed governor of Egypt in 1714, ordered Qaytas' execution the following year; at the same time, he systematically eliminated Ifranj Ahmed's supporters. Following Qaytas' execution, the governor's troops razed the bey's mansion, the seat of his household.[2] This in itself was not unusual; in fact, it was the typical dénouement to a grandee's downfall. But, the chronicler points out, the governor's men also took an axe to the enormous mulberry tree that grew in Qaytas Bey's garden and under which he had constructed a council chamber, or *divanhane*, where the household head received people, heard complaints, and plotted strategy. Indeed, such "at-homes" were a typical feature of what David Ayalon has called the "open house" (*bayt maftūḥ*): the mansion of a grandee turned into a political headquarters, rivaling the governor's council in Cairo's citadel.[3]

Qaytas Bey, however, was the only grandee known to have held his "at-homes" under a mulberry tree. And this was no ordinary mulberry tree, either. "Nothing like this tree had ever been seen in Cairo," Ahmed Çelebi marvels, "for it was nearly 500 years old."[4] At this point, the chronicler, whose tree fetish is noticeable at various points in his lengthy work,[5] abandons Qaytas Bey while he expounds on the tree. But he doesn't go all the way back to the tree's genesis, presumably during the Ayyubid era. Instead, he focuses on one of the tree's illustrious previous owners, Sudun al-ᶜAjami, commander (*atabek*) of the Mamluk sultan Qaytbay's armies, who had been active some 150 years earlier, when the tree was a youthful 350 or so. Ahmed Çelebi identifies the historical Sudun al-ᶜAjami with the legendary father of Dhu'l-Faqar and Qasim Beys, the namesakes of the Faqari and Qasimi factions. In order to keep his two sons from running off and joining Sultan Qansuh al-Ghuri's futile defense against the Ottomans, in fact, Sudun supposedly imprisoned them in two enclosures (s. *bāb*) that he constructed near his house. Qaytas Bey's tree, then, provides the chronicler with a transition to his own version of the factional origin myth. Why he places the origin myth at this curious juncture is a question we shall explore presently.

Ahmed Çelebi is, to my knowledge, the only chronicler to link the mulberry tree to the origin myth. Al-Damurdashi certainly remarks on Qaytas Bey's possession of the tree; he has the unfortunate bey desperately gathering mulberries as a present for the governor in the hope that this feeble offering will stave off his execution.[6] Does the mulberry tree have implications for the origin myth, or does Ahmed Çelebi pay it special attention just because he has an obsession with trees in general? As it happens, the mulberry tree does have certain mythological and religious connotations in a variety of cultural contexts. In European literature, the mulberry tree is most famous for its role in Ovid's version of the Greek myth of Pyramus and Thisbe.[7] Notwithstanding, those myths pertaining to mystical beliefs and foundation traditions of the Chinese and Turco-Iranian cultural spheres turn out to shed more light on this particular incarnation of the origin myth. Accordingly, this chapter will use these mythical traditions to ascertain the symbolic function of the mulberry tree in the myth of the Faqari and Qasimi factions' emergence.

The Yazidi Connection

Qaytas Bey, as it happens, was a Kurd, although neither Ahmed Çelebi nor any other chronicler tells us anything about his background before he became Ibrahim Bey b. Dhu'l-Faqar's client.[8] We do know, however, that Kurdish mountain tribespeople who rebelled sporadically against Ottoman authority were not infrequently captured and sold as slaves; quiescent tribes, meanwhile, were occasionally recruited as military irregulars.[9] Some of these tribal populations adhered to the Yazidi religion, a much-maligned and much misunderstood Kurdish sect that centers on a cult of angels headed by Malik Taʾus, whom Yazidis regard as the supreme angel. (Because an alternative name for Malik Taʾus is Shaytan, or "Satan," Muslims typically identify him with the devil; thus, some Muslim—and non-Muslim—commentators have labeled the Yazidis "devil-worshippers.")[10] What is significant for our purposes is the fact that certain groups of Yazidis hold the mulberry tree, as well as other trees, to be sacred for reasons that remain obscure.[11] If the tree were indeed planted or transplanted in Cairo under the Ayyubids, whose elite were ethnically Kurdish, then it is possible that some lingering Yazidi significance attached to it. It is also possible that Qaytas Bey was himself a converted Yazidi who attached particular significance to the tree that grew in his garden. These are, of course, only conjectures; corroborative evidence is lacking.

Chopping down the defeated bey's mulberry tree would not have been an extraordinary action on the part of the governor's men, under the circumstances. It was part of the grandee's ruination, along with the destruction of his house; as such, it bears comparison to the earliest Muslims' practice of cutting down the date palms of their defeated adversaries.[12] A few years after Qaytas' execution, in fact, Nasuh Pasha, the governor of Damascus, sent his corps of Baltacıs (axemen) to cut down the enormous mulberry trees of the Druze in eastern Lebanon.[13] These ancient Arabian date palms and Druze mulberry trees, however, were economic resources; by cutting them down, the Prophet and his companions, on the one hand, and the Ottoman governor of Damascus, on the other, were destroying their adversaries' livelihood. This was not the case for Qaytas Bey. He did not, so far as we know, use his mulberry tree to grow silkworms; the climate of Lower Egypt was not suitable to sericulture, nor would a single tree, however ancient and huge, have been a practical way to attempt it.[14] Al-Damurdashi's description of Qaytas' frantically gathering mulberries for the governor suggests that the bey and his entourage ate the fruit, but it can hardly have been a source of significant income. Cutting down the ancient mulberry tree must have been, above all else, a symbolic gesture, as it were a posthumous slap in the face. It rendered the site of Qaytas' house, the locus of his power, barren, not unlike scorching the earth or sowing it with salt. Perhaps it was, in addition, a rebuke of Qaytas' hypothetical Yazidi origins.

Sufi Connections

The mulberry tree has yet other associations in the Middle East and Central Asia, notably a not insignificant connection with the Bektashi mystical, or Sufi, order, to which the Ottoman Janissaries traditionally adhered. When Hajji Bektash Veli was appointed to Rum, or Asia Minor, he threw a flaming mulberry branch into the air as a signal to the dervishes in Anatolia; the branch landed at the threshold of what would become Hajji Bektash's house outside Konya in central Anatolia. There, it immediately sprouted and grew into an enormous mulberry tree that is said to be still burning at its tip. Later, the tree would mark the site of the tomb of the fifteenth-century Bektashi leader Balım Sultan.[15] In a Serbian Orthodox parallel to this tradition, the mulberry tree growing in the churchyard of the Patriarchate of Pec in southwestern Kosovo was, according to legend, planted by Saint Sava (1169–1236), founder of the Serbian Orthodox Church, who brought a mulberry branch from Jerusalem.[16] The mulberry is not, however, the only tree boasting mystical associations. The juniper tree was long considered a "shamanic tree" because the wood, when burned, can produce an hallucinogenic effect if the smoke is inhaled. The juniper is regarded as sacred by the Tahtacıs, an intensely ʿAlid, even Kızılbash population concentrated on and near the Kazdağı in western Anatolia.[17]

Curiously enough, even modern Egyptian literature gives us a hint of an association between mulberry trees and foreign, specifically Persian, Sufi orders. The celebrated Nobel prizewinning Egyptian novelist Naguib Mahfouz, in *Stories of Our Quarter*, recalls the mulberry tree that grew in the garden of an ancient Sufi lodge, walled off from the rest of the neighborhood; as a child, he had what amounted to a mystical vision of the lodge's shaykh, who declaimed a cryptic line of Persian, then vanished.[18] The tree itself seems to embody exoticism; like the Persian Sufi lodge, it is a foreign transplant on Egyptian soil. Indeed, in a far more general, and even nebulous, sense, the mulberry tree in an Egyptian context seems to connote foreignness. The tree is certainly not native to Egypt; any specimens would have to be imported from Syria, Anatolia, northern Iran, or other cooler, more mountainous, and somewhat moister climates. Even then, they would not flourish in Egypt's exceptionally hot, dry climate unless carefully tended.

In a curious twist on the mulberry tree-foreign Sufi association, the redoubtable *Sīrat al-Ẓāhir Baybars* contains an episode in which Baybars experiences a mystical vision of a huge fruit-bearing tree (though what sort of fruit is not specified). He hears voices speaking to him from the tree and ultimately discovers that the figure responsible for his vision is the great thirteenth-century Egyptian Sufi master Ahmad al-Badawi (d. 1276), arguably as close to a Muslim patron saint as Egypt has had. Al-Badawi, so far from being a Persian emigré, lived in the Nile Delta town of Tanta, where his tomb still stands and where his birthday is still celebrated by hordes of visitors from throughout the country. The shaykh would still have been alive when Baybars came to prominence in Egypt. In the story, al-Badawi takes Baybars under his protection on the understanding that after he dies, Baybars will build him a tomb in Tanta.[19] The tale exploits the mystical associations of trees in general, albeit not in the context of specifically Persian Sufism and not to make a point concerning exotic imports to Egypt. On the contrary, the connection to the quintessentially Egyptian shaykh Ahmad al-Badawi gives Baybars special legitimacy within Egypt itself.

Perhaps, then, Ahmed Çelebi means to evoke this exoticism in his version of the factional origin myth. It seems impossibly pat to suggest that he is pointing out the alien, un-Egyptian quality of the entire "Mamluk system," introduced to Egypt by the Ayyubids, who were presumably responsible for transplanting the mulberry tree, as well. But perhaps he is hinting, more subtly, that the mulberry tree, like Sudun "al-ᶜAjami" (the Persian, the foreigner), and all the other Suduns who populated the Mamluk elite, was a foreign transplant that took root and thrived in Egypt. Sultan Selim, so far from destroying this tree, honors its then-owner, Sudun, and frees his two sons, imprisoned nearby, thus contributing to the tree's nurturing. In the same sense that Selim displaces Sudun as a father figure to Qasim and Dhu'l-Faqar (see the preceding chapter), so he displaces him as tender of the mulberry tree.

Given this context, we may regard the tree's destruction two hundred years later as part and parcel of the "rottenness" of Egypt's circumstances that the chroniclers, particularly al-Damurdashi, sense in the twelfth Islamic century. The tree's demise seems to bear out the warning, "Woe to him who has reached the year 1113 [1701 C.E.]!" that al-Damurdashi puts in the mouth of the grandee Hasan Agha Bilifya.[20] By this time, things appeared to be changing fundamentally in Egypt; institutions and mores—and trees—that had lasted for five hundred years were now vanishing or being wantonly destroyed. Nothing illustrated this more clearly than the peculiar series of contretemps that engulfed Egypt's military and administrative elite between 1711 and 1715, when the old, messy but dependable factional feud ruptured to reveal a complex new web of alliances and counteralliances that transcended the factional dichotomy. Qaytas Bey, himself a Faqari chieftain, split his own faction and dragged the Qasimis into the resulting quarrel. By "hiding his head under the skirt" of the Qasimi leader ᶜIvaz Bey, he ultimately brought on the latter's assassination.[21] This is the picture we get from al-Damurdashi's chronicle, in any case. To Ahmed Çelebi, whose version of the origin myth is uniquely pro-Faqari, the destruction of Qaytas' tree must have represented and epitomized the Ottoman administration's hostility toward the Faqari faction, to which it now attempted to deal a deathblow.

Trees in Global Perspective

The motif of chopping down the ancient tree gains even greater resonance when we consider the importance to Ottoman mythology of trees in general. In the Ottoman dynasty's own foundation myth, Osman, the regional Anatolian lord who founded the line of sultans that would bear his name, has a dream in which a tree springs from his navel and grows to shade the entire world. The tree symbolizes the Ottoman royal house, which will nourish and protect the subjects and territories that enjoy its beneficent and expansive shade.[22] Chopping down this tree would strike at the roots of an entire civilizational edifice. Indeed, the tree as metaphor for a state, dynasty, or civilization was widespread and uniquely effective, as witness the infamous British political cartoon, published during the furor over the Ottoman suppression of the 1876 Bulgarian nationalist uprising, of Prime Minister Benjamin Disraeli warning Liberal leader William Gladstone, "Woodman, spare that tree!"—the tree in question being the Ottoman Empire itself.[23] In chapter 10, we shall observe Ridvan Bey Abu'l-Shawarib's genealogist lauding the bey's sons as "the branches of this tree"—meaning Abu'l-Shawarib's own household.[24]

Curiously, there is even an alleged ancient Egyptian precedent for building a council chamber beneath a tree. Evliya Çelebi, describing the Nile Delta town of Manuf, northwest of Cairo, comments on the town's main mosque, in whose courtyard three date trees grow. "According to what they say," the traveler relates, "before Pharaoh, Queen (*Melike*) Delüke planted [the trees] and held a *divan* in their shade."[25] Big, old trees have a certain romance about them because of the events they are imagined to have witnessed. As a result, they naturally lend themselves to fanciful origin myths of the sort just related, to say nothing of the factional origin myth transmitted by Ahmed Çelebi.

In a far more global sense, the tree can be a cosmic symbol. In the Book of Genesis, to choose the most obvious example, the Tree of the Knowledge of Good and Evil becomes the source of original sin while the Tree of Life provides immortality (Gen. 2:9, 17; 3:2–7, 22–24). Norse mythology, popularized in Richard Wagner's *Ring* cycle, features the primordial World Ash Tree (as the comedienne Anna Russell says of the character Hunding, "He has an ash tree with a sword stuck in it growing through his living-room floor.")[26] In Greek mythology, the Garden of the Hesperides lies at the western end of the world, and in it grows a tree bearing golden apples, three of which Heracles/Hercules picks as his eleventh labor.[27] Ancient Chinese myth held that an enormous mulberry tree, whose fruit bestowed immortality, stood in the sea at the eastern edge of the world. In its branches perched ten suns, one of whom traversed the sky each day until the day when all ten decided to appear together; the resulting inferno prompted the lord of heaven to send a legendary archer to shoot nine of the suns down.[28]

The Turkic peoples of Central and Inner Asia cultivated variations on a common origin myth in which the primordial founders of the people in question emerge from the trunk of a tree, or from a space or natural formation between two trees. The tree, in turn, is explicitly or implicitly linked with the cosmic poplar tree (Bay Terek), which symbolizes the axis of the universe. This people first enters history when they break out of an enclosed "homeland," such as the mythic Mongol/Turkic homeland, Ergenekon, typically led by a (human or animal) culture hero.[29] In similar fashion, Sultan Selim enables Dhu'l-Faqar and Qasim to break out of the enclosures—and the chains—within which their father has imprisoned them. In a more negative light, we might compare this breaking out to the breaching of the legendary wall constructed by Alexander the Great in the far northern reaches to hem in the destructive forces of Gog and Magog—two entities, like Saᶜd-Haram and Faqari-Qasimi, that seem to exist only in tandem.[30] In Ahmed Çelebi's origin myth, then, the motif of the mulberry tree dovetails with that of Selim as catalyst to the factions' emergence.

The tree's destruction, on the other hand, signals the end of the factional reality that Selim, according to the myth, brought into being, and presumably the beginning of a new, postfactional reality. By the same token, when the "Huns" north of the Caucasus converted to Armenian Orthodoxy, their new bishop ordered a tree dedicated to their Turkic god, Tengri, cut down so that the Huns would no longer be tempted to sacrifice horses to it.[31] Here, cutting down the tree symbolized the demise of the Huns' former, pagan way of life, which gave way before Christianity. In parallel, if more apocalyptic, terms, the splitting of the World Ash Tree in Wagner's *Ring* betokens the Twilight of the Gods.[32]

There seems to be a fundamental human respect, in any case, for trees as symbols of literal rootedness, of timeless solidity, continuity, and stability. By the same token, destroying a tree or illicitly picking its fruit is almost universally seen as a sign of instability, if not chaos and apocalypse. Qaytas Bey's mulberry tree, both as a tree and as a particular kind of tree, serves its ominous rhetorical purpose admirably. So far as the Faqari and Qasimi factions are concerned, the tree's destruction constitutes Qaytas' posthumous punishment for violating the factional dichotomy; at the same time, it acts as a harbinger of the end of the two-faction system.

9

The Competitive Feasts of Qasim and Dhu'l-Faqar Beys

In the Damurdashi group of chronicles and in al-Jabarti's narrative, an alternative origin myth appears that does not draw on the tradition of Sudun and his sons. According to this myth, the Faqari and Qasimi factions originate in two beys named, naturally, Dhu'l-Faqar and Qasim, whom Selim I appointed pilgrimage commander (*amīr al-ḥājj*) and financial administrator (*defterdar*), respectively, of Egypt. According to the myth, "Qasim Bey loved buildings, and Dhu'l-Faqar Bey loved numbers." The story, as reproduced by al-Jabarti, continues:

> It is agreed that . . . Qasim Bey built a reception hall in his house, decorated it lavishly, then prepared a great reception in it for Dhu'l-Faqar Bey the pilgrimage commander. [Dhu'l-Faqar] came to his [house] and dined there with a small entourage. Then Dhu'l-Faqar Bey said to [Qasim], "You, too: be my guest tomorrow." And Dhu'l-Faqar gathered his mamluks that day, *sancak beys* and emirs and officers (*ikhtiyāriyya*) of the regiments. Qasim arrived with ten men from his entourage, and two personal servants (*khawāṣak*)[1] behind him and some messengers and a valet (*sarrāj*),[2] and went into the house. Dhu'l-Faqar ordered that no one should disturb them . . . until they had finished their feast, and sat down with [Qasim], at which Qasim Bey asked, "What about the *sancak beys* and officers?" Dhu'l-Faqar replied, "They will eat after us. All of them are my mamluks; when I die, they will pray for mercy for me. When you die, will your hall pray for you? You have wasted your wealth on bricks and mortar."[3]

Whatever the "truth" behind it, this story is clearly very much a story; indeed, it resembles in form and tone a fable or parable. I am reminded of another parable from seventeenth-century Cairo, a variation on the familiar "Country Mouse and City Mouse" fable that the late S. D. Goitein found in the Cairo Geniza and, somewhat reluctantly, published at the insistence of his colleague, the late Gabriel Baer.[4] The Geniza document consists of a dialogue between two characters, one of whom extols the virtues of life in the countryside, the other who speaks in favor of city life, with specific reference to Cairo. The final portion of the dialogue has not been recovered, so that we cannot tell whether the fable ends with a resolution in favor of country or city. In our chroniclers' parable, Qasim Bey could be the Country Mouse and Dhu'l-Faqar Bey the City Mouse (or vice versa)—with this difference, however: this fable comes down in favor of Dhu'l-Faqar Bey's preference for amassing mamluks rather than building grandiose halls. To create an enduring household, the tale seems to tell us, buildings are not enough; the important thing is to have large numbers of clients who will carry on the household after one is gone. This, at least, is the conclusion that scholarship on Ottoman Egypt has consistently endorsed.[5] This chapter, however, takes a closer look at this alternative myth. After first determining from internal evidence that the myth probably dates to the period of the factions' desuetude in the early eighteenth century, we proceed to an alternative interpretation of what this myth intends to convey.

Dating the Myth

A crude version of this tale, featuring two nameless grandees, was apparently circulating by the late seventeenth century; in this barebones form, the story's parable-like quality would have been especially evident.[6] When it is specifically linked to Dhu'l-Faqar and Qasim Beys, however, the tale seems not to be pointing a moral truth so much as explaining, implicitly, why Dhu'l-Faqar, and hence the Faqari faction, was ultimately more successful and longer-lived than Qasim and the Qasimi faction. This leads to the suspicion that this version of the parable must date from the early eighteenth century, like the chronicles in which it appears. Only by about 1730 was it clear that the Faqari faction had indeed outlasted the Qasimis. This was the date of the Faqaris' decimation of the Qasimis after the assassination of Ismail Bey b. ᶜIvaz and the death of Çerkes Mehmed Bey. By then, the Qasimi faction was already in deep trouble, having divided against itself as a result of the rivalry between Ibn ᶜIvaz and Çerkes Mehmed. Al-Damurdashi hints at an early deficiency in the Qasimis' numbers when he recounts how, in 1107/1695–96, the Qasimis managed to acquire a majority of the subprovincial governorships, but how the departure of the Qasimi beys to their posts left Ibrahim Bey Abu Shanab as the only Qasimi bey in Cairo.[7] The ultimate hegemony of the Faqaris is apparent in al-Jabarti's obituary of Hasan Agha Bilifya, in which he points out that "most of the emirs of Egypt and its leaders trace their descent to (*yarjaᶜūna fī'l-nisba ilā*) one of two houses: the Bilifya house or the house of Ridvan Bey [al-Faqari]."[8]

A second clue to the relatively late provenance of this parable is the exclusive prominence of the offices of pilgrimage commander (*amīr al-ḥājj*) and *defterdar*, as well as their assignment to two beys. Neither office is mentioned in the 1525 *Kanunname-i Mısır*, and nowhere is it stipulated that either post must be filled by a bey. Beys began to monopolize the two posts only at the beginning of the seventeenth century; during the sixteenth century, both offices were held at various times by efendis, specifically judges and other functionaries in the Ottoman provincial bureaucracy.[9] Even after beys began to dominate these two posts, furthermore, it was by no means clear that these were the most influential positions in the provincial administration, or even the most influential positions held by beys. The governor of the Upper Egyptian superprovince of Jirja was arguably just as influential as the pilgrimage commander and *defterdar*, and probably a good deal wealthier than either of them. If Egypt were the breadbasket of the Ottoman Empire, then Jirja was the breadbasket of Egypt; the governor was responsible for ensuring that the province's prodigious grain output made it down the Nile to Cairo and, ultimately, across the Red Sea to the Holy Cities. This entailed a number of daunting responsibilities, including ensuring that irrigation was maintained, and that the powerful bedouin tribes of the region disrupted neither the cultivation of the grain nor its transshipment. Initially left under the administration of Arab tribal chieftains, the Upper Egyptian subprovinces were consolidated in 1576 into one huge unit, Jirja, administered by a bey. As if in recognition of the extraordinarily heavy responsibilities he bore and the extraordinarily vast resources he commanded, this bey, unlike other subprovincial governors, bore the title *ḥākim*; his subprovince was termed not *vilayet* but *iqlīm*, literally "clime."[10] In the seventeenth century, this bey found himself practically administering a separate province. It would not be an exaggeration to say that Jirja rivaled Cairo as a regional capital during this period. The beys who governed Jirja were aware of this reality and made the most of it; in the most spectacular case, "Jalali" Mehmed Bey rebelled against the administration in Cairo in 1659, forcing the governor to send thousands of troops to subdue him.[11]

Had our parable achieved its definitive form in the seventeenth century, then, it might have included a third character in the role of governor of Jirja. By the early eighteenth century, however, this post had lost some of its clout, not because Upper Egypt was any less important but because Cairo was increasingly dominant. This leads to a further point regarding the dating of the tale. By 1730, a new beylical position had come to the fore: that of *shaykh al-balad*. Originally a title assumed by the bedouin headman of a particular district, it came to denote the most powerful bey in Cairo, a sort of *primus inter pares*. The Qasimi chieftain Çerkes Mehmed Bey seems to have been the first to take this title, prompting a flurry of outraged directives from Istanbul.[12] By the end of the eighteenth century, however, so far from having been abolished, the office was clearly the chief locus of power in Egypt; its holder was considerably more powerful than either the pilgrimage commander or the *defterdar*—and ultimately than the Ottoman governor. If our parable dated from much after 1730, therefore, it would surely have had to include a *shaykh al-balad* character. In sum, the tale probably attained the form in which it appears in our chronicles, showcasing two beys named Qasim and Dhu'l-Faqar who served as *defterdar* and pilgrimage commander, early in the eighteenth century, just in time for the factions' slow fade into irrelevance. This would be in keeping with the other origin traditions, which crystallized just before the twilight of the two-faction system.

The Myth as Cautionary Parable

Even more than offering an explanation of why the Faqari faction ultimately "succeeded" where the Qasimis "failed," this parable seems to take on the character of a cautionary tale. In effect, it warns the listener or reader not to put his faith in buildings. In this sense, the fable is reminiscent of Percy Bysshe Shelley's famous poem "Ozymandias," which some readers of this book will have been obliged to read—even to memorize—in grammar school English class. Shelley's "traveler from an antique land" reports the existence of "two vast and trunkless legs of stone" in the desert. The poet's point is that all that remains of Ozymandias is the shattered remnants of the statues and edifices that he built to glorify himself. Presumably, he did not amass large numbers of mamluks who would carry on his name.

Obviously, al-Damurdashi and al-Jabarti cannot have been familiar with Shelley. They were probably, however, familiar with similar parables from Islamic history and lore. The most famous "lavish building" parable in Islamic lore is doubtless that of the many-columned city of Iram, which, according to the Qurʾan, was built by Shaddad, ruler of the kingdom of ʿAd. Shaddad, as befits a self-aggrandizing ruler, believed that he had built paradise on Earth and that therefore belief in God and the Last Day was now irrelevant. Shaddad and the ʿAdites refused to heed the admonitions of the pre-Islamic prophet Hud, and thus brought the wrath of God down upon their heads: the city and everyone in it were utterly destroyed in an earthquake.[13] (Interestingly, a plausible prototype for this city is the lost city of ʿUbar in southern Oman, which has now been located with the help of satellite imagery from the space shuttle and Landsat spacecraft.)[14] As the Qurʾan asks, "Have you not seen what your Lord did to ʿAd? Iram of the lofty pillars, the like of which have not been created in [any] land" (89:7).[15] In the fifteenth-century Persian poet Nizami's *Hamsa*, Alexander the Great, searching for the water of life, stumbles across the ruins of Iram; on the entrance portal, he reads the inscription, "Life in these lands is not for all eternity. Think not thy realm will last. Prepare to die."[16] Other tales of the long-lost ruins and treasures of Iram existed and can be found in, for example, the *Thousand and One Nights*.[17] A rather striking parallel to Iram can be found in the fate of the fabulous palace of the famously just Sasanian emperor Khusrau I Anushirvan (r. 531–79 C.E.) at Ctesiphon in what is now central Iraq; the remains of the palace stand to this day. The Prophet Muhammad was born during Anushirvan's reign, and at the moment of his birth, according to tradition, the dramatic arch of Anushirvan's palace ruptured and nearly collapsed.[18] The similarity to Iram's destruction following Hud's prophecy cannot be coincidental. Like Qasim Bey's great hall, like Iram, Anushirvan's palace was only a transient bit of vanity.

This same moral lesson is present in the Qasim-Dhu'l-Faqar parable, although it is at first, perhaps, overshadowed by the bilateral, city mouse-country mouse structure of the tale, which, characteristically, gives each character a chance to state his position. At the end of the tale, however, Dhu'l-Faqar Bey clearly "wins," and not just because his mamluks could tear down Qasim Bey's hall if they wanted to. Dhu'l-Faqar never claims that his mamluks will enable him to vanquish Qasim *in this life*. Instead, he implies that in acquiring mamluks, he has taken thought for his soul's salvation, for after his death, his mamluks will intercede for him with God. Thus, he, like a good Muslim, has heeded the lesson of Iram: "Think not thy realm will last. Prepare to die." Qasim Bey, on the other hand, has fallen into the trap of Iram by placing his faith in grandiose buildings, which, as Iram and Anushirvan's arch testify, will only end in dust. Thus, he has squandered the wealth he amassed in life, for it will yield no benefit after his death. Here, then, as in the other origin myths, the character of Qasim fills the role of the "bad guy," or, in this case, the misguided materialist. Dhu'l-Faqar, in contrast, takes the part of the good Muslim.

Rhetorically, then, this origin myth is consistent with the myth of Sudun's two sons jousting before Selim, and with that of Saᶜd and Haram. It is unlikely, of course, that either the Damurdashi chroniclers or al-Jabarti intended to portray the Faqaris as good and the Qasimis as evil. Once again, the structure of the tale imposes such a presentation, and some sort of rhetorical tradition dictates that Qasim play the "loser." In this case, there may be a hint of historical corroboration for the factions' differing priorities: the Faqaris did seem to have numbers on their side, although there is no evidence that their palaces and foundations were any less imposing than those of the Qasimis. But the point of this parable is not, as we have seen, simply that manpower is a much more secure investment than real estate, although this may seem at first blush to be the central lesson. Instead, like the other origin myths, this story is at least implicitly a tale of good and evil, or at least of the right path and the wrong path. And, as in the other origin myths, Dhu'l-Faqar/Saᶜd takes the right path while Qasim/Haram takes the wrong path.

10

Qasimi Genesis?

Qansuh's Slave Troop and Ridvan's Circassian Geneaology

Thus far, we have been treating the Faqari and Qasimi factions in tandem, as part of a single two-faction phenomenon whose roots we are seeking. Yet in the introduction, I hinted that in "reality," the two factions may have come into being through two very different, nonparallel processes, which could explain why the factional labels "Faqari" and "Qasimi" do not appear to come into widespread use until the early eighteenth century. I have collected a handful of pieces of evidence, from disparate and rather unlikely sources, that point to the stirrings of factional consciousness during the seventeenth century. The Qasimis stir earlier, in the early decades of the seventeenth century, and for that reason supply the subject of the first of two chapters examining this evidence.

The earliest hint I have found of what would later be known as the Qasimi faction occurs in Haci ᶜAli's Turkish continuation of al-Nahrawali al-Makki's *Al Barq al yamānī (The Yemeni Lightning)*, dealing almost exclusively with Yemen. A roughly contemporary indicator of Qasimi ethnic, if not yet factional, consciousness, is the extraordinary genealogy of Abu'l-Shawarib Ridvan Bey, which glorifies the bey's Circassian ancestry and points to a critical mass of Circassians among the early Qasimis. Both sources, interestingly enough, underline the Yemeni connection that seems to haunt the two factions, and particularly the Qasimis.

Qansuh Bey's *Bölük*

In her admirable book *Egypt's Adjustment to Ottoman Rule,* Doris Behrens-Abouseif identifies a Qasim Bey who was active in the 1620s and 1630s, and posits him as a plausible candidate for eponymous founder of the Qasimi faction. In this, she echoes P. M. Holt, who similarly identified this Qasim Bey in his seminal article "The Beylicate in Ottoman Egypt during the Seventeenth Century."[1] Haci ᶜAli's translation/amendation of al-Nahrawali provides an unexpected piece of corroborative evidence for this claim. Recounting how Qasim's mamluk Qansuh Bey was appointed governor of Yemen in 1629, Haci ᶜAli explains:

> Because to this day, it is customary for one party (*taife*) to dominate in the province of Egypt, Qasim Bey the Great's followers (*tevābi*ᶜ) dominated all the governors and authorities. One of [his followers], an emir of Egypt who was at the time pilgrimage commander, Qansuh Bey, amassed majesty, wealth, property, and power, and collected followers from the soldiers and sultan's servants (*kullar*). Because he was amoral and given to ostentation, and at base oblivious to the consequences, he always antagonized the authorities. When his intentions were thwarted, he wrought outrage and havoc. He never kept still, and it was impossible to curb his thousands of *kul*s and followers. The inevitable result of his remaining in Egypt was upheaval and rebellion.[2]

In desperation, the governor of Egypt obtained an imperial order to pack Qansuh off to Yemen. In this fashion, he attained the rank of pasha and became Yemen's last Ottoman governor until the second Ottoman occupation of Yemen in 1872.[3] Qasim Bey's *taife* may have been the germ of the Qasimi faction. It seems, moreover, that his mamluk Qansuh, in preparation for his campaign in Yemen, amassed a party of his own: "In Egypt, he immediately assembled a troop *(bölük)* of different races, all, like him, foreign slaves *(kölemen celbāları)*.[4]

Haci ᶜAli's observations are striking in two almost contradictory ways. On the one hand, he implies that the factional system, or at least a system in which one party dominated all positions, was already established in Egypt by the 1620s. Qasim Bey's followers constituted such a dominant party. In describing this group, nonetheless, Haci ᶜAli avoids the term *farīq* or any of its variants. The word he does use, *taife* (*ṭāʾifa*), is a generic term for a grouping; it can apply to artisan guilds, merchant consortia, interest groups, factions, Sufi brotherhoods, and a host of other social bodies. When it comes to Qansuh Bey's group, on the other hand, the chronicler is clearly groping for words to describe an unfamiliar phenomenon. He employs none of the vocabulary typical of descriptions of elite households.[5] *Bölük*, in contrast, has unmistakable military connotations. A *bölük* was a division or troop of soldiers; the imperial Janissaries were divided into *bölük*s, with the critical exception of the corps of irregular mercenaries, or *sekbans*, which was incorporated into the Janissary regiment in the fifteenth century and consisted of thirty-four *bölük*s. The *bölük* seems to have been the elemental formation of these mercenaries.[6] The chronicler's use of this term implies that Qansuh collected the group specifically for the Yemen campaign, and even that it was organized according to the army's preexisting regimental structure.[7]

This *bölük* accompanied Qansuh to Yemen, along with a "group of Rumis" (*taifet-i Ervām*) appointed directly from Istanbul. The combined force numbered eight thousand, of whom, Haci ᶜAli grimly reports, only one hundred escaped.[8] They proceeded to Yemen by way of Mecca, where they intervened in the struggle between two descendants of the Prophet for the post of *sharīf* of Mecca. An unruly lot, the soldiers murdered one of the competing *sharīf*s and abandoned their regiments, so that of the force that started out from Cairo, only a fraction made it to Yemen to fight the Zaydi imam.[9]

Qansuh Bey's *bölük*, then, was evidently a subunit of an emerging Qasimi faction. It formed under pressure of the Ottoman military operation in Yemen and may have adopted the organization of an army regiment. Perhaps it would have formed the core of the Qasimi faction in later years had a substantial portion of its members managed to make it out of Yemen. When Qansuh Pasha left Mocha in 1631, however, he left virtually alone. What remained of his forces stayed behind to help Arnavud Mustafa Bey try to defend the city. Presumably, the "100 who escaped" were among the seven hundred Ottoman soldiers who finally gave up and decamped to Egypt with Mustafa Bey.[10] One can only imagine that any loyalty they may have had to Qansuh had by then vanished.

Abu'l-Shawarib Ridvan Bey's Circassian Genealogy

The future of the Qasimi faction, as it turned out, lay not with Qansuh Pasha, who died in Istanbul in 1054–1644,[11] but with a younger and somewhat less conspicuous follower of Qasim Bey, Ridvan Bey Abu'l-Shawarib (moustachioed). Abu'l-Shawarib himself does not stand out as one of Egypt's formidable grandees; he was no match for his namesake, the ambitious pilgrimage commander Ridvan Bey al-Faqari. Nor does he appear to have amassed an unusually large or influential following, as did Qasim Bey's later follower Qansuh Bey (the younger). Instead, his son Özbek Bey took over his household when he died, and launched a line of mamluks that would carry the Qasimis into the eighteenth century.

What is distinctive about Abu'l-Shawarib is his ethnic consciousness and how it lent itself to an early sense of factional cohesion. He was one of many Circassian mamluks resident in Egypt during the seventeenth century, and seems to have attempted to parlay his ethnic heritage into a claim to critical administrative positions in Ottoman Egypt, most notably that of pilgrimage commander, which during the 1630s and 1640s was monopolized by the other Ridvan Bey—al-Faqari. This, at least, seems to me the most logical explanation for the appearance in the 1630s of an anonymous genealogy tracing Ridvan's descent to the first Circassian Mamluk sultan, Barquq (r. 1382–99), thence to the Prophet Muhammad's tribe of Quraysh.

I should hasten to add that I am the first to suggest that this genealogy was commissioned by Abu'l-Shawarib. The genealogist provides no identifying sobriquet for his patron, calling him only Ridvan Bey; meanwhile P. M. Holt's seminal article "The Exalted Lineage of Ridwan Bey" has codified the identification of this Ridvan Bey with the longtime Faqari pilgrimage commander.[12] Yet the text of the genealogy gives Ridvan Bey's title not as pilgrimage commander (*amīr al-ḥājj*) but as "servant of the Prophetic litter" (*khādim al-maḥmil al-Muḥammadī*), referring to the symbolic litter that was carried to Mecca from Egypt as part of the pilgrimage.[13] This title could be a virtual synonym for pilgrimage commander, as Holt asserts, but it could also be a calculated attempt to point up Ridvan's devotion to the pilgrimage and the holy places while avoiding the actual title of pilgrimage commander. More damningly, Ridvan Bey al-Faqari was not himself Circassian but Georgian.[14] Most damning of all is the genealogy's assertion that the Ridvan Bey who commissioned the work has two sons (of a total of seven) named Özbek and Khushqadam, as did Abu'l-Shawarib. Ridvan Bey al-Faqari, in contrast, left no sons.[15] The weight of the evidence, then, points to Abu'l-Shawarib as the commissioner of this genealogy.

A second misconception may prove more tenacious. This genealogy is typically adduced as evidence of an attempt to revive the political culture of the Mamluk sultanate, or at least as a bid for provincial autonomy at the expense of Ottoman authority.[16] Such an interpretation, however, discounts the fact that the Ottomans had defeated the Mamluk sultanate over a century before the genealogy appeared; by the 1630s, they were, obviously, certain that it would not be resurrected. An evocation of the Mamluk sultanate in 1632 was far different from such an evocation in 1524, when it would justifiably have been construed as an attempt to resurrect the defeated regime—and indeed, the Ottomans had had to put down three such revolts in the years immediately following the conquest.[17] Seventeenth-century evocations of the Mamluk sultanate must, in contrast, be interpreted as taking place within an Ottoman provincial context, for reasons specific to that context. To do otherwise would be anachronistic and acontextual.

Ridvan's genealogy is a short work of twenty folios or so, depending on which manuscript one consults. Manuscripts exist in one library in the United States and two libraries in England.[18] The purpose of this work appears to be twofold: on the one hand, to trace Ridvan Bey's lineage to Barquq and to the Quraysh; on the other, to demonstrate that Ridvan's ancestors have consistently been devoted servants of the Ḥaram al-Sharīf—that is, the scared mosque of Mecca. This latter agenda, as Holt recognized, seems to be directed to the office of pilgrimage commander, or *amīr al-ḥājj*.[19]

Abu'l-Shawarib's genealogy combines a widespread Circassian origin myth with more subtle and occasionally abstruse allusions to other bodies of myth and lore—all, however, myths that would have been familiar to educated Ottoman Muslims. His genealogist's starting point is an established Circassian tradition of descent from Arabs, which in turn spins off of the legend surrounding the fate of the last ruler of the southern, or Yemeni, Arab kingdom of Ghassan. The historical Ghassanids are known to have migrated fairly extensively in the course of their checkered history. Although they originated in the Yemen, the Ghassanids evidently migrated northward in the early centuries of the Common Era for reasons that remain shrouded in the mists of time.[20] They seem to have converted to Monophysite Christianity from what is now known as Greek Orthodox Christianity in the sixth century.[21] They were already established as quasi-autonomous local rulers under Byzantine suzerainty in what are now Jordan and southern Syria by the time the series of disasters that befell Yemen in the sixth century C.E., notably the collapse of the ancient Maʾrib Dam,[22] triggered a new wave of northward migrations. As Byzantine clients, they fled into Byzantine-ruled Anatolia after the Sasanian conquest of Syria from the Byzantines early in the seventh century, then returned following the Byzantine reconquest of Syria in 628 C.E.[23] When the armies of the early Muslim state, led by the general Khalid b. al-Walid, swept northward and overran Ghassan, the monarch decamped again to Anatolia.[24]

The fate of this last Ghassanid king, Jabala b. al-Ayham, and his descendants quickly became a source of legend, and a variety of cultures fastened on it. A prevalent tradition held that Jabala and his brothers became the ancestors of the Albanians, the Circassians, and a number of the peoples of the Caucasus and the Black Sea region. By the fifteenth century, Ghassanid lineage had become an article of faith among certain of the Circassian Mamluk sultans of Egypt; it is featured in two fifteenth-century chronicles composed by the historian al-ʿAyni.[25]

The genealogist's account of Circassian origins is similar in a number of respects to an origin tradition reported by the seventeenth-century Ottoman traveler Evliya Çelebi in the section of his travelogue dealing with the Caucasus, where he spent considerable time en route to an Ottoman campaign against the Russians. Both accounts focus not so much on Jabala b. al-Ayham as on a character named Kisa, who in Evliya's account is Jabala's brother but who in Ridvan's genealogy is a neighboring but unrelated ruler. In Evliya's travelogue, Jabala flees after putting out the eye of an Arab with a lance during a chivalric exercise. In Ridvan's genealogy, Jabala accepts Islam at the hands of the future caliph ʿUmar b. al-Khattab, then accompanies him on the pilgrimage, in the course of which he puts out the eye of a bedouin Arab who treads on his cloak; in a parallel incident, Kisa puts out the eye of a bedouin with his lance while playing *jirit*.[26] This Kisa takes refuge with the Byzantine emperor, who grants him land "between the east of Constantiniyya and the west of it."[27] The ethnic designation "Circassians" (*Sarākisa*) derives from the Arabic for "Kisa fled" (*sarā Kisā*).[28] As for Jabala, he settles in the "Mountains of the Albanians" (*Jabal Arnāwūd*), which would have been in the same general region, far to the east of present-day Albania,[29] and becomes the progenitor of the Albanians (fo. 12r). Here, both Evliya and Ridvan's genealogist draw on an extensive body of origin traditions that exploit the familiar motif of a patriarch and his sons, each of whom gives rise to a different people. The archetype of this tradition is the myth, widespread in medieval Islamic literature, of the sons of Noah: Shem, Ham, and Japheth, who supposedly gave rise to the different races of humankind.[30] Ridvan's genealogist, although he rejects the notion that Kisa and Jabala are brothers, traces Ridvan's lineage all the way back to Shem son of Noah, thence to Adam, the first man (fo. 19r–v).

According to Ridvan's genealogy, Kisa takes refuge with the Byzantine emperor, who grants him "land between the east of Constantiniyya and the west of it." This phrase can hardly describe the Byzantine capital. In the context of the narrative as a whole, it should logically denote the region of the Caucasus, between the Black and Caspian seas. The narrative notes that this region had previously been held by the Bulgars and, in antiquity, by the Armenians, remnants of whom still existed in the area. Kisa named the new settlement Basna. If the region in which Kisa allegedly settled is really Circassia, then "Basna" must be the district of Besne in the central region of Circassia known as Kabardia. Indeed, the nineteenth-century Circassian historian Shora Bekmursin Nogmov connects the legend of Kisa or Kessa/Kess and his brothers specifically to the Kabards, who were the largest and culturally the dominant subpopulation of the Circassian people.[31]

To press the Circassian claim to preeminence in Egypt, the genealogist demonstrates that a number of the Arab-descended Circassians who had fled northward and mingled with the settled population ultimately returned to the Islamic lands. One of these was none other than the future Mamluk sultan Barquq b. Anas "al-Jarakisi al-Bulghari al-ᶜUthmani." According to the genealogy, Barquq was not a military slave, or mamluk, but a free Circassian who was kidnapped by Bulgar thieves and sold to the "Ayyubid" sultan al-Mansur ᶜAli b. al-Ashraf Barsbay (fo. 12v). There is obviously some confusion in the genealogist's chronology. No Ayyubid sultan bore the name Barsbay, while the Mamluk sultan Barsbay reigned from 1422–37. Barquq was in fact the mamluk of the Mamluk emir Yelbugha; the genealogy, however, claims that Yelbugha was Barquq's grandfather (fos. 13r, 19r). In any event, the Circassian sultanate that Barquq, in fact, inaugurated is portrayed as a restoration of Qurayshi rule to Egypt.

Ridvan's genealogy, unlike the lore transmitted by Evliya Çelebi or Shora Bekmursin Nogmov, adds a distinctively Ottoman-era element to the evidence for Circassian legitimacy. When Sultan Selim I conquered the Mamluk sultanate in 1517, according to the genealogist's account, a number of the routed Circassians returned from Egypt to their ancestral homeland. Among those who returned was the thirteen-year-old emir Rustam b. Timraz, supposedly the descendant of al-Ashraf Barsbay. A merchant from the northern Lebanese port of Tripoli supposedly observed Rustam while trading in Circassia and recognized his noble lineage. On returning to the Ottoman realm, the merchant informed Özdemir Pasha, a Circassian who had served as Ottoman governor of Yemen and Abyssinia.[32] Özdemir in turn informed the admiral and sometime governor of Egypt and Yemen, Sinan Pasha, who ordered Rustam to "return to Bāb al-ᶜUthmānī" (fo. 18r). Rustam, however, refused to comply out of fear for his life; he remained in Circassia until his death, during the reign of Selim II. His line was not restored to the Ottoman Empire until his grandson, Ridvan Bey, was brought to Egypt.

Such is the genealogist's attempt to demonstrate the ties of blood and life experience that bound Ridvan's ancestors to the Holy Cities and to Egypt. Even apart from the main thrust of the genealogy, however, historical resonances and recognized touchstones of legitimacy abound in this work. If we look closely, we can detect a number of tropes that prompt the reader to make associations with well-known bodies of regional mythology and Islamic lore and, in the process, to affirm Ridvan's legitimacy by ancestral association with these legends. To make the process of trope-stalking as straightforward as possible, I shall proceed according to the chronological order of events in the genealogy's story.

Quraysh

To begin with, there is the question of Kisa's Arab ancestry. Evliya Çelebi unwittingly contradicts himself in portraying Kisa, the ancestor of the Circassians, as both a Qurayshi and the brother of the Ghassanid leader Jabala b. al-Ayham, for the Ghassanids were southern, or Yemeni, Arabs while the Quraysh were Qaysis, or northerners.[33] Unlike Evliya, Ridvan Bey's genealogist seems to realize the contradiction of transforming a Ghassanid into a Qurayshi; he thus abandons altogether the kinship between Jabala and Kisa. While Jabala remains a Ghassanid, and therefore a Yemeni, as well as a Christian by birth, Kisa is cast as the Muslim chief of the Qurayshi tribe of the Banu ʿAmir.[34] Our genealogist is likewise careful to point out that Kisa spearheaded a migration parallel to but separate from that of the Ghassanids. Only by presenting Kisa as utterly separate from the Ghassanids can the genealogist convincingly connect him to the Qaysi Arabs, let alone to the Quraysh.

But the genealogist is careful not to go too far in demonstrating Ridvan's membership of the Quraysh. Spinning out the lineage of Rustam b. Timraz, the descendant of Kisa who was urged to return to Egypt from Circassia, the genealogist traces Rustam's bloodline back through Barsbay, Barquq, and Kisa to Qusayy, the sixth-century founder of the Qurayshi tribal conglomerate; then to ʿAdnan, legendary ancestor of the northern, or Qaysi, Arabs; and ultimately all the way back to Shem, Noah, and Adam (fo. 19r). Thus, he shows Ridvan Bey to be convincingly Qaysi and Qurayshi. However, he stops short of claiming that Ridvan is descended from the Prophet. In this way, Ridvan could assert Qurayshi legitimacy without taking the highly suspect step of falsifying a claim of Prophetic descent. Such a claim might have offended or offered an implicit challenge to several potent religious and political figures in Egypt and outside, notably the leader of Egypt's population of descendants of the Prophet (*naqīb al-ashrāf*), who at this time was a Turcophone efendi appointed from Istanbul.[35]

Migration Myths

Migration narratives have played critical legitimating roles in shaping the histories of numerous peoples. Nicholas Howe has pointed out how successive generations of medieval Anglo-Saxon chroniclers expolited the biblical motif of the Exodus of the Children of Israel from Egypt to buttress their claims to England and, ultimately, the legitimacy of their Christianizing mission to the Germany from which their ancestors had come.[36] By the same token, Ridvan's genealogist spins a double tale of exodus from the Islamic realm to Circassia and return. Here, however, the archetypal exodus motif is not that of Moses—although Jabala's and Kisa's blinding of a bedouin is reminiscent of Moses' killing of the Egyptian—but of the Prophet Muhammad, who led the first Muslims from a hostile Mecca to the haven of Medina, only to return in triumph eight years later. The consistent devotion of Ridvan and his putative ancestors to the Kaᶜba supplies the link between Ridvan and the Prophet that his genealogist dare not attempt to provide through fabricated bloodlines. This link, though not made explicit in the geneaology, would have been unmistakable to readers and would arguably have made as strong an impression as any of Ridvan's ostensible kinship ties.

Khalid b. al-Walid

The Muslim general from whom both Kisa and Jabala b. al-Ayham are supposed to have fled is the renowned yet problematic hero Khalid b. al-Walid. A relatively late convert to Islam from among the inhabitants of Mecca, Khalid appears in a rather ambivalent light in many *ḥadīths*, or traditions of the Prophet.[37] Although his military prowess was undeniable, his piety was occasionally suspect. In Ottoman collective memory, he held the dubious distinction of being the person who introduced bribery into Islamic government.[38] The genealogist can play on his faintly suspect reputation in presenting Khalid as the scourge of Kisa and his descendants; his implication is that by driving Kisa out of his homeland, Khalid is acting as the enemy of Islam, the more so since, as the genealogist has already shown, Kisa and his ancestors have proven themselves servitors of the Muslim holy places.

Yet there are deeper resonances to Khalid's appearance in the narrative. A certain strand of Ottoman collective memory depicts Khalid as the ancestor of the İsfendiyaroğulları, or "sons of Isfendiyar," to whom the sixteenth-century Ottoman grand vizier Şemsi Pasha belonged.[39] In the same way that Khalid is supposed to have introduced bribery into the original Muslim polity, Şemsi Pasha is supposed to have persuaded the Ottoman sultan to accept bribes.[40] Whatever their connection to Khalid, the İsfendiyaroğulları were a local Turkic dynasty who ruled the region around the Black Sea port of Sinop in northern Anatolia until they were conquered by the Ottoman sultan Mehmed II in 1460; by corrupting a later sultan, Şemsi Pasha claimed to have avenged his family's defeat.[41] Notwithstanding, the dynasty evokes, even though it did not claim descent from, the Persian hero İsfendiyar (Esfandiyar), who figures prominently in the *Shahname,* the tenth-century epic of the pre-Islamic Iranian kings. In the *Shahname,* Esfandiyar slays the simurgh, the mythical bird, resembling the Chinese phoenix, who protects the hero Zal and his son, the Herculean figure Rustam. By virtue of being immersed in the simurgh's blood, Esfandiyar is rendered invulnerable, with the exception of his eyes, which he closes against the blood. He subsequently comes into conflict with Rustam, who ultimately slays him by shooting a double-tipped arrow into Esfandiyar's eyes.[42]

It can hardly be a coincidence that Rustam, the legendary strongman of the *Shahname,* has the same name as the ancestor of Ridvan Bey who was urged to return from Circassia following the Ottoman conquest of Egypt. Rustam was not a common name among Circassians in Egypt or elsewhere during the seventeenth century; the name would almost inevitably evoke the hero of the Persian epic. In the *Shahname,* Esfandiyar, having in the course of his own adventures slain Rustam's protector, the simurgh, seeks to "fetter" Rustam and thus to end his sway over the southeastern Iranian territory known as Sistan.[43] In the same fashion, Khalid b. al-Walid sought to end the rule of Jabala b. al-Ayham and of Kisa over northern Jordan and southern Syria. But just as Rustam of the *Shahname* ultimately won his revenge against Esfandiyar, so Rustam the descendant of Kisa won his revenge against Khalid when his grandson returned to Ottoman territory.

We could easily read an anti-Ottoman message into these associations: by forcing the latter-day Rustam to flee Egypt for Circassia, the Ottomans arguably committed the same sort of injustice as Esfandiyar, who attacked the original Rustam. Such an anti-Ottoman streak could have been identified by any well-read Ottoman functionary, for most Ottoman functionaries, even in Egypt, would have been familiar with the *Shahname.* Indeed, the work had been translated into Turkish at the court of the Mamluk sultan Qansuh al-Ghuri (r. 1501–16) in Cairo.[44] Here, however, the objective seems to be not to condemn the Ottomans but to demonstrate a prior claim: Kisa and his ancestors were servitors of the holy places before Khalid b. al-Walid launched his military campaigns; they were heirs to the Byzantines long before the

Ottomans conquered Constantinople; they had claims in Egypt before the Ottoman conquest in 1517.

The Byzantines

The Byzantine Empire looms large in the genealogy's account of the patriarch Kisa, who founds Circassia by the grace of the Byzantine emperor. Byzantine intervention in Muslim affairs was, or course, an historical reality; after the defeat of the Sasanian empire in 634 C.E., the Byzantines were for centuries the chief enemy of a series of Muslim empires. During the initial Muslim drive into Byzantine territory, there were doubtless numerous opponents and victims of the Muslim advance who fled to the Byzantines, and whom the Byzantines actively courted; the most notable is the historical Ghassanid Jabala b. al-Ayham, who, after his resounding defeat by Khalid in 636 C.E., returned to Anatolia for good.[45] In addition, flight to the Byzantine court is a recognizable trope in several strands of heroic and/or origin legend; perhaps the most famous example is the episode of the pre-Islamic warrior-poet Imru al-Qays' being summoned to the Byzantine court and asked to serve in the Byzantine army.[46] Imru al-Qays was himself a member of a southern, or Yemeni, Arab tribe distantly related to the Ghassanids. The story of the last Ghassanid's flight to Byzantium, though based in fact, could conceivably draw on motifs of the earlier quasi-historical tale of Imru al-Qays. Even after the Muslims were well-established in Greater Syria, the legends of the half-Arab, half-Greek border warrior Digenes Akrites[47] clearly attest that the Arab-Byzantine border region, like the later Ottoman-Byzantine border region, was highly volatile and fluid; crossing over from one domain to another, along with shifting loyalties, was not uncommon.

Yet what separates Kisa, to say nothing of Jabala b. al-Ayham, from a border personality such as Digenes Akrites is his personal intercession with the Byzantine emperor. This gives Kisa a certain stamp of legitimacy, albeit an alternative legitimacy not dependent on the authority of the preeminent Muslim ruler of the day (in this case, the second caliph, ᶜUmar b. al-Khattab [r. 634–44 C.E.]). If Ridvan Bey, by virtue of his descent from Kisa, partakes of this Byzantine legitimacy, then he, too, enjoys a legitimacy independent of the authority of the preeminent Muslim ruler of *his* day: namely, the Ottoman sultan. In an Ottoman context, of course, Byzantine legitimacy was far more highly charged, for the Ottoman Empire had brought the Byzantine Empire to an end in 1453 and, indeed, purported to be its heir.[48] The genealogist's suggestion that Kisa and, indirectly, Ridvan, has a much more venerable claim to Byzantine legitimacy can be seen as a challenge to the Ottoman sultan, but it can also be interpreted as yet another example of a prior claim that would provide a provincial grandee with a legitimacy that complemented, rather than challenging, the legitimacy of the Ottoman sultan as Byzantine heir. This was the sort of complementary legitimacy sought by the Phanariot Greeks whom the Ottoman sultan appointed to govern the principalities of Moldavia and Wallachia (modern Romania) in the eighteenth century, and who portrayed themselves as literal heirs to the Byzantines to the extent of adopting the elaborate formalities of the long-defunct Byzantine imperial court.[49] Their motive—and, I would argue, Ridvan's, too—was not to challenge the Ottoman sultan but to demonstrate an older regional authority independent of yet complementary to the authority they derived from the sultan.[50] This sort of venerable pedigree made them more, rather than less, attractive to the sultan as potential servants of the Ottoman state.[51]

The Genealogy's Purpose

But if Ridvan did not want to assert himself against the Ottoman sultan, then why did he commission this genealogy? Whom was it meant to impress, and for what purpose? The most likely target, it seems to me, is Tabanı Yası (flat-foot) Mehmed Pasha, who had been governor of Egypt during Qansuh Bey's escapades and who, by 1632, the date of the genealogy's completion,[52] was grand vizier. And what did Ridvan Bey want to persuade Tabanı Yası Mehmed to do? Probably to appoint him pilgrimage commander. Consider that in 1632, Ridvan Bey "al-Faqari" had been pilgrimage commander for only one year; it was not yet a certainty that he would be reappointed. And given the dominance of Abu'l-Shawarib's patron, Qasim Bey, his clients would seem to have been strong candidates for the position. Add to this Abu'l-Shawarib's participation in Qasim's pilgrimage-cum-expedition to the Holy Cities in 1631, which enabled him to claim the title "servant of the Prophetic litter." In this context, the Circassian genealogy was the icing on the cake, so to speak, particularly since the rival Ridvan Bey could claim no such exalted lineage.

In closing the genealogy, the author enthuses over Abu'l-Shawarib's seven sons. The implication here is that the bey's sons will ensure a second generation of worthy Circassian servants of the Holy Cities, as well as future generations, whether through their own sons or through their clients. In stark contrast, Ridvan Bey al-Faqari, though he ultimately amassed a large number of clients, had no sons and could guarantee no such continuity. On the other hand, Abu'l-Shawarib had to contend with the fact that the rival Ridvan Bey had rebuilt the Kaᶜba in his first year as pilgrimage commander[53]—just when Qansuh Pasha (formerly Bey) was proving a spectacular disaster in Yemen.

Yemen

Ridvan's genealogy provides yet another example of Yemen lurking behind the scenes of the emerging Qasimi-Faqari factional rivalry. For Yemen is quietly yet consistently present in the genealogist's account. The Ghassanids, whose migration allegedly paralleled Kisa's, originated in Yemen, and the division between Qaysi (northern) and Yemeni (southern) Arabs plays a critical, if not explicit, part in the definition of Kisa's, and ultimately Ridvan's, heritage. Furthermore, Rustam, who flees Egypt at the time of the Ottoman conquest, is ordered back by Sinan Pasha, the Ottoman admiral who "reconquered" Yemen following Imam al-Mutahhar's rebellion (see chapter 4). Sinan apparently received word of Rustam from "Özdemir the Great"—namely, Özdemir Pasha, a former Mamluk emir who served as Ottoman governor of Yemen under Süleyman I and later conquered Abyssinia for him.[54]

It seems, then, that the people who most desire Rustam's return to Ottoman service are veterans of the Ottoman administration of Yemen. Their enthusiasm for a Circassian prince who has no connection to Yemen, who is not even descended from Yemeni Arabs, makes little sense in and of itself. If, however, we recall Abu'l-Shawarib Ridvan's associate, the hapless Qansuh Pasha, it suddenly seems more comprehensible. Qansuh had covered himself with shame both in Egypt and in Yemen, and had been instrumental in the Ottoman loss of the latter province. His younger comrade, Ridvan, may have been trying to make the case that despite his links to Qansuh, he could be trusted to succeed where Qansuh had failed; the best he could do to attest to this, however, was to highlight the esteem in which his ancestor was held by Ottoman governors of Yemen.

Not coincidentally, Yemen had its own historical claim to the service of the Holy Cities. According to legend, the first person ever to have draped the Kaᶜba with a *kiswa*, or cloth covering, was Asᶜad al-Himyari, king of the ancient northern Yemeni kingdom of Himyar, centuries before the advent of Islam.[55] During the Middle Ages, the Rasulid dynasty, which ruled Yemen from its capital at the southern city of Zabid, made much of its sponsorship of a pilgrimage caravan. Significantly, the Rasulids claimed descent from Ghassan and habitually referred to themselves as Ghassanids.[56] Moreover, they claimed ᶜAbbasid legitimacy inasmuch as the dynasty's founder was the ambassador or messenger (*rasūl*) of the ᶜAbbasid caliph.[57] After declaring independence from the Ayyubid sultanate in Cairo, the Rasulids attempted to extend their sway over the Hijaz. They were thwarted in this attempt by the early Mamluk sultans.[58]

This Yemeni claim to service of the Holy Cities may partially explain the lengths to which Ridvan's genealogist goes to demonstrate that Ridvan himself is descended not from Yemeni Arabs but from the Qays via Quraysh. Genealogically, Ridvan Bey represents a competing Qaysi/Qurayshi claim to the Holy Cities. Through Rustam, he is descended from the Mamluk sultans, who countered the Rasulid/Ghassanid claim to the Holy Cities. Through Kisa, whom the genealogist carefully differentiates from Jabala b. al-Ayham, he is descended from the Prophet's clan of Quraysh, if not from the Prophet himself.

Unalluded to in the genealogy is the claim to control of the Holy Cities by the Zaydi imams, who were at the time completing their ouster of the Ottomans from Yemen. I find it hard to believe that, given the events unfolding in Yemen, the Zaydi imam was not on the genealogist's mind. The presence in the immediate vicinity of the Holy Cities of a hostile Muslim state must have been cause for considerable concern among the Ottomans; three centuries earlier, the Zaydi imam had held sway over Mecca and Medina before being routed by the Mamluks.[59] Moreover, the imam's lineage trumped even the most creative effort Abu'l-Shawarib's genealogist could produce. The imam was a descendant not only of the Quraysh but of the Prophet, via Hasan b. ᶜAli, and a genuine Arab, not an Arab many times removed. In depicting Ridvan Bey as one shade removed from an Arab descendant of the Prophet, the genealogy could, in some vague, implicit sense, be an answer to an unvoiced challenge by the Zaydi imam to Ottoman control of the Holy Cities.

Conclusion

Abu'l-Shawarib Ridvan Bey's eccentric genealogy is best interpreted as one up-and-coming young Circassian grandee's attempt to persuade the Ottoman grand vizier to appoint him pilgrimage commander. His chief rival for this post was the formidable Ridvan Bey "al-Faqari," although it would be unwise to jump to the conclusion that the other Ridvan was his only rival, or even that commander of the Egyptian pilgrimage was the only post for which Abu'l-Shawarib was aiming. He might well have settled for the command of the pilgrimage caravan from Damascus; a few years later, the Albanian Mustafa Bey, who remained in Mocha after Qansuh Pasha had fled, received this post as a reward for his perseverance.[60] The potential effect of Qansuh's disgraceful performance on the fortunes of other members of the emerging Qasimi faction should not be underestimated, and it seems likely that one purpose of the genealogy was to ward off such professional damage. Abu'l-Shawarib perhaps hoped that his fictive lineage and his fictive forebears' lengthy tradition of service to Mecca would transcend his connection to Qansuh.

The genealogy appears at an interesting conjuncture in Egyptian and in Ottoman history. Circassians were becoming quite numerous among Egypt's grandees. The Circassian custom known as the *ataliqate*, whereby a young boy was sent away from his parents' home to be raised by strangers, made Circassian youths uniquely suited for recruitment to distant military service. Even the children born to Circassians and the ethnically related Abkhazians in Egypt and Istanbul were sent back to the ancestral homeland to be raised; this had been the experience of Evliya Çelebi's patron.[61] This ancient Circassian custom may provide a template for the comings and goings described in the origin myth, buttressing the narrative strategy of alluding to archetypal migration motifs.

Nonetheless, this was also a time when ethnic consciousness was unusually high in Ottoman military and administrative circles as a result of the 1622 Genç Osman affair, when Sultan Osman II had vainly attempted to offset the Janissaries, who were largely *devshirme* recruits from the Balkans, with a new army of mercenaries, or *sekbans*, recruited from the empire's Asiatic provinces.[62] Noteworthy in this context are the genealogist's efforts to demonstrate the esteem in which Ridvan's Circassian ancestors are held by Ottoman administrators, as well as his skirting of Ridvan's lack of training in the imperial palace. Indeed, one of these Ottoman administrators, Özdemir Pasha, serves as an example of a Circassian former Mamluk who proved a valuable and unfailingly loyal servant of the sultan; his son even became a powerful grand vizier.[63]

In the event, Abu'l-Shawarib's scheme did not succeed. Ridvan al-Faqari remained pilgrimage commander until his death in 1656. Afterward, Abu'l-Shawarib assumed paramount power in conjunction with other Qasimi leaders until his own death in the late 1650s; by this time, however, the central authority had already thrown its support to an elite of Bosnians whom it had probably injected into the Qasimi faction.[64] The era of Circassian assertion in Egypt was, at least temporarily, over.

Nonetheless, Abu'l-Shawarib reaped a sort of posthumous victory, for his son Özbek Bey would ensure the continuation of the Qasimi faction. He held several posts in the Ottoman Egyptian administration, including that of pilgrimage commander, as well as governor of Jirja. Evliya Çelebi refers to him as the founder of a great household (*ulu hanedan*) with a private army of five hundred soldiers.[65] His clients included Murad Bey the *defterdar*, patron of the famous early eighteenth-century Qasimi chieftains Ibrahim Bey Abu Shanab and ᶜIvaz Bey.

And ultimately, it was Abu'l-Shawarib, rather than Qasim Bey, whom Qasimi grandees of a later epoch remembered and revered as a factional "founding father" figure. In the early eighteenth century, when the Qasimi faction split into two rival camps headed by Ismail Bey b. ᶜIvaz and Çerkes Mehmed Bey, Ismail's camp was known as the Shawariba.[66] Following his assassination in 1724, Ismail Bey was buried in Abu'l-Shawarib's tomb, alongside his father, the Circassian mamluk ᶜIvaz Bey.[67] Qasim Bey may, in actual fact, have founded the Qasimi faction and served as its namesake, and Qansuh Pasha may have added to its ranks while bungling the Ottoman defense of Yemen, but Abu'l-Shawarib Ridvan Bey would survive in collective memory as the grand old man of the Qasimis.

11

Faqari Genesis?

ᶜAli Bey's Mosque and the Ottoman Dhu'l-Faqar Sword

In the mid-seventeenth century, at roughly the same time that the Qasimi faction was apparently beginning to coalesce around Qasim Bey and his followers, the germ of what would later be known as the Faqari faction becomes vaguely discernible. This faction's genesis was, however, not at all parallel to that of its eventual rival. Most obviously, no one named Dhu'l-Faqar Bey played anything like the "founding father" role taken by Qasim Bey in the formation of the Qasimi faction. Instead, the label "Zülfikari" attached to ᶜAli Bey, the powerful governor of the Upper Egyptian superprovince of Jirja, because he carried a facsimile of the early Islamic hero ᶜAli b. Abi Talib's magical sword Dhu'l-Faqar. Accordingly, this chapter consists of an examination of ᶜAli Bey in connection with the probable first conflict between the nascent Faqari and Qasimi factions, followed by an examination of this extraordinary sword and the importance of its image to Ottoman military formations.

Zülfikari ᶜAli Bey

With one exception, which we shall encounter at the end of this chapter, the only mention Evliya Çelebi makes of either Qasimis or Faqaris is a reference to the Turkish inscription on a mosque in Jirja by the endower, ᶜAli Bey, who governed Jirja from the early 1630s through 1653. To the left of the mosque's *miḥrāb*—that is, the niche indicating the direction of Mecca—Evliya read:

Now the governor of Jirja, lion of God, of the people of beneficence,
Zülfikari Mir ʿAli, master of drum [i.e., a military band] and standard,
With the divine order, with divine blessing as a guide,
Has constructed this noble mosque, together with two fountains.
His scribe said, "Know its date, o great prince.
It was built in 1061 [1651]." The End.

—*Seyahatname,* vol. 10:522.[1]

Shortly thereafter, Evliya refers to the mosque as the "Circeli ʿAli Bey mosque," that is, the mosque of ʿAli Bey of Jirja.[2]

This ʿAli Bey was the collaborator of Ridvan Bey al-Faqari, the Georgian mamluk who held the post of pilgrimage commander for an extraordinary twenty-five years, from 1631 until his death in 1656. ʿAli Bey, meanwhile, established himself in Jirja, which during the seventeenth century, as noted in chapter 9, rivaled Cairo as a center of political and economic influence. ʿAli Bey seems to have established his own demesne in Jirja, although he never rebelled against the governor in Cairo, as did his successor Mehmed Bey in 1659 (see chapters 6 and 9). He did, however, amass a formidable military force consisting largely of Rumi, or Balkan and western Anatolian, mercenaries.[3] With Ridvan Bey, ʿAli formed a formidable, if unofficial, partnership: ʿAli controlled the supply of Upper Egyptian grain that the pilgrimage caravan, directed by Ridvan, transported each year to the Holy Cities. Ridvan, in turn, had access to the considerable commercial traffic that accompanied the pilgrimage.

In the 1640s, Ridvan's and ʿAli's political and economic dominance came under attack from a rival partnership of two Circassian beys, Qansuh and Memi (or Mamay). Qansuh was another mamluk of Qasim Bey, although he was evidently a different Qansuh from the final governor of Yemen. With the backing of the governor of Egypt, the Ottoman central authority appointed Qansuh pilgrimage commander, replacing Ridvan, and Memi governor of Jirja, replacing ʿAli. Ridvan, meanwhile, was "rewarded" for his long years of service with the governorship of Abyssinia—a standard tactic designed to remove him from any center of political influence. Ridvan steadfastly refused the appointment while ʿAli marched toward Cairo from Jirja with an enormous army. In the face of these developments, the governor, none other than Haydar Aghazade Mehmed Pasha, withdrew his support from Qansuh and Memi, and ultimately had them executed.[4] This confrontation between the two rival pairs of beys is the "event" of which al-Hallaq speaks with regard to Mehmed Pasha's tenure (see chapter 4).

This confrontation is, I believe, the first glimpse we have of what would become the insistent rivalry between the Qasimis and the Faqaris. Qansuh and, perhaps, Memi belonged to the formidable household of Qasim Bey furthered by the elder Qansuh Bey, although there is no evidence of their taking the sobriquet Qasimi. On the other hand, ᶜAli Bey, if not Ridvan, regarded himself as a "Zülfikari."

What did Zülfikari mean in this context? The line of poetry in which ᶜAli Bey had it inscribed is one long allusion to ᶜAli b. Abi Talib: "lion of God, of the people of beneficence" (*şir-i Ḫüdā, ehl-i kerem*) are traditional ascriptions to this much-revered figure. "Zülfikari" is, first and foremost, one of these allusions: ᶜAli b. Abi Talib was "Zülfikari" inasmuch as he carried the famous double-bladed sword Dhu'l-Faqar. And if ᶜAli Bey meant to compare himself to his namesake as a "lion of God" and as one of the "people of beneficence," he must also have meant to invite comparison as a wielder of Dhu'l-Faqar. He could not wield the sword itself, which had vanished many centuries before. But he may well have wielded a banner emblazoned with the image of Dhu'l-Faqar. Such banners, bearing a peculiarly Ottoman representation of the sword, were quite common among the Ottoman armies, and were associated particularly with the Janissaries. Since ᶜAli Bey's army consisted of young men from the Balkans and western Anatolia, traditionally candidates for the *devshirme*, some of whom may well have been former Janissaries, it is all the more likely that he carried such a banner and that, therefore, his sobriquet and, ultimately, the name of the Faqari faction derive from this sword.

The Sword Dhu'l-Faqar and the Dhu'l-Faqar Banner

The sword Dhu'l-Faqar is as old as Islam itself—or, according to Shiᶜite belief, as old as humanity. Shiᶜite tradition holds that Adam carried the sword out of the Garden of Eden with him, along with the Ark of the Covenant, Moses' staff, and his own coffin.[5] According to the Prophetic biographical (*sīra*) literature, the sword originally belonged to a wealthy leader of the pagan community in Mecca who was an implacable enemy of the early Muslims.[6] Although the sword's maker was said to have been an Arabian smith, it has also been asserted that the sword was of Indian workmanship; Indian swordsmiths were well-known for the quality of their steel swords.[7] Evliya Çelebi, however, recounts an eccentric tradition that "the king of Egypt, Mukavkis," when he swore allegiance to the Prophet, sent him as presents the concubine Mariya, three Coptic girls, a mule, and a sword. The sword was, of course, Dhu'l-Faqar, which the Prophet later gave to ᶜAli, along with the mule, Duldul.[8] One suspects this bit of lore comes from an Egyptian source, perhaps one influenced by Coptic traditions, for "Mukavkis," or Muqawqis, was the derogatory nickname applied by the Copts to Cyrus, the Greek Orthodox (Chalcedonian) patriarch of Alexandria at the time of the Muslim conquest.[9] Indeed, Evliya seems to have stumbled across a strain of Coptic tradition associated with ᶜAli; deep in Upper Egypt, he came across a church called Umm ᶜAli because "our Coptic kings" sent ᶜAli's mother as a gift to ᶜAli's grandfather, who gave her to Abu Talib.[10] If anything, these traditions would only have made Upper Egypt all the more fertile ground for the cultivation of a sort of Dhu'l-Faqar cult.

A substantial mythology grew up surrounding accounts that Dhu'l-Faqar was double-bladed; as we shall see, the two blades would loom large in later Muslim iconography. Some modern scholars have posited that the sword was double-bladed in the sense that many swords of Indian manufacture were double-bladed: the blade consisted of two sheets of steel molded around a hollow tube, similar to the human spinal column; hence the name Dhu'l-Faqar, "having a spine." In this sense, the sword had two blades, although the blades would have met in a single point.[11] The Prophetic biographical literature, however, maintains that the sword took its name from small hollows or grooves (s. *fuqra*) in the blade, "for more easy cleaving of coats of mail."[12]

According to the *sīra* literature, the Prophet acquired Dhu'l-Faqar when the sword's Meccan owner was slain while fighting the Muslims at the battle of Badr in 624 C.E.[13] Early Muslim sources are not clear as to whether the Prophet fought with Dhu'l-Faqar in subsequent battles. The Prophet owned and used a number of swords, all with different names, as did his companions.[14] According to widespread Sunni and Shiᶜite traditions, however, the Prophet bequeathed the sword, along with his ring and the rest of his weapons, to his cousin and son-in-law, ᶜAli b. Abi Talib, at the battle of Uhud, where the Meccans defeated the Muslims in 625 C.E.[15] ᶜAli subsequently became the fourth caliph, or leader of the Muslim community, following the Prophet's death. It is as ᶜAli's sword that Dhu'l-Faqar is chiefly remembered; indeed, the extensive mythology surrounding the sword centers on ᶜAli's possession of it. The lore of the Prophet and his companions clearly links the sword to ᶜAli, who emerges as the superhero of early

Islam, capable of prodigious feats on the battlefield. The proverbial expression "There is no young man but ᶜAli, and no sword but Dhu'l-Faqar" (*Lā fatā illā ᶜAlī, wa-la sayfa illā Dhū'l-Faqāri*) is well-known among Muslims.[16] In later Muslim, above all Shiᶜite or Shiᶜite-influenced, lore, Dhu'l-Faqar acquired magical properties. It was said to be the longest sword in the world. The sword's two blades, by then construed as two separate points, were said to serve the purpose of putting out the eyes of enemies of Islam.[17] This belief may in turn have been influenced by the legend, transmitted in the Iranian epic *Shahname* and recounted in the preceding chapter, of the hero Rustam slaying Esfandiyar by shooting a double-tipped arrow into his eyes, his only vulnerable spot.

On ᶜAli's death, Dhu'l-Faqar passed into the hands of his sons Hasan and Husayn. The fate of Dhu'l-Faqar following the martyrdom of Husayn in 680 C.E. is shrouded in mystery, made all the more opaque by the allegiances of the various communities who have laid claim to the sword. In the early centuries of Islam, Dhu'l-Faqar came to be regarded as a symbol of ᶜAlid legitimacy; those who professed to possess the sword by the same token professed to represent the family of the Prophet (*ahl al-bayt*), whom various proto-Shiᶜite groups regarded as the only legitimate claimant to leadership of the Muslim community. Indeed, Twelver Shiᶜite tradition maintains that the sword remained within the ᶜAlid line until the disappearance of the Twelfth Imam in 873 C.E.[18] The ᶜAbbasid caliphs, who initially posed as the defenders of the *ahl al-bayt*'s right to the caliphate, are the first ruling dynasty said to have had the sword Dhu'l-Faqar in their possession. Supposedly, the renowned ᶜAbbasid caliph Harun al-Rashid (r. 786–809 C.E.) allowed one of his generals to use the sword in battle.[19] The last ᶜAbbasid caliph said to have possessed Dhu'l-Faqar was al-Muqtadir (r. 908–32 C.E.). According to some traditions, the Fatimids, proponents of an Ismaili counter-caliphate, stole (or liberated, depending on one's viewpoint) the sword from the ᶜAbbasid palace during the tumultuous days following al-Muqtadir's murder by one of his generals, and carried it off to what was then their capital in Tunisia.[20] A couple of decades later, the Fatimid caliph supposedly wielded the sword against the infamous sectarian Berber rebel known to posterity as the Man on the Donkey.[21]

The great Ismaili jurist known as the Qadi al-Nuᶜman (d. 974), to whom we owe the report of Dhu'l-Faqar's theft, claims to have seen the sword at the court of the Fatimid caliph al-Muᶜizz (r. 953–75), the founder of Cairo. He describes it as "all of iron, with hilt and blade made of one piece . . . ; at its tip it was pointed like the tip of a lance, so that it could be used both for striking and for piercing. It had two edges; in the middle [of the blade] was a ridge (ʿ*amūd*), which, however, was barely visible."[22] Heinz Halm suggests that it may have been a Roman *gladius*: a small, plain, workmanlike iron sword that gave its name to the gladiators who used it. Even if the Qadi al-Nuʿman did not really see the sword, or even if the sword that he saw were not really Dhu'l-Faqar, his description illustrates a distinctly Ismaili conception of the sword as a realistic, even mundane weapon having a single blade with two edges.

Dhu'l-Faqar as Image

After the fourteenth century, the whereabouts of the sword Dhu'l-Faqar no longer occupy a prominent place in various sectarian traditions. The image of the sword, however, remained vital to the self-presentation of the chief contenders for religious legitimacy and military supremacy in the reconfigured Muslim world of the premodern era. Some of the earliest pictorial representations of the sword can be found in manuscripts produced under the Mongol Ilkhanid regime, which ruled from its capital Tabriz in northwestern Iran during the late thirteenth and the fourteenth centuries. An illuminated manuscript of the polymath al-Biruni's (973?–1048) *Chronology of Ancient Peoples*, produced in Tabriz in 1307–08, includes representations of the sword as a scimitar with a forked blade.[23] Since this depiction arguably displays no original Mongol influences,[24] we may speculate that this image of Dhu'l-Faqar derives from regional pre-Mongol pictorial traditions. Given the early Ilkhanids' flirtation with Sufism and Shiʿism, as well as strong ʿAlid and mystical tendencies in the Tabriz vicinity during the Middle Ages,[25] these traditions may reflect those influences, as well.

Among both the Ottomans and the Safavids, who seized control of most of Iran early in the sixteenth century, the image of Dhu'l-Faqar was closely tied to veneration of ʿAli. Although the Safavids espoused a militant brand of mystical Shiʿism, characterized by fervent devotion to ʿAli and his descendants, Dhu'l-Faqar does not appear to have had the iconographic significance in Safavid art and heraldry that it did among the Ottomans. In the period immediately preceding the Safavid conquest of Iran, however, when Iran was divided into various Timurid, and later Turcoman, principalities, there are faint indications of the sword's symbolic importance. An illumination from a late fifteenth-century Iranian manuscript of an epic biography of ʿAli depicts ʿAli displaying his prowess in arms before the

Prophet. ᶜAli carries Dhu'l-Faqar, which appears as a scimitar with two separate, curving blades. The blades appear almost to overlap, so that the sword resembles nothing so much as a pair of gardening shears.[26] Beneath the hooves of ᶜAli's mule Duldul lies the corpse of one of the enemies of Islam whom ᶜAli has vanquished; his garment is pierced with two pairs of puncture wounds—presumably the work of Dhu'l-Faqar.[27] This manuscript was produced in the southern Iranian city of Shiraz, then under the rule of the Kara Koyunlu (Black Sheep) Turcoman dynasty. Remarkably, the artist has painted the faces of both ᶜAli and the Prophet; in most traditions, rendering the features of any of the Abrahamic prophets or of Muhammad's family is strictly taboo. Here, however, both men resemble fifteenth-century Persian gentlemen, painted in the rather stubby, truncated style favored by the Shiraz school throughout most of the fifteenth century.[28] Sixteenth-century Ottoman miniatures of ᶜAli and Husayn feature similar versions of Dhu'l-Faqar, although in at least one manuscript, the sword's two blades are more widely splayed.[29]

The Ottoman Dhu'l-Faqar Tradition

Under the Ottomans, Dhu'l-Faqar came to be associated in particular with the Janissary corps, the elite corps of Ottoman infantry, which originated in the fourteenth century.[30] The Janissaries' attachment to Dhu'l-Faqar is part and parcel of their devotion to ᶜAli and, by extension, of their association with the Bektashi Sufi order, an order noted for its pronounced ᶜAlid tendencies. Hajji Bektash Veli, the medieval Anatolian mystic who inspired the order and who plays a key role in Janissary origin myth, is not himself supposed to have possessed Dhu'l-Faqar, although Bektashi doctrine speaks of an invisible sword with which to combat one's base passions.[31] On the other hand, the legendary medieval dervish Sarı Saltuk, whose influence was especially strong in the Balkans, was actually thought to have come into possession of Dhu'l-Faqar, as well as various other possessions of the early caliphs.[32]

Aside from their Bektashi affiliation, the Janissaries' devotion to ᶜAli was most clearly manifested in the corps' deployment of representations of the sword Dhu'l-Faqar. Dhu'l-Faqar figures prominently in the insignia of several companies (s. *orta*) of the imperial Janissaries, quartered in Istanbul.[33] The *Codex Vindobonensis*, a sixteenth-century compilation of Viennese paintings of Ottoman officials, depicts Janissaries marching in processions carrying outsized wooden replicas of Dhu'l-Faqar.[34] Janissary and Bektashi tombstones also bore carved images of the sword and related Shiᶜite-influenced imagery. Some of the most anthropomorphic examples of Dhu'l-Faqar occur on Janissary tombstones.[35]

The most famous and widespread of these representations, however, was the image of Dhu'l-Faqar emblazoned on the Janissaries' battle flags. According to legend, Orhan had emblazoned the image of Dhu'l-Faqar on the banner he gave to the Janissaries on their creation, so as to place the new corps under the protection of ᶜAli.[36] In later Ottoman history, these flags were carried not only by the Janissaries but by the sultan himself. Inasmuch as the Janissaries were the sultan's personal corps of soldiery, composed of his servants (s. *kul*), who surrounded his person on the battlefield, the Dhu'l-Faqar banner was not simply a Janissary banner but a sultanic banner. It was inextricably linked to the sultan's power and legitimacy.

The Ottoman Dhu'l-Faqar banner took the shape of a pointed rectangle, a triangle, or a forked pennant. Its ground was either red, the Ottoman dynastic color (*al*), or white (*ak*), the color of the Janissaries' headgear. The sword was depicted on the banner in highly stylized fashion, with two separate, often widely splayed blades (fig. 11.1). Often, the sword image was composed of lines of calligraphy, containing the proverb "There is no young man but ᶜAli, and no sword but Dhu'l-Faqar." Zdsislaw Zygulski has pointed out the anthropomorphism of the sword as portrayed on Ottoman Dhu'l-Faqar flags: the blades resemble legs, the quillons arms, the pommel a head.[37] Moreover, the sword always stands alone; it is never depicted in the hand of a warrior. Zygulski speculates that this anthropomorphism may stem from a form of Turkish "nostalgia," and given the anthropomorphic Dhu'l-Faqar's frequent association with hand motifs (interpreted in an Islamic context as the hand of ᶜAli, Husayn, or Fatima), we may speculate that it is influenced in part by Central Asian shamanistic traditions.

According to the late Mamluk chronicler Ibn Iyas, who witnessed the Ottoman conquest of Egypt, Sultan Selim, on entering Cairo, pitched his campaign tent on the island of Rawda in the Nile, and planted a red and a white banner in front of it.[38] These banners in all probability bore the image of Dhu'l-Faqar. Indeed, the Topkapı Palace museum collection contains a red Dhu'l-Faqar banner that Selim carried to Egypt.[39] Just how widespread the use of the Dhu'l-Faqar banner was among Ottoman armies during the sixteenth and seventeenth centuries can be surmised from the widely dispersed specimens, most of them captured by the Ottomans' adversaries, still to be found in various European museums. The visitor to the former Doge's palace in

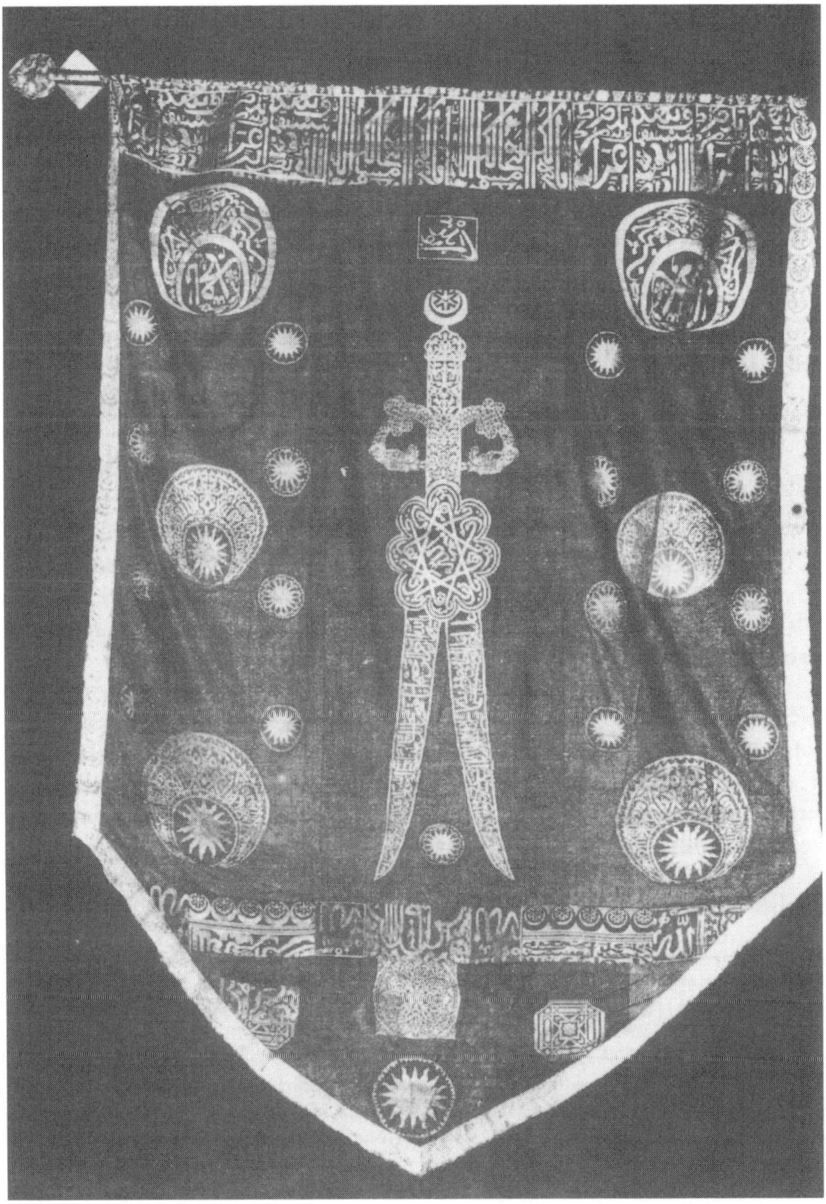

Fig. 11.1. An Ottoman Zülfikar banner (sixteenth century). Topkapı Palace Museum 1/824. (By permission of the Topkapı Palace Museum.)

Venice may be surprised to see, on looking up while walking through one of the exhibition rooms, a large, red, triangular Dhu'l-Faqar banner draped across the ceiling.[40]

Intriguingly, however, Ottoman miniatures, ordinarily an invaluable source for details of design in textiles and architecture, seldom depict the designs on battle flags with any precision. The same is true of contemporary European paintings and engravings of the Ottoman armed forces. A rare exception to this rule is a miniature of the vessels bearing ᶜAli Pasha to his new post as governor of Egypt in the seventeenth century. Flying from his ships' masts are forked pennants, each bearing the image of Dhu'l-Faqar.[41] Here, the sword's blade divides in two only toward the bottom; nonetheless, the effect of the splayed blade is compounded by the fork of the pennant itself. Seen from afar, these long, fluttering pennants must have created a striking visual effect; the distinctive image of the sword could have left no doubt in the observer's mind as to who was approaching. That Dhu'l-Faqar was associated with the governor of Egypt, among other Ottoman figures, argues for the continuing resonance of the sword's image in that province, where it had been closely associated with the Ottoman conquest.

By at least the fifteenth century, then, the sword Dhu'l-Faqar had undergone a transformation within the Ottoman cultural context from an actual sword used by ᶜAlid leaders in battle, to the image of a sword displayed on a banner. This transformation gave the sword a widespread popular appeal that it arguably could not previously have had. A banner, after all, could be seen and embraced by a far greater number of people, military and otherwise, than an actual sword. It could also be reproduced, so that armies in various locales and various divisions of a single army could carry their own banners. These sorts of considerations gained importance as Muslim armies grew more numerous and defended increasingly large and diffuse territories. By the sixteenth century, Ottoman armies were routinely engaged on two fronts: the western front against the Hapsburg Empire, and the eastern front against Safavid Iran. These were, in addition, enormous armies totaling possibly hundreds of thousands, composed of imperial forces stationed in the capital combined with levies from the provinces.[42] A typical levy from Egypt alone by the early eighteenth century consisted of three thousand soldiers.[43] By contrast, the Muslim army at Badr numbered roughly 300, the defeated Meccan force one thousand;[44] even the Muslim army that took Yarmuk in what is now Jordan from the Byzantines in 636 C.E. (prompting the flight of the Ghassanid king Jabala b. al-Ayham) numbered only forty-six thousand.[45]

In these changed circumstances, the transformation of Dhu'l-Faqar from a single material object to a mass-produced symbol presented unsuspected opportunities. The cult of the sword, if we may call it that, was far more easily spread by means of images displayed on banners and wooden replicas than it could ever have been by the sword itself. It was perhaps by means of its dissemination through these banners and wooden replicas, with their accompanying mythology, that Dhu'l-Faqar acquired its iconographic status. In this respect, the sword's dissemination and popularization resemble those of notable Christian icons, such as the Virgin of Guadalupe, whom Father Miguel Hidalgo, the hero of Mexican independence, chose as the symbol of his movement in 1810. The Virgin's image on flags, signboards, votive candles, and, most recently, T-shirts has consolidated her status as a national symbol of Mexico.[46] Just as one need not have a personal vision of the Virgin, or contact with someone who has experienced such a vision, in order to revere her, so one need not see the actual sword Dhu'l-Faqar, or have contact with a hero who has wielded it, in order to regard the sword with near religious awe.

Historians and anthropologists have asserted that the widespread popularity of the Virgin of Guadalupe in Mexico drew (and draws) on pre-Columbian beliefs in fertility goddesses.[47] In like fashion, among the Ottoman Janissaries, the lore of Dhu'l-Faqar resonated with the sword legends that abounded in other cultures with which Janissary recruits had come in contact. Until the seventeenth century, a large proportion of the Janissary corps, both in Istanbul and in the provinces, consisted of *devshirme* recruits: young boys from the Christian population of the Balkans and Anatolia removed from their families, converted to Islam, and trained as infantrymen. The Janissaries also included prisoners of war and mercenaries of various stripes from both the European and the Iranian theatres.[48] These recruits could well have been familiar with a mélange of sword legends, which meshed easily with the tales of Dhu'l-Faqar. Thus, Konstantin Mihalowicz, a Serbian soldier who, after his capture in 1455 by Mehmed II's forces south of Belgrade, served for twelve years as a Janissary auxiliary, recounts in his memoirs a tale of Dhu'l-Faqar that draws on elements of the Arthurian legends of the sword in the stone and Excalibur. On Muhammad's death, according to Michalowicz, ᶜAli, wishing to destroy Dhu'l-Faqar, struck the sword against a rock "until it was completely hidden in the rock." When his own hour drew nigh, ᶜAli threw the sword into the sea, which "bubbled and seethed" for three days in mourning for ᶜAli.[49] Here, Muhammad plays the part of King Arthur while ᶜAli takes the role of the Round Table knight Percival, who later recovered the Holy Grail. Meanwhile, soldiers from eastern Anatolia, the Caucasus, and the Kurdish regions may have been familiar with what Mehrdad R. Izady calls "the ancient Iranic rite of worshipping the deity represented as a sword stuck into the ground," practiced currently among Kurdish Alevis in eastern Anatolia.[50] Michele Membré, a Venetian envoy en route to the Safavid court in 1539, noticed outside a church in Georgia "a wooden mast with three or four of their daggers . . . and two swords all stuck into the said wood."[51] Similar tales of magical swords and spears from other bodies of European and Iranian mythology may well have filtered into Dhu'l-Faqar lore: for example, the Nordic *Nibelungenlied*; the Welsh *Mabinogian*; the *Chanson de Roland*;[52] the tales of the Byzantine border soldiers known as *akritoi*, epitomized by the epic of Digenes Akrites; the legends of Alexander the Great; the Iranian epic *Shahname*; the *Thousand and One Nights*.[53] Special mention should be made in this regard of the tales of King Solomon, loosely based on the Qurʾanic accounts of Solomon (Sulayman), regarded by Muslims as a prophet. Solomon's vizier Asaf was said to have possessed a magic sword that, like Dhu'l-Faqar, became a Holy Grail-like icon; Sayf ben Dhi Yazan, the mythic culture hero of pre-Islamic Yemen, supposedly steals it from the father of the African princess "Takrur." Like Excalibur, furthermore, Asaf's sword is thrown into the sea.[54] Indeed, the compatability of the Dhu'l-Faqar legend with these various traditions must partially explain the readiness of Janissaries from such disparate backgrounds to revere the sword and the man who wielded it.

If ᶜAli Bey carried a flag bearing the image of the Ottoman version of Dhu'l-Faqar, whether on a white or on a red ground, then he must have known full well the loyalty this symbol would inspire among Rumis who had previously been in Ottoman military service, particularly in the Janissary regiment. Likewise, he knew full well what he was doing when he compared himself to ᶜAli b. Abi Talib. Jirja under his governorship must have been a "Zülfikari" bastion, and when he brought his army down to Cairo, his banners advertised him and his symbolic allegiance.

Following his death, his client and successor in Jirja, the rebellious Mehmed Bey, also brought an army to Cairo, where it was observed by the French merchant Jean de Thévenot. Thévenot, as we saw in chapter 6, described Mehmed Bey's *tuğ*, which, he reports, was followed by "a great big flag" (*un beau grand drap-peau* [*sic*]). It is possible, even likely, that this was an Ottoman Dhu'l-Faqar flag, but alas, Thévenot does not elaborate! Perhaps he couldn't see the flag clearly, or if he could, perhaps he didn't know what to make of the strange blazon in its center.[55]

The Yemeni Dhu'l-Faqar Tradition

In the case of ᶜAli Bey's Ottoman Dhu'l-Faqar banner, as in the case of Abu'l-Shawarib Ridvan Bey's genealogy, a shadowy Yemeni/Zaydi counterpoise lurks in the background. There is also a Zaydi version of the Dhu'l-Faqar legend and of the Dhu'l-Faqar flag. Zaydi tradition holds that when the authority of the ᶜAbbasid caliph began to be diluted by autonomous regional powers early in the tenth century C.E., the Zaydi imam al-Hadi claimed the title "sword of the caliphs" (*sayf al-khulafāʾ*), and migrated from Medina to Yemen, carrying the sword Dhu'l-Faqar with him.[56] (This account, incidentally, contradicts the story of the sword's theft from Baghdad by the Fatimids.) For centuries, the sword remained in the hands of the Zaydi imams, who wielded it in battle. The last imam to fight with Dhu'l-Faqar was supposedly al-Mahdi Muhammad b. al-Mutahhar (r. 1301–28), who was expelled from Mecca by the Mamluk sultan as part of a broad Mamluk campaign to "Sunnify" the Holy Cities and reinforce Mamluk suzerainty over them.[57]

Yet even Sunni tradition maintains that the sword was held by the Rasulid sultans, who ruled most of Yemen from their capital at the southern city of Zabid during the thirteenth and fourteenth centuries.[58] Although, as we saw in the preceding chapter, the Rasulids claimed descent from the Ghassanids, the dynasty was founded in the twelfth century by a Turkic supporter of the ᶜAbbasid caliph who claimed to have been the caliph's envoy (*rasūl*). Originally vassals of the Ayyubid dynasty, the Rasulids asserted their independence in the early thirteenth century.[59] Their alleged possession of Dhu'l-Faqar, added to their purported connection to the ᶜAbbasids, gave them an aura of Sunni legitimacy that approached, if it did not match, that of the Mamluks, who had saved the ᶜAbbasid caliphate from extinction.[60]

The whereabouts of the sword following its use by the imam al-Mahdi remain unclear. Yet the association of the Zaydi imam with Dhu'l-Faqar seems to have persisted. Although the sword did not become as widespread a symbol among Zaydi sympathizers as it did among the Ottoman Janissaries, its image was evidently emblazoned on Zaydi banners in much the same fashion as on Ottoman banners. The British traveler Robert Playfair, in a late eighteenth-century memoir of his travels in southern Arabia, notes that the armies of the Zaydi imam carried a red flag displaying the image of Dhu'l-Faqar.[61] He does not describe the sword's appearance on this banner, but we may assume that it was considerably different from the image of the sword that appeared on Ottoman banners. Later Zaydi flags, including the national flag of Yemen in use until the Zaydi monarchy's overthrow in 1962, bear an image of Dhu'l-Faqar as a single-bladed scimitar.[62] This image may more closely reflect the sword's actual appearance than the fanciful forked Ottoman version, for, as we have seen, Dhu'l-Faqar most probably consisted of a single blade bearing a ridge or notches, or of two steel plates forming a single blade. If anything, this depiction of Dhu'l-Faqar would imply that the Zaydi imams of Yemen were more familiar with the actual sword than the Ottoman sultan or Janissaries could possibly have been.

Over and above their knowledge of the sword's true appearance, the Zaydi imams had a greater stake than any Ottoman group in the sword's physical presence. The theory of the imamate in Zaydi Shiᶜism entails the so-called imam of defense (*imām al-difāᶜ*)—that is, a leader (caliph or imam) of the Muslim community who assumes that position by virtue of his ability to defend the Muslim community, by armed might if necessary. This pattern can be observed in the careers of various lines of imams in medieval and early modern Yemen, up to and including the Qasimi imams: following the death of a recognized imam, a purported successor, who might or might not belong to the deceased's bloodline, would proclaim his *daᶜwa*, or "call," and seek recognition in various territories, in the process often fighting off rival claimants to the imamate, as well as Sunni and Ismaili adversaries.[63] This practice allowed for multiple lines of Zaydi imams who competed for recognition, and hence multiple Zaydi dynasties over the centuries.

As caliph and battle commander, the Zaydi imam, at least in the eyes of his followers, took on a character similar to the great heroes of the early Muslim community, notably ᶜAli himself. He thus arguably possessed greater personal charisma than any single Ottoman sultan or vizier, and as a consequence, his physical presence on the battlefield was more highly charged. The sword he wielded could acquire the same mythic status that the swords of the early heroes of Islam had acquired. Thus, the imam wielding Dhu'l-Faqar or its image arguably acquired a spiritual significance with which the Ottomans were unacquainted.

It is very tempting to imagine the two Dhu'l-Faqar traditions meeting and clashing during the tortuous Ottoman struggle to hold Yemen during the 1620s and 1630s: in Yemen's ruggedly unforgiving mountains and broiling coastal plains, the Ottoman armies, carrying banners emblazoned with the anthropomorphic, two-pronged Dhu'l-Faqar, confronting the armies of the Zaydi imam, whose flag bore an image of Dhu'l-Faqar that resembled an ordinary scimitar. Unfortunately, this is a bit of a leap: the Ottomans probably did carry their signature Dhu'l-Faqar banners, but we can't be sure that the imam carried the same banner observed by Playfair over a century later, still less the Dhu'l-Faqar banner of the twentieth-century dynasty of imams.

The dynasty who ousted the Ottomans was the Qasimi dynasty, named after its founder, the imam al-Mansur al-Qasim (r. 1598–1620). We can hardly fail to notice that this dynasty, by an amazing coincidence, bore the same name as the Egyptian faction founded by Qasim Bey—which, moreover, took shape amidst the Ottoman struggle to keep Yemen from these very Qasimi imams. Could the faction possibly have adopted the Zaydi Dhu'l-Faqar flag, and perhaps the very name Qasimi, from this line of imams? There was certainly no lack of contact between the two sides. Quite a number of Ottoman soldiers, many sent from Egypt, deserted to the imam's army to escape the disease, food and ammunition shortages, lack of reinforcements, and nonpayment of salaries that plagued the Ottoman camp.[64] Those captured by the imam's forces, meanwhile, were distributed among the Zaydi tribes as agricultural laborers.[65] Some of them may have returned to Egypt after the Ottomans had been expelled. Likewise, Turkish mercenaries and Caucasian mamluks employed by the imam himself[66] may have found their way to Egypt. As we saw in chapter 4, bedouins known as Zayidiyya inhabited the countryside of the Nile Delta early in the eighteenth century. The circumstantial evidence is indeed compelling, even startling, but I doubt that it is conclusive. The Qasimi *faction* is clearly associated with Qasim Bey. If anything, it seems more likely that the Qasimi faction adopted the Zaydis' red, single-bladed Dhu'l-Faqar flag than that they borrowed the dynasty's name. If they did appropriate the flag, though, it was only as a marker of identity and not as an ideological symbol. Intriguing as this notion is, it is impossible to verify in the absence of direct written or material evidence.

It is important to bear in mind that by the early eighteenth century, at any rate, the factions were distinguished by the *colors* of their flags, not by the images emblazoned on their flags—or at least, people noticed that they carried red and white flags. I once speculated that if both the Faqaris' and the Qasimis' flags bore the sword Dhu'l-Faqar, then the sword was not a *distinguishing* feature, as the contrasting colors of the flags were. Now, however, I am more inclined to think that colors are mentioned as distinguishing features for the same reason that *tuğ*s and *ᶜalem*s, or knobs and disks, are mentioned: they are clearly visible and contrastable in a large procession and from a long distance. Those observing the factions in the eighteenth century may not have recognized the sword at all; this could explain why neither al-Damurdashi nor al-Jabarti mentions the sword, but only the colors of the rival factions' banners. It is perhaps significant in this regard that Ottoman miniatures, as noted above, almost never portray the designs on battle flags with any degree of precision.[67] Nor, for the most part, do the paintings of European observers, which rarely depict anything beyond a suggestion of calligraphy on Ottoman banners. While a Dhu'l-Faqar banner would have been visible to far more people than the sword itself could ever have been, from the vantage point of the average soldier, it may have looked like nothing so much as a red or white flag with an amorphous blob in the middle. Thus, ironically, the sword that was the namesake of one of our two factions ultimately took a back seat to the color of the flag on which it was emblazoned.

What About Ridvan Bey and Dhu'l-Faqar Bey?

To put forward the sword Dhu'l-Faqar as the namesake of the Faqari faction, and ᶜAli Bey as the "first Faqari," means to reject Ridvan Bey and Dhu'l-Faqar Bey as candidates for faction-founder. It is worth stressing that the notion that Ridvan Bey "al-Faqari" founded the Faqari faction originated in two cautious footnotes to P. M. Holt's "Al-Jabarti's Introduction to the History of Ottoman Egypt" and *Egypt and the Fertile Crescent*; here, Holt speculated that Dhu'l-Faqar might have been one of Ridvan's titles.[68] There is, however, no concrete evidence that Ridvan Bey actually used the sobriquet Faqari, to say nothing of the title Dhu'l-Faqar—nor, indeed, did Holt ever claim that there was. Given what we have learned about ᶜAli Bey, on the other hand, I think it is safe to say that he makes a far more plausible "first Faqari" than Ridvan. This is not to say, however, that Ridvan was not just as influential in Egyptian society as ᶜAli, or that he did not have as many clients or leave behind as many architectural monuments. We know that he was at least as prominent a figure as ᶜAli—perhaps more prominent. In the sense of laying the economic and political foundations for what would later be known as the Faqari faction, he played a role similar to that of Ridvan Bey Abu'l-Shawarib vis-à-vis the Qasimi faction; that is why the two Ridvans had become fabled "great men" by the eighteenth century. But he did not supply the faction's name and quite possibly never applied it to himself.

In her book, meanwhile, Doris Behrens-Abouseif argues for a relatively straightforward solution to the mystery of Faqari and Qasimi origins: namely, that the same Qasim Bey cited above was the eponymous founder of the Qasimis while a far less prominent early seventeenth-century grandee named Dhu'l-Faqar Bey was the eponymous founder of the Faqaris. I believe she was right about Qasim Bey, but I would have remained skeptical had I not discovered Haci ᶜAli's description of Qasim's entourage. So far as Dhu'l-Faqar Bey is concerned, there is simply no evidence linking him either to a large military grouping or to the sobriquet Zülfikari or any variation thereon. All he has to recommend him are his name and the period during which he was active, and these, I would argue, are simply not enough to be convincing. My own candidate for faction-founder, or at least sobriquet-coiner, was not named Dhu'l-Faqar at all but identified himself as Zülfikari because of his allegiance to ᶜAli b. Abi Talib and his sword.

It is important to bear in mind, however, that ᶜAli Bey's appropriation of this sobriquet appears to have been rooted in his identification with ᶜAli b. Abi Talib and his sword rather than with a recognized faction. Although he did have an enormous household, he may not have been a faction-founder in the way that Qasim Bey seems to have been. If, indeed, the Faqari faction took its name so directly from the Ottoman Dhu'l-Faqar banner, then perhaps the name attached to the general body of grandees, troops, and tribesmen who came down on the side of ᶜAli and Ridvan in their apparently definitive struggle with Qansuh and Memi. By the same token, the name of Qansuh's patron, the veteran household-builder Qasim Bey, may have attached to the opposing side. In other words, as I suggested in the introduction, the origins and early development of the two factions were by no means parallel or symmetrical. Instead, this was an uneven, uncertain, and rather messy process.

The Factions and the East-West Dichotomy

This apparent first major confrontation between the nascent Faqaris and Qasimis occurred at a highly charged juncture in provincial and imperial history. In chronicles covering this period, the conflict occurs shortly after an imperial order arrives, demanding the expulsion from Egypt's regiments of Ottoman soldiery of all "sons of the Arabs" (*awlād al-ᶜArab*), who seem to comprise the bulk of Qansuh and Memi Beys' troops. ᶜAli Bey proposes replacing the *awlād* with a clear alternative, namely, *Rum oğlanı* (literally, sons of the Anatolians [or Greeks]), from whom he has recruited his own army.[69] As I have pointed out elsewhere, *awlād al-ᶜArab* probably refers to mercenaries from among the local populations of the Ottoman Arab provinces, and Asiatic regions more generally, regardless of whether they were ethnically Arab in the modern sense.[70] ᶜAli Bey's *Rum oğlanı* are likewise mercenaries, but from the Balkan and western Anatolian populations that comprised the traditional pool of the *devshirme*. In effect, then, the conflict between Ridvan-ᶜAli and Qansuh-Memi was a contest between *Rum oğlanı* and *awlād al-ᶜArab*, who, like the factions themselves, represented an either-or contrast. This confrontation, in turn, partook of an empire-wide friction between "westerners," typically palace-trained recruits from the Balkans, and "easterners," mercenaries from Asia.[71] Such a dichotomy lay at the heart of the deposition of the young sultan Osman II (r. 1618–22), who had sought to overcome the power of the palace *devshirme* recruits (*kullar*) by recruiting a new army of Asiatic mercenaries.[72] The broader east-west ethnogeographical antagonism would continue through the seventeenth century. Until the introduction into the Qasimi faction of a Bosnian leadership stratum, itself probably palace-trained, in the 1660s,[73] the Faqaris probably represented a "western," Rumi option while the Qasimis were a haven for "eastern" Asiatics, or *awlād al-ᶜArab*. Although it lies beyond the scope of the present study to demonstrate this ethnic dimension in detail, such a dimension would further emphasize the distinctively Ottoman character of the factions' origins, which were linked to this specific feature of the broader seventeenth-century crisis.

The Factions in Evliya Çelebi's Travelogue

By way of stressing the messy, assymetrical nature of the factions' genesis, I shall let the redoubtable Evliya Çelebi have the last word. The first mention I have found of the Qasimis and Faqaris as full-fledged factions occurs in the tenth volume of Evliya's *Book of Travels*, which covers his travels in Egypt and eastern Africa, and which he probably composed toward the end of a nine-year sojourn in Cairo (roughly 1673–82).[74]

By the time Evliya settled in Cairo, to judge from the manner in which he refers to them, the two factions were already fully formed, indeed well-known quantities. However, they seem almost to exist in the background of political events; atypically, Evliya does not pay them special attention, nor does he supply an excursus on their origins. He mentions Qasim Bey and marks the date of his death, but does not connect him to a faction. So it is all the more surprising when, toward the end of volume ten, he suddenly puts forth,

> From time to time, enmity breaks out between the Kasımlıs and the Zülfikarlıs, and a great battle erupts on Rumayla Square [in front of the Citadel]. Sometimes, they gather on the Black Square (Kara Meydan) like black crows or black mountains;[75] sometimes, they close the Sultan Hasan and Sultan Muʾayyad mosques, and a big battle ensues. Finally, someone like [the governor] Ömer Pasha will roll out the cannon, bombard the Muʾayyad Mosque and destroy the bandits and rebels, chop them into bits inside the mosque, and leave Cairo in peace (*Seyahatname*, vol. 10: 720).

Clearly, these factional battles were a fairly routine occurrence by the 1670s or 1680s; likewise, the two factions themselves were well-known quantities. Indeed, Evliya's depiction of the two factions here is reminiscent of Shirbini's portrayal of the Saʿd and Haram (see chapter 3): they are standard features of Egyptian life, and one is inconceivable without the other.

But although the two factions seem to be already entrenched by the time Evliya describes them, we may be able to tease out of his passage a couple of clues to their evolution. For one thing, Evliya identifies the factions as Kasımlı and Zülfikarlı rather than as Qasimi and Faqari, or even Kasımlı and Fakarlı. This indicates that he is at least dimly aware that they originated with two figures named Qasim and Dhu'l-Faqar. Turcophone chroniclers as late as Mehmed b. Yusuf al-Hallaq, who wrote c. 1715, identify them in this fashion, as well. In the Arabic chronicles, by contrast, the faction is always Faqari, minus the *dhū* prefix, and aside from the Sudun origin myth, no mention is made of the name's derivation from Dhu'l-Faqar. Yet the name Faqari is syntactically incomplete. One would never call the actual sword—or, indeed, an actual person—simply Faqar, "backbone." The truncated name seems to bespeak a forgetfulness of its source. By the same token, al-Damurdashi and Ahmed Çelebi give the name of the seventeenth-century grandee Dhu'l-Faqar Bey as Zayn al-Faqar, "ornament of the spine," although conceivably *zayn* could have derived from the honorific *zaynī* that seems occasionally to be applied to regimental officers.[76] By the time al-Damurdashi wrote, it seems to me, the very lexical connection between Dhu'l-Faqar and Faqari had been forgotten.

A less obvious clue is Evliya's observation that every so often, "enmity breaks out" (*birbirleriyle öyle düşman olup*, literally, they become one another's enemy) between the two factions. This at least seems to imply that the factions did not originate as enemies, in the manner of Ahmed Çelebi's origin myth, but may have come into existence autonomously before clashing. By the 1670s and 1680s, the two factions, like the Saʿd and Haram bedouin, may have become a byword for factional strife; still, we sense a lingering awareness of their separate genesis some decades earlier.

Conclusion

How the Factions Formed

I started this project with the aim of solving the mystery of the origins of the Faqari and Qasimi factions. I think I have done this; at least I have proposed a solution that I think is more plausible than any previously put forward. The Qasimi faction, indeed, originated with the influential early seventeenth-century grandee Qasim Bey. His mamluk Qansuh Bey, who on being appointed governor of Yemen in 1629 became Qansuh Pasha, built on his patron's foundations by amassing an entourage of slaves, presumably mamluks of various kinds, who accompanied him to Yemen. Nonetheless, the later Qasimi faction stemmed largely from the household of Ridvan Bey Abu'l-Shawarib.

The Faqari faction, in contrast, took its name not from an eponymous founder but from the Ottoman Dhu'l-Faqar banner, which was carried by ʿAli Bey, governor of Jirja during the 1630s and 1640s, who therefore presumed to compare himself to ʿAli b. Abi Talib, owner of the pictured sword. The future of this faction, however, seems to have lain with ʿAli's comrade, (the other) Ridvan Bey.

The two factions seem to have come to the fore as a result of the conflict in the 1640s between a second Qansuh Bey, also a mamluk of Qasim Bey, and his ally Memi Bey, on the one hand, and ʿAli Bey and his ally Ridvan Bey, on the other. This conflict revolved around what were then the two most lucrative and politically influential administrative offices that beys could attain in Egypt: those of pilgrimage commander and governor of Jirja. Later, the factional rivalry would come to center on the offices of pilgrimage commander and *defterdar*, or financial director, as the governorship of Jirja took a back seat to Cairene posts. One version of the myth of the factions' origins probably coalesced during this later period, in the late seventeenth or early eighteenth century, and thus featured an eponymous Dhu'l-Faqar Bey the pilgrimage commander and Qasim Bey the *defterdar.* The other origin myths, featuring Sultan Selim as catalyst to the enmity between the brothers Qasim and Dhu'l-Faqar, and the binary opposition between Faqari/Saᶜd and Qasimi/Haram, do not seem to have crystallized until the early eighteenth century, although their antecedents are arguably visible in the late seventeenth century.

As for Saᶜd and Haram, they were two conglomerations of bedouin tribes that probably originated in Yemen but that were present in Egypt as early as the fifteenth century. The Haram seem to have had a more sustained presence in Egypt through the pre-Ottoman period. The association of Saᶜd and Haram with the Faqari and Qasimi factions, respectively, appears to date from the factions' emergence in the early seventeenth century. The Haram apparently included elements associated with the Ottoman campaigns in Yemen, which acted as catalysts to the formation of the Qasimi faction. In Egypt, in any event, the rivalry of the two bedouin blocs constituted a rural counterpart to the Faqari-Qasimi rivalry; meanwhile, grandees from the Faqari and Qasimi factions arguably provided a measure of unity to the disparate tribes that made up each bedouin faction. Both the Faqaris and Qasimis and their bedouin counterparts seem to have tapped into preexisting traditions and motifs of factional rivalry, notably the red-white color dichotomy of the Qaysi and Yemeni Arab factions, to which the Saᶜd and Haram may have had direct, if distant, links.

The Function of Factional Origin Myths

Obviously, the various myths of the factions' origins have obscured the historical realities of the factions' development from the eyes of inquisitive historians. Here, I have tried to get at both the historical reality—which, as is so often the case with historical realities, is far more mundane, random, and gradual than mythic—and the myths themselves. This has meant approaching the myths on their own terms and wrestling with the numerous symbols, tropes, and allusions that adorn them. Why bother doing this? Because the myths are as important as the reality, although for a different reason. The myths provided a framework within which a factional identity could be constructed. They served to fix and to legitimize the factions by linking them to an heroic past, whether fictive (Kisa) or, more commonly, fictionalized (Baybars, Jabala b. al-Ayham, the Hilalis, the *Shahname,* even some of the legends of the Prophet's companions). The characters and tropes to which the myths alluded were eminently adaptable, with parallels in the multifarious cultures from which recruits to the factions came. Likewise, the recruits contributed to the myths themselves, incorporating heroes and motifs, however vaguely misremembered, from their home cultures. By listening to and telling stories, new and not so new recruits reinforced the identities of the factions to which they belonged. At the same time, through this form of participation, they reinforced their own membership in these factions.

The individual symbols and motifs contained in the myths, meanwhile, allow us entry into the culture of the large, diffuse military-administrative society of seventeenth- and eighteenth-century Egypt. This was a veritable society within a society: a large, heterogeneous mass in which many different groups could participate at different times and to different degrees. Men and women; mamluks, mercenaries, and *devshirme* boys; bedouin tribesmen and lifelong city dwellers; Arabs, Turks, Rumis, Circassians, Persians, Africans, and a host of other peoples participated in this culture. Through the intricate process of deciphering the symbolism of the origin myths and assessing their resonance to the people among whom they circulated, we can gain some inkling of how members of this society made sense of the culture in which they participated. These were the stories they told themselves about this society that they had joined or into which they had been cast, and about their particular places in it.

And they did, I am certain, tell these stories, perhaps most frequently in a barracks or barracks-like setting, but also perhaps at the "open houses" of various grandees, while on the pilgrimage, while on campaign, and, of course, in coffeehouses. Women, meanwhile, no doubt partook of the same or parallel stories in the harems, or private quarters, of great houses, or perhaps at the public baths; the prominence of heroic female characters in some of the most popular epics makes one wonder if such stories had a special resonance for the women of the factions, some of whom became powerful figures in their own right.[1]

Faction members also acted out these tales in a certain sense; the processions in which the Faqaris and Qasimis marched made publicly visible the standards, flags, and insignia that were the stuff of their legends. Even the predictable battles in which they faced off, described so succinctly by Evliya Çelebi, gave them a chance to parade this self-created image of themselves, which in turn linked them back to the myths. We have numerous examples from other societies of processions and public rituals that served a similar purpose; a number of them have come up in the course of this book. But we also have examples of the extraordinary hold that such stories can exert within relatively circumscribed military societies in particular. Enlisted men in the British army in India, for instance, indulged in a pastime known as "spinning cuffers," that is, telling stories after lights out in the barracks. Although some of these were quite mundane stories about civilian activities, they "lived" for the soldiers and were sometimes appropriated as "factual" narratives in journals and letters home.[2] An even more compelling parallel comes from the Faqaris' and Qasimis' near contemporaries in Spanish America: the soldiers who manned Spain's colonial garrisons, who routinely participated in processions designed, like those in Cairo, to welcome a new governor or to celebrate a royal wedding or a military victory. These pageants featured heroes of popular Castilian chivalric romances, notably Amadis of Gaul; once Miguel de Cervantes' *Don Quixote* had crossed the Atlantic, the soldiers and their commanders lost no time in adding the would-be knight and his squire, Sancho Panza, to their festivities.[3] Here, fiction threatened to cross the boundary separating it from "reality," just as it does in Cervantes' novel, in which Don Quixote attempts to act out venerable tales of chivalry. Yet this is not so very different from what members of the Faqari and Qasimi factions did when they conceptualized the rivalry between their factions in terms of familiar heroic stories. In a very real sense, the storytelling and the rituals constituted two forms of public performance.

Factions in Prenationalist Societies

It is all very well to demonstrate that the stories legitimized the factions, but why did the factions need to be legitimized in the first place? Each faction provided cohesion to a wildly disparate membership, many of whom were newcomers to Egypt from vastly different climes. The stories, as well as the colors, standards, and various rituals—that is, the invented traditions—that each faction cultivated buttressed its identity and enabled it to be longer lived and historically more resonant than a mere household or gang. Moreover, the fact that there were two factions, and the ingrained rivalry between these two factions, fostered identity and relative longevity. The danger of being defeated or bested by the competing faction itself provided, as Roy P. Mottahedeh puts it, a negative loyalty.[4] In short, a key part of a faction's identity consisted in not being the other faction, or, in fact, being its opposite.

Indeed, the culture of bilateral factionalism was arguably peculiarly suited to prenationalist societies, in particular territorially vast, ethnically diffuse empires. This may explain the multiplicity of bilateral factional systems in premodern societies, from Qaysis and Yemenis through Blues and Greens, Guelphs and Ghibellines, and Haydaris and Ni^cmatis to Hatfields and McCoys. Each of these factions had a "package" of invented traditions that reinforced its identity and legitimacy, often through fictive links or allusions to earlier prototypes. All the factions just listed had their origin myths; most also had distinctive colors, emblems, and/or territories. The origin myths in particular could provide the factions and their leaders with a legitimacy that complemented that of the empire or other prenationalist polity to which they belonged. Each faction, as we have seen, could provide a sense of community to a disparate population that otherwise would have little to keep it together. The opposing faction provided the "common foe" that galvanized its members.

These considerations almost inevitably lead to the question of the state's role in the formation of factions. In an emerging nation-state, the state itself typically appropriates the nationalist project.[5] If, however, there is no nationalist project to appropriate, but only two nonnationalist factions, the state can manipulate them, either by favoring one (as did the Byzantine emperors and numerous Ottoman provincial governors) or by playing one off against the other (as did the Buyids, Seljuks, and Safavids in Iran).[6] This is not to say, however, that the state's role is one of utterly cynical manipulation, or that the state somehow transcends the forces that shape the factions. If we regard the premodern state not as an abstract yet coherent entity, but as a network of interest groups, we can easily see how various figures and groups within the state could, in various circumstances, participate in or come into conflict with a two-faction system.

This, in turn, raises the question of the particular role of the Ottoman state in the formation of the Faqari and Qasimi factions. I have shown throughout the book how various figures and interest groups associated with the Ottoman central authority interacted with Egypt from its conquest by Selim I through the factions' demise. More generally, the emergence of the two factions partakes of the seventeenth-century crisis within the Ottoman Empire. Toward the end of the sixteenth century, the series of Long Wars with the Hapsburg Empire impelled the Ottoman armies to recruit peasant mercenaries, who were supplied with firearms. In the face of the ruinous inflation that was either triggered or exacerbated by an influx of silver from Spain's New World colonies, these mercenaries found their salaries, when they were paid, to be worthless and, in response, left the battlefield and spread terror throughout the countryside, causing massive flight of the settled agricultural population. This was, then, a time when the Ottoman armed forces were becoming increasingly "*sekban*-ized" (*sekban* being the typical term for such a mercenary) while massive population movement was occurring.[7]

At the same time, these *sekban*s became available for the armies of provincial governors, who began building powerful households quite separate from the imperial palace. The assassination in 1622 of Sultan Osman II (Genç Osman) by palace *kullar* after he attempted to supplement the imperial Janissary corps with an army of *sekban*s from the Asian provinces was part and parcel of this competition between palace *kul*s and provincial *sekban*s. Abaza Mehmed Pasha of Erzurum rebelled in 1624, supposedly to avenge Osman II, and led a *sekban* army toward Istanbul.[8] Four decades later, Abaza Hasan Pasha of Aleppo launched a similar rebellion that was stopped by the reforming grand vizier Mehmed Köprülü.[9] Although Egypt produced no such *jalālī* governors, rebellious beys such as "Jalali" Mehmed Bey, who succeeded his patron ᶜAli Bey as governor of Jirja and rebelled against the governor in 1659, were their direct parallels.[10]

And the war in Yemen? Yemen provided an uncomfortable, disease-ridden crucible in which the Qasimi faction, at least in part, seems to have been forged. In a certain sense, Yemen was a particularly intense and unpleasant microcosm of the seventeenth-century Ottoman Empire as a whole: an arena through which a crazy quilt of peoples of many different locales, ethnicities, kin groups, faiths, and life-styles passed and in which they met and interacted. Once what was left of the Ottoman garrison force quit Yemen, this morass spilled back into Egypt, which was already absorbing its own motley crew of new arrivals from Istanbul and from other Ottoman provinces, while coping with rapid shifts among its tribal populations.

In short, the movement of peoples amid new economic and political stresses that characterized the Ottoman Empire in the seventeenth century formed the backdrop for the emergence of the Faqari and Qasimi factions in Egypt. Thus, the emergence of these factions was symptomatic of the broader seventeenth-century crisis in the Ottoman Empire and elsewhere. The Faqari and Qasimi factions, who recruited heavily from different geographical pools of *sekban*s and mamluks (think of ᶜAli Bey's Rumis and Abu'l-Shawarib's Circassian pride), and who were, to varying degrees, involved with Yemen, reflected and were shaped by this demographic flux. Indeed, the incident that provided the first hint of the Faqari-Qasimi rivalry—the conflict between Qansuh/Memi and Ridvan/ᶜAli—was, as noted in chapter 11, in some respects a competition between "eastern" and "western" pools of personnel and, at the same time, a competition between rival conglomerations of mercenaries from outside the imperial palace.

In the aftermath of Ridvan's and ᶜAli's victory over Qansuh and Memi, Bosnians suddenly appeared among the Qasimis. In particular, Ahmed Bey Bushnaq (the Bosniak) suddenly took over the post of pilgrimage commander in 1660; he was not only a Bosnian but evidently someone who had served in the imperial capital, to judge from his sobriquet, Yeni Kapılı.[11] I suspect, although I am far from having the evidence to prove, that Ahmed Bey was injected into the Qasimi faction by the reforming grand vizier Mehmed Köprülü, to whose entourage he may even have belonged. To be frank, I suspect that Köprülü sought to appoint Bosnian clients to key positions in Egypt in order to rein in the ambitions of just such "eastern" types as the two Ridvan Beys, while making sure that no one else, regardless of ethnicity, could establish a semiautonomous bailiwick within the province. What is interesting, however, is that these Bosnians were absorbed by one of the factions, despite their ethnic difference from most of the factions' members; they were seemingly unable to operate outside the factional system. Indeed, Köprülü or any grand vizier arguably sought to manipulate the existing factional system rather than to subvert it. In any case, the interventionist policies of Mehmed Köprülü and his son and successor, Fazıl Ahmed, toward Egypt and the Ottoman provinces—and the connections between those policies and their position in the palace—deserve closer study.[12]

I shall close with the story with which I began—modified, however, to reflect what we have learned from this undertaking. Nearly four centuries ago in the land of Egypt, two factions slowly and fitfully emerged. The first was named after the bey who founded it; the second took its name from the sword emblazoned on the flag carried by one of the beys who launched it. Over the years, these origins were forgotten, and people came to believe that the factions had existed ever since the Ottomans conquered Egypt in 1517. The two factions competed for key administrative positions. Meanwhile, the Ottoman government favored first one, then another, but seemed always to count on their rivalry.

The myths are more compelling, aren't they?

Notes

Introduction

1. Alan Cameron, *Circus Factions: Blues and Greens at Rome and Byzantium* (Oxford: Clarendon Press, 1976); Carol Lansing, *The Florentine Magnates: Lineage and Faction in a Medieval Commune* (Princeton, NJ: Princeton University Press, 1991).

2. Patricia Crone, "Were the Qays and Yemen of the Umayyad Period Political Parties?" *Der Islam* 71, no. 1 (1994): 1–57; Julius Wellhausen, *The Arab Kingdom and Its Fall*, trans. Margaret Graham Weir (Beirut: Khayats, 1927), pp. 68–71, 207–11, 250–51, 259–61, 320–22, 359–60, 387, chapter 8 passim.

3. Jane Hathaway, *The Politics of Households in Ottoman Egypt: The Rise of the Qazdağlıs* (Cambridge: Cambridge University Press, 1997), chapter 2; idem, "The Military Household in Ottoman Egypt," *International Journal of Middle East Studies* 27, no. 1 (1995): 39–52.

4. *EI*², *s.v.* "Mamlūk," by David Ayalon; *s.v.* "Mamlūks," by P. M. Holt.

5. *EI*², *s.v.* "Mamlūk," by David Ayalon; *s.v.* "Mamlūks," by P. M. Holt; Michael Winter, *Egyptian Society under Ottoman Rule, 1517–1798* (London and New York: Routledge, 1992), pp. 47ff.; Daniel N. Crecelius, *The Roots of Modern Egypt: A Study of the Regimes of ᶜAli Bey al-Kabir and Muhammad Bey Abu al-Dhahab, 1760–1775* (Minneapolis and Chicago: Bibliotheca Islamica, 1981), pp. 22–34.

6. For example, Winter, *Egyptian Society under Ottoman Rule*; Crecelius, *Roots of Modern Egypt*; Doris Behrens-Abouseif, *Egypt's Adjustment to Ottoman Rule: Institutions,* Waqf, *and Architecture in Cairo (Sixteenth-Seventeenth Centuries)* (Leiden: Brill, 1994). Note also the pointed use of the adjective "indigenous" in Nelly Hanna, *Making Big Money in 1600: The Life and Times of Ismail Abu Taqiyya, Egyptian Merchant* (Syracuse: Syracuse University Press, 1998), pp. xxii, 19, 44, 95, 136, 167.

7. Thus, *EI*², *s.v.* "Mamlūks," by Holt.

8. P. M. Holt, *Egypt and the Fertile Crescent: A Political History, 1516–1922* (Ithaca and London: Cornell University Press, 1966), pp. 113ff.; *EI*², *s.v.* "Kays ᶜAylān: Kays and Yaman in the Ottoman Period," by Gabriel Baer and Miriam Hoexter.

9. Abdul-Karim Rafeq, *The Province of Damascus, 1723–1783* (Beirut: Khayats, 1966), pp. 100–01, 109, 113, 137, 139–42, 145–46, 171–75, 187, 206, 209–12, 223–26, 240; Karl K. Barbir, *Ottoman Rule in Damascus, 1708–1758* (Princeton, NJ: Princeton University Press, 1980), pp. 89–94.

10. Herbert L. Bodman, Jr., *Political Factions in Aleppo, 1760–1826* (Chapel Hill, NC: University of North Carolina Press, 1963), esp. pp. 55–139; Abraham Marcus, *The Middle East on the Eve of Modernity: Aleppo in the Eighteenth Century* (New York: Columbia University Press, 1989), pp. 88–92; Holt, *Egypt and the Fertile Crescent*, pp. 103, 106–11, 132, and especially pp. 132–33, where Holt seems to recognize the similarity of these factional systems.

11. Hossein Mirjafari, "The Haydari-Niᶜmati Conflicts in Iran," trans. and adapted by J. R. Perry, *Iranian Studies* 12, no. 3–4 (1979): 147–48. I am grateful to Sholeh Quinn for recommending this article and providing me with a copy.

12. Hathaway, *Politics of Households*, pp. 6–7 and the sources cited there.

13. On Ottoman Egyptian institutions, see Stanford J. Shaw, *The Financial and Administrative Organization and Development of Ottoman Egypt, 1517–1798* (Princeton, NJ: Princeton University Press, 1962), passim.; Hathaway, *Politics of Housholds*, pp. 8–9, 11–14.

14. On this point, see, for example, Ariel Salzmann, "An Ancien Régime Revisited: `Privatization' and Political Economy in the Eighteenth-Century Ottoman Empire," *Politics and Society* 21, no. 4 (1993): 399ff.; A. A. ᶜAbd al-Rahim, "Land Tenure in Egypt and Its Social Effects on Egyptian Society: 1798–1813," in *Land Tenure and Social Transformation in the Middle East*, ed., Tarif Khalidi (Beirut: American University in Beirut Press, 1984), pp. 237–48; Shaw, *Financial and Administrative Organization*, pp. 30ff.; Abdul-Rahim Abu-Husayn, "The *Iltizām* of Mansur Furaykh: A Case Study of *Iltizām* in Sixteenth-Century Syria," in *Land Tenure and Social Transformation*, pp. 249–56.

15. Barbir, *Ottoman Rule in Damascus*, chapter 3, esp. pp. 151–67.

16. Dina Rizk Khoury, *State and Provincial Society in the Ottoman Empire: Mosul, 1540–1834* (Cambridge: Cambridge University Press, 1997), pp. 47–48, 64; Jean-Louis Bacqué-Grammont, *Les Ottomanes, les Safavides, et leurs voisins: Contribution à l'histoire des relations internationales dans l'Orient islamique de 1514 à 1524* (Istanbul: Nederlands Historisch-Archaeologisch Instituut, 1987), pp. 235–71, 310ff.; Géza Dávid and Pál Fodor, eds., *Hungarian-Ottoman Military and Diplomatic Relations in the Age of Süleyman the Magnificent* (Budapest: Loránd Eötvös University, Department of Turkish Studies, Hungarian Academy of Sciences, Institute of History, 1994); idem, eds., *Ottomans, Hungarians, and*

Hapsburgs in Central Europe: The Military Confines in the Era of Ottoman Conquest (Leiden: Brill, 2000); Michael R. Hickok, *Ottoman Military Administration in Eighteenth-Century Bosnia* (Leiden: Brill, 1997), pp. 8–9.

17. Hathaway, *Politics of Households,* pp. 21, 23, 24–25, 27, 53, chapter 8, 103.

18. Mustafa Akdağ, *Celali İsyanları (1550–1603)* (Ankara: Türk Tarih Kurumu, 1963); Suraiya Faroqhi, "Crisis and Change, 1590–1699," in *An Economic and Social History of the Ottoman Empire,* ed., Halil Inalcik with Donald Quataert, part 2 (Cambridge: Cambridge University Press, 1994), pp. 433–41; idem, "Rural Society in Anatolia and the Balkans during the Sixteenth Century," *Turcica* 9 (1977): 161–96, and 11 (1979): 103–53; Halil Inalcik, "Military and Fiscal Transformation in the Ottoman Empire, 1600–1700," *Archivum Ottomanicum* 6 (1980): 286–88.

19. Ina Baghdiantz McCabe, *The Shah's Silk for Europe's Silver: The Eurasian Trade of the Julfa Armenians in Safavid Iran and India (1530–1750),* University of Pennsylvania Armenian Texts and Studies (Atlanta: Scholars Press, 1999), chapter 2; Rudolph P. Matthee, *The Politics of Trade in Safavid Iran: Silk for Silver, 1600–1730* (Cambridge: Cambridge University Press, 1999), pp. 44, 67, 74, 76, 84–89.

20. Hathaway, *Politics of Households,* pp. 44–46, 55, 62, 70–72, 80, 101–06.

21. See, for example, Suraiya Faroqhi, "Crisis and Change," pp. 413–14, 468–70, 572–73; Linda T. Darling, *Revenue Raising and Legitimacy: Tax Collection and Finance Administration in the Ottoman Empire, 1560–1660* (Leiden: Brill, 1996), pp. 2–16.

22. See, for example, Shaw, *Financial and Administrative Organization,* pp. 3–6, 36, 37. For a brief discussion of this problem, see Dror Ze᾿evi, *An Ottoman Century: The District of Jerusalem in the 1600s* (Albany: State University of New York Press, 1996), pp. 194–95.

23. Holt, *Egypt and the Fertile Crescent,* pp. 77–101; Winter, *Egyptian Society under Ottoman Rule,* pp. 49ff., 253–54; Crecelius, *Roots of Modern Egypt,* pp. 22–34; Hanna, *Making Big Money,* pp. xvi, 10, 71–72, 101, 114–16, 124, 172.

24. See, for example, Winter, *Egyptian Society under Ottoman Rule,* pp. 31, 46, 76–77, 254; Behrens-Abouseif, *Egypt's Adjustment to Ottoman Rule,* pp. 106–08, 137; Hanna, *Making Big Money,* pp. xvi, xxv, 19, 44, 95, 105, 136, 167.

25. See, for example, Gabriel Baer, "Shirbini's *Hazz al-quḥūf* and Its Significance," in *Fellah and Townsman in Ottoman Egypt: Studies in Social History,* by Gabriel Baer (London: Frank Cass and Co., 1982), pp. 3–47.

26. André Raymond, "Soldiers in Trade: The Case of Ottoman Cairo," *British Society for Middle Eastern Studies Bulletin* 18, no. 1 (1991): 16–37; Hathaway, *Politics of Households,* p. 39.

27. On the political history, see Holt, *Egypt and the Fertile Crescent*, pp. 71–101; Hathaway, *Politics of Households*, pp. 5–106; Crecelius, *Roots of Modern Egypt*, pp. 11–168; Winter, *Egyptian Society under Ottoman Rule*, chapter 2. For a more encyclopaedic perspective, see M. W. Daly, ed., *The Cambridge History of Egypt: Modern Egypt from 1517 to the End of the Twentieth Century*, vol. 2 (Cambridge: Cambridge University Press, 1998): Michael Winter, "Ottoman Egypt, 1525–1609," in *The Cambridge History of Egypt*, pp. 1–33; Jane Hathaway, "Egypt in the Seventeenth Century," in *The Cambridge History of Egypt*, pp. 34–58; Daniel Crecelius, "Egypt in the Eighteenth Century," in *The Cambridge History of Egypt*, pp. 59–86.

28. P. M. Holt, "Al-Jabarti's Introduction to the History of Ottoman Egypt," *BSOAS* 25, no. 1 (1962): 38–51.

29. Mustafa b. Ibrahim al-Maddah al-Qinali, *Majmūᶜ laṭīf* (to 1739), Vienna, Nationalbibliothek, MS Hist. Osm. 38, quoted in Holt, "Al-Jabarti's Introduction," p. 43; ᶜAbd al-Rahman b. Hasan al-Jabarti (1754–1825), *ᶜAjāʾib al-āthār fi'l-tarājim wa'l-akhbār* (Cairo: Lajnat al-Bayan al-ᶜArabi, 1958-67; hereafter *ᶜAjāʾib* [Cairo]), vol. 1: 71.

30. Al-Jabarti, *ᶜAjāʾib* (Cairo), vol. 1: 71; Ahmed Çelebi b. ᶜAbd al-Ghani, *Awḍaḥ al-ishārāt fi man tawalla Miṣr al-Qāhira min al-wuzarāʾ wa'l-bāshāt* (c. 1737), ed. A. A. ᶜAbd al-Rahim (Cairo: Maktabat al-Khanji, 1978), pp. 283–84.

31. Ahmed Kâhya ᶜAzeban al-Damurdashi, *Al-durra al-muṣāna fi akhbār al-Kināna*, British Museum, MS Or. 1073–74, p. 2; al-Jabarti, *ᶜAjāʾib* (Cairo), vol. 1: 71.

32. Winter, *Egyptian Society under Ottoman Rule*, pp. 21, 50–51, 58, 66, 102–03; P. M. Holt, "The Beylicate in Ottoman Egypt during the Seventeenth Century," *BSOAS* 24, no. 2 (1961): 226, 242.

33. Behrens-Abouseif, *Egypt's Adjustment to Ottoman Rule*, pp. 116–25.

34. Ibid., pp. 121–22.

35. Holt, "The Beylicate," pp. 226, 242.

36. Holt, "Al-Jabarti's Introduction," p. 44 n. 2; idem, *Egypt and the Fertile Crescent*, p. 80 n. 1.

37. One of the earliest criticisms of this approach with specific reference to Islamic historiography is Marilyn R. Waldman, *Toward a Theory of Historical Narrative: A Case Study in Perso-Islamicate Historiography* (Columbus, OH: Ohio State University Press, 1980), chapter 1.

38. See Hathaway, *Politics of Households*, p. 75 and n. 89.

39. See Cemal Kafadar, *Between Two Worlds: The Origins of the Ottoman State* (Berkeley: University of California Press, 1995), pp. 95–105; Halil Inalcik, "The Rise of Ottoman Historiography," in *Historians of the Middle East*, eds.,

Bernard Lewis and P. M. Holt (London: Oxford University Press, 1962), pp. 152–67; V. L. Ménage, "The Beginnings of Ottoman Historiography," in *Historians of the Middle East*, eds., Lewis and Holt, pp. 168–79.

40. See chapter 2, n. 28.

41. See Hathaway, *Politics of Households*, pp. 75–76, 116; and more generally, pp. 60–106.

42. Ismail al-Khashshab, *Tadhkira li-ahl al-baṣāʾir wa'l-abṣār maʿ wajh al-ikhtiṣār*, Paris, Bibliothèque Nationale, MS Arabe 1858; Hathaway, "Mamluk 'Revivals' and Mamluk Nostalgia in Ottoman Egypt," in *The Mamluks in Egyptian and Syrian Politics and Society*, eds., Amalia Levanoni and Michael Winter (Leiden: Brill, forthcoming).

43. On this point, see David Ayalon, "The Historian al-Jabarti and His Background," *BSOAS* 23 (1960): 223, and n. 1.

44. Al-Khashshab, *Tadhkira li-ahl al-baṣāʾir*, fo. 2r.

45. Ibid., fo. 5v.

46. Ahmad al-Rammal b. Zunbul (d. 1553), *Wāqiʿat al-Sulṭān al-Ghawrī maʿ Salīm al-ʿUthmānī*, ed. ʿAbd al-Munʿam ʿAmir (Cairo: Al-Haʾya al-Misriyya al-ʿAmma li'l-Kitab, 1997), pp. 139, 188, 202; Anonymous, *Nisba sharīfa wa-risāla munīfa tashtamil ʿalā dhikr nasab al-Jarākisa min Quraysh*, Princeton, NJ: Princeton University, Garrett Manuscripts Collection, MS 186H, fos. 17r–18v.

47. David Ayalon, "Studies in al-Jabarti I: Notes on the Transformation of Mamluk Society in Egypt under the Ottomans," *Journal of the Economic and Social History of the Orient* 3, no. 2 (1960): 148–74; 3, no. 3 (1960): 275–325; Winter, *Egyptian Society under Ottoman Rule*, pp. 47ff.; Gabriel Piterberg, "The Formation of an Ottoman Egyptian Elite in the Eighteenth Century," *International Journal of Middle East Studies* 22, no. 3 (1990): 282–83, 287.

48. On the broader theme of provincial contribution to central Ottoman culture, see Khoury, *State and Provincial Society*, chapter 6.

49. Eric Hobsbawm and Terrence Ranger, eds., *The Invention of Tradition* (Cambridge: Cambridge University Press, 1983).

50. On this point, see Nicholas Howe, *Migration and Mythmaking in Anglo-Saxon England* (New Haven, CT: Yale University Press, 1989; paperback Notre Dame, IN: University of Notre Dame Press, 2001), pp. 34–35. My thanks to Gabriel Piterberg for drawing my attention to this book and to the author for providing me with a copy.

51. M. C. Lyons, *The Arabian Epic: Heroic and Oral Story-Telling, Texts*, vol. 3 (Cambridge: Cambridge University Press, 1995), pp. 237–300.

52. See, for example, Powys Mathers, trans., *The Book of the Thousand Nights and One Night*, trans. into French by J. C. Mardrus (New York: St. Martin's Press, 1972), vol. 4: 531–37.

53. James Winny, ed. and trans., *Sir Gawain and the Green Knight*, Middle English text with facing translation (Peterborough, Ont.: Broadview Press, 1992), pp. 4, 6 (Middle English); 5, 7 (translation).

54. See, for example, al-Damurdashi, *Al-Durra al-muṣāna*, pp. 161, 176; Ahmed Çelebi, *Awḍaḥ*, pp. 386, 388, 389, 391, 396, 397, 420, 428, 431, 476, 496, 502, 508, 509, 518, 543, 565, 567, 568, 571. Even al-Jabarti incorporates one of these; see *ᶜAjāʾib* (Cairo), vol. 1: 67.

55. Holt, "Al-Jabarti's Introduction," p. 51. See also Waldman, *Toward a Theory of Historical Narrative*, p. 11.

56. On the Damurdashi chronicles, see Holt, "Al-Jabarti's Introduction;" idem, "Ottoman Egypt (1517–1798): An Account of Arabic Historical Sources," in *Political and Social Change in Modern Egypt*, ed., P. M. Holt (Oxford and London: Oxford University Press, 1968), pp. 3–12; Daniel N. Crecelius, "Ahmad Shalabi ibn ᶜAbd al-Ghani and Ahmad Katkhuda ᶜAzaban al-Damurdashi: Two Sources for al-Jabarti's *ᶜAjāʾib al-āthār fī'l-tarājim wa'l-akhbār*," in *Eighteenth Century Egypt: The Arabic Manuscript Sources*, ed., Daniel N. Crecelius (Claremont, CA: Regina Books, 1990), pp. 89–102.

Appendix Notes: Origin Myths of the Factions

1. Ahmed Çelebi b. ᶜAbd al-Ghani, *Awḍaḥ al-ishārāt fī man tawalla Miṣr al-Qāhira min al-wuzarāʾ wa'l-bāshāt*, ed., A. A. ᶜAbd al-Rahim (Cairo: Maktabat al-Khanji, 1978), pp. 283–84 (translation author's).

2. Mustafa b. Ibrahim al-Maddah al-Qinali, *Majmūᶜ laṭīf*, Vienna, Nationalbibliothek, MS Hist. Osm. 38, as reproduced in Holt, "Al-Jabarti's Introduction," pp. 42–43 (my translation differs slightly from Holt's).

3. Anonymous, *Kitāb al-durra al-munṣāna fī waqāīᶜ [sic] al-Kināna*, University of Oxford, Bodleian Library, MS Bruce 43, as reproduced in Holt, "Al-Jabarti's Introduction," pp. 43–44 (my translation differs slightly from Holt's).

4. Ahmed Kâhya ᶜAzeban al-Damurdashi, *Al-durra al-muṣāna fī akhbār al-Kināna*, British Museum, MS Or. 1073, p. 2 (translation author's). See also Holt, "Al-Jabarti's Introduction," pp. 44–45.

Chapter 1: Bilateral Factionalism in Ottoman Egypt

1. On the Mamluk system, see David Ayalon, "Aspects of the Mamluk Phenomenon," parts 1–2, *Der Islam* 53 (1976): 196–225; 54 (1977): 1–32; idem, *L'esclavage du mamelouk* (Jerusalem: Magnes Press, 1951); idem, "Mamlūk," *EI*[2]; idem, "Studies on the Structure of the Mamluk Army," parts 1–3, *BSOAS* 15, no. 2 (1953): 203–28 and 448–76; 16, no. 1 (1954): 57–90.

2. See Ayalon, *L'esclavage du mamelouke*, pp. 30ff.; idem, "Mamlūk," *EI*[2]; Robert Irwin, "Factions in Medieval Egypt," *Journal of the Royal Asiatic Society* 1986, no. 2: 228–46; idem, *The Middle East in the Middle Ages: The Early Mamluk Sultanate, 1250–1382* (London and Sydney: Croom Helm, 1986), pp. 88–90, 152–56.

3. Hathaway, *Politics of Households*, pp. 17–27; idem, "The Military Household in Ottoman Egypt," pp. 41, 43–47.

4. Hathaway, *Politics of Households*, chapter 4; idem, "The Household of Hasan Ağa Bilifya: An Assessment of Elite Politics in Seventeenth-Century Ottoman Egypt," *Turcica* 27 (1995): 135–51.

5. Ahmed Çelebi, *Awḍaḥ*, pp. 369–70, 372, 397, 464, 476, 477, 486, 504, 523, 535, 554, 569.

6. Al-Jabarti, *ʿAjāʾib al-āthār fī'l-tarājim wa'l-akhbār*, 3 vols. (Beirut: Dar al-Jil, 1983; hereafter *ʿAjāʾib* [Beirut]), vol. 1: 486.

7. Hathaway, *Politics of Households*, pp. 18–20; Ehud R. Toledano, "The Emergence of Ottoman-Local Elites in the Middle East and North Africa (1700–1900): A Framework for Research," in *Middle Eastern Politics and Ideas: A History from Within—Essays in Honour of Albert Hourani*, eds., Ilan Pappé and Moshe Maʾoz (London and New York: I. B. Tauris, 1997), pp. 156–57. *Kapı* was distinct from *hane*, the basic family production unit among the masses of taxpaying reaya: see Halil Inalcik, "The Ottoman State: Economy and Society, 1300–1600," in *An Economic and Social History of the Ottoman Empire*, ed., Halil Inalcik with Donald Quataert, part 1 (Cambridge: Cambridge University Press, 1994), chapter 6.

8. Hathaway, *Politics of Households*, p. 20.

9. Leslie P. Peirce, *The Imperial Harem: Women and Sovereignty in the Ottoman Empire* (New York and Oxford: Oxford University Press, 1993), pp. 6–12. Even the Assyrian palace at Nineveh was divided into an interior (*bītanu*, or our house), and an exterior (*bābanu*, or our doorway). See John Malcolm Russell, *Sennacherib's Palace Without Rival at Nineveh* (Chicago: University of Chicago Press, 1991). I am grateful to Professor Howard Crane for this reference.

10. *EI*[2], *s.v.* "Mamlūk," by Ayalon.

11. Al-Damurdashi, *Al-Durra al-muṣāna*, p. 2; al-Jabarti, *ʿAjāʾib* (Cairo), vol. 1: 70. For similar examples from the medieval Hadramawt, southern Egypt, and seventeenth-century Ottoman naval warfare, see respectively R. B. Serjeant, *The South Arabian Hunt* (London: Luzac, 1976), p. 38; Martin Hinds and Victor Ménage, *Qasr Ibrim in the Ottoman Period: Turkish and Further Arabic Documents* (London: Egypt Exploration Society, 1991), Arabic Text no. 78, pp. 54–55; Kâtib Çelebi, *Tuḥfet ül-kibār fī esfār ül-biḥār* (Istanbul: Matbaʿat-i Bahriye, 1329/1911), pp. 62, 73, 75, 76, 77, 107, 130; Fevzi Kurtoğlu, *1877–1878 Türk-Rus Harbinde Deniz Hareketleri* (Istanbul: Deniz Matbaası, 1935), pp. 26, 47. I am

grateful to Colin Heywood for drawing my attention to the second source and to William Blair for drawing my attention to the last two sources.

12. For example, Jamal al-Ghitani, ed., *Sīrat al-Ẓāhir Baybars*, 50 parts in 5 vols. (Cairo: Al-Haʾya al-Misriyya al-ʿAmma li'l-Kitab, 1996), vol. 1: 182, 523, 689, the last referring to *farīq fī'l-janna wa-farīq fī'l-saʿīr* (the faction in heaven and the faction in hell); Kâtib Çelebi, *Tuḥfet ül-kibār*, p. 124; Wilferd Madelung, *Religious Trends in Early Islamic Iran* (New York: The Persian Heritage Foundation, Bibliotheca Persica, 1988), pp. 26–38.

13. See, however, Roy Mottahedeh, *Loyalty and Leadership in an Early Islamic Society* (Princeton, NJ: Princeton University Press, 1980), p. 159, where he notes that in the Buyid period (945–1055) in Iraq and Iran, "a faction is sometimes called a *farīq*, 'division,' but is more often called a *ṭāʾifah*," and cites an Arabic source in which the words are used interchangeably (n. 61).

14. Mehmed b. Yusuf al-Hallaq, *Tārīḫ-i Mıṣr-ı Ḳāhire* (to 1715), Istanbul University Library, T.Y. 628, fo. 189r; al-Jabarti, *ʿAjāʾib* (Cairo), vol. 1: 71.

15. Holt, *Egypt and the Fertile Crescent*, pp. 90–91; Hathaway, *Politics of Households*, chapters 4–5.

16. Al-Jabarti, *ʿAjāʾib* (Cairo), vol. 2: 202–03, 286–87, 290, 306–07; Holt, *Egypt and the Fertile Crescent*, p. 94; Crecelius, *Roots of Modern Egypt*, pp. 50–51, 54–58; Hathaway, *Politics of Households*, p. 85 n. 132.

17. *EI*^{2}, *s.v.* "Mamlūks," by P. M. Holt.

18. Anonymous, *Akhbār al-nuwwāb min dawlat Āl ʿUthmān min ḥīn istawla ʿalayhā al-sulṭān Salīm Khān* (to 1715), Istanbul, Topkapı Palace Library, MS Hazine 1623, fo. 55r.; al-Jabarti, *ʿAjāʾib* (Cairo), vol. 1: 267.

19. Dante Alighieri, *Inferno*, ed. and trans. Elio Zappulla (New York: Pantheon Books, 1998), pp. 97–101. These two blocs themselves grew out of multiple neighborhood rivalries; see Lansing, *The Florentine Magnates*, pp. 181–84.

20. Mirjafari, "Haydari-Niʿmati Conflicts."

21. Ibid., p. 152: the Haydaris with the Fuladlu, the Niʿmatis with the Qojabiglu (Kocabeylu), both branches of the Shahiseven tribe.

22. Cameron, *Circus Factions*, pp. 12, 45–73, 231.

23. Ibid., pp. 41, 191, 198–99, 201–13, 314–17.

24. Ibid., pp. 215–22, 234–38, 244–48, 308.

25. Ibid., pp. 65–70.

26. Ibid., pp. 75–79, 296; Speros Vryonis, Jr., "Byzantine Circus Factions and Islamic *Futuwwa* Organizations," *Byzantinische Zeitschrift* 58 (1965): 47–48, 56. See also Cameron's critique of Vryonis, *Circus Factions*, pp. 341–43. Despite

the assertions of some scholars, neither faction appears to have represented certain social classes or exhibited heterodox religious tendencies, nor did either act as a political party: see Cameron, *Circus Factions*, pp. 80–86, 126–53, 271–96. Patricia Crone makes strikingly similar arguments about Qays and Yemen under the Umayyads; see Crone, "Qays and Yemen of the Umayyad Period," especially p. 43.

27. Vryonis, "Circus Factions and Islamic *Futuwwa* Organizations," pp. 52–53; Cameron, *Circus Factions*, pp. 76, 108–09.

28. Vryonis, "Circus Factions and Islamic *Futuwwa* Organizations," p. 57; Cameron, *Circus Factions*, pp. 182–83.

29. Quoted in Vryonis, "Circus Factions and Islamic *Futuwwa* Organizations," p. 58; Cameron, *Circus Factions*, p. 258.

30. Cameron, *Circus Factions*, p. 308.

31. Irfan Shahid, *Byzantium and the Arabs in the Fifth Century* (Washington, DC: Dumbarton Oaks Research Library and Collection, 1989), pp. 338–43. Shahid argues that on purely linguistic grounds, the southern Arabians were not, strictly speaking, Arabs. Interestingly, this is also the opinion of the Yemeni chronicler Ibn al-Dayba^c with regard to the Himyarites; see ^cAbd al-Rahman b. ^cAli b. al-Dayba^c, *Tuḥfat al-zaman fī faḍā^ɔil ahl al-Yaman*, ed., Sayyid Kusrawi Hasan (Beirut: Dar al-Kutub al-^cIlmiyya, 1992), p. 29. See also ^cAbd al-Rahman b. Muhammad b. Khaldun (1332–1406), *The Muqaddimah: An Introduction to History*, trans. Franz Rosenthal, abridged and ed. N. J. Dawood (Princeton, NJ: Princeton University Press, 1967), pp. 99–100, 115.

32. 1 Kings 10 is the well-known story of the Queen of Sheba's visit to the court of King Solomon. On archaeological and epigraphic evidence for the kingdom of Sheba/Saba^ɔ, see Muhammad ^cAbd al-Qadir Bafaqih, *L'Unification du Yémen antique: La lutte entre Saba^ɔ, Himyar, et le Hadramawt du Ier au IIIème siècle de l'ère chrétienne* (Paris: Librairie Orientaliste Paul Geuthner, 1990), pp. 139–56.

33. John Noble Wilford, "Ruins in Yemeni Desert Mark Route of Frankincense Trade," *New York Times*, 28 January 1997, pp. B9–10.

34. Shahid, *Byzantium and the Arabs in the Fifth Century*, p. 175; idem, *Byzantium and the Arabs in the Sixth Century* (Washington, DC: Dumbarton Oaks Research Library and Collection, 1989), part 1, pp. 53–54, 144–47; part 2, pp. 728–31. The Ethiopians, and likewise many Yemeni Christians, were Monophysites. On the Himyarites generally, see Bafaqih, *L'unification du Yémen antique*, pp. 175–93. For the story of the last Himyarite king, Dhu Nuwas, converting to Judaism, see Muhammad b. Ishaq (d. ca. 768), *The Life of Muhammad*, ed. ^cAbd al-Malik b. Hisham (d. 834), trans. and with an introduction and notes by Alfred Guillaume (Lahore, Karachi, Dacca: Oxford University Press, Pakistan Branch, 1955, 1968, 1970), pp. 14, 17–20.

35. Wendell Phillips, *Qataban and Sheba: Exploring the Ancient Kingdoms on the Biblical Spice Routes of Arabia* (New York: Harcourt, Brace and Co., 1955), pp. 221–23. The dam was erected as early as the eighth century B.C.E. See also "Ibn Hisham's Notes" to Ibn Ishaq, *Life of Muhammad*, pp. 693–94. The Qur'an refers to the dam break as divine punishment for the "Sabians'" ingratitude to God for the bounty of their land; see sura 34:15–16.

36. Shahid, *Byzantium and the Arabs in the Sixth Century*, part 1, pp. 365–67 (where he verifies the date of the invasion), 547.

37. Crone, "Qays and Yemen of the Umayyad Period," pp. 2–3, 44–53. On the Mudar, see Ibn Khaldun, *Muqaddimah*, pp. 99, 107, 115.

38. Matthew S. Gordon, *The Breaking of a Thousand Swords: A History of the Turkish Military of Samarra, A.H. 200–235/815–889 C.E.* (Albany: State University of New York Press, 2001), pp. 37–38, 185 n. 254.

39. Holt, *Egypt and the Fertile Crescent*, chapter 8.

40. Miriam Hoexter, "The Role of the Qays and Yaman Factions in Local Political Divisions: Jabal Nablus Compared with the Judean Hills in the First Half of the Nineteenth Century," *Asian and African Studies* 9 (1973): 249–311; Salim Tamari, "Factionalism and Class Formation in Recent Palestinian History," in *Studies in the Economic and Social History of Palestine in the Nineteenth and Twentieth Centuries*, ed., Roger Owen (London: Macmillan; Oxford: St. Antony's, 1982), pp. 177–202; Baruch Kimmerling and Joel S. Migdal, *Palestinians: The Making of a People* (New York: The Free Press, 1993), pp. 7, 40–41, 72.

41. Khalid Yahya Blankinship, *The End of the Jihad State: The Reign of Hisham Ibn ʿAbd al-Malik and the Collapse of the Umayyads* (Albany: State University of New York Press, 1994), p. 46; *EI*[2], *s.v.* "Kays ʿAylān: Kays and Yaman in the Ottoman Period," by Baer and Hoexter.

42. Ibn al-Daybaʿ, *Kitāb Qurrat al-ʿuyūn bi-akhbār al-Yaman al-maymūn*, ed., Muhammad b. ʿAli al-Akwaʿ al-Hiwali, 2 vols. (Cairo: Matbaʿat al-Saʿada, 1977), vol. 2: 189. *EI*[1], *s.v.* "Ḥāshid and Bakīl," by J. Schleifer, cites an ancient Himyarite town called, appropriately, *Ḥamr*; according to al-Hamdani, it was the birthplace of the great third-century C.E. *tubbaʿ* Asʿad al-Himyari.

43. Al-Damurdashi, *Al-Durra al-muṣāna*, p. 2; al-Jabarti, *ʿAjāʾib* (Cairo) vol. 1: 70–71.

44. Shahid, *Byzantium and the Arabs in the Fifth Century*, pp. 338, 340.

45. Thus, for example, the popular Ottoman-era oral narrative of the life of Baybars al-Bunduqdari, founder of the Mamluk sultanate, refers to the Prophet Muhammad as *walad ʿAdnān*, or son of ʿAdnan; for one of many examples, see *Sīrat al-Ẓāhir Baybars*, vol. 2: 808. Meanwhile, an Arab nationalist manifesto published at the beginning of World War I appealed to Arabs as "sons of Qahtan and descendants of ʿAdnan": Anonymous, "Announcement

to the Arabs, Sons of Qahtan," in *Al-Qaḍiyya al-ʿarabiyya* by Ahmad ʿIzzat al-Aʿzami, 4: 108-17, reprinted in *Arab Nationalism: An Anthology,* ed., Sylvia Haim (Berkeley: University of California Press, 1962, 1976), pp. 83-88.

46. See, for example, Anonymous, *Nisba sharīfa,* fo. 19r–v; Ibn Khaldun, *Muqaddimah,* pp. 59–61. Irfan Shahid provides an extensive discussion of "Ishmaelism;" see Shahid, *Byzantium and the Arabs in the Fifth Century,* pp. 155–59, 166–80, 332–50, 382–83.

47. Anonymous, *Nisba sharīfa,* fo. 19r–v.

48. P. M. Holt, "The Exalted Lineage of Ridwan Bey: Some Observations on a Seventeenth-Century Mamluk Genealogy," *BSOAS* 22, no. 2 (1959): 221–30.

49. For Ridvan al-Faqari's biography, see al-Jabarti, *ʿAjāʾib* (Cairo), vol. 1: 234, 237.

50. Genesis 4: 1–16; 25: 21–34; 27: 1–45; 32–33; Robert Graves, *The Greek Myths,* 2 vols., revised ed. (London: Penguin Books, 1960), vol. 1: 237–38.

51. Mirjafari, "Haydari-Niʿmati Conflicts," pp. 148–49.

52. Muhammad b. Jarir al-Tabari, *The History of al-Tabari,* vol. 31, *The War between Brothers,* trans. Michael Fishbein (Albany: State University of New York Press, 1992). For an example of such a portent, see idem, *Al-Tabari: The Early ʿAbbasi Empire,* vol. 2, *The Son and Grandsons of al-Mansur; the Reigns of al-Mahdi, al-Hadi, and Harun al-Rashid,* trans. John Alden Williams (Cambridge: Cambridge University Press, 1989), p. 298.

53. Sudun al-ʿAjami was killed after the battle of Marj Dabiq in Syria, where Selim defeated Qansuh al-Ghuri, and could therefore not have encountered Selim in Cairo. Furthermore, he had only one son, Sharaf al-Din Yunus. See Muhammad b. Ahmad b. Iyas, *An Account of the Ottoman Conquest of Egypt in the Year* A.H. *922 (*A.D. *1516),* trans. W.H. Salmon (London: Royal Asiatic Society, 1921), pp. 112–15; idem, *Journal d'un bourgeois du Caire,* trans. Gaston Wiet, 2 vols. (Paris: Armand Colin, 1955), vol. 1: 341, 344; vol. 2: 2, 39.

54. Ahmed Çelebi, *Awḍaḥ,* pp. 283–84; al-Jabarti, *ʿAjāʾib* (Cairo), vol. 1: 67–71.

55. Al-Damurdashi, *Al-Durra al-muṣāna,* p. 2.

56. Evliya Çelebi (c. 1611–c. 1682), *Narrative of Travels in Europe, Asia, and Africa,* trans. Josef von Hammer-Purgstall, 2 vols. in 3 (London: Parbury, Allen, 1834; reprint Johnson Reprint Corp., 1968), vol. 1: 169, 170, 173.

57. Two of the most distinctive are that of the Medici, bearing six balls, and that of the Visconti, showing a serpent devouring a child (personal observation in Florence, Siena, and Milan).

58. Fulcher of Chartres, *Chronicle of the First Crusade*, trans. Martha Evelyn McGinty (Philadelphia: University of Pennsylvania Press, 1941), p. 18; Stephen Runciman, *The First Crusade*, abridged ed. (Cambridge: Cambridge University Press, 1980), p. 62; *EI*², *s.v.* "Hilāl," by Richard Ettinghausen.

59. On Mamluk blazons, see L. A. Mayer, *Saracenic Heraldry: A Survey* (Oxford: Clarendon Press, 1953).

60. As quoted in Holt, "Al-Jabarti's Introduction," pp. 42–43; my translation differs very slightly from Holt's.

61. Mirjafari, "Haydari-Niᶜmati Conflicts," pp. 137–44.

62. Mottahedeh, *Loyalty and Leadership*, pp. 158–67.

63. Robert C. Davis, *The War of the Fists: Popular Culture and Public Violence in Late Renaissance Venice* (New York and Oxford: Oxford University Press, 1994).

64. Mirjafari, "Haydari-Niᶜmati Conflicts," pp. 144, 146, 147, 151, 153–54.

65. See, for example, Cameron, *Circus Factions*, pp. 12, 19, 67–70, 194–96, 201–13.

66. *EI*², *s.v.* "Kays ᶜAylān: Kays and Yaman in the Ottoman Period," by Baer and Hoexter.

67. Evliya Çelebi, *Narrative of Travels*, vol. 1, part 2, section 80. The procession in question celebrated Murad IV's reconquest of Baghdad in 1638.

68. Ibid., vol. 1, part 2, section 78.

69. For a striking illustration of this phenomenon in modern Egypt, see Dwight F. Reynolds, *Heroic Poets, Poetic Heroes: The Ethnography of Performance in an Arabic Oral Epic Tradition* (Ithaca and London: Cornell University Press, 1995), pp. 59–61. I am grateful to Stephen Dale for drawing my attention to this source.

70. Metin Kunt, "Ethnic-Regional (*Cins*) Solidarity in the Seventeenth-Century Ottoman Establishment," *International Journal of Middle East Studies* 5 (1974): 233–39.

71. Al-Hallaq, *Tārīḫ-i Mıṣr-ı Ḳāhire*, fo. 157v.; Ahmed Çelebi, *Awḍaḥ*, p. 155. P. M. Holt interpreted the ambiguous word *ajnabī*, or "foreigner," as connoting someone from "outside the Mamluk system" (Holt, "Beylicate," p. 225). A more likely connotation is, on the one hand, a stranger or an outsider—someone who suddenly entered Egypt's military elite from outside—or, on the other hand, a foreigner in the modern sense of the word: in this case, a Bosnian as opposed to a Circassian or other Caucasian. See Gyula Kaldy-Nágy, "The 'Strangers' (*Ecnebiler*) in the Sixteenth-Century Ottoman Military Organization," in *Between the Danube and the Caucasus: Oriental Sources*

on the History of the Peoples of Central and South-Eastern Europe, ed., György Kara (Budapest: Akadémiai Kiadó, 1987), pp. 165–69.

72. Benedict Anderson, *Imagined Communities: Reflections on the Origin and Spread of Nationalism*, revised and extended ed. (London and New York: Verso, 1991 [1983]), chapter 2.

73. Hathaway, *Politics of Households*, pp. 75–76.

74. Ibid., pp. 73–74.

75. Amalia Levanoni's recent research demonstrates, however, that in the Circassian phase of the Mamluk sultanate, two *de facto* factions took shape under the *laqab*s Zahiri and Ashrafi; household heads exploited fictive patron-client ties in order to claim one of the two sobriquets.

Chapter 2: Bir Varmış, Bir Yokmuş

1. I am grateful to Devin Stewart for drawing my attention to the Persian expression.

2. For folklore types, see the classic study by Antti Aarne, *The Types of the Folktale*, trans. and enlarged by Stith Thompson (Helsinki: Academia Scientarum Fennica, 1961).

3. I use the terms "folkloric," "folklore," and "folktales" as layperson's terms, not intending to invoke the theoretical issues attached to the academic discipline of folklore studies. The terms "popular histories" and "popular narratives" could also be applied to the sorts of stories I discuss here.

4. Al-Damurdashi, *al-Durra al-muṣana*, p. 1.

5. The "brothers" he mentions may be Sufis; *ikhwān* would not typically be used to specify soldiers. On al-Damurdashi's Sufi connections, see below, n. 50.

6. For a plot synopsis, see John W. Freeman, *Stories of the Great Operas* (New York and London: W. W. Norton and Co., 1984), pp. 465–67.

7. Samuel Peterson, "*Taʿziyeh*: Parts and Plays in Worship," in *Taʿziyeh: Ritual and Popular Belief in Iran: Essays Prepared for a Drama Festival and Conference Held at Trinity College, Hartford Seminary, April 30–May 2, 1988*, ed., Milla Cozart Riggio (Hartford, CT: Trinity College, 1988), p. 25. On the *taʿziyeh* in general, see this collection and Peter J. Chelkowski, *Taʿziyeh: Ritual and Drama in Iran* (New York: New York University Press, 1979). On the *taʿziyeh* in Trinidad, see Frank J. Koram and Peter J. Chelkowski, "Community Process and the Performance of Muharram Observances in Trinidad," *The Drama Review* 38, no. 2 (1994): 150–75.

8. Bafaqih, *L'Unification du Yémen antique*, chapter 2.

9. Robert L. Playfair, *A History of Arabia Felix or Yemen*, (1859; reprint, Amsterdam: Philo Press; St. Leonards: Ad Orientem, Ltd., 1970), p. 47.

10. Ibn Ishaq, *Life of Muhammad*, pp. 7, 9; Ibn Khaldun, *Muqaddimah*, pp.14–16; Ibn al-Daybaᶜ, *Tuḥfat al-zaman*, p. 29; Anonymous, *Taʾrīkh Ṣanᶜāʾ [al-] Yaman*, Istanbul, Süleymaniye Library, MS Ayasofya 3048, fos. 165r, 167v, 169v; Rumuzi, *Tārīḫ-i fetḥ-i Yemen* (to 1568), Istanbul: Topkapı Palace Library, MS Revan 1297, fo. 28r; *EI*², *s.v.* "Kaᶜba," by A.J. Wensinck-J. Jomier. This ruler (Asᶜad al-Himyari) is probably the "Tubbaᶜ" mentioned in the Qurʾan, 44:37 and 50:14.

11. *EI*², *s.v.* "al-Basūs," by J. W. Fück; *s.v.* "Kulayb b. Rabīᶜa," by Giorgio Levi Della Vida. See also Reynold A. Nicholson, *A Literary History of the Arabs* (Cambridge: Cambridge University Press, 1969), pp. 55–61; Adel Sulayman Gamal, "The Beginnings of Classical Arabic Poetry," in *Literary Heritage of Classical Islam: Arabic and Islamic Studies in Honor of James A. Bellamy*, ed., Mustansir Mir (Princeton, NJ: The Darwin Press, Inc., 1993), pp. 45–54. I am grateful to Adel Sulayman and Irfan Shahid for drawing my attention to this connection, and to Adel Sulayman for recommending the last two sources. See also Mathers, trans., *The Thousand Nights and One Night*, pp. 459–61.

12. *EI*², *s.v.* "Kulayb b. Rabīᶜa," by Levi della Vida.

13. Lyons, *The Arabian Epic*, vol. 3: 651–60.

14. Ibid., vol. 3:. 651. As P. M. Holt notes, one of these manuscripts has *al-wazīr*; see Holt, "Al-Jabarti's Introduction," p. 43 and n. 4.

15. Shahid, *Byzantium and the Arabs in the Fifth Century*, pp. 338–39.

16. *EI*², *s.v.* "Kulayb b. Rabīᶜa," by Levi della Vida.

17. M. A. Shaban, *The ᶜAbbasid Revolution* (Cambridge: Cambridge University Press, 1970); Blankinship, *End of the Jihad State*, pp. 66–67, 98–99, 126, 179.

18. *EI*², *s.v.* "Bakr," by W. Caskel; *s.v.* "Kays ᶜAylān," by W. Montgomery Watt. Two alternative but less likely possibilities are (1) that "Akri" is really the Ottoman spelling of the Turkish *eğri*, "crooked"—in which case, *Akrī wa-Qaysī* might really be *eğri ve kısa*, Turkish for "crooked and short," a possible reference to the Faqaris' Dhu'l-Faqar banner (see chapter 11), although *kısa* is typically written with a *kef* rather than a *qaf*; (2) that "Akri" refers to the Byzantine border warriors known as *akritoi*, the most famous of whom was the legendary half-Arab/half-Greek Digenes Akrites.

19. *Sīrat Banī Hilāl al-kubrā*, *Taghrībāt Banī Hilāl*, and *Sīrat Banī Hilāl fī qiṣṣat Abī Zayd al-Hilālī wa'l-Nāᶜisa wa-Zayd al-ᶜAjjāj*: Lyons, *The Arabian Epic*, vol. 3: 237–300; *EI*², *s.v.* "Hilāl: The Saga of the Banī Hilāl," by J. Schleifer; Reynolds, *Heroic Poets*, pp. 13–18.

20. Edward W. Lane, *An Account of the Manners and Customs of the Modern Egyptians*, 5th ed., ed., Edward Stanley Poole, new introduction by John Manchip White (New York: Dover Publications, 1973), pp. 364–65.

21. *EI*², *s.v.* "Hilāl," by Hadi Roger Idris. Evliya Çelebi claims that several Hilali chieftains were buried in the Upper Egyptian district of al-Bahnasa; see *Evliya Çelebi Seyahatnamesi*, ed., Mehmed Zillîoğlu, vol. 10 (Istanbul: Üçdal Neşriyat, 1966), p. 695. All references to vol. 10 are to this edition.

22. *EI*², *s.v.* "Hilāl," by Idris. The epic in question is *Sīrat al-amīra dhāt al-himma*; see Lyons, *The Arabian Epic*, vol. 3: 296, 301, 380, 398, 446–47, 499–500. See also Lane, *Manners and Customs*, pp. 414–20. Lane notes that this epic, along with the tales of Sayf b. Dhi Yazan and the *1001 Nights*, was no longer frequently recited because of the lack of copies—which suggests that by this time, the tales were derived from a written source.

23. *EI*², *s.v.* "Hilāl," by Idris. The other two subdivisions were Athbaj and Riyah. See also Reynolds, *Heroic Poets*, pp. 14, 70–71.

24. Lyons, *The Arabian Epic*, vol. 3: 287, 292; *EI*², *s.v.* "Hilāl: The Saga of the Banī Hilāl," by J. Schleifer. See also Lane, *Manners and Customs*, pp. 391–94.

25. These events are described in some detail in Irwin, *The Middle East in the Middle Ages*, pp. 22–34. This section of the present chapter benefits from the comments and criticisms of Reuven Amitai-Preiss.

26. Ibid., pp. 62–65.

27. See Amalia Levanoni, *A Turning Point in Mamluk History: The Third Reign of al-Nasir Muhammad ibn Qalawun (1310–1341)* (Leiden: Brill, 1994).

28. Reuven Amitai-Press, *Mongols and Mamluks: The Mamluk-Ilkhanid War, 1260–1281* (Cambridge: Cambridge University Press, 1995), pp. 146–47; Amina A. Elbendary, "The Sultan, the Tyrant, and the Hero: Changing Medieval Perceptions of al-Zahir Baybars," *Mamluk Studies Review* 5 (2001): 150. At least two versions of the *Sīra* have been or are being published: Jamal al-Ghitani, ed., *Sīrat al-Ẓāhir Baybars*, 50 parts in 5 vols. (Cairo: Al-Haʾya al-Misriyya al-ʿAmma li'l-Kitab, 1996); Georges Bohas and Jean-Patrick Guillaume, eds., *Le Roman de Baïbars*, 11 vols. (Paris: Actes Sud/Sindbad, 1985–98). The Topkapı Palace Library also owns two unpublished manuscripts, MS Revan 1606–07. See also Lane, *Manners and Customs*, pp. 400ff. Lane himself bought a manuscript, which he judged to be roughly a century old, in which case it would have dated to about the mid-eighteenth century.

29. See, for example, *Sīrat al-Ẓāhir Baybars*, vol. 2: 821.

30. *Sīrat al-Ẓāhir Baybars*, vol. 1: 277, 295, 703–04; vol. 3: 1480–87.

31. David Ayalon, "The Wafidiyya in the Mamluk Kingdom," *Islamic Culture* 25 (1951): 94–97. As Ayalon points out, A. N. Poliak erroneously held that the Mamluks were vassals of the Golden Horde Mongols, and that Baybars named his son after the Golden Horde ruler Berke Khan b. Jushi.

32. Irwin, *The Middle East in the Middle Ages*, pp. 17–18, 33, 49.

33. *Sīrat al-Ẓāhir Baybars*, vol. 2: 783, 823–26, 992, 1016. This is also the case in the manuscript Lane consulted; see *Manners and Customs*, p. 412.

34. *Les Enfances de Baïbars, Roman de Baïbars*, trans. and annotated by Georges Bohas and Jean-Patrick Guillaume, vol. 1 (Paris: Actes Sud/Sindbad, 1985), pp. 37–38. I am grateful to Linda Northrup for relaying the translated text of this incident. In the manuscript summarized by Lyons, it is "ᶜAla al-Din," another mamluk, who complains of Baybars' physical maladies; see *The Arabian Epic*, vol. 3: 82.

35. For example, *Le Procès du moine maudit, Roman de Baïbars*, trans. and annotated by Georges Bohas and Jean-Patrick Guillaume, vol. 10 (Paris: Actes Sud/Sindbad, 1998), p. 148. See also Irwin, *The Middle East in the Middle Ages*, p. 64.

36. On ᶜAntar, see Lyons, *The Arabian Epic*, vol. 3: 17–76. For instances of reference to the *Shahname* in an oral narrative, see ibid., vol. 3: 377, 399; Warren S. Walker, ed., *A Turkish Folktale: The Art of Behçet Mahir* (New York and London: Garland Publishing, Inc., 1996), pp. 3–8, 11–12.

37. Holt, "Al-Jabarti's Introduction," p. 43 n. 1.

38. André Raymond, "Une 'Révolution' au Caire sous les Mamelouks: La Crise de 1123/1711," *Annales Islamologiques* 6 (1966): 97.

39. This is especially true of Ismail Bey b. ᶜIvaz: for example, al-Damurdashi, *Al-Durra al-muṣāna*, pp. 199, 266, 272–75.

40. Ahmed Çelebi, *Awḍaḥ*, pp. 283–84.

41. On this point, see Hathaway, *Politics of Households*, pp. 44–46, 101–03.

42. See ibid., pp. 57, 61–62, 71 and n. 79, 103–05.

43. I am grateful to Beth Baron and Magda al-Nowaihi for pointing this out.

44. Konstantin Mihalowicz, *Memoirs of a Janissary*, trans. Benjamin Stolz, historical commentary and notes by Svat Soucek (Ann Arbor, MI: Dept. of Slavic Languages and Literatures, University of Michigan, 1975), pp. 7, 9.

45. See chapter 11, below; Qurʾan, sura 8; "Ibn Hisham's Notes" to Ibn Ishaq, *Life of Muhammad*, p. 756 n. 616; al-Tabari, *History of al-Tabari*, vol. 9: *The Last Years of the Prophet*, ed. and trans. Ismail K. Poonawala (Albany: State University of New York Press, 1990), p. 154 n. 1049, and the sources cited there; *EI*[2], *s.v.* "Badr," by W. Montgomery Watt; *s.v.* "Dhū'l-Faḳār," by E. Mittwoch; John Renard, *Islam and the Heroic Image: Themes in Literature and the Visual Arts* (Columbia, SC: University of South Carolina Press, 1993), pp. 105, 207, 295 n. 12.

46. See, for example, Lyons, *The Arabian Epic*, vol. 3: 78, 154–55, 157–58, 164, 167, 179, 207–08, 212, 216, 243, 587, 605–09, 615, 622, 624, 633, 634, 635, 639.

47. On presentations of ᶜAli, see Jan Knappert, *Islamic Legends: Stories of the Heroes, Saints, and Prophets of Islam*, 2 vols. (Leiden: E. J. Brill, 1985), vol. 1: 223–27, 238–42, 248, 250–68, 275, 280–83.

48. Muhyi-yi Gülşeni, *Menâḳib-i İbrâhîm-i Gülşenî ve Şemleli-zâde Aḥmed Efendi, Şive-i Ṭarîḳat-i Gülşenîye*, ed., Tahsin Yazıcı (Ankara: Türk Tarih Kurumu Basımevi, 1982), pp. 367, 370, 373–80, 397, 400, 406, 443–49; Ibn Zunbul, *Wāqiᶜat*, p. 178; B. G. Martin, "A Short History of the Khalwati Order of Dervishes," in *Scholars, Saints, and Sufis: Muslim Religious Institutions since 1500*, ed., Nikki R. Keddie (Berkeley: University of California Press, 1972), p. 296. See also Lane, *Manners and Customs*, pp. 243–44; J. Spencer Trimingham, *The Sufi Orders in Islam*, with a new foreword by John O. Voll (New York and Oxford: Oxford University Press, 1998 [1971, 1973]), pp. 74–78.

49. Evliya Çelebi, *Seyahatname*, vol. 10: 415–16; see also pp. 504, 613.

50. See al-Damurdashi, *Al-Durra al-muṣāna*, pp. 161, 165; Ernst Bannerth, "La Khalwatiyya en Égypte: Quelques aspects de la vie d'une confrérie," *Mélange de l'Institut Dominicain d'Études Orientales* 8 (1960): 1–74; Martin, "A Short History of the Khalwati Order of Dervishes," pp. 290–97.

51. On this point, see Walker, ed., *The Art of Behçet Mahir*, pp. xxff.

52. For example, al-Damurdashi, *Al-Durra al-muṣāna*, pp. 125, 142, 198–99, 219, 239–40, 259–60, 348–49, 402, 429, 439, 482, 514–15, 526, 546, 563, 585; Muhammad ᶜAbd al-Muᶜti al-Ishaqi, *Kitāb akhbār al-uwal fī man taṣarrafa fī Miṣr min arbāb al-duwal* (1623) (Bulaq: Al-Matbaᶜa al-ᶜUthmaniyya, 1304/1887), p. 156.

53. Evliya Çelebi, *Seyahatname*, vol. 10: 552, 573, 587, 597, 603, 604, 607, 614, 629, 645, 690, 691, 692, 693, 694 (Noah's sons); 614–15, 698, 699, 700–01, 710–11 (Joseph); 552, 553, 590, 600, 609, 624, 633, 634, 690, 710 (Moses, Pharaoh, Haman); 647, 648, 666, 682 (Solomon, Asaf); 695 (Hilalis); 550, 612, 629, 632, 634, 691 (Sayf ben Dhi Yazan); 638 (ᶜAntar).

54. Ibn Zunbul, *Wāqiᶜat*, pp. 97, 116–20 (esp. pp. 118–19).

55. Ahmed Çelebi, *Awḍuḥ*, p. 528.

56. Carsten Niebuhr, *Travels through Arabia and Other Countries in the East*, trans. Robert Heron, 2 vols. (Edinburgh: R. Morrison and Sons, Booksellers, Perth; G. Mudie, Edinburgh; and T. Vernor, London, 1792; reprint Beirut: Librairie du Liban, n.d.), vol. 2: 265. In Niebuhr's rather garbled rendition, these are "Autar," "Rustam Sal," and "Beber, king of Egypt." He also notes stories of the Ayyubids and the life of "Bahluldan," a jester at Harun al-Rashid's court.

57. On this point, see Howe, *Migration and Myth-Making,* chapter 3 and pp. 130–32.

58. Ahmed Çelebi, *Awḍaḥ,* p. 283.

59. Rajaʾ al-Naqqash, *Naguib Mahfouz: Ṣafaḥāt min mudhakkirātihi wa-aḍwāʾ jadīda ʿalā adabihi wa-ḥayyātihi* (Cairo: Markaz al-Ahram li'l-Tarjama wa'l-Nashr, 1997), p. 25 (translation author's). On identification with ancient factions and with the characters in the Banu Hilal epic, see further Reynolds, *Heroic Poets,* pp. 60–61, 73; for contrasting attitudes toward this epic, see ibid., pp. 91–92, 139.

60. On this point, see Jonathan Berkey, "Storytelling, Preaching, and Power in Mamluk Cairo," *Mamluk Studies Review* 4 (2000): 53–73, esp. p. 65.

61. Footage of this may be seen in David Wallace, dir., *In the Footsteps of Alexander the Great,* 2 parts, Maya Vision production for the British Broadcasting Corporation and Maryland Public Television (Alexandria, VA: PBS Home Video, 1997), part 2.

Chapter 3: Saʿd and Haram

1. Al-Qinali, *Majmūʿ laṭīf,* as quoted in Holt, "Al-Jabarti's Introduction," pp. 42–43.

2. Al-Damurdashi, *Al-Durra al-muṣāna,* p. 4.

3. Bafaqih, *L'unification du Yémen antique,* pp. 157–63; *EI*[1], *s.v.* "Ḥāshid and Bakīl," by Schleifer; Crone, "Qays and Yemen of the Umayyad Period," p. 15; Shaban, *ʿAbbasid Revolution,* p. 73.

4. Numbers 32:33; 34:14–15; Deuteronomy 3:13; Joshua 1:12; 13:7–8, 29; 14:4; 17; 22:1, 7. The expression in biblical Hebrew is *hatzi-shevet Menasheh* or *hatzi-mateh Menasheh,* literally, "half the staff of Manasseh," referring, perhaps, to the staff borne by the leader of each of the twelve tribes (*mateh* is also used for the legendary staff of Moses). See Numbers 17: 17–20, where God instructs Moses to inscribe the name of each chief of the twelve tribes on a separate staff, then to place all the staves in the tabernacle.

5. Respectively, Joshua 17:2, 22:7, and Judges 7:23.

6. Although some commentaries assert that we should not take "half" in this context literally, they concede that it nonetheless connotes a portion of a tribe. See, for example, J. H. Hertz, ed., and trans., *The Pentateuch and Haftorahs,* 2d ed. (London: Soncino Press, 1981), p. 710 n. 33.

7. For a lucid discussion of the connotations of the word in the context of a royal household, see Peirce, *The Imperial Harem,* pp. 3–6. The form actually used in Arabic for the women's quarters is *ḥarīm.*

8. *EI*[2], *s.v.* "Kaᶜba," by Wensinck-Jomier.

9. Arabic, *makrūh*. The other categories are *wājib* or *farḍ* (obligatory); *mandūb, mustaḥabb, sunna* (recommended); and *mubāḥ* (neutral). For a discussion of these distinctions, see Joseph Schacht, *An Introduction to Islamic Law* (1995; reprint, Oxford: Oxford University Press, 1964), pp. 120–21; H. A. R. Gibb, *Mohammedanism: An Historical Survey*, 2d ed. (Oxford: Oxford University Press, 1970), p. 69.

10. See Deuteronomy 2:34; 7:2, 26; 13:16, 18; 20:17; Joshua 2:10; 6:17, 18; 7:1, 11–13, 15; 10:28, 35, 37, 39, 40; 11:11, 12, 21; also Numbers 21:2. In Exodus 22:19, the same root is used to refer to the proscription of any of the Children of Israel who sacrifices to a god other than the god of Israel.

11. See the Jewish Publication Society Hebrew-English *Tanakh [Torah, Nevi'im, Kethuvim]: The Traditional Hebrew Text and the New JPS Translation*, 2d ed. (Philadephia: Jewish Publication Society, 1999), at the verses cited in n. 10. In rabbinical usage, not coincidentally, *herem* came to mean a ban of excommunication, that is, a complete cutting-off from the Jewish community; see Marcus Jastrow, *A Dictionary of the Targumim, the Talmud Babli and Yerushalmi, and the Midrashic Literature*, 2 vols. (New York: Traditional Press, Inc., 1903), vol. 1: 503–04.

12. It was evidently used in late nineteenth-century Yemen for brigands; see Albert Deflers, *Voyage au Yémen: Journal d'une excursion botanique faite en 1887 dans les montagnes de l'Arabie Heureuse* (Paris: Paul Klincksieck, 1889), p. 96. For a similar meaning, see Evliya Çelebi, *Seyahatname*, vol. 10: 586, 591, 605, 615, 733, 735, 736.

13. For examples of this pejorative usage, see *Sīrat al-Ẓāhir Baybars*, vol. 2: 982, 1016, 1043, 1465; Abu'l-Mahasin Yusuf b. Taghri Birdi (1410–70), *History of Egypt, 1382–1469 A.D.*, 7 vols., trans. William Popper (Berkeley: University of California Press, 1954–60), vol. 1: 118.

14. Bafaqih, *L'Unification du Yémen antique*, p. 302.

15. Ibid., pp. 300–02.

16. Yahya b. al-Husayn b. al-Qasim (1625–89), *Ghāyat al-amānī fī akhbār al-quṭr al-yamānī*, ed., Saᶜid ᶜAbd al-Fattah ᶜAshur, 2 vols. (Cairo: Dar al-Katib al-ᶜArabi, 1968), vol. 1: 437.

17. ᶜAbdallah Muhammad b. Ibrahim b. Battuta (1304–77), *Riḥlat Ibn Baṭūṭa*, introduction by Karam al-Bustani (Beirut: Dar Sadir, Dar Bayrut, 1964), pp. 246–47.

18. Niebuhr, *Travels through Arabia*, pp. 242–43.

19. Ibn Battuta, *Riḥla*, p. 247; see also Mathers, trans., *The Thousand Nights and One Night*, vol. 4: 504.

20. Ibn Ishaq, *Life of Muhammad*, p. 292. On the battle of Badr generally, see ibid., pp. 289–314, 321–60.

21. Qutb al-Din Muhammad b. Ahmad al-Nahrawali al-Makki (1511–82) identifies him as Mustafa Bey al-Rumuzi, *defterdar* of Yemen: *Al-Barq al-yamānī fī'l-fatḥ al-ᶜuthmānī*, a.k.a. *Ghazwāt al-Jarākisa wa'l-Atrāk fī janūb al-jazīra*, ed., Jasir Hamad (Riyadh: Dar al-Yamama, 1968), p. 430. See also Rumuzi, *Tārīḫ-i feth̲-i Yemen*, fo. 65r, where he describes himself as an historian and a poet (*müverraḫ ve şāᵓir*).

22. On the genre, see Geoffrey L. Lewis, "The Utility of Ottoman *Fethnames*," in *Historians of the Middle East*, eds., Bernard Lewis and P. M. Holt (London: Oxford University Press, 1962), pp. 192–96.

23. Reinhart Dozy, *Supplément aux dictionnaires arabes*, 2 vols. (Leiden: E. J. Brill, 1927), vol. 1: 811.

24. Kâtib Çelebi, *Tuḥfet ül-kibār*, p. 27.

25. Al-Nahrawali, *Al-Barq al-yamānī*, pp. 184, 188. "Come to the best of works" is, however, included in the Zaydi call to prayer today.

26. There were (and are) indeed tribes in geographical Yemen known as the Banu Yazid and Banu Muᶜawiya. Both are subunits of the Bakil confederation. See Paul Dresch, *Tribes, Government, and History inYemen* (Oxford: Clarendon and Oxford University Press, 1989), pp. 24–25, 321–23; Yahya b. al-Husayn, *Ghāyat al-amānī*, vol. 2: 736, 798; A. S. Tritton, *The Rise of the Imams of Sanaa* (London: Oxford University Press, 1925; reprint Westport, CT: Hyperion Press, Inc., 1981), pp. 67, 68; R. B. Serjeant, "The Coastal Population of Socotra," in *Socotra: Island of Tranquility*, compiler, Brian Doe (London: IMMEL Publishing, Ltd., 1992), p. 165.

27. Yahya b. al-Husayn, *Ghāyat al-amānī*, vol. 2: 634, 650, 646.

28. Manfred Kropp, "The Realm of Evil: The Struggle of Ottomans and Zaidis in the 16th–17th Centuries as Reflected in Historiography," in *Yemen—Present and Past*, eds., B. Knutsson, V. Mattsson, and M. Persson (Lund, Sweden: Lund University Press, 1994), p. 91.

29. *Minhum quḍāh wa-fuqahāᵓ wa-ᶜudāl wa-mashāyikh al-bilād*: quoted in Abu'l-Fawz Muhammad Amin al-Suwaydi, *Sabāᵓik al-dhahab fī maᶜrifat qabāᵓil al-ᶜArab*, British Museum Library, MS Or. 1543, p. 69. I am grateful to Dina Rizk Khoury for providing me with this text.

30. Ibn Iyas, *Histoire des Mamlouks circassiens*, trans. Gaston Wiet, 2 vols. (Cairo: Institut Français d'Archéologie Orientale, 1945), vol. 2: 65.

31. Süheyli Efendi, *Tevārīḫ-i Mıṣīr [sic] ül-ḳadīm* (c. 1630), Istanbul, Süleymaniye Library, MS Fatih 4229, fo. 137v; Anonymous, *Kitāb-i tevārīḫ-i Mıṣr-ı Ḳāhire-i ḫaṭṭ-ı Ḥasan Paşa* (to 1683), Istanbul, Süleymaniye Library, MS Haci Mahmud Efendi 4877, fo. 12v.

32. Ibn Iyas, *Histoire des Mamlouks circassiens,* vol. 2: 65.

33. Ibid., vol. 2: 77, 117, 402, 407, 415.

34. Ibid., vol. 2: 78–79.

35. Ibn Iyas, *Journal d'un bourgeois du Caire,* vol. 2: 130; Süheyli, *Tevārīḫ-i Mısīr,* fos. 110v, 112r.

36. Ibn Iyas, *Journal d'un bourgeois du Caire,* vol. 2: 188, 191, 202, 210–11, 229, 261–62, 382, 416. See also Winter, *Egyptian Society under Ottoman Rule,* pp. 81, 87, 89–90.

37. On this point, see Winter, *Egyptian Society under Ottoman Rule,* pp. 92–93.

38. Ahmed Çelebi, *Awḍaḥ,* pp. 395, 396, 428.

39. Al-Damurdashi, *Al-Durra al-muṣāna,* pp. 114, 201. Ibn Iyas makes repeated references to Hasan al-Mar[ɔ]i, the bedouin chieftain of Buhayra at the time of the Ottoman conquest, but it is not clear whether he is a member of the Haram. See *Journal d'un notable du Caire,* vol. 2: 169, 189, 190, 211, 215, 250, 251, 283–84 (where they are inexplicably called shaykhs of Gharbiyya). Hasan's chief claim to fame is that he turned the fleeing Tumanbay over to Selim. See also Winter, *Egyptian Society under Ottoman Rule,* pp. 80–83.

40. See Baer, "Shirbini's *Hazz al-quḥūf.*"

41. Yusuf b. Muhammad b. [c]Abd al-Jawad al-Shirbini (fl. late seventeenth century), *Hazz al-quḥūf fī sharḥ qaṣīd Abī Shādūf,* ed., Shaykh Mahmud Musa (Bulaq: Al-Matba[c]a al-Amiriyya, 1308/1890–91), p. 6. I am grateful to Doris Behrens-Abouseif for bringing this reference to my attention. Note the apparent appropriation of this phrase by al-Jabarti in his version of the seventeenth-century origin myth.

42. On this point, see especially Baer, "Shirbini's *Hazz al-quḥūf,*" pp. 36–37.

43. Lane, *Manners and Customs,* p. 196. He also makes an analogy to the Qays and Yemen of Syria.

44. Mirjafari, "Haydari-Ni[c]mati Conflicts," pp. 135–36.

45. Evliya Çelebi, *Seyahatname,* vol. 10: 552, 553, 591, 607, 729–30. Ibn Khaldun mentions a (presumably Yemeni) tribe named Judham; see *Muqaddimah,* p. 99.

46. Al-Damurdashi, *al-Durra al-muṣana,* pp. 187–88.

47. Ibid., pp. 364–67.

48. Ahmed Çelebi, *Awḍaḥ,* p. 528.

49. See *EI*[2], *s.v.* "Hilāl," by Idris; "Hilāl: The Saga of the Banī Hilāl," by Schleifer; Lyons, *The Arabian Epic*, vol. 3: 237–300.

50. Ibn al-Daybaᶜ, *Qurrat al-ᶜuyūn*, vol. 2: 133, 160, 172, 174–75, 225; al-Nahrawali, *Al-Barq al-yamānī*, pp. 20, 21, 27, 28, 49, 289; Yahya b. al-Husayn, *Ghāyat al-amānī*, vol. 2: 645. See also Wellhausen, *The Arab Kingdom and Its Fall*, pp. 384–85, where the term applies to the original followers of Zayd b. ᶜAli.

51. See, for example, al-Jabarti, *ᶜAjāʾib* (Cairo), vol. 2: 287, 289; vol. 3: 314–17; vol. 4: 128–29.

52. On the Qazdağlıs, see Hathaway, *Politics of Households*, esp. chapter 4; on the Shanabis, see Ahmed Çelebi, *Awḍaḥ*, pp. 372, 464; on the Shawarabis, see ibid., pp. 369–70, 397, 476, 477, 486, 504, 523, 535, 554, 569.

53. Bernard Lewis, *The Arabs in History*, rev. ed. (New York: Harper and Row, 1966), p. 34.

54. Wasim (literally, handsome in Arabic) may have appealed to the Zayidiyya because of its prime grazing land; Ibn Taghri Birdi notes horses being tethered there in the spring to take advantage of the rich spring grass (*History of Egypt*, vol. 2, part 4: 8). In Mamluk and Ottoman times, its tax revenues were endowed to the *waqf*s of the Holy Cities of Mecca and Medina; see Heinz Halm, *Ägypten nach den mamlukischen Lehensregistern*, 2 vols. (Wiesbaden: Reichert, 1979), vol. 1: 210; Topkapı Palace Archives, D. 2520/3 (1166–67/1752–54), D. 7662 (1163/1750).

55. On this point, see Ömer Lütfi Barkan, ed., "Mısır Kanunnâmesi," in *XV ve XVIıncı asırlarda Osmanlı İmparatorluğunda Ziraî Ekonominin Hukukî ve Malî Esasları*, ed., Barkan, vol. 1: *Kanunlar* (Istanbul: İstanbul Üniversitesi Edebiyat Fakültesi Yayınları, 1943), chapter 105, p. 359; Shaw, *Financial and Administrative Organization*, pp. 196–97.

56. Hathaway, *Politics of Households*, pp. 38, 40–41.

57. Haci ᶜAli, *Aḫbār ül-yamānī*, fos. 210r–218r; Anonymous, *Tevārīḫ-i Mıṣr-ı Ḳāhire*, fos. 36v–37r, 39v, 43v; Anonymous, *Akhbār al-nuwwāb*, fo. 18v; Ahmed Çelebi, *Awḍaḥ*, p. 141. On his career in Egypt and rivalry with Ridvan Bey, see al-Hallaq, *Tārīḫ-i Mıṣr-ı Ḳāhire*, fos. 143v–147v; Anonymous, *Tevārīḫ-i Mıṣr-ı Ḳāhire*, fos. 53r–59r; Anonymous, *Akhbār al-nuwwāb*, fo. 24v.

58. Anonymous, *Tevārīḫ-i Mıṣr-ı Ḳāhire*, fos. 36r, 39v.

59. Ibn Ishaq, *Life of Muhammad*, pp. 70–71.

60. Ibid., pp. 118, 281, 283, 286, 377, 381; Evliya Çelebi, *Evliya Çelebi Seyahatnamesi*, ed., Ahmed Cevdet, 10 vols. (Istanbul: Ikdâm Matbaası, 1314/1896–7—1938), vol. 1: 28; idem, *Narrative of Travels*, vol. 1: 2.

61. Ibn Ishaq, *Life of Muhammad*, pp. 200–01, 206–07, 453, 463–64, 683–87. Al-Suwaydi, *Sabāʾik al-dhahab*, p. 69, presents the "Saᶜāda" as a branch of the Khazraj clearly related to the Banu Haram.

62. J. R. L. Carter, *Tribes in Oman* (London: IMMEL Publishing, Ltd., 1982), pp. 43–45, 116; *EI*[1], *s.v.* "Hadramawt," by J. Schleifer. R. B. Serjeant also notes, citing ᶜAbd al-Razzaq Khalidi, that Saᶜd and its derivatives dominate names among the population of Socotra; see "The Coastal Population of Socotra," p. 162.

63. Carter, *Tribes in Oman*, pp. 116, 117.

64. C. van Arendonk, *Les Débuts de l'imamat zaidite au Yémen*, trans. Jacques Ryckmans (Leiden: E. J. Brill, 1960), pp. 135, 189.

65. Yahya b. al-Husayn, *Ghāyat al-amānī*, vol. 2: 803, 813.

66. Al-Nahrawali, *Al-Barq al-yamānī*, p. 172.

67. Hathaway, *Politics of Households*, p. 65; idem, "Household of Hasan Ağa Bilifya," pp. 139–44.

68. Al-Damurdashi, *Al-Durra al-muṣāna*, p. 12. A notable exception to this breakdown is the allegiance of the Nisf Haram to the late eighteenth-century grandee Hüseyin Bey al-Sabunci, who ultimately became a client of Ibrahim Kâhya al-Qazdağlı; the Haram evidently had a long-standing allegiance to the founder of the Sabunci household, Ibrahim Çorbacı al-Sabunci. See al-Jabarti, *ᶜAjāʾib* (Cairo), vol. 2: 117–18; on the Sabunci household, see Hathaway, *Politics of Households*, pp. xvi, 42, 132.

69. On changes in Egypt's land tenure, see Hathaway, *Politics of Households*, pp. 8–11, and the sources cited there.

70. Ibid., pp. 158–59; Hathaway, "Household of Hasan Ağa Bilifya," pp. 142–43; idem, "The Role of the Kızlar Ağası in 17th–18th Century Ottoman Egypt," *Studia Islamica* 75 (1992): 154–55.

71. See Ahmed Çelebi, *Awḍaḥ*, p. 416; and nn. 36–39 above.

72. Al-Damurdashi, *Al-Durra al-muṣāna*, pp. 364–67; Ahmed Çelebi, *Awḍaḥ*, p. 528.

73. Süheyli, *Tevārīḫ-i Mıṣīr*, fo. 137v; Anonymous, *Tevārīḫ-i Mıṣr-ı Ḳāhire*, fo. 12v. On Sulayman, see Ibn Iyas, *Histoire des Mamlouks circassiens*, vol. 2: 402; idem, *Journal d'un bourgeois du Caire*, vol. 1: 51; Anonymous, *Tevārīḫ-i Mıṣr-ı Ḳāhire*, fo. 12v.

74. Ahmed Çelebi, *Awḍaḥ*, pp. 182, 237, 240, 281, 338–41, 343, 345, 354–56, 361–62, 365–66, 373–74, 376, 385, 394–95, 556, 598, 616; al-Damurdashi, *Al-Durra al-muṣāna*, pp. 178, 192–98, 213–17, 244–45, 444–51.

75. Al-Damurdashi, *Al-Durra al-muṣāna*, pp. 535–37. See also Winter, *Egyptian Society under Ottoman Rule*, pp. 105–07.

76. See Winter, *Egyptian Society under Ottoman Rule*, pp. 103, 106.

77. See Heinz Halm, *The Empire of the Mahdi: The Rise of the Fatimids*, trans. Michael Bonner (Leiden: Brill, 1996), pp. 102, 174–75, 197, 199, 268, 270, 306, 314, 318, 338, 392–93; *EI*², *s.v.* "Hawwāra," by T. Lewicki; William Popper, *Systematic Notes to Ibn Taghri Birdi's Chronicles of Egypt and Syria under the Circassian Sultans, 1382–1468 (Cont'd)* (Berkeley: University of California Press, 1957), p. 6; *EI*², *s.v.* "Hawwāra—Egypt and the Sudan," by P. M. Holt; Ibn Taghri Birdi, *History of Egypt*, vol. 1: 32, 85; vol. 2: 59; Ibn Iyas, *Histoire des Mamlouks circassiens*, vol. 2: 143, 156–57, 161, 223, 247, 262, 276, 287, 334, 399, 402, 453. Michael Winter's assertion that they migrated during the sixteenth century is clearly erroneous: see Winter, *Egyptian Society under Ottoman Rule*, p. 105.

78. For example, Ahmed Çelebi, *Awḍaḥ*, pp. 237, 529–31. For a list of administrators of Upper Egypt in the sixteenth and seventeenth centuries, see Jean-Claude Garcin, "Émirs Hawwâras et beys de Ǧirǧa aux XVIe et XVIIe siècles," *Annales Islamologiques* 12 (1984): 245–55.

79. Al-Jabarti, *ᶜAjāᵓib* (Cairo), vol. 2: 351–52.

80. Ibid., vol. 2: 349–51; Winter, *Egyptian Society under Ottoman Rule*, pp. 69, 105.

Chapter 4: The Yemeni Connection to Egypt's Factions

1. Ibn al-Daybaᶜ, *Qurrat al-ᶜuyūn*, vol. 1: 167–69; Madelung, *Religious Trends in Early Islamic Iran*, pp. 87–88. Madelung explains that al-Hadi even visited Tabaristan before his relocation to Yemen and attracted numerous Tabari Zaydis to Yemen as his supporters.

2. Madelung, *Religious Trends in Early Islamic Iran*, pp. 86–87; Farhad Daftary, *The Ismailis: Their History and Doctrines* (Cambridge: Cambridge University Press, 1990; repr. 1995), pp. 69–70, 74–76, 166; Paul Dresch, "Imams and Tribes: The Writing and Acting of History in Upper Yemen," in *Tribes and State Formation in the Middle East*, eds., Philip S. Khoury and Joseph Kostiner, (Berkeley: University of California Press, 1990), p. 266; Nahida Coussonnet, "Les assises du pouvoir zaydite au XIIIe siècle," in *Le Yémen, Passé et présent de l'unité, Revue du Monde Musulman et de la Méditerranée* no. 67, ed., Michel Tuchscherer (Paris: Édisud, 1994), p. 30; François Blukacz, "Le Yémen sous l'autorité des imams zaidites au XVIIe siècle: Une éphémère unité," in *Le Yémen*, p. 40; Bernard Haykel, "Al-Shawkani and the Jurisprudential Unity of Yemen," in *Le Yémen*, p. 56; Kropp, "Realm of Evil," p. 90.

3. Ibn al-Daybaᶜ, *Qurrat al-ᶜuyūn*, vol. 1: 178–220; Daftary, *The Ismailis*, p. 118.

4. Van Arendonk, *Les Débuts de l'imamat zaidite*, p. 221.

5. *EI*^{2}, *s.v.* "Ḥāshid wa-Bakīl," by G. Rentz; Ibn al-Dayba^{c}, *Qurrat al-^{c}uyūn*, vol. 1: 241–50; Yahya b. al-Husayn, *Ghāyat al-amānī*, vol. 1: 237, 253–57; Daftary, *The Ismailis*, pp. 209–10.

6. See ^{c}Ali b. al-Hasan al-Khazraji (d. 1410), *The Pearl-Strings: A History of the Resuliyy Dynasty of Yemen*, trans., introduction, annotations, index, tables, and maps by Sir. J. W. Redhouse; ed., E. G. Brown, R. A. Nicholson, and A. Rogers, E. J. W. Gibb Memorial Series, 2 vols. (Leiden: E. J. Brill; London: Luzac and Co., 1906); Yahya b. al-Husayn, *Ghāyat al-amānī*, vol. 1: 321–vol. 2: 650; Ibn al-Dayba^{c}, *Qurrat al-^{c}uyūn*, vol. 1: 372–vol. 2: 235; idem, *Bughyat al-mustafīd fī taʾrīkh madīnat Zabīd*, ed., ^{c}Abdallah al-Hibshi (San^{c}a: Markaz al-Dirasat wa'l-Buhuth al-Yamani, 1979), pp 69–214; *EI*^{1}, *s.v.* "Rasūlids," by A. S. Tritton.

7. On Portuguese messianic visions of destroying Mecca and Medina, then ultimately conquering Jerusalem, see Sanjay Subrahmanyam, "Du Tage au Gange au XVIe siècle: Une conjoncture millénariste à l'échelle eurasiatique," *Annales: Histoires, Sciences Sociales* 56, no. 1 (2001): 52–54, 77–81. My thanks to Geoffrey Parker for referring me to this article.

8. Ibn al-Dayba^{c}, *Qurrat al-^{c}uyūn*, vol. 2: 216–35; Yahya b. al-Husayn, *Ghāyat al-amānī*, vol. 2: 630–31, 640–54; al-Nahrawali, *Al-Barq al-yamānī*, pp. 16–32. See also M. Yakub Mughul, "Portekizli'lerle Kızıldeniz'de Mücadele ve Hicaz'da Osmanlı Hâkimiyetinin Yerleşme hakkında bir Vesika," *Belleten* 2, nos. 3–4 (1965): 39.

9. Al-Nahrawali, *Al-Barq al-yamānī*, pp. 32–59; Yahya b. al-Husayn, *Ghāyat al-amānī*, vol. 2: 668–85. *Levend* can refer to any type of mercenary; however, it is frequently applied to naval personnel. See the references to *levendler-i donanma-ı Hümāyūn* (*levends* of the imperial navy) in Istanbul, Başbakanlık Arşivi, Kamil Kepeci, Kahve Rusumu 4519 (1129–1717). See also Gustav Bayerle, *Pashas, Begs, and Effendis: A Historical Dictionary of Titles and Terms in the Ottoman Empire* (Istanbul: Isis Press, 1997), p. 102; Mughul, "Portekizli'lerle Kızıldeniz'de Mücadele," p. 46; Riza Nour, "L'Histoire du croissant," *Revue de Turcologie* 1, no. 3 (February 1933): 88/317.

10. See, for example, Istanbul, Başbakanlık Arşivi, Mühimme Defteri 3, No. 245 (Rebiülevvel 967/December 1559); Mühimme Defteri 6, nos. 257, 272 (Rebiülevvel 972/October 1564).

11. Al-Nahrawali, *Al-Barq al-yamānī*, pp. 19, 35, 42–43, 49, 53. Al-Nahrawali mistakenly gives Salman's name as Süleyman. M. Yakub Mughul has published a letter dated 25 Rebiülevvel 923/ 17 April 1517 from Salman Reis to Selim I, then in Egypt (Topkapı Palace Archives, E. 8337), along with commentary; see "Portekizli'lerle Kızıldeniz'de Mücadele," pp. 37–47. See also Kâtib Çelebi, *Tuḥfet ül-kibār*, pp. 24–25.

12. Playfair, *A History of Arabia Felix*, p. 101.

13. Al-Nahrawali, *Al-Barq al-yamānī*, pp. 70, 80–84; Yahya b. al-Husayn, *Ghāyat al-amānī*, vol. 2: 667–68, 684; Kâtib Çelebi, *Tuḥfet ül-kibār*, pp. 57–58. See also Evliya Çelebi, *Seyahatname*, vol. 10: 585, 634, for a much more favorable account of Süleyman Pasha.

14. Al-Nahrawali, *Al-Barq al-yamānī*, pp. 85–86.

15. Ibid., pp. 87–92; Yahya b. al-Husayn, *Ghāyat al-amānī*, vol. 2: 685.

16. Yahya b. al-Husayn, *Ghāyat al-amānī*, vol. 2: 756–81; al-Ishaqi, *Akhbār al-uwal*, p. 167. It was during Hasan Pasha's tenure that the Qasimi revolt against the Ottomans began.

17. Istanbul, Başbakanlık Arşivi, Mühimme Defteri 1, Nos. 1303 (Muharrem 962/November–December 1554); 1478, 1636, 1637 (all Safer 962/December 1554–January 1555); Mühimme Defteri 2, Nos. 42, 132 (both Rebiülevvel 963/ January–February 1556); 193, 226 (both Rebiüssani 963/February–March 1556); 716 (Receb 963/May–June 1556); 1213, 1245 (both Ramazan 963/July–August 1556); 1281, 1351 (both Şevval 963/August–September 1556), 1472, 1476, 1478, 1485 (all Zilkade 963/September–October 1556); 2025 (Rebiüssani 964/February–March 1557); Mühimme Defteri 3, Nos. 252 (Zilkade 966/September 1559); 550 (Rebiülevvel 967/December 1559); Mühimme Defteri 4, No. 2013 (Cumazeülahır 968/February–March 1561); Mühimme Defteri 5, Nos. 720 (Cumazeülevvel 973/November–December 1565); 731, 739 (Cumazeülahır 973/ January 1566); 1754, 1756 (Zilkade 973/May–June 1566); Mühimme Defteri 6, no. 382 (Rebiüssani 972/November 1564); Mühimme Defteri 10, No. 89 (Ramazan 978/February 1571); Shams al-Din ᶜAbd al-Samad b. Ismail al-Mawzaᶜi, *Dukhūl al-ᶜUthmāniyyīn al-awwal ilā al-Yaman*, a.k.a. *Al-Iḥsān fī dukhūl mamlakat al-Yaman taḥta ẓill ᶜadālat Āl ᶜUthmān*, ed., ᶜAbdallah Muhammad al-Hibshi (Beirut: Dar al-Tanwir, 1986), pp. 131, 167–68, 225.

18. Mühimme Defteri 1, Nos. 428, 1204 (both Zilkade 961/October 1554); 1224 (9 Muharrem 962/December 1554); Mühimme Defteri 2, Nos. 300 (Rebiüssani 963/March 1556); 1473–74, 1479 (all Zilkade 963/October 1556); Mühimme Defteri 4, Nos. 540, 580, 596 (all Receb 967/April–May 1560); 644, 667 (both Şaban 967/May–June 1560); Mühimme Defteri 5, Nos. 780 (Cumazeülahır 973/January 1566); 1756 (12 Zilkade 973/June 1566); al-Mawzaᶜi, *Dukhūl al-ᶜUthmāniyyīn*, pp. 86, 90, 92, 96, 134, 143, 153–54, 161, 169–70, 192, 212, 221, 222, 225. The smaller, less commercially and strategically critical towns, such as Taᶜizz, Mawzaᶜ, and al-Hujuriyya, were evidently administered by aghas or beys with the rank of agha—i.e., below the rank of *sancak beyi*. On Egypt's land tenure system, see "Mısır Kanunnâmesi," ed., Barkan; Shaw, *Financial and Administrative Organization*, pp. 28ff., 60–62.

19. Al-Nahrawali, *Al-Barq al-yamānī*, pp. 98–120; Yahya b. al-Husayn, *Ghāyat al-amānī*, vol. 2: 698–715; Holt, *Egypt and the Fertile Crescent*, pp. 52–54. See also Evliya Çelebi, *Seyahatname*, vol. 10: 634, 674, 675, 676, 677, 678–79, 722.

20. Mühimme Defteri 5, nos. 710, 711, 718 (5 Cumazeülahır 973/28 December 1565); 752 (9 Cumazeülahır 973/1 January 1566); 1236 (20 Şaban 973/12 March 1566). See also al-Nahrawali, *Al-Barq al-yamānī*, p. 159; Yahya b. al-Husayn, *Ghāyat al-amānī*, vol. 2: 724.

21. Mühimme Defteri 5, Nos. 710, 711, 718, 720, 731, 752, 780 (9 Cumazeülahır 973/1 January 1566), 1702 (6 Zilkade 973/25 May 1566); al-Nahrawali, *Al-Barq al-yamānī*, p. 159.

22. This was the same Mahmud Pasha who, as governor of Egypt, would be assassinated by an unknown gunman in 1567. His mosque in Cairo is still standing. See al-Nahrawali, *Al-Barq al-yamānī*, pp. 154–55. Ridvan Pasha, meanwhile, founded an influential family of notables in Ottoman Palestine; see Ze᾿evi, *An Ottoman Century*, pp. 39–41, 45, 48, 49, 50, 52, 53, 55–57.

23. Ralph S. Hattox, *Coffee and Coffeehouses: The Origins of a Social Beverage in the Medieval Near East* (Seattle: University of Washington Press, 1985), pp. 11ff.; Yahya b. al-Husayn, *Ghāyat al-amānī*, vol. 2: 689; Kropp, "Realm of Evil," p. 93. On coffee cultivation and preparation in the region, see Richard Pankhurst, *Economic History of Ethiopia, 1800–1935* (Addis Ababa: Haile Sellassie I University Press, 1968), pp. 198–203.

24. Hattox, *Coffee and Coffeehouses*, pp. 17–28, 74–76; al-Nahrawali, *Al-Barq al-yamānī*, pp. 128, 401.

25. Hattox, *Coffee and Coffeehouses*, pp. 26–41, 76–81; Mühimme Defteri 5, No. 612 (Cumazeülevvel 973/November 1565); Mühimme Defteri 7, Nos. 377, 389 (Rebiüssani 975/October 1567) (on closing down coffeehouses in Jerusalem and Cairo). See also Lane, *Manners and Customs*, pp. 332–33.

26. Haci ᶜAli, *Aḫbār ül-yamānī*, fo. 206v; Evliya Çelebi, *Seyahatname*, vol. 10: 609; see also p. 675.

27. Evliya Çelebi, *Seyahatname*, vol. 10: 551, 592, 600, 605, 606, 624, 675; see also Jane Hathaway, "The Wealth and Influence of an Exiled Ottoman Eunuch in Egypt: The *Waqf* Inventory of ᶜAbbas Agha," *Journal of the Economic and Social History of the Orient* 37 (1994): 296, 302, 307–08, 317.

28. André Raymond, *Le Caire des Janissaires: L'Apogée de la ville ottomane sous ᶜAbd al Rahman Katkhuda* (Paris: Éditions CNRS, 1995), pp. 55–56; Hattox, *Coffee and Coffeehouses*, p. 72.

29. Niebuhr, *Travels*, pp. 55, 68, 94 (on growing and trading regions), 265–66, 280, 299, 307, 309, 314, 333, 350. See also Deflers, *Voyage au Yémen*, pp. 29, 31, 38, 40, 52, 78, 80, 82, 86, 88, 93, 98, 100, 103, 105.

30. On their locations, see Deflers, *Voyage au Yémen*, pp. 38, 40–41, 46–47, 50.

31. Mühimme Defteri 3, Nos. 1493, 1499 (6 Zilhicce 967/28 August 1560).

32. Yahya b. al-Husayn, *Ghāyat al-amānī*, p. 726; al-Nahrawali, *Al-Barq al-yamānī*, pp. 165–69, 227; Istanbul, Başbakanlık Arşivi, Maliyeden Müdevver 4118 (1000/1591–92), pp. 32, 38, 41. See also Rumuzi, *Tārīḫ-i fetḥ-i Yemen*, fos. 44r, 45v.

33. Al-Nahrawali, *Al-Barq al-yamānī*, pp. 227–30, 269, 297, 323–27; Rumuzi, *Tārīḫ-i fetḥ-i Yemen*, fos. 45v, 65r–v, 88v–89r. Deflers notes that before the second Ottoman conquest of Yemen in 1872, a Hamdani missionary controlled the area north of Sanʿa; see *Voyage au Yémen*, pp. 40–41, 46–47.

34. Al-Nahrawali, *Al-Barq al-yamānī*, pp. 167–70.

35. Ibid., pp. 184, 188, 289. See also chapter 3, n. 25.

36. Mühimme Defteri 5, Nos. 720, 760 (both Cumazeülahır 973/December 1565–January 1566); 1754 (Zilkade 973/May 1566); Mühimme Defteri 7, Nos. 584, 585, 589, 595, 611–18 (all Cumazeülahır 975/December 1567–January 1568); 1168–69 (Ramazan 975/March–April 1568); 1269 (14 Şevval 975/12 April 1568); 1330, 1332, 1333, 1348, 1361, 1376, 1455 (all Zilkade 975/May–June 1568); 1508 (Zilhicce 975/June 1568); 1793 (Muharrem 976/July 1568); 2251 (Rebiüssani 976/September–October 1568); 2621 (Cumazeülahır 976/November–December 1568); 2738 (Zilkade 976/April–May 1569); 2764 (Cumazeülahır 977/November–December 1569); 2769 (Şaban 977/January–February 1570); Mühimme Defteri 9, No. 73 (Ramazan 977/February–March 1570); Mühimme Defteri 10, Nos. 45 (? 979/1570–71), 461 (Cumazeülahır 979/October–November 1571); Rumuzi, *Tārīḫ-i fetḥ-i Yemen*, fo. 39r; al-Nahrawali, *Al-Barq al-yamānī*, p. 199.

37. Al-Ishaqi, *Akhbār al-uwal*, p. 154.

38. Mühimme Defteri 5, No. 1756 (12 Zilkade 973/31 May 1566).

39. Al-Nahrawali, *Al-Barq al-yamānī*, p. 393. P. M. Holt also notes several thousand troops who stopped in Cairo en route to Yemen in 1613–14 but refused to leave Cairo; see Holt, "Beylicate," p. 230. A similar incident is reported by al-Ishaqi, *Akhbār al-uwal*, p. 170.

40. Al-Nahrawali, *Al-Barq al-yamānī*, pp. 196, 270, 388–89. For an Ottoman miniature of an incident in which prisoners in a weapons storehouse near Sanʿa escaped, fought their way past the Ottoman guard, and joined al-Mutahhar (*Al-Barq al-yamānī*, p. 189), see R. B. Serjeant and Ronald Lewcock, eds., *Sanʿaʾ: An Arabian Islamic City* (London: World of Islam Festival Trust, 1983), p. 416.

41. Rumuzi, *Tārīḫ-i fetḥ-i Yemen*, fo. 44v; al-Nahrawali, *Al-Barq al-yamānī*, p. 393. On the Egyptian bedouin and Ismailis, see ibid., pp. 269, 297, 304–05, 323, 395.

42. Ibn al-Daybaʿ, *Qurrat al-ʿuyūn*, vol. 2: 225; Yahya b. al-Husayn, *Ghāyat al-amānī*, vol. 2: 644; al-Nahrawali, *Al-Barq al-yamānī*, p. 21; Rumuzi, *Tārīḫ-i fetḥ-i Yemen*, fos. 42v, 69r.

43. Mühimme Defteri 7, Nos. 1174, 1176 (28 Ramazan 975/27 March 1568); 1250, 1256 (13 Şevval 975/11 April 1568).

44. Al-Nahrawali, *Al-Barq al-yamānī*, pp. 182–96.

45. Ibid., pp. 205–13; al-Ishaqi, *Akhbār al-uwal*, p. 154.

46. Al-Nahrawali, *Al-Barq al-yamānī*, pp. 218–443; al-Mutahhar's surrender occurs on pp. 427–30.

47. Yahya b. al-Husayn, *Ghāyat al-amānī*, vol. 2: 736–67.

48. Ibid., vol. 2: 769–814; Haci ᶜAli, *Aḫbār ül-yamānī*, fo. 221r–v.

49. Haci ᶜAli, *Aḫbār ül-yamānī*, Istanbul, Süleymaniye Library, MS Hamidiye 886.

50. Haci ᶜAli notes that Fazli Pasha, governor from 1622–24, could expect no help from the capital in the wake of the Janissary rebellion that resulted in the murder of Sultan Osman II (1618–22), and its aftermath. See *Aḫbār ül-yamānī*, fo. 205v. Fazli Pasha served on Crete in 1647; see Kâtib Çelebi, *Tuḥfet ül-kibār*, p. 123.

51. R. R. Palmer and Joel Coulton, *A History of the Modern World to 1815*, 5th ed. (New York: Alfred A. Knopf, Inc., 1978), pp. 120, 128, 138, 157, 162–63; Dorothy M. Vaughan, *Europe and the Turk: A Pattern of Alliances, 1350–1700* (Liverpool: University of Liverpool Press, 1954; repr. New York: AMS Press, 1976), pp. 165–69.

52. Haci ᶜAli, *Aḫbār ül-yamānī*, fos. 210v–216r; Yahya b. al-Husayn, *Ghāyat al-amānī*, p. 831; al-Mawzaᶜi, *Dukhūl al-ᶜUthmāniyyīn*, p. 218; Anonymous, *Tevārīḫ-i Mıṣr-ı Ḳāhire*, fo. 36r; Tritton, *The Rise of the Imams of Sanaa*, pp. 94, 97.

53. Haci ᶜAli, *Aḫbār ül-yamānī*, fos. 214v, 217r.

54. Ibid., fo. 218r; Yahya b. al-Husayn, *Ghāyat al-amānī*, p. 839. On the Kaᶜba restoration, see Anonymous, *Tevārīḫ-i Mıṣr-ı Ḳāhire*, fos. 37v–38r; Suraiya Faroqhi, *Pilgrims and Sultans: The Hajj under the Ottomans* (Cambridge: Cambridge University Press, 1994), pp. 114–16.

55. Haci ᶜAli, *Aḫbār ül-yamānī*, fos. 217r–220r; Yahya b. al-Husayn, *Ghāyat al-amānī*, p. 839.

56. Haci ᶜAli, *Aḫbār ül-yamānī*, fos. 205r–208r.

57. Yahya b. al-Husayn, *Ghāyat al-amānī*, pp. 819–30 passim. This view is shared by R. Strothmann; see *EI*², *s.v.* "Ṣanᶜāʾ."

58. J. A. B. Palmer, "The Origin of the Janissaries," *Bulletin of the John Rylands Library* 35 (1952–53): 452, quoting the chronicles of Uruc and Aşıkpaşazade.

59. Although curiously, Mehmed Süreyya, the compiler of the *Sicill-i ᶜOsmānī*, has no biography of Haydar Agha but a relatively long and laudatory biography of Haydar Aghazade Mehmed; see *Sicill-i ᶜOsmānī*, 4 vols. (Istanbul, 1308–15/1890–97; republished Westmead, Farnborough, Hants., England: Gregg International Publishers, Limited, 1971), vol. 4: 169.

60. Al-Jabarti, *ᶜAjāʾib* (Cairo), vol. 1: 71.

61. Al-Hallaq, *Tevārīḫ-i Mıṣr-ı Ḳāhire*, fo. 140v.

62. Maliyeden Müdevver 4442 (1010–14/1601–06), fos. 84v, 93v, 126r, notes a Haci Memi, follower (*tābiᶜ*) of Qansuh Pasha the governor of Yemen, shipping Indian provisions to Yemen. A Memi Kashif is also described as assisting Sinan Pasha's invasion of Yemen; see al-Nahrawali, *Al-Barq al-yamānī*, p. 233; Rumuzi, *Tārīḫ-i fetḥ-i Yemen*, fo. 55r; see also al-Mawzaᶜi, *Dukhūl al-ᶜUthmāniyyīn*, p. 164. Whether this is the same Memi is uncertain.

63. Al-Hallaq, *Tarīḫ-i Mıṣr-ı Ḳāhire*, fos. 140v–153v. See also Anonymous, *Tevārīḫ-i Mıṣr-ı Ḳāhire*, fos. 45r–59r; Holt, "The Beylicate," pp. 231–32.

64. Kâtib Çelebi, *Tuḥfet ül-kibār*, pp. 127, 145.

65. Anonymous, *Akhbār al-nuwwāb*, fo. 24r; Ahmed Çelebi, *Awḍaḥ*, pp. 151–52.

66. Anonymous, *Tevārīḫ-i Mıṣr-ı Ḳāhire*, fos. 58r, 68r. See also Holt, "Beylicate," pp. 244–45. Yemenli Fazli is not to be confused with Fazli Pasha, governor of Yemen 1622–24; see Haci ᶜAli, *Aḫbār ül-yamānī*, fos. 204v–206r; Yahya b. al-Husayn, *Ghāyat al-amānī*, vol. 2: 816.

67. On this point, see Haci ᶜAli, *Aḫbār ül-yamānī*, fo. 210r.

68. See note 45, above, and al-Nahrawali, *Al-Barq al-yamānī*, pp. 205–40 passim.; Yahya b. al-Husayn, *Ghāyat al-amānī*, vol. 2: 731.

69. Haci ᶜAli, *Aḫbār ül-yamānī*, fo. 217r; al-Nahrawali, *Al-Barq al-yamānī*, pp. 128, 196, 269, 388; Yahya b. al-Husayn, *Ghāyat al-amānī*, vol. 2: 697, 774, 799; R. B. Serjeant, "The Post-Medieval and Modern History of Sanᶜaʾ and the Yemen, ca. 953–1382/1545–1962," in *Sanᶜaʾ*, eds., Serjeant and Lewcock (London: World of Islam Festival Trust, 1983), p. 80. Agricultural workers are mentioned specifically by Yahya b. al-Husayn, *Ghāyat al-amānī*, vol. 2: 804.

70. Evliya Çelebi, *Seyahatname*, vol. 10: 677; Niebuhr, *Travels*, p. 91.

71. Maliyeden Müdevver 4118 (1000/1591–92), pp. 35, 40, 48; 7555 (1009/1600–01), pp. 18, 49, 72, 99, 107, 108, 111, 160, 172, 197, 221, 227, 228, 248 (Ibrahim b. al-Mutahhar listed as a spy); Yahya b. al-Husayn, *Ghāyat al-amānī*, vol. 2: 729, 776–77.

72. Evliya Çelebi, *Seyahatname*, vol. 10: 711.

73. Hathaway, *Politics of Households*, pp. 77 and n. 102, 134–37; Raymond, *Le Caire des Janissaires*, pp. 80–85; Doris Behrens-Abouseif, *Azbakiyya and Its*

Environs: From Azbak to Ismail, 1476–1879 (Cairo: Institut Français d'Archéologie Orientale, 1985), pp. 55–60, 63–67.

74. Niebuhr reports that the imam got one-quarter of the retail price of all coffee sold. See *Travels*, p. 88. See also Dresch, "Imams and Tribes," p. 267; Tritton, *Rise of the Imams of Sanaa*, p. 119. Blukacz notes a tax on profits from the India trade imposed by the expansionist imam al-Mutawakkil Ismail (r. 1644–76) on the Hadramawti port of Shihr (in today's western Oman) after his conquest of this region in 1655; see "Le Yémen sous l'autorité des imams zaidites," p. 48.

75. ᶜAbd al-Rahman b. Hasan al-Bahkali, *Quintessence de l'or du règne du Chérif Muhammad b. Ahmad*, ed. and trans. Michel Tuchscherer as *Imams, notables et bédouins du Yémen au XVIIIe siècle*, TAIE 30 (Cairo: Institut Français d'Archéologie Orientale, 1992), p. 175.

76. Playfair, *History of Arabia Felix*, pp. 114–15. On French incursions into Egypt's coffee trade, see Hathaway, *Politics of Households*, pp. 46, 137, and the sources cited there.

77. Ayalon, "The Historian al-Jabarti," pp. 224–28; John O. Voll, "Linking Groups in the Networks of Eighteenth-Century Revivalist Scholars: The Mizjaji Family in Yemen," in *Eighteenth-Century Renewal and Reform in Islam*, eds., John O. Voll and Nehemiah Levtzion (Syracuse: Syracuse University Press, 1987), p. 79. See also al-Jabarti, *ᶜAjāʾib* (Cairo), vol. 1: 167; idem, *ᶜAjāʾib* (Beirut), vol. 2: 103–14.

78. Al-Nahrawali, *Al-Barq al-yamānī*, p. 251. His history is *Taʾrīkh al-nār al-ṣāfir ᶜan akhbār al-qarn al-ᶜāshir*.

79. Ibn al-Daybaᶜ, *Bughyat al-mustafīd*, pp. 136, 145, 148, 149, 150, 180; Yahya b. al-Husayn, *Ghāyat al-amānī*, vol. 2: 650; al-Mawzaᶜi, *Dukhūl al-ᶜUthmāniyyīn*, p. 203. On Zabid's intellectual prominence, see also Deflers, *Voyage au Yémen*, p. 102.

80. Shams al-Din ᶜAbd al-Samad b. Ismail al-Mawzaᶜi, *Dukhūl al-ᶜUthmāniyyīn al-awwal ilā al-Yaman*, a.k.a. *Al-Iḥsān fī dukhūl mamlakat al-Yaman taḥta ẓill ᶜadālat Āl ᶜUthmān*, ed., ᶜAbdallah Muhammad al-Hibshi (Beirut: Dar al-Tanwir li'l-Tibaᶜa wa'l-Nashr, 1986). A translation of this chronicle appears in Frédérique Soudan, *Le Yémen ottoman d'après la chronique d'al-Mawzaᶜi* (Cairo: Institut Français d'Archéologie Orientale, 1999), pp. 43–229; the author is apparently unaware of the 1986 edition.

81. J. Heyworth-Dunne, *An Introduction to the History of Education in Modern Egypt* (London: Luzac and Co., 1938), pp. 25–26 and n. 4; Bayard Dodge, *Al-Azhar: A Millennium of Muslim Learning*, memorial ed. (Washington, DC: Middle East Institute, 1974), p. 104, and appendix 4, esp. p. 203.

82. Voll, "The Mizjaji Family in Yemen," passim.

Chapter 5: Red and White

1. Holt, "Al-Jabarti's introduction," pp. 42–43. The translations are my own and differ very slightly from Holt's. There are actually two nearly identical manuscripts of the anonymous chronicle, as Holt explains on p. 42.

2. Vryonis, "Circus Factions and Islamic *Futuwwa* Organizations," p. 58; Cameron, *Circus Factions*, p. 258.

3. Nour, "L'Histoire du croissant," p. 66/295. See also Ibn Khaldun, *Muqaddimah*, pp. 214–15.

4. Martin Hinds, "The Banners and Battle Cries of the Arabs at Siffin (A.D. 657)," in *Studies in Early Islamic History*, by Martin Hinds, ed. Jere Bacharach, Lawrence I. Conrad, and Patricia Crone, with an introduction by G. R. Hawting (Princeton, NJ: The Darwin Press, 1996), pp. 97–142, esp. pp. 134–42.

5. Muhammad b. Yazid b. Maja (d. 887), *Sunan*, ed. Muhammad Fuʾad ʿAbd al-Baqi, 2 vols. (Cairo: Halabi, 1372/1952), vol. 2: 1366–67; ʿAla al-Din ʿAli b. Husam al-Din al-Muttaqi (1477–1567), *Kanz al-ʿummāl*, 8 parts (Hyderabad: Daʾirat al-Maʿarif, 1312/1894–95), part 3: 203; part 4: 38, 39, 45, 53; cited in Bernard Lewis, ed. and trans., *Islam from the Prophet Muhammad to the Capture of Constantinople*, vol. 2: *Religion and Society* (1974; reprint, New York and Oxford: Oxford University Press, 1987), pp. 51–53.

6. Hilal al-Sabiʾ (970–1056), *Rusūm dār al-khilāfa: The Rules and Regulations of the ʿAbbasid Court*, trans. with introduction and notes by Elie A. Salem (Beirut: American University in Beirut Press, 1977), pp. 61–62, 73–75. On the other hand, only the caliph could wear red shoes. The justification that al-Sabiʾ gives for this is that "red is the color of the caliph and of those who rebel against his authority" (p. 61). To what rebels he refers is unclear. On the use of black, see also Abdel Rahman Zaki, *Aʿlām al-duwal al-ʿarabiyya wa'l-islāmiyya* (Cairo: Matbaʿat al-Tahrir, 1958), pp. 27–28; idem, *Al-Aʿlām wa-shārāt al-mulk fī wādī al-Nīl* (Cairo: Dar al-Maʿaref, 1948), pp. 27–28.

7. See Yacoub Artin, *Contribution à l'étude du blason en Orient* (London: B. Quaritch, 1902); Nour, "L'Histoire du croissant," p. 66/295; Whitney Smith, *Flags through the Ages and across the World* (New York: McGraw-Hill, 1975), pp. 41–42; Zaki, *Aʿlām al-duwal al-ʿarabiyya*, pp. 26–27; idem, *Al-Aʿlām wa-shārāt al-mulk*, pp. 26–27. On early Islamic banner colors in general, see also Wellhausen, *The Arab Kingdom and Its Fall*, p. 533 n. 1.

8. Al-Sabiʾ, *Rusūm dār al-khilāfa*, pp. 76–77. Al-Sabiʾ notes that "it has been said that one banner was for the East, the other for the West" (p. 76); perhaps these associations recall the civil war between al-Amin and al-Maʾmun, the sons of Harun al-Rashid, whose armies presumably carried different-colored banners. Otherwise, the comment may reflect the faint influence of the Chinese association of geographical quadrants with colors.

9. Halm, *Empire of the Mahdi*, pp. 186, 414; Paula Sanders, *Ritual, Politics, and the City in Fatimid Cairo* (Albany: State University of New York Press, 1994), pp. 31; 88–89; 170 n. 196; Irene A. Bierman, *Writing Signs: The Fatimid Public Text* (Berkeley: University of California Press, 1998), pp. 21, 36, 105, 120.

10. Halm, *Empire of the Mahdi*, pp. 186, 413–14—although Wellhausen notes that white was early on the color of ʿAlid opponents of the ʿAbbasids; see *The Arab Kingdom and Its Fall*, p. 533 n. 1.

11. Halm, *Empire of the Mahdi*, pp. 147, 320, 324–25, 354; Sanders, *Ritual, Politics, and the City*, p. 96; Bierman, *Writing Signs*, pp. 74, 121–22, 125.

12. Evliya Çelebi, *Seyahatname*, vol. 10: 366; Bierman, *Writing Signs*, pp. 121–22. The lion is uncharacteristic of Fatimid textiles, however, so this banner may have been a Mamluk product.

13. Ramazan Şeşen, *Salâhaddin Eyyûbi ve Devri*, 2d printing, foreword by Ekmeleddin İhsanoğlu (Istanbul: İslam Tarih, Sanat ve Kültürünü Araştırma Vakfı, 2000), pp. 232–33. I am grateful to Dr. Cüneyt Kanat for bringing Şeşen's work to my attention.

14. Ahmad b. ʿAli al-Qalqashandi (1365/6–1418), *Ṣubḥ al-aʿshʾā fī ṣināʿat al-inshā*, 14 vols. (Cairo: Al-Muʾassasa al-Misriyya al-ʿAmma li'l-Taʾlif wa'l-Tarjama wa'l-Tibaʿa wa'l-Nashr, 1964), vol. 4: 57; Şeşen, *Salâhaddin Eyyûbi*, p. 233; L. A. Mayer, *Mamluk Costume: A Survey* (Geneva: A. Kundig, 1952), p. 46. I thank Amalia Levanoni for her insight into this issue.

15. Bethany J. Walker, "Rethinking Mamluk Textiles," *Mamluk Studies Review* 4 (2000): 190 and figure 18. On Mamluk blazons generally, see Mayer, *Saracenic Heraldry*.

16. Ibn Taghri Birdi, *History of Egypt*, vol. 2: 47.

17. See the full discussion in Zygulski, *Ottoman Art in the Service of the Empire*, pp. 17–24. Fındıklılı Silahdar Mehmed Agha's *Silāḥdār Tārīḫi* is cited on p. 19.

18. Zygulski, *Ottoman Art in the Service of the Empire*, pp. 6, Figure 3b; 7–8.

19. Ibid., pp. 5, Figure 2d–e; 7; 8; 72, Figure 16; 74–75; 83–84. For Ilkhanid and Timurid images of flags with *tuğs*, see Basil Gray, *Persian Painting*, 2d ed. (1961; reprint, New York: Rizzoli, 1977), pp. 43, 89.

20. On this point, see Faruk Sümer, Ahmet E. Uysal, and Warren S. Walker, eds. and trans., *The Book of Dede Korkut: A Turkish Epic* (Austin: University of Texas Press, 1972, 1991), p. 190 n. 12.

21. Nour, "L'histoire du croissant," pp. 51/280, 65/294. On the Oghuz, see, for example, Sümer, et al., eds. and trans., *Book of Dede Korkut*, pp. x–xviii.

See, however, Colin Heywood's revisionist theory of Ottoman origins: "Filling the Black Hole: The Emergence of the Bithynian Atamanates," in *The Great Ottoman Turkish Civilisation*, eds., Kemal Çiçek, Ercüment Kuran, Nejat Göyünç, and İlber Ortaylı, 4 vols. (Ankara: Yeni Türkiye Yayınevi, 2000), vol. 1: 107–15.

22. Nour, "L'Histoire du croissant," pp. 51/280, 65/294, 113/342. See also Evliya Çelebi, *Seyahatname*, vol. 10: 89. On the Rum Seljuks, see Mehmed Fuad Köprülü, *The Seljuks of Anatolia: Their History and Culture according to Local Muslim Sources*, trans. Gary Leiser (Salt Lake City: University of Utah Press, 1992).

23. Köprülü, *The Seljuks of Anatolia*, pp. 47–48.

24. Ibid., pp. 42–43.

25. Sümer, et al., eds. and trans., *Book of Dede Korkut*, pp. 44, 164, 165.

26. Ibid., pp. 21, 24, 25–26, 32, 35, 48, 62, 68, 116, 134, 146, 173.

27. Ibid., pp. 9–10, 65 and p. 193 n. 42. On the other hand, Azrail, the angel of death, is described as "red-winged;" see pp. 90–93.

28. Ibid., p. 51. Cf. the many references to red as the color of blood and, therefore, death in the *Thousand Nights and One Night.*

29. Sümer, et al., eds. and trans., *Book of Dede Korkut*, pp. 16, 22, 24, 52–53, 55, 59, 60, 71, 109, 120, 128, 138, 146, 151, 155, 172, 173. Correspondingly, Edward Lane reports that dreams in which the colors white and green appear are thought to be good while those in which red and black appear are thought to be bad; see *Manners and Customs*, p. 261.

30. Palmer, "Origin of the Janissaries," p. 452; Irène Mélikoff, *Hadji Bektach: Une mythe et ses avatars—Genèse et évolution du soufisme populaire en Turquie* (Leiden: Brill, 1998), pp. 101–03.

31. Palmer, "Origin of the Janissaries," p. 474; Mélikoff, *Hadji Bektach*, pp. 80–81. Konstantin Mihalowicz transmits what seems to be a garbled version of this origin myth; see *Memoirs of a Janissary*, p. 35. He also has Osman hanging a red flag from his tent (p. 31).

32. Köprülü, *The Seljuks of Anatolia*, p. 59.

33. Mélikoff, *Hadji Bektach*, p. 74.

34. Nour, "L'Histoire du croissant," p. 111/340; see also Zaki, *Aʿlām al-duwal al-ʿarabiyya*, pp. 35, 37–40; idem, *Al-Aʿlām wa-shārāt al-mulk*, pp. 30–33, 39.

35. Şiri ʿAli, *Tārīḫ-i fetḥ-i Mıṣır*, Topkapı Palace Library, MS Eminet Hazinesi 1433/2 (fos. 219r–268v, following the *Tārīḫ-i Āl-i ʿOsmān*), fo. 248 v. This Sinan Pasha was later killed in battle by Kurtbay (see chapter 7).

36. Fairfax Downey, *Soliman le Magnifique*, trans. S. M. Guillemin (Paris: Payot, 1930), cited in Nour, "L'Histoire du croissant," p. 112/341.

37. Luigi Ferdinando Marsigli, *Stato militare dell'impèrio ottomano*, vol. 2, plate 20, and supplement to plates 20–22, cited in Zygulski, *Ottoman Art in the Service of the Empire*, pp. 29–30. See also İ. H. Uzunçarşılı, *Osmanlı Devleti Teşkilâtından Kapukulu Ocakları*, 2 vols. (Ankara: Türk Tarih Kurumu Basımevi, 1943), vol. 1: 294–305; Fevzi Kurtoğlu, *Türk Bayrağı ve Ay Yıldız* (Ankara: Türk Tarih Kurumu, 1938, 1987, 1992), pp. 64–66. Mihalowicz asserts that a white flag with gold letters represents the emperor's power, while the *sipahi* cavalry's flag is red, and the Janissaries' flags are red and green or red and gold; see *Memoirs of a Janissary*, p. 165. Kâtib Çelebi notes the ships of the Ottoman navy flying red and yellow flags supplied by the central government (*miriden*); see *Tuḥfet ül-kibār*, p. 157. See also Zaki, *Aᶜlām al-duwal al-ᶜarabiyya*, pp. 37, 40; idem, *Al-Aᶜlām wa-shārāt al-mulk*, pp. 30–31.

38. Lane, *Manners and Customs*, pp. 241–42. There is also some indication that Ibrahim-i Gülşeni, head of an offshoot of the Khalwati order, also favored white; see Muhyi-i Gülşeni, *Menâḳib-i İbrâhîm-i Gülşenî*, vol. 3, no. 9, p. 469.

39. Al-Damurdashi, *Durra*, pp. 472–73. See also Hickok, *Ottoman Military Administration in Eighteenth-Century Bosnia*, pp. 1–2, 21–36. The dream account is evidently taken from a panegyric biography of Hekimoğlu ᶜAli by his son; see ibid., p. xxii. I believe that Banja Luka, not Belgrade, is intended where al-Damurdashi has "Budin."

40. Lane, *Manners and Customs*, p. 492.

41. Robert S. Lopez, "Silk Industry in the Byzantine Empire," *Speculum* 20 (1945): 10–11, 14–15, 42. Zaki, *Aᶜlām al-duwal al-ᶜarabiyya*, pp. 35, 37, stresses that the Ottoman flag in Egypt was red.

42. Haci ᶜAli, *Ahbār ül-yamānī*, fos. 205v–208v.

43. Ibid., fos. 205v–206v, 221v; Yahya b. al-Husayn, *Ghāyat al-amānī*, vol. 2: 800, 818.

44. Halm, *Empire of the Mahdi*, p. 186.

45. Tritton, *Rise of the Imams of Sanaa*, p. 125.

46. Playfair, *History of Arabia Felix*, p. 29.

47. The name is spelled with a *te*, as opposed to a *ṭa*, which would normally indicate that it should be pronounced Tevkli and carry the first meaning. However, *tok*, denoting the salivary gland, can also be spelled with a *te*; thus *toklu* could also mean "having swollen or pendulant salivary glands" (the chief symptom of mumps).

48. Mühimme Defteri 3, Nos. 316 (8 Zilhicce 966/3 September 1559); 607 (11 Rebiülevvel 967/11 December 1559); 772 (15 Cemazeülevvel 967/12 February

1560); 792 (18 Cemazeülevvel 967/15 February 1560); 1458 (26 Zilkade 967/18 August 1560).

49. On this point, see Anonymous, *Tevārīḫ-i Mıṣr-ı Ḳāhire*, fo. 67v.

50. Mathers, trans., *The Thousand Nights and One Night*, vol. 4: 503. See also pp. 460–61, where the tribe of Bakr is repeatedly associated with red; and pp. 465–66, where the tents of Kudaid, the enemy of the Kinda leader Hujr, are described as red.

51. Mühimme Defteri 5, No. 428 (27 Rebiülevvel 973/22 October 1565).

52. Ignaz Goldziher, *Muslim Studies*, ed. S. M. Stern, trans. C. R. Barber and S. M. Stern, 2 vols. (Chicago: Aldine Publishing Co., 1968), vol. 1: 78–79.

53. Holt, *Egypt and the Fertile Crescent*, pp. 113–23; Mikhayil Mishaqa (1799–1888), *Murder, Mayhem, Pillage, and Plunder: The History of Lebanon in the Eighteenth and Nineteenth Centuries*, trans. Wheeler M. Thackston, Jr. (Albany: State University of New York Press, 1988), pp. 6, 7.

54. Goldziher, *Muslim Studies*, vol. 1: 79.

55. Lyons, *The Arabian Epic*, vol. 3: 651.

56. Ibid., vol. 3: 653.

57. *EI²*, *s.v.*"Kulayb b. Rabīᶜa," by Levi Della Vida.

58. Playfair, *History of Arabia Felix*, p. 47. Curiously, the Mühimme records a district called *Levn-i Ḥamrāᵓ*, or "Red Color," in the vicinity of Sanᶜaᵓ in the sixteenth century: Mühimme Defteri 5, No. 1226 (20 Şaban 973/12 March 1566).

59. Ibn Ishaq, *Life of Muhammad*, p. 9.

60. See n. 3, above.

61. Ibn Ishaq, *Life of Muhammad*, pp. 150, 413, 484–85.

62. Chelkowski, "When Time Is No Time and Space Is No Space: The Passion Plays of Husayn," in *Taᶜziyeh*, ed. Milla Cozart Riggio (Hartford, CT: Trinity College, 1988) esp. p. 16; see also p. 39, figures 23–24; idem, "Taᶜziyeh: Indigenous Avant-Garde Theatre of Iran," in *Taᶜziyeh: Ritual and Drama in Iran,* ed., Peter J. Chelkowski (New York: New York University Press and Soroush Press, 1979) p. 9; Andrzej Wirth, "Semiological Aspects of the *Taᶜziyeh*," in *Taᶜziyeh: Ritual and Drama*, p. 35.

63. Chelkowski, "Taᶜziyeh," p. 3. See also Yitzhak Nakash, "An Attempt to Trace the Origin of the Rituals of ᶜĀshurāᵓ," *Die Welt des Islams* 33 (1993): 161–81.

64. Chelkowski, "Taᶜziyeh," p. 4.

65. Mirjafari, "Haydari-Niᶜmati Conflicts," esp. pp. 144–47, 151.

66. Evliya Çelebi, *Seyahatname*, vol. 10: 696; Lane, *Manners and Customs*, p. 428. Lane also notes (pp. 451, 466) that the celebration of the birthday (*mawlid*) of the "Hasanayn"—that is, Husayn and his older brother Hasan—was second only to the Prophet's birthday in spiritual significance.

67. Evliya Çelebi, *Seyahatname*, vol. 10: 415; Lane, *Manners and Customs*, pp. 214–16. See also Naguib Mahfouz, *Palace Walk* [*Bayn al-Qaṣrayn*], trans. William Maynard Hutchins and Olive E. Kenny (1956; reprint, New York: Doubleday, 1990), pp. 48–49. The Umayyad Mosque in Damascus also claims to be the resting place of Husayn's head.

68. Winter, *Egyptian Society under Ottoman Rule*, p. 118.

69. On this point, see al-Jabarti, *ᶜAjāʾib* (Cairo), vol. 2: 252–54; vol. 4: 43, 47, 85, 245–46; Lane, *Manners and Customs*, pp. 461–62.

70. Martin, "Khalwati Order of Dervishes," pp. 276–78; Doris Behrens-Abouseif, "Four Domes of the Late Mamluk Period," *Annales Islamologiques* 17 (1981): 191–201; idem, "An Unlisted Monument of the Fifteenth Century: The Dome of Zāwiyat al-Damirdaš," *Annales Islamologiques* 18 (1982): 105–21; Doris Behrens-Abouseif and Leonor Fernandes, "Sufi Architecture in Early Ottoman Cairo," *Annales Islamologiques* 20 (1984): 103–14.

71. Al-Jabarti, *ᶜAjāʾib* (Cairo), vol. 1: 70. The Arabic phrase is *ḥattā fī awānī al-mutanāwilā wa'l-maʾkūlāt wa'l-mashrūbāt*, which can be translated "even cutlery and dishes for food and drink" or, alternatively, "even dishes and food and drink," depending on whether or not we interpret the entire phrase as a compound (*iḍāfa*) with *awānī* (vessels). Holt translates it as "even in the table implements and utensils for food and drink." See "Al-Jabarti's Introduction," p. 48.

72. Cameron, *Circus Factions*, p. 54.

73. Sümer, et al., eds. and trans., *Book of Dede Korkut*, pp. 12, 16, 59, 60.

74. It is worth noting in this connection that the Haydaris regarded the Niᶜmatis as ritually impure and would not eat with them, intermarry with them, or visit their bathhouses; see Mirjafari, "Haydari-Niᶜmati Conflicts," pp. 147, 154.

75. Jaroslav Stetkevych, *Muhammad and the Golden Bough: Reconstructing Arabian Myth* (Bloomington, IN: Indiana University Press, 1996), pp. 22 23. See Genesis 25: 25, 29–34.

76. Holt, "Al-Jabarti's Introduction," pp. 42–45; al-Damurdashi, *Durra*, p. 2 (where he refers to Saᶜd and Haram, not Faqari and Qasimi, in processions).

77. Al-Jabarti, *ᶜAjāʾib* (Cairo), vol. 1: 71.

78. See, for example, the painting "Procession of the pasha at his arrival in Cairo" by the late eighteenth-century French painter Cassas, reproduced in Behrens-Abouseif, *Egypt's Adjustment to Ottoman Rule*, plate 1.

Chapter 6: The Knob and the Disk

1. On these processions, see Behrens-Abouseif, *Egypt's Adjustment to Ottoman Rule*, pp. 54–60.

2. H. B. Paksoy, "Two Altaic Games: 'Chelik-Chomak' and 'Jirid Oyunu,' " in *Aspects of Altaic Civilization III*, ed., Denis Sinor (Bloomington, IN: Indiana University Research Institute for Inner Asian Studies, 1990), pp. 187–96; Özdemir Nutku, *IV. Mehmed'in Edirne Şenliği (1675)* (Ankara: Türk Tarih Kurumu Basımevi, 1972, 1987), pp. 107–08. See also Lane, *Manners and Customs*, pp. 351–52.

3. Zygulski, *Ottoman Art in the Service of the Empire*, pp. 74–75.

4. Ibid., pp. 74–75; p. 72, fig. 16.d.

5. Smith, *Flags through the Ages*, p. 62; Zygulski, *Ottoman Art in the Service of the Empire*, p. 5, fig. 2.d.

6. Zygulski, *Ottoman Art in the Service of the Empire*, p. 75 and illus. 13.

7. Reproduced in Robert Irwin, *Islamic Art in Context: Art, Architecture and the Literary World* (New York: Harry N. Abrams/Prentice Hall, 1997), p. 231, fig. 194.

8. Wheeler M. Thackston, ed., trans., and annotator, *The Baburnama: Memoirs of Babur, Prince and Emperor* (New York and Oxford: Oxford University Press, in association with the Freer Gallery of Art and the Arthur M. Sackler Gallery, Washington, DC, 1996), p. 136. Zygulski, *Ottoman Art in the Service of the Empire*, p. 89, has Babur oiling the standards rather than throwing *koumiss* at them.

9. Mehrdad R. Izady, *The Kurds: A Concise Handbook* (Washington, DC: Taylor and Francis, Inc., 1992), p. 151.

10. See, for example, Paul Dundas, *The Jains* (London and New York: Routledge, 1992), pp. 175–81.

11. Stuart Cary Welch, *Imperial Mughal Painting* (New York: George Braziller, 1978), pp. 45 (plate 3), 62–63 (plates 12–13).

12. For both types, see, e.g., Gray, *Persian Painting*, pp. 134–35; Yuri A. Petrosyan, Marie Lukens Swietochowski, and Stefano Carboni, *Pages of Perfection: Islamic Paintings and Calligraphy from the Russian Academy of Sciences, St. Petersburg* (Lugano: Art Restoration for Cultural Heritage Foundation; Milan: Electa, 1995), p. 253. It seems to have been only under the Qajars that a finial in the form of a hand, typically associated with Husayn's standard-bearer ᶜAbbas, became widespread. See, for example, Layla S. Diba, ed., with Maryam Ekhtiar, *Royal Persian Paintings: The Qajar Epoch, 1785–1925* (Brooklyn: Brooklyn Museum of Art, in association with I. B. Tauris Publishers, 1998), p. 201, fig. 52.

13. Metin And, *Ritüelden Drama: Karbelâ-Muharrem-Taʾziye* (Istanbul: Yapıkredi Yayınları, 2002), pp. 334–36, 339, 340.

14. Cozart Riggio, ed., *Taʿziyeh*, back inside cover.

15. Niebuhr, *Travels*, p. 381.

16. Zygulski, *Ottoman Art in the Service of the Empire*, pp. 21–22, 32. See also Lane, *Manners and Customs*, pp. 247, 438–40. Lane reports that such Qurʾans, known as *muṣḥafs*, were attached to the *maḥmil*, the symbolic litter that accompanied the Egyptian pilgrimage caravan, and that they were even worn on the right side by individuals.

17. Hülya Tezcan and Turgay Tezcan, *Türk Sancak Alemleri* (Ankara: Türk Tarih Kurumu Basımevi, 1992), plates 34–40, 42–54.

18. As the botanist Albert Deflers explained in the late nineteenth century, "[T]he reason for the dove replacing the crescent over the minarets was to be found in the legend that when the Prophet took refuge in a cave on Jabal Thawr [en route from Mecca to Medina], two doves hung their nests over the entrance and, when pursuers arrived, were cooing with such tranquillity that it seemed impossible that there could be anyone inside": Deflers, *Voyage au Yémen*, pp. 59–60, quoted in R. L. Bidwell, "Western Accounts of Sanʿaʾ, 1510–1962," in *Sanʿaʾ: An Arabian Islamic City*, eds., R. B. Serjeant and Ronald Lewcock (London: World of Islam Festival Trust, 1983), p. 113. This would seem to be one of the many variations on the story of the Prophet and Abu Bakr sheltering in a cave, over whose entrance a spider spun a web.

19. *Türk Ansiklopedisi*, *s.v.* "Monçuk," by H. Eren; *s.v.* "Boncuk" (author not given).

20. Niebuhr, *Travels*, p. 381.

21. F. Steingass, *Persian-English Dictionary* (Beirut: Librarie du Liban, 1892, 1970), p. 398.

22. Dozy, *Supplément aux dictionnaires arabes*, vol. 1: 204.

23. Zygulski, *Ottoman Art in the Service of the Empire*, p. 73, fig. 17.b. It is also possible that al-Damurdashi's account conflates the Ottoman *tuğ* (knob) with the Ottoman *ʿalem* (a circular metal plate at the top of a flagstaff).

24. Jean de Thévenot, *Relation d'un voyage fait au Levant . . .* (Paris: T. Iolly, 1665), p. 470; see also p. 469.

25. Zygulski, *Ottoman Art in the Service of the Empire*, p. 89.

26. Şükrü Bitlisi, *Selimname* (1525), Istanbul, Topkapı Palace Library, MS Hazine 1597–98, fo. 113a. Interestingly, the text takes up the color of the Ottoman banner: "The air was filled with the red and green flag. The sky, which had been blue, turned black as pitch. The shah of the east [i.e., Selim] was the dawn of that day; the flag removed the bandage from [all] eyes." (Āl-yeşil

bayrāḳla tutdi hava. Laciverd iken sipsiyah oldu semāʾ. Şarḳ şāhi dāḫi ol gün ṣubḥdem. Çeşmet [*sic*] ile bendi kaldırdı ᶜalem.) Reading *ᶜalem* as a misspelling of *ᶜālem* (world) would give the alternative ". . . [Selim] removed the bandage from the eyes of the world." I am grateful for Boğaç Ergene's suggestions in deciphering this text.

27. For examples, see Petrosyan, et al., *Pages of Perfection*, pp. 284–85.

28. George F. Scanlon, ed. and trans., *A Muslim Manual of War* (Cairo: American University in Cairo Press, 1961).

29. Gabriella Uluhogian, *Un' antica mappa dell'Armenia: monasteri e santuari dal 1. al 17. secolo* (Ravenna: Longo, 2000).

Chapter 7: Selim and Sudun in the Origin Myths

1. Al-Damurdashi, *al-Durra al-muṣāna*, p. 2; al-Qinali, *Majmūᶜ laṭīf*, as quoted in Holt, "Al-Jabartī's Introduction," pp. 42–43.

2. Ahmed Çelebi, *Awḍaḥ*, pp. 283–84; al-Jabarti, *ᶜAjāʾib* (Cairo), vol. 1: 68–71.

3. Cornell H. Fleischer, *Bureaucrat and Intellectual in the Ottoman Empire: The Historian Mustafa Ali (1541–1600)* (Princeton, NJ: Princeton University Press, 1986), pp. 279–80.

4. For example, ᶜAbd al-Rauf b. Taj al-Arifih al-Munawi (d. 1621), *Al-Tasyīr bi-sharḥ al-Jāmiᶜ al-ṣaghīr fī aḥādith al-bashīr al-naḍīr*, commentary on Jalal al-Din ᶜAbd al-Rahman al-Suyuti (1445–1505), *Al-Jāmiᶜ al-ṣaghīr . . .* (Cairo: Al-Matbaᶜa al-Misriyya, 1286/1869–70), vol. 2: 290. See also Stephane Yérasimos, *Légendes d'empire: La formation de Constantinople et de Sainte-Sophie dans les traditions turques* (Paris: Institut Français d'Études Anatoliennes d'Istanbul and Jean Maisonneuve Successeur Librairie d'Amérique et d'Orient, 1990), pp. 187–92; Nadia M. El-Cheikh, "Constantinople through Arab Eyes: A Mythology," in *Myths, Historical Archetypes, and Symbolic Figures in Arabic Literature: Towards a New Hermeneutic Approach—Proceedings of the International Symposium in Beirut, June 25th–30th, 1996*, eds. Angelika Neuwirth, Birgit Embaló, Sebastian Günther, and Maher Jarrar (Stuttgart: Franz Steiner Verlag, 1999), p. 527.

5. R. W. Southern, *Western Views of Islam in the Middle Ages* (Cambridge, MA: Harvard University Press, 1962), pp. 84ff.

6. Mihalowicz, *Memoirs of a Janissary*, p. 115.

7. Bacqué-Grammont, *Les Ottomanes, les Safavides, et leurs voisins*, pp. 50–293 passim.; Holt, *Egypt and the Fertile Crescent*, pp. 40–45.

8. Celalzade Mustafa Çelebi (d. 1567), *Selīm-Nāme*, ed. Ahmet Uğur and Mustafa Çuhadar (Ankara: Başbakanlık Basımevi, 1990), pp. 418, 420, 424–25. See also Şiri ᶜAli, *Tārīḫ-i fetḥ-i Mıṣır*, fos. 257v–258r.

9. It has been pointed out that "classical" Ottoman legal structures were already in place before Süleyman's reign. See Halil Inalcik, "Suleiman the Lawgiver and Ottoman Law," *Archivum Ottomanicum* 1 (1969): 105–38; Uriel Heyd, *Studies in Old Ottoman Criminal Law*, ed. V. L. Ménage (Oxford: Clarendon Press, 1973), pp. 7–33.

10. Barkan, ed., "Mısır Kanunnâmesi."

11. Cornell H. Fleischer, "The Lawgiver as Messiah: The Making of the Imperial Image in the Reign of Süleymân," in *Soliman le Magnifique et son temps: Actes du Colloque de Paris Galeries Nationales du Grand Palais, 7–10 mars 1990*, ed., Gilles Veinstein (Paris: La Documentation Française, 1992), pp. 160–74; Cemal Kafadar, "The Myth of the Golden Age: Ottoman Historical Consciousness in the Post-Süleymânic Era," in *Süleymân the Second [sic] and His Time*, eds., Halil Inalcik and Cemal Kafadar (Istanbul: Isis Press, 1993), pp. 38–45; Barbara Flemming, "Public Opinion under Sultan Süleymân," in *Süleymân the Second*, eds. Inalcik and Kafadar, pp. 53–57; Halil Inalcik, "State, Sovereignty, and Law during the Reign of Süleymân," in *Süleymân the Second*, eds., Inalcik and Kafadar, pp. 59–69, 76.

12. Fleischer, "The Lawgiver as Messiah," pp. 163–64. See also Subrahmanyam, "Du Tage au Gange," p. 59.

13. Fleischer, *Bureaucrat and Intellectual*, pp. 279–80. See also idem, "The Lawgiver as Messiah," pp. 162–63.

14. Al-Ishaqi, *Akhbār al-uwal*, p. 163. See also Subrahmanyam, "Du Tage au Gange," pp. 66–67 and n. 49.

15. The three epics are Ferdowsi's *Shahname*; Ahmedi's *Iskendername*, itself derived from a Byzantine source; and Nizami's *Khamsa*; see *EI*², *s.v.* "*Iskandarname*," by A. Abel. See also Ferdowsi (c. 940–c. 1022), *The Epic of the Kings: Shāh-Nāma of Ferdowsi*, abridged trans. by Reuben Levy, foreword by Ehsan Yarshater, preface by Amin Banani, introduction by Dick Davis (Costa Mesa, CA, and New York: Mazda Publishers, in association with Bibliotheca Persica, 1996), pp. 232–50. Evliya Çelebi briefly discusses different versions of the Iskender stories; see his *Seyahatname*, vol. 10: 574, 600. See also Mather, trans., *The Thousand Nights and One Night*, vol. 4: 520, where a king is described thus: ". . . whose glory surpassed the glory of Feridun [a hero of the *Shahname*], whose star was the star of Alexander, whose fortune was the fortune of the Persian Anushirwan."

16. For examples, see Gray, *Persian Painting*, pp. 28–29, 32, 74, 76, 97, 128, 131, 140; Filiz Çağman, *Traditional Turkish Arts: Miniature* (Ankara: Turkish Republic, Ministry of Culture and Tourism, General Directorate of Fine Arts, n.d. [1987?]), p. 46.

17. Stephen F. Dale, "The Legacy of the Timurids," *Journal of the Royal Asiatic Society* 8, no. 1 (1998): 45–58; idem, "The Poetry and Autobiography of

the *Bâbur-nâma*," *Journal of Asian Studies* 55, no. 3 (1996): 635–64. For an interesting comparison of Selim to Timur, see Ibn Zunbul, *Wāqiᶜat*, p. 51.

18. Celalzade Salih Çelebi, *Tārīḫ-i Mışr-ı cedīd*, Istanbul, Süleymaniye Library, MS Çelebi Abdullah Efendi 248, fo. 123v.

19. Abdullah Çelebi Ridvan Paşazade, *Tārīḫ-i Mışır*, Istanbul, Süleymaniye Library, MS Fatih 4362, fo. 106v; Şiri ᶜAli, *Tārīḫ-i fetḥ-i Mışır*, fo. 248r.

20. Evliya Çelebi, *Seyahatname*, vol. 10: 365, 366–67.

21. Al-Ishaqi, *Akhbār al-uwal*, p. 144.

22. Evliya Çelebi, *Seyahatname*, vol. 10: 529. In this same passage, Bayezid rejects the idea of making a bid for the New World. The *Kızıl Elma*, a perennial goal of Ottoman conquest, is conventionally identified with Vienna or Rome (neither of which, obviously, Süleyman managed to conquer). On the *Kızıl Elma* motif, see *EI*², *s.v.* "Kızıl Elma," by Pertev Naili Boratov.

23. For example, Ridvan Paşazade, *Tārīḫ-i Mışır*, fo. 128v; Keşfi Mehmed Çelebi (d. 1524), *Selimname*, Istanbul, Süleymaniye Library, MS Esad Efendi 2147, fos. 69r, 78v; Süheyli Efendi, *Tevārīḫ-i Mışīr*, fo. 81v; Celalzade Mustafa, *Selīm-Nāme*, p. 426.

24. Süheyli Efendi, *Tevārīḫ-i Mışīr*, fos. 99v–100r; Keşfi Mehmed, *Selimname*, fo. 80r; Şiri ᶜAli, *Tārīḫ-i fetḥ-i Mışır*, fo. 255r; Yusuf Efendi, *Tārīḫ-i Mışır*, Istanbul, Süleymaniye Library, MS Esad Efendi 2148, fo. 52r; al-Ishaqi, *Akhbār al-uwal*, p. 147.

25. Ibn Zunbul, *Wāqiᶜat*, pp. 70–74, 165; Şiri ᶜAli, *Tārīḫ-i fetḥ-i Mışır*, fo. 258v; Süheyli Efendi, *Tevārīḫ-i Mışīr*, fos. 101r–v, 116v; Yusuf Efendi, *Tārīḫ-i Mışır*, fo. 41v.

26. Evliya Çelebi, *Seyahatname*, vol. 10: 364–66.

27. Al-Ishaqi, *Akhbār al-uwal*, pp. 145–47. This is also true of Muhyi-yi Gülşeni, *Menâḳib-i İbrâhîm-i Gülşenî*, p. 352.

28. Ibn Zunbul, *Wāqiᶜat*, pp. 110–11, 140–41; see also p. 188.

29. Behrens-Abouseif, *Egypt's Adjustment to Ottoman Rule*, pp. 121–22.

30. For a single example, see Richard W. Kaeuper and Elspeth Kennedy, eds. and trans., *The Book of Chivalry of Geoffroi de Charny: Text, Context, and Translation* (Philadelphia: University of Pennsylvania Press, 1996), esp. pp. 86–87, 94–95.

31. Wellhausen, *The Arab Kingdom and Its Fall*, pp. 322–23, 419.

32. See the following chapters in María Rosa Menocal, Raymond P. Scheindlin, and Michael Sells, eds., *The Literature of al-Andalus* (Cambridge: Cambridge University Press, 2000): Dwight Reynolds, "Music," pp. 69–72;

Tovah Rosen, "The Muwashshah," pp. 177–78, 186 n. 11; Lourdes María Alvárez, "Petrus Alfonsi," p. 282; Devin J. Stewart, "Ibn Zaydun," p. 314; Karla Mallette, "Poetries of the Norman Courts," pp. 377–86 passim..

33. See, for example, Scanlon, ed. and trans., *A Muslim Manual of War;* see also Ayalon, "*Furūsiyya* Exercises."

34. On this point, see David Ayalon, "The Circassians in the Mamluk Kingdom," *Journal of the American Oriental Society* 69, no. 3 (1949): 144–45; idem, *Gunpowder and Firearms in the Mamluk Kingdom: A Challenge to Medieval Society* (London: Vallentine, Mitchell, and Co., Ltd., 1956), pp. 52–57.

35. Rhoads Murphey's *Ottoman Warfare, 1500–1700* (New Brunswick, NJ: Rutgers University Press, 1998) casts doubt on the accuracy of this claim, since the author argues convincingly that the Ottomans relied preponderantly on their mastery of older techniques of warfare during this period; see pp. 14–15, 32, 35–36, 109–10.

36. Ayalon, *Gunpowder and Firearms,* pp. 63–82.

37. See chapter 6, n. 2.

38. *Sīrat al-Ẓāhir Baybars,* vol. 2: 856–59, 1289–92, 1297; vol. 3: 1497; Lyons, *The Arabian Epic,* vol. 3: 130, 145, 220, 238, 310, 311, 334, 380, 439, 447, 473, 479.

39. Ibn Taghri Birdi, *History of Egypt,* vol. 2, part 3: *1412–1422* A.D., p. 80.

40. Ibn Iyas, *Journal d'un bourgeois du Caire,* vol. 1: 341, 344; vol. 2: 2, 39, 65–68; idem, *An Account of the Ottoman Conquest,* pp. 112–15.

41. See Ibn Taghri Birdi, *History of Egypt,* vols. 1–2, passim.

42. Ayalon, "*Furūsiyya* Exercises," p. 59.

43. This derives from several mentions of Haman in the Qurʾan in connection with Pharaoh: Qurʾan 28:5, 9, 37; 40:23, 36.

44. Ibn Taghri Birdi, *History of Egypt,* vol. 1, part 1: 1–4.

45. Ibn Iyas, *Badāʾiʿ al-zuhūr fī waqāʾiʿ al-duhūr,* ed. Muhammad Mustafa, vol. 5 (922–28/1516–22) (Cairo: Al-Haʾya al-Misriyya al-ʿAmma li'l-Kitab, 1404/1984), p. 151. See also idem, *Journal d'un bourgeois du Caire,* vol. 2: 145. Wiet's translation of *malak al-Rūm* as "kings of Anatolian origin" is open to question, however.

46. For example, the famous story from Ferdowsi's *Shahname* of Anushirvan overhearing two owls lamenting the state of ruin to which Anushirvan's policies have brought their village. This story was appropriated by al-Turtushi (ca. 1059–1126), who, in his *Sirāj al-mulūk,* replaced Anushirvan with the ʿAbbasid caliph al-Maʾmun (r. 809–33 C.E.). See Lewis, ed. and trans., *Islam . . . ,* vol. 2: 134–35. See also Ibn Khaldun, *Muqaddimah,* pp. 40–42, 238–39 (where the story

is applied to Bahram b. Bahram); Mathers, trans., *The Thousand Nights and One Night*, pp. 260, where a king is lauded with "his justice passed the justice of Khusrau-Anushirwan, and his generosity exceeded the generosity of Hatim of the tribe of Taiy."

47. Evliya Çelebi, *Narrative of Travels*, pp. 169, 170, 173; idem, *Seyahatname*, vol. 10: 696.

Chapter 8: The Mulberry Tree

1. Jane Hathaway, "Sultans, Pashas, *Taqwīms*, and Mühimmes: A Reconsideration of Chronicle-Writing in Eighteenth-Century Ottoman Egypt," in *Eighteenth-Century Egypt: The Arabic Manuscript Sources*, ed., Daniel N. Crecelius (Claremont, CA: Regina Press, 1990), p. 66.

2. Ahmed Çelebi, *Awḍaḥ*, pp. 271–83.

3. Ayalon, "Studies in al-Jabarti I," pp. 293–97.

4. Ahmed Çelebi, *Awḍaḥ*, p. 283.

5. In addition to p. 283, see ibid., pp. 352, 415, 480, 482.

6. Al-Damurdashi, *Al-Durra al-muṣāna*, p. 206.

7. Ovid, *Selections from the Metamorphoses and Heroides of Publius Ovidius Naso, with a Literal and Interlinear Translation*, trans. Hamilton, ed. Thomas Clark and George William Heilig (New York: Charles De Silver and Sons; David McKay Co., Inc., 1889), pp. 131–38. I am grateful to Richard Groening for alerting me to this connection.

8. Al-Jabarti, *ʿAjāʾib* (Cairo), vol. 1: 254.

9. Khoury, *State and Provincial Society in the Ottoman Empire*, pp. 40–41, 62, 65, 190.

10. Izady, *The Kurds*, pp. 137–45.

11. Philip G. Kreyenbroek, *Yezidism: Its Background, Observances and Textual Tradition* (Lewiston, NY: The Edwin Mellen Press, Ltd., 1995), pp. 73–74, 78, 88 n. 77, 80, 113–14, 148; Chris Hedges, "Satan's Alive and Well, but the Sect May be Dying," *New York Times*, 31 May 1993, p. A2.

12. See, for example, Muhammad b. ʿUmar al-Waqidi (747 or 8–823), *Kitāb al-Maghāzi*, ed. Marsden Jones, 3 vols. (London: Oxford University Press, 1966), vol. 1: 372–73, quoted in Norman A. Stillman, *The Jews of Arab Lands: A History and Source Book* (Philadelphia: Jewish Publication Society, 1979), p. 134. See also Qurʾan 59:5.

13. Ahmed Çelebi, *Awḍaḥ*, p. 352.

14. Silk fiber was widely traded in the Egyptian delta during the Middle Ages; however, this fiber was imported from Syria, Italy, and other regions where silk was cultivated. See S. D. Goitein, *A Mediterranean Society*, vol. 1: *Economic Foundations* (Berkeley: University of California Press, 1967), pp. 101–04, 154, 193, 200, 222–24, 454–55 n. 53; Jane Hathaway, "A Twelfth-Century Partnership in Silk-Trading in the Egyptian Delta: A Geniza Study," *Journal of the Middle East Studies Society at Columbia University* 2, no. 1 (1988): 23–37. For a description of silk making, transport, and trade during the seventeenth century, see Matthee, *The Politics of Trade in Safavid Iran*, chapter 2. In addition, silkworms evidently do not like the leaves of older mulberry trees: ibid., p. 34.

15. John K. Birge, *The Bektashi Order of Dervishes* (London: Luzac and Co., 1937), pp. 37, 57; Mélikoff, *Hadji Bektach*, p. 71.

16. See www.studioa.co.yu/manastiri/ manastiri_cl.html, pp. 1–2; www.heritage.org.yu/kosovo. html; ww.gov.yu/kosovo.facts/index.html.

17. *Türk Ansiklopedisi*, *s.v.* "Tahtacılar," by E. R. Fiğlalı.

18. Naguib Mahfouz, *Ḥikāyāt ḥāratinā*, translated as *Fountain and Tomb*, trans. Soad Sobhy, Essam Fattouh, and James Kenneson (Washington, DC: Three Continents Press, 1988), pp. 11–12, 115–17.

19. *Sīrat al-Ẓāhir Baybars*, vol. 1: 719–31.

20. Al-Damurdashi, *Durra*, p. 78.

21. Ibid., p. 190.

22. Aşıkpaşazade (b. 1400), *Die altosmanische Chronik des Aşikpaşazade*, ed. Friedrich Giese, vol. 1: *Text und Variantenverzeichnis* (Leipzig: Otto Harrassowitz, 1929), pp. 9–11, cited in Rudi Paul Lindner, *Nomads and Ottomans in Medieval Anatolia* (Bloomington, IN: Research Institute for Inner Asian Studies, Indiana University, 1983), p. 37.

23. Cartoon by Sir John Tenniel, *Punch* 1876; reproduced in the British Library exhibition "The Eastern Question: Gladstone and Bulgaria," 21 February–10 May 1992. The tree is labeled "Turkish Rule."

24. Anonymous, *Nisba sharīfa*, fo. 20r.

25. Evliya Çelebi, *Seyhatname*, vol. 10: 553.

26. H. R. Ellis Davidson, *Myths and Symbols in Pagan Europe: Early Scandinavian and Celtic Religions* (Manchester: Manchester University Press, 1988), pp. 23–25, 168–71, 179–81; Freeman, *Stories of the Great Operas*, pp. 518–19; Anna Russell, "*The Ring of the Nibelungs* (An Analysis)," *Anna Russell Sings! Again?*, recorded at Town Hall, New York, 23 April 1953; rereleased on *The Anna Russell Album?*, Columbia Records, New York, 1972.

27. Graves, *The Greek Myths*, vol. 2: 145–46. The Norse/Teutonic gods are supposed to remain eternally young by virtue of eating golden apples tended

by Freia, goddess of spring, a feature that would seem to tie all three myths together; see Ellis Davidson, *Myths and Symbols in Pagan Europe*, pp. 175, 181, 213.

28. Jan and Yvonne Walls, eds. and trans., *Classical Chinese Myths* (Hong Kong: Joint Publishing Co., 1984), pp. 65–69. For a variation on this tale, see Edward T. C. Werner, *Ancient Tales and Folklore of China*, 2d ed. (1922; reprint, London: Bracken Books, 1986), pp. 181–82, 186–87. In a rare instance of the mulberry tree as a bad omen, two mulberry trees supposedly sprang up in the palace of a Shang-dynasty emperor (1637 B.C.E.) and grew at a prodigious rate until he reformed his conduct; see Herbert A. Giles, *Religions of Ancient China* (London: Archibald Constable and Co., Ltd., 1906), pp. 10–11.

29. Devin DeWeese, *Islamization and Native Religion in the Golden Horde: Baba Tükles and Conversion to Islam in Historical and Epic Tradition* (University Park, PA: Pennsylvania State University Press, 1990), pp. 43–49, 273–90, 495, 500, 512. Thanks to Carter Findley for bringing this source to my attention.

30. Ibid., pp. 286–88. See also Subrahmanyam, "Du Tage au Gange," p. 76 and n. 67.

31. DeWeese, *Islamization and Native Religion*, pp. 292–97.

32. *Götterdämmerung*, act 1, scene 1; Freeman, *Stories of the Great Operas*, p. 525.

Chapter 9: The Competitive Feasts

1. This appears to be a form of *khaṣṣakiyya*, which under the Mamluk sultanate denoted the sultan's "bodyguard and select retinue," consisting of his own mamluks. See Ayalon, "Studies on the Structure of the Mamluk Army," 1, pp. 213–16.

2. On this office, see Hathaway, *Politics of Households*, pp. 55, 57–58, 63.

3. Al-Jabarti, *ʿAjāʾib* (Cairo), vol. 1: 71; al-Damurdashi, *Al-Durra al-muṣāna*, pp. 2–4. Al-Damurdashi's version is slightly longer and more elaborate.

4. S. D. Goitein, "Townsman and Fellah: A Geniza Text from the Seventeenth Century," *Asian and African Studies* 8, no. 3 (1972): 257–61.

5. Holt, "Al-Jabarti's Introduction," p. 51; Behrens-Abouseif, *Egypt's Adjustment to Ottoman Rule*, pp. 118–19.

6. Holt, "Al-Jabarti's Introduction," p. 44 n. 1; Behrens-Abouseif, *Egypt's Adjustment to Ottoman Rule*, p. 118.

7. Al-Damurdashi, *Durra*, p. 30.

8. Al-Jabarti, *ʿAjāʾib* (Cairo), vol. 1: 234.

9. For example, *Akhbār al-nuwwāb*, fo. 8v. The chief judge, or *qāḍī ʿaskar*, was often named *qāʾim maqām*, the stand-in for a deposed governor, during this period; see ibid., fos. 5v, 6v, 17v. See also Holt, "Beylicate," pp. 221–22.

10. Barkan, ed., "Mısır Kanunnâmesi," p. 365; Shaw, *Financial and Administrative Organization*, p. 15; Holt, *Egypt and the Fertile Crescent*, p. 51; idem, "Beylicate," pp. 220–21; Hathaway, *Politics of Households*, p. 9.

11. Al-Hallaq, *Tārīḫ-i Mıṣr-ı Ḳāhire*, fos. 160r–176r.

12. See Jane Hathaway, "Çerkes Mehmed Bey: Rebel, Traitor, Hero?" *Turkish Studies Association Bulletin* 22, no. 1 (1998): 110.

13. Qurʾan 89: 5–7; Renard, *Islam and the Heroic Image*, pp. 167–68. See Ibn Khaldun's skeptical view of the city's identity: *Muqaddimah*, pp. 17–18.

14. Wilford, "Ruins in Yemeni Desert," pp. B9–10.

15. Ahmed Ali, trans., *The Qurʾan: A Contemporary Translation*, 2d rev. ed. (Princeton, NJ: Princeton University Press, 1988), p. 535 (translation slightly modified).

16. Renard, *Islam and the Heroic Image*, p. 168.

17. See, for example, Mathers, trans., *The Thousand Nights and One Night*, vol. 4, pp. 3, 438.

18. Renard, *Islam and the Heroic Image*, p. 169.

Chapter 10: Qasimi Genesis?

1. Behrens-Abouseif, *Egypt's Adjustment to Ottoman Rule*, pp. 119–20; Holt, "Beylicate," p. 242.

2. Haci ʿAli, *Aḫbār ül-yamānī*, fo. 210r: "Vilāyet-i Mıṣır'da ilā yevminā hazhā bir ṭaife'nin taġallub ve istīlāsı muʿtād olduğu gibi, ol ʿaṣırda Ḳoca Ḳāsim Bik tevābiʿi cümlīye ġalebe ve ḥukkām üzerine musellaṭ olub, mā beynlerinde ümerāʾ-i muḥāfiẓīn-i Mıṣır'dan ol vaḳit emīr ül-ḥāc olan Qānṣūh Bik ziyādet-i şevket ve māl ve menāl ve ḳüvvet ṣāḥibi olub, ve üzerine kesret ile ʿasker ve ḳūl ṭaifesinden tevābiʿāt irküb, nefisinde ḫafīf ve dārāta māʾil ve aṣlında taʿzīl ve ʿāḳibetkyārından ġāfil olmaġla, dāʾimen ḥukkāma ḳarşu koyub, ve maḳṣūdunca musāʿadet olunmadıkca, ġuluvv ve hengyāme ḳoparub, ve hiç tek ṭurmiyub, Mıṣır'da ḳūl ve nice bin tevābiʿāt içinde defʿi dāḫi mümkün olmiyub, diyār-i Mıṣır'da ḳarāri lābud ʿāḳibet fitne ü fesād-i ʿaẓīme müteveffiḳ olmaḳ muḳarrer iduġin . . ."

3. Ibid., fo. 210v. It appears that Haci ʿAli was one of the soldiers sent to Yemen under Qansuh's command.

4. Ibid., fo. 211r: "Mıṣır'da hemān bir bölük-i ecnās-i muḫtalife ve kendü gibi kölemen celbālarını başına evşirmek." Here, the chronicler combines *jalbā*,

the Arabic plural of *jalīb* (imported/foreign slave; an alternative plural is *julabāʾ*) with the Turkish *-lar* plural suffix.

5. Such terms would include *bayt, kapı, tābiʿ*, and, of course, mamluk. See Hathaway, *Politics of Households*, pp. 17–21; Toledano, "Emergence of Ottoman-Local Elites," pp. 154, 156–57.

6. Uzunçarşılı, *Kapukulu Ocakları*, vol. 1: 293, 444; Bayerle, *Pashas, Begs, and Effendis*, pp. 23–24, 133.

7. This would seem to support my argument in *Politics of Households* that households could form within the regiments. See pp. 20–21, 37–46.

8. Haci ʿAli, *Aḫbār ül-yamānī*, fo. 215r; Anonymous, *Tevārīḫ-i Mıṣr-ı Ḳāhire*, fo. 36v.

9. Haci ʿAli, *Aḫbār ül-yamānī*, fos. 211v–212v; Anonymous, *Tevārīḫ-i Mıṣr-ı Ḳāhire*, fo. 37r.

10. Haci ʿAli, *Aḫbār ül-yamānī*, fos. 219r–220r.

11. Ibid., fo. 218r.

12. See chapter 1, n. 48.

13. Anonymous, *Nisba sharīfa*, fo. 2v.

14. Al-Jabarti, *ʿAjāʾib* (Cairo), vol. 1: 234.

15. Anonymous, *Nisba sharīfa*, fos. 19v–20r; Holt, "Exalted Lineage of Ridwan Bey," p. 226; al-Jabarti, *ʿAjāʾib* (Cairo), vol. 1: 234.

16. Holt, "Exalted Lineage of Ridwan Bey," p. 230.

17. Those of Canverdi (Janbirdi) al-Ghazali in 1520–21, the *kāshifs* Canım and Inal in 1522, and Haʾin Ahmed Pasha in 1524; see Holt, *Egypt and the Fertile Crescent*, pp. 46–51.

18. Anonymous, *Nisba sharīfa wa-risāla munīfa tashtamil ʿala dhikr nasab al-Jarākisa min Quraysh*, Princeton University Library, Garrett Manuscript Collection, MS 186H. Holt consulted manuscripts in the John Rylands Library, Manchester, England; and in the British Museum. He also had access to a published edition entitled *Kitāb qahar al-wujūh al-ʿābisa bi-dhikr nasab al-Jarākisa min Quraysh*, published under the auspices of one Muhammad Efendi Hafiz al-Jarkasi al-Baji by al-Matbaʿa al-Bahiyya al-Misriyya in 1316/1898–99. In this edition, *Nisba sharīfa . . .* is the first line of text after the opening invocations. I am grateful to Professor Holt for supplying me with a copy of this publication.

19. Holt, "Exalted Lineage of Ridwan Bey," p. 229.

20. See Irfan Shahid, *Byzantium and the Arabs in the Fourth Century* (Washington, DC: Dumbarton Oaks Research Library and Collection, 1984), pp. 119–21, on possible Ghassanid presence at Hira in the northeastern Arabian

peninsula, part of the Sasanian empire's sphere of influence, before their migration to the Byzantine-dominated northwestern region. Arab tradition, however, asserts that the Ghassanids descended from the southern Arabian tribe of Azd, who left Yemen for Mecca when the Maʾrib Dam broke in 550 C.E. See *EI*[1], *s.v.* "Ghassān," by J. Schleifer.

21. Shahid, *Byzantium and the Arabs in the Fifth Century*, pp. 75, 91, 374–75, 526–27.

22. See chapter 1, nn. 34–36.

23. Marshall G. S. Hodgson, *The Venture of Islam: Continuity and Change in a World Civilization*, 3 vols. (Chicago: University of Chicago Press, 1974), vol. 1: 151–54, 188–89, 200–05; Irfan Shahid, "Ghassan Post Ghassan," in *The Islamic World from Classical to Modern Times: Essays in Honor of Bernard Lewis*, eds., C. E. Bosworth, Charles Issawi, Roger Savory, and A. L. Udovitch (Princeton, NJ: The Darwin Press, 1989), p. 323.

24. Shahid, "Ghassan Post Ghassan," pp. 323–25.

25. P. M. Holt, "Literary Offerings: A Genre of Courtly Literature," in *The Mamluks in Egyptian Politics and Society*, eds., Thomas Philipp and Ulrich Haarmann (Cambridge: Cambridge University Press, 1998), pp. 8–11. The chronicles are *Al-Sayf al-muhannad fī sīrat al-Malik al-Muʾayyad* and *Al-Rawḍ al-zāhir fī sīrat al-Malik al-Ẓāhir* composed for the sultans al-Muʾayyad Shaykh (r. 1412–21) and al-Zahir Tatar (r. 1421). See also Behrens-Abouseif, *Egypt's Adjustment to Ottoman Rule*, p. 133 and n. 126.

26. Anonymous, *Nisba sharīfa*, fos. 10r–v; Evlıya Çelebi, *Seyahatname*, vol. 2: 101. This story bears an obvious resemblance to the Qurʾanic and biblical story of Moses' flight from Egypt after accidentally killing an Egyptian (Qurʾan 28:15–22, Exodus 2:11–15).

27. Anonymous, *Nisba sharīfa*, fo. 10r.

28. Ibid., fo. 11r; Evliya Çelebi, *Seyahatname*, vol. 2: 102.

29. Movses Dasxuranci, *The History of the Caucasian Albanians*, trans. C. J. F. Dowsett (London and New York: Oxford University Press, 1961); Subrahmanyam, "Du Tage au Gange," p. 63.

30. See Ibn Khaldun, *Muqaddimah*, pp. 59–62. Evliya ascribes the foundations of most major locales in Egypt to Noah's sons, indicating that the myth was alive and well in Egypt during his residence there in the late seventeenth century; see *Seyahatname*, vol. 10: 552, 573, 587, 596, 603, 604, 607, 614, 629, 645, 690, 692–93, 694.

31. Shora Bekmursin Nogmov (Schora Bekmursin Nogmow, 1794–1844), *Die Sagen und Lieder des Tscherkessen-Volks*, trans. Adolf Bergé (Leipzig: Verlag von Otto Wigand, 1866), pp. 44–46. On Nogmov, see also Amjad Jaimoukha, *The Circassians: A Handbook* (New York: Palgrave, 2001), pp. 37, 281; on the Kabardians, ibid., pp. 19, 49–52.

32. On Özdemir's career, see Holt, *Egypt and the Fertile Crescent*, pp. 52–54.

33. Evliya Çelebi, *Seyahatname*, vol. 2: 100–01.

34. Anonymous, *Nisba sharīfa*, fos. 10v, 11v–12r. See also Holt, "Exalted Lineage of Ridwan Bey," pp. 228–29.

35. In the eighteenth century, native Egyptian *ashrāf* took over the post. Toward the end of that century, the post was monopolized by the Bakri family.

36. Howe, *Migration and Myth-Making*, pp. 34–35, 41–42, chapter 3, 138–39.

37. Ibn Ishaq, *Life of Muhammad*, pp. 373, 485; *EI*², *s.v.* "Khālid b. al-Walīd," by Patricia Crone.

38. Fleischer, *Bureaucrat and Intellectual*, p. 296.

39. Ibid. According to J. H. Mordtmann, Şemsi Pasha fabricated a genealogy going back to Khalid; see *EI*², *s.v.* "Isfendiyār Oghlu."

40. Fleischer, *Bureaucrat and Intellectual*, p. 296; al-Ishaqi, *Akhbār al-uwal*, pp. 148–49.

41. Kâtib Çelebi, *Tuḥfet ül-kibār*, p. 13; Fleischer, *Bureaucrat and Intellectual*, p. 296.

42. Ferdowsi, *Epic of the Kings*, pp. 193–211. For an illustration from the Demotte *Shahname*, see Oleg Grabar and Sheila Blair, *Epic Images and Contemporary History: The Illustrations of the Great Mongol Shahname* (Chicago: University of Chicago Press, 1980), p. 21.

43. Rustam was originally a hero of Scythian epic lore whose exploits were ultimately incorporated into the legends of the Iranian kings. Sistan (Sakastan) takes its name from the Scythians, or Saka. See Richard N. Frye, *The Heritage of Central Asia* (Princeton, NJ: Markus Wiener Publishers, 1996), pp. 191–92; Ferdowsi, *Epic of the Kings*, pp. 196–97.

44. Ananiasz Zajaczkowski, "La plus ancienne traduction turque en vers du *Šâh-nâme* de l'état mamelouk d'Égypte (XV–XVIe siècles)," Türk Dili Araştırmaları Yıllığı, *Belleten* 3 (1966): 51–63; Barbara Flemming, "Šerif, Sultan Gavrî, und die «Perser»," *Der Islam* 45 (1969): 81–93; Benjamin Lellouch, "Le Douzième *ǧuzʾ* perdu des *Badāʾiʿ al-zuhūr* d'Ibn Iyas à la lumière d'une chronique turque d'Égypte," *Arabica* 45 (1998): 97.

45. Shahid, "Ghassan Post Ghassan," pp. 323–25.

46. A. J. Arberry, ed. and trans., *The Seven Odes: The First Chapter in Arabic Literature* (London: George Allen and Unwin; New York: MacMillan, 1957), pp. 31–39.

47. John Mavrogordato, ed. and trans., *Digenes Akrites* (Oxford: Clarendon Press, 1956).

48. Halil Inalcik, "The Policy of Mehmed II toward the Greek Population of Istanbul and the Byzantine Buildings of the City," *Dumbarton Oaks Papers* 23–25 (1969–70): 231–49.

49. William H. McNeill, *Europe's Steppe Frontier, 1500–1800* (Chicago and London: University of Chicago Press, 1964), pp. 107–10, 140–41, 173–76.

50. I have made the same argument elsewhere: see Hathaway, *Politics of Households*, p. 170; idem, " 'Mamluk Households' and 'Mamluk Factions' in Ottoman Egypt: A Reconsideration," in *The Mamluks in Egyptian Politics and Society*, eds., Thomas Philipp and Ulrich Haarmann (Cambridge: Cambridge University Press, 1998), pp. 113–14.

51. The fortunes of the former Byzantine royal families under Mehmed II are suggestive in this regard; see Halil Inalcik, "Greeks in Ottoman Economy and Finances, 1453–1500," in *Essays in Ottoman History* by Halil Inalcik (Istanbul: Eren Yayıncılık, 1998), pp. 384–87.

52. This is the date given in the Rylands manuscript examined by Holt; see Holt, "Exalted Lineage of Ridwan Bey," p. 221.

53. Faroqhi, *Pilgrims and Sultans*, pp. 11, 115–19.

54. Holt, *Egypt and the Fertile Crescent*, pp. 52–54. See also chapter 4 of the present work.

55. See, for example, Anonymous, *Taʾrīkh Ṣanʿāʾ [al-]Yaman*, fos. 164r–165r.

56. See, for example, al-Khazraji, *The Pearl-Strings*, vol. 1, passim.

57. Van Arendonk, *Les Débuts de l'imamat Zaidite*, p. 221 n. 8.

58. Al-Khazraji, *The Pearl-Strings*, vol. 1: 87–88.

59. Serjeant, "The Mosques of Sanʿaʾ," p. 312.

60. Haci ʿAli, *Aḫbār ül-yamānī*, fo. 220v.

61. Jaimoukha, *The Circassians*, pp. 159, 175–77, 166–68 (on the traditional distance between fathers and children); Evliya Çelebi, *The Intimate Life of an Ottoman Statesman: Melek Ahmed Pasha (1588–1662) as Portrayed in Evliya Çelebi's Book of Travels*, translation and commentary by Robert Dankoff, historical introduction by Rhoads Murphey (Albany: State University of New York Press, 1991), p. 49. See also Evliya Çelebi, *Seyahatname*, vol. 2: 104. Jaimoukha's discussion of the consonant-rich and vowel-poor Circassian language (p. 247) leads me to suspect that the word derives not from a Circassian root but from the Turkish *atalık*, literally, "fatherhood."

62. Gabriel Piterberg, "The Alleged Rebellion of Abaza Mehmed Paşa: Historiography and the Ottoman State in the Seventeenth Century," in *Mutiny and Rebellion in the Ottoman Empire*, ed., Jane Hathaway (Madison, WI: University of

Wisconsin Press, 2002), pp. 13–19; Baki Tezcan, "The 1622 Military Rebellion in Istanbul: A Historiographical Journey," in *Mutiny and Rebellion*, pp. 25–35. See also Holt, "Exalted Lineage of Ridwan Bey," p. 228 n. 1, where he notes the polarization between the imperial household, dominated by Caucasians, and the grand vizierate, dominated by Rumis.

63. See chapter 4, nn. 45, 68.

64. Al-Jabarti, *ᶜAjāʾib* (Cairo), vol. 1: 237; Hathaway, "Egypt in the Seventeenth Century," pp. 48–49.

65. Evliya Çelebi, *Seyahatname*, vol. 10: 527, 610, 692; ᶜAbdülkerim b. ᶜAbdurrahman, *Tārīḫ-i Mıṣır* (to 1715), Istanbul, Süleymaniye Library, MS Hekimoğlu Ali Paşa 705, fos. 78v, 91v.

66. For example, Ahmed Çelebi, *Awḍaḥ*, pp. 397, 476, 477, 486, 504, 523, 535, 569.

67. Al-Damurdashi, *Al-Durra al-muṣāna*, p. 265.

Chapter 11: Faqari Genesis?

1. "Şimdi Circe ḥākimi şir-i Ḫüdā, ehl-i kerem / Zülfikārī Mīr ᶜAlī der ṣāḥib-i ṭabl ü ᶜalem / Emr-i Ḥak'la feyż-i Rabbānī ana oldu delīl / Bu müşerref cāmie yapdı dāḫi iki sebīl. / Kātibi didi, 'Anın tārīḫini bil ey hümām. / Sene bin altmış birinde bu bīnā oldu,' tamām."

2. Evliya Çelebi, *Seyahatname*, vol. 10: 624.

3. Al-Hallaq, *Tārīḫ-i Mıṣr-ı Ḳāhire*, fos. 109r–v.

4. Ibid., fo. 140v.

5. Muhammad Baqir al-Majlisi, *Biḥār al-anwār*, 3rd printing (Beirut: Dar Ihyaʾ al-Turath al-ᶜArabi, 1403/1983), vol. 42: 57; Renard, *Islam and the Heroic Image*, p. 96. Other Shiᶜite traditions hold that the angel Gabriel descended from the sky with the sword and gave it to the Prophet; that the sword was the gift of Balqis, the Queen of Sheba, to Solomon; and that a palm frond that the Prophet spat out became the sword; see *Biḥār al-anwār*, vol. 42: 57, 58. I am grateful to Mohammed Ajami for directing me to *Biḥār al-anwār*. See also Sümer, et al., eds. and trans., *The Book of Dede Korkut*, p. 33, where the hero Uruz extols a tree as the source of the gates of Medina and Mecca, the staff of Moses, the saddle of ᶜAli, the handle and sheath of Dhu'l-Faqar, and the cradle of Hasan and Husayn.

6. Al-Majlisi, *Biḥār al-anwār*, vol. 42: 58; Ibn Ishaq, *Life of Muhammad*, pp. 307, 338, 345. The Meccan was al-ᶜAs b. Munabbih b. al-Hajjaj. Another Shiᶜite tradition holds that the sword was taken from al-ᶜAs' father, Munabbih b. al-Hajjaj, after he was slain in the raid on the Banu al-Mustaliq; see *Biḥār al-anwār*, vol. 42: 58.

7. A. Rahman Zaky, "On Islamic Swords," in *Studies in Islamic Art and Architecture in Honour of Professor K. A. C. Cresswell* (Cairo: The American University in Cairo Press, published for the Center for Arabic Studies, 1965), pp. 270–71; 271 n. 1; 277; 279; 282; 284; 287; Zygulski, *Ottoman Art in the Service of the Empire*, p. 49. See also Ibn Ishaq, *Life of Muhammad*, pp. 587, 601. A Shiʿite tradition holds that the sword was forged for ʿAli by ʿUmayr "the Polisher" from iron in Yemen, to which ʿAli was directed by Gabriel; see al-Majlisi, *Biḥār al-anwār*, vol. 42: 58.

8. Evliya Çelebi, *Seyahatname*, vol. 10: 553–54, 575.

9. Sawirus b. al-Muqaffaʿ, *Taʾrīkh baṭārika al-kanīsa al-miṣriyya/History of the Patriarchs of the Egyptian Church*, vol. 3, part 1, ed. and trans. Antoine Khater and O. H. E. KHS-Burmester (Cairo: Société d'Archéologie Copte, 1968), pp. 490–91 and p. 491 n. 1. The name apparently means "Colchian," that is, someone from ancient Colchis, modern Georgia.

10. Evliya Çelebi, *Seyahatname*, vol. 10: 628.

11. Zygulski, *Ottoman Art in the Service of the Empire*, pp. 46, 48. Two Shiʿite traditions likewise hold that the sword had a ridge in the middle that looked like the spinal column; see al-Majlisi, *Biḥār al-anwār*, vol. 42: 58.

12. Al-Tabari, *History of al-Tabari*, vol. 9: 154 n. 1049, and the sources cited there. See also David C. Nicolle, *Arms and Armour of the Crusading Era, 1050–1350* (White Plains, New York: Kraus International Publications, A Division of Kraus-Thomson Organization, Ltd., 1988), vol. 1: *Commentary*, p. 149; see also Renard, *Islam and the Heroic Image*, p. 207. Only one Shiʿite tradition agrees that the sword contained multiple grooves; see al-Majlisi, *Biḥār al-anwār*, vol. 42: 58.

13. Qurʾan, sura 8; *EI*^{2}, *s.v.* "Badr," by W. Montgomery Watt. In canonical Sunni *ḥadīth*, the sword is mentioned by name in Ibn Hanbal 1: 271, and Ibn Maja, "Jihād," 18; the sword as part of the spoils of Badr is mentioned in Abu Dawud, "Jihād," 139, 144; al-Tirmidhi, "Tafsīr," 8:7; and Ibn Hanbal 3:497.

14. Al-Tabari, *History of al-Tabari*, vol. 9: 153–54; Zaky, "On Islamic Swords," pp. 270–71; Zygulski, *Ottoman Art in the Service of the Empire*, p. 48.

15. See Renard, *Islam and the Heroic Image*, p. 105. One Shiʿite tradition holds that the Prophet gave the sword to ʿAli at Badr; see al-Majlisi, *Biḥār al-anwār*, vol. 42: 58.

16. *EI*^{2}, *s.v.* "Dhū'l-Faḳār," by E. Mittwoch; Zaky, "On Islamic Swords," p. 270; Zygulski, *Ottoman Art in the Service of the Empire*, p. 49. According to various Shiʿite traditions, this was Gabriel's or another angel's exclamation on the day of either Badr or Uhud; or the Prophet's exclamation on first seeing ʿAli wield the rather cumbersome sword. See al-Majlisi, *Biḥār al-anwār*, vol. 42: 58; Renard, *Islam and the Heroic Image*, pp. 207, 295 n. 12. According to Ibn Hisham, someone else uttered this sentence: "Ibn Hisham's Notes" to Ibn Ishaq, *Life of Muhammad*, p. 756 n. 616.

17. *EI*², *s.v.* "Dhū'l-Fakār," by E. Mittwoch; Renard, *Islam and the Heroic Image,* p. 207; al-Majlisi, *Biḥār al-anwār,* vol. 42: 58 (on the sword's length).

18. Renard, *Islam and the Heroic Image,* pp. 105, 142.

19. Friedrich Wilhelm Schwarzlose, *Die Waffen der alten Araber aus ihren Dichtern dargestellt* (Hildesheim and New York: Georg Olms Verlag, 1982), p. 152; Zygulski, *Ottoman Art in the Service of the Empire,* p. 46.

20. Halm, *Empire of the Mahdi,* p. 353. I am grateful to Professor Paul E. Walker for bringing this incident to my attention in his paper "Purloined Insignia: Stolen Symbols of Legitimacy in the ʿAbbasid-Fatimid Rivalry," delivered at the Middle East Studies Association conference, Providence, RI, November 1996, pp. 1–5.

21. Halm, *Empire of the Mahdi,* pp. 319–20.

22. Quoted in ibid., p. 353. On Qadi al-Nuʿman more generally, see Bierman, *Writing Signs,* pp. 63, 66–67.

23. Nicolle, *Arms and Armour of the Crusading Era,* vol. 1: *Commentary,* p. 149; vol. 2: *Illustrations,* p. 708, figs. 388A (fo. 92r), 388D (fo. 161r), 388E (fo. 162r).

24. Ibid., vol. 1: 149.

25. See, for example, Trimingham, *The Sufi Orders in Islam,* pp. 55, 69, 74–78, 82, 90–91, 99–101; David Morgan, *The Mongols* (Oxford and New York: Basil Blackwell, 1986), pp. 144, 161; Hodgson, *The Venture of Islam,* vol. 2: *The Expansion of Islam in the Middle Periods,* pp. 499–500.

26. Gray, *Persian Painting,* p. 105. The work in question is Ibn Husam's *Khawārname.*

27. I am grateful to Barbara McFarland of the University of Texas, College of Liberal Arts, for pointing this out.

28. For other examples of the fifteenth-century Shiraz style, see Gray, *Persian Painting,* pp. 66, 73–77, 79, 97, 98, 102–03, 106–07.

29. Zygulski, *Ottoman Art in the Service of the Empire,* plate 2: Lamiʾi Çelebi (1472–1532), *Maqtāl-i Ḥażret-i Imām Ḥüseyin,* Cracow, Czartoryski Library, MS 2327; see also pp. 49, 65 n. 101. Filiz Çağman and Zeren Tanındı, *The Topkapı Saray Museum: The Albums and Illuminated Manuscripts,* trans., expanded, and ed. J. M. Rogers (London: Thames and Hudson, 1986), p. 239 and plates 167–68: Mustafa Darir Erzurumlu, *Siyer-i Nebi* (1594), MS Hazine 1223, fos. 298a and 70b.

30. Palmer, "The Origin of the Janissaries."

31. Mélikoff, *Hadji Bektach,* p. 111.

32. Köprülü, *The Seljuks of Anatolia*, p. 46.

33. Luigi Ferdinando Marsigli, *Stato militare dell'impèrio ottomano/L'État militaire de l'empire ottoman*, vol. 2: 53, plates 20–22, cited in Zygulski, *Ottoman Art in the Service of the Empire*, pp. 28–30.

34. *Codex Vindobonensis*, Vienna, Österreiche Nationalbibliothek, MS 8626, cited in Zygulski, *Ottoman Art in the Service of the Empire*, p. 149.

35. The tomb of one Molla Mehmed, son of Tavergalı (?) Mehmed Agha (d. 1235/1819–20), lies outside the exit door of the Naval Museum in Istanbul. On both the head- and footstones is an image of Dhu'l-Faqar resembling those found on battle flags, except for the addition of hair-like projections to the pommel, and finger-like projections to the quillons.

36. Nour, "L'Histoire du croissant," pp. 115–16/344–45.

37. Zygulski, *Ottoman Art in the Service of the Empire*, pp. 50–51, 53. In the Historical Museum of the City of Vienna is a painting by Niklas Meldemann (Nuremberg, 1530) of the first Ottoman siege of Vienna in 1529. One Ottoman flag bears an image that resembles a human figure, perhaps an archer. It must surely be Dhu'l-Faqar, which, naturally, the German painter did not recognize.

38. Cited in Nour, "L'Histoire du croissant," p. 117/346.

39. Kurtoğlu, *Türk Bayrağı ve Ay Yıldız*, p. 77, figure 48.

40. Personal visit to the museum of the Doge's palace, Venice, June 1995. See also Smith, *Flags through the Ages*, p. 55, for the Bey of Tunis' colorful, busy Dhu'l-Faqar flag in the nineteenth century.

41. Kurtoğlu, *Türk Bayrağı ve Ay Yıldız*, p. 99.

42. Caroline Finkel, *The Administration of Warfare: The Ottoman Military Campaigns in Hungary, 1593–1606*, 2 vols. (Vienna: VWGÖ, 1988), vol. 1: 62–63, notes the difficulty of estimating the size of an Ottoman army; she cites various European sources as giving estimates of 500,000, 300,000, and 100,000. See also Murphey, *Ottoman Warfare*, pp. 35–49; Murphey points out that the number of soldiers who actually made it to the battlefield was typically much smaller than the numbers listed in the salary registers.

43. Istanbul, Başbakanlık Osmanlı Arşivi, Maliyeden Müdevver 7069 (1150/1737–38); al-Damurdashi, *Al-Durra al-muṣāna*, pp. 5–6, 17, 222.

44. *EI*[2], *s.v.* "Badr," by W. Montgomery Watt.

45. Al-Tabari, *The History of al-Tabari*, vol. 11: *The Challenge to the Empires*, trans. Khalid Yahya Blankinship (Albany: State University of New York Press, 1993), pp. 87–88.

46. Jaroslav Pelikan, *Mary through the Centuries: Her Place in the History of Culture* (New Haven, CT: Yale University Press, 1996), pp. 176–82; Smith,

Flags through the Ages, p. 74; and my own observations in San Antonio, TX. See also the numerous World Wide Web pages devoted to the Virgin of Guadalupe.

47. Pelikan, *Mary through the Centuries*, pp. 180–81; Smith, *Flags through the Ages*, p. 74.

48. Palmer, "Origins of the Janissaries;" V. L. Ménage, "Sidelights on the Devshirme from Idris and Sa[c]duddin," *BSOAS* 18 (1956): 181–83; Paul Wittek, "Devshirme and Shari[c]a," *BSOAS* 17 (1955): 271–78.

49. Mihalowicz, *Memoirs of a Janissary*, pp. 7, 9.

50. Izady, *The Kurds*, p. 151. Indeed, Izady asserts that this ritual may be directly related to the Arthurian legends via a legion of the Iranic people known as Sarmatians stationed in the British Isles by the Roman emperor Marcus Aurelius in the second century C.E.

51. Michele Membré, *Mission to the Lord Sophy of Persia*, ed. and trans. A. H. Morton (London: School of Oriental and African Studies, University of London, 1993), p. 13.

52. In fact, a large steel sword that hung over the door of Bursa's citadel in the sixteenth century was thought by European visitors to be Roland's sword Darandal; by the late seventeenth century, this sword had been conflated with the sword of the Bektashi saint Abdal Murad. See Heath W. Lowry, "The 'Sword of Roland' and the 'Sword of Abdal Murad': A Note on the History of Brusa (Bursa) in the Light of Six Centuries of Travellers' Accounts (1325–1925)," in *Aptullah Kuran için Yazılar/Essays in Honour of Aptullah Kuran*, eds., Çiğdem Kafescioğlu and Lucienne Thys-Şenocak (Istanbul: Yapı Kredi Yayınları, 1999), pp. 233–52.

53. In a tale from the *Thousand and One Nights*, the hero is given the bow of the prophet Salih, Solomon's sword, and a dagger forged by Tammuz; see Mathers, trans., *The Thousand Nights and One Night*, vol. 4: 274.

54. Lyons, *The Arabian Epic*, vol. 3: 587, 605, 606, 607, 608, 609, 615, 622, 624, 633, 634, 635, 639. Asaf is also supposed to have had an enormous impact on Sudan; see Evliya Çelebi, *Seyahatname*, vol. 10: 646, 647, 666.

55. Thévenot, *Relation d'un voyage fait au Levant . . .*, p. 470. Meldemann's painting of the siege of Vienna is suggestive in this regard; see n. 37, above.

56. Van Arendonk, *Imamat zaidite*, p. 221; Fuad Ishaq Khuri, *Imams and Emirs: State, Religion, and Sects in Islam* (London: Saqi, 1990), p. 120; Hugh Scott, *In the High Yemen* (London: John Murray, 1942), pp. 222–23.

57. Serjeant, "The Mosques of San[c]a[ɔ]," p. 312; Irwin, *The Middle East in the Middle Ages*, p. 120; Shaun E. Marmon, *Eunuchs and Sacred Boundaries in Islamic Society* (Oxford and New York: Oxford University Press, 1995), pp. 49–53, 55–61.

58. Van Arendonk, *Imamate zaidite*, p. 221 n. 8.

59. Al-Khazraji, *The Pearl-Strings*, vol. 1: 74–91; Yahya b. al-Husayn, *Ghāyat al-amānī*, vol. 1: 410–21; Ibn al-Daybaᶜ, *Qurrat al-ᶜuyūn*, vol. 2: 1–3; *EI*[1], *s.v.* "Rasūlids," by A. S. Tritton; Shahid, "Ghassan Post Ghassan," pp. 331–33.

60. P. M. Holt, "Some Observations on the ᶜAbbasid Caliphate of Cairo," *BSOAS* 47 (1984): 501–07.

61. Playfair, *History of Arabia Felix*, p. 29.

62. Scott, *In the High Yemen*, pp. 222–23; H. Gresham Carr, *Flags of the World*, based on F. Edward Hulme, *The Flags of the World and Their History, Blazonry, and Associations*, 1897 (London and New York: Frederick Warne and Co., Ltd., 1953), p. 163 and Plate 25, no. 3.

63. For example, Ibn al-Daybaᶜ, *Qurrat al-ᶜuyūn*, vol. 1: 228–29, 238, 239–40, 290–92, 301–02.

64. Haci ᶜAli, *Aḫbār ül-yamānī*, fos. 209v ff.

65. Serjeant, "The Post-Medieval and Modern History of Sanᶜaʾ," p. 73.

66. Ibid., p. 80.

67. A curious exception to this rule is an Ottoman plan of Vienna drawn shortly after the second siege in 1683 and preserved in the Historical Museum of the City of Vienna (the source is given as the secret archive [Geheimarchiv] of the grand vizier Aynacı Süleyman Pasha, 1688). One Ottoman battle flag bears a single-bladed sword in green on a yellow-white ground.

68. Holt, "Al-Jabarti's Introduction," p. 44 n. 2; idem, *Egypt and the Fertile Crescent*, p. 80 n. 1.

69. Hallaq, *Tārīḫ-i Mıṣr-ı Ḳāhire*, fos. 109r–v.

70. Jane Hathaway, "Osmanlı Mısır'ında Yerli Askerî Unsurlar ve Yeniçeriler," in *Türkler*, eds., Hasan Celâl Güzel, C. Cem Oğuz, and Osman Karatay, 20 vols. (Ankara: Yeni Türkiye Yayınları, 2002), vol 10: 172–79.

71. Kunt, "Ethnic-Regional (*Cins*) Solidarity."

72. Piterberg, "Alleged Rebellion of Abaza Mehmed Paşa," pp. 14–19; Tezcan, "1622 Military Rebellion in Istanbul," pp. 25–35.

73. Hathaway, *Politics of Households*, p. 35.

74. *EI*[2], *s.v.* "Ewliyā Çelebi," by J. H. Mordtmann [H. W. Duda].

75. They may appear "black" because of their armor, or Evliya may simply be attempting a word play involving the name of the square, Kara Meydan.

76. See the brief discussion in the glossary of Hinds and Ménage, *Qasr Ibrim*, p. 111, and documents no. 64 (pp. 24–25), 66 (pp. 27–29), 74 (pp. 46–47), 76 (pp. 50–51), 79 (pp. 56, 58), 85 (pp. 71–73).

Conclusion

1. See Hathaway, *Politics of Households*, chapter 7; idem, "Marriage Alliances among the Military Households of Ottoman Egypt," *Annales Islamologiques* 29 (1995): 133–49.

2. Peter Stanley, "Military Culture and Military Protest: The Bengal Europeans and the `White Mutiny' of 1859," in *Rebellion, Repression, Reinvention: Mutiny in Comparative Perspective*, ed., Jane Hathaway (Westport, CT, and London: Praeger, 2001), p. 107.

3. Irving A. Leonard, *Books of the Brave: Being an Account of Books and of Men in the Spanish Conquest and Settlement of the Sixteenth-Century New World* (Cambridge, MA: Harvard University Press, 1949), pp. 300–03, 314–15. I am grateful to Geoffrey Parker for directing me to this source.

4. Mottahedeh, *Loyalty and Leadership*, p. 160.

5. On this point, see Eric Hobsbawm, "Introduction: Inventing Traditions," in *The Invention of Tradition*, eds., Eric Hobsbawm and Terrence Ranger, pp. 11–14; Anderson, *Imagined Communities*, pp. 86ff.

6. Mottahedeh, *Loyalty and Leadership*, pp. 160, 164–66; Mirjafari, "Haydari-Niᶜmati Conflicts," pp. 146–48. One foreign observer even accused the Safavid Shah ᶜAbbas (r. 1588–1629) of creating the factions in order to prevent "anti-government alliances" (ibid., p. 147).

7. On this series of crises, see Ömer Lütfi Barkan, "The Price Revolution of the Sixteenth Century: A Turning Point in the Economic History of the Near East," *International Journal of Middle East Studies* 6 (1975): 3–28; M. A. Cook, *Population Pressure in Rural Anatolia, 1450–1600* (New York and Oxford: Oxford University Press, 1972); Suraiya Faroqhi, with Leila Erder, "Population Rise and Fall in Anatolia, 1550–1620," *Middle Eastern Studies* 15 (1979): 322–45; Faroqhi, "Crisis and Change, 1590–1699," pp. 433–441; Halil Inalcik, "The Socio-Political Effects of the Diffusion of Fire-Arms in the Middle East," in *War, Technology and Society in the Middle East*, eds., V. J. Parry and Malcolm Yapp (London and New York: Oxford University Press, 1975), pp. 195–217; idem, "Military and Fiscal Transformation," 286–88.

8. Piterberg, "Alleged Rebellion of Abaza Mehmed Paşa," p. 31.

9. Holt, *Egypt and the Fertile Crescent*, p. 105.

10. Al-Hallaq, *Tārīḫ-i Mıṣr-ı Ḳāhire*, fos. 159v–179r. It is noteworthy that al-Hallaq interrupts his report on the governor's campaign against Mehmed Bey with the news that Abaza Hasan Pasha has been defeated and executed (fo. 173v).

11. Hathaway, *Politics of Households*, p. 35. Surely these, rather than the fact that he "stood outside the Mamluk system," were the reasons that the

Faqaris, when he was appointed pilgrimage commander, objected to him as an *ajnabī*: Holt, "Beylicate," p. 225; see also Kaldy-Nágy, "The *Ecnebiler*."

12. An admirable step in this direction is Zeʾevi, *An Ottoman Century*, pp. 57–59, 83–84, 159.

Bibliography

Primary Sources

ʿAbdülkerim b. ʿAbdurrahman. *Tārīḫ-i Mıṣır* (to 1715). Istanbul: Süleymaniye Library, MS Hekimoğlu Ali Paşa 705.

Ahmed Çelebi b. ʿAbd al-Ghani. *Awḍaḥ al-ishārāt fī man tawalla Miṣr al-Qāhira min al-wuzarāʾ wa'l-bāshāt* (c. 1737). Edited by A. A. ʿAbd al-Rahim. Cairo: Maktabat al-Khanji, 1978.

Ali, Ahmed, trans. *The Qurʾan: A Contemporary Translation*. 2d rev. ed. Princeton: Princeton University Press, 1988.

ʿAli, Haci. *Aḫbār ül-yamānī* (1666–67). Istanbul: Süleymaniye Library, MS Hamidiye 886.

Alighieri, Dante. *Inferno*. Edited and translated by Elio Zappulla. New York: Pantheon Books, 1998.

Anonymous. *Akhbār al-nuwwāb min dawlat Āl ʿUthmān min ḥīn istawla ʿalayhā al-sulṭān Salīm Khān* (to 1715). Istanbul: Topkapı Palace Library, MS Hazine 1623.

Anonymous. "Announcement to the Arabs, Sons of Qahtan." In *Al-Qaḍiyya al-ʿarabiyya*, by Ahmad ʿIzzat al-Aʿzami, vol. 4: 108–117. Reprinted in *Arab Nationalism: An Anthology*. Edited by Sylvia Haim, 83–88. Berkeley: University of California Press, 1962, 1976.

Anonymous. *Kitāb al-durra al-munṣāna fī waqāʿ [sic] al-Kināna*. Oxford: University of Oxford, Bodleian Library, MS Bruce 43.

Anonymous. *Kitāb-i tevārīḫ-i Mıṣr-ı Ḳāhire-i ḫaṭṭ-ı Ḥasan Paşa* (to 1683). Istanbul: Süleymaniye Library, MS Haci Mahmud Efendi 4877.

Anonymous. *Nisba sharīfa wa-risāla munīfa tashtamil ʿala dhikr nasab al-Jarākisa min Quraysh* (1632?). Princeton, NJ: Princeton University, Garrett Manuscripts Collection, MS 186H.

Anonymous. *Taʾrīkh Ṣanʿāʾ [al-] Yaman* (mid-eighteenth century). Istanbul: Süleymaniye Library, MS Ayasofya 3048.

Arberry, A. J., ed. and trans. *The Seven Odes: The First Chapter in Arabic Literature*. London: George Allen and Unwin; New York: MacMillan, 1957.

Aşıkpaşazade (b. 1400). *Die altosmanische Chronik des Aşıkpaşazade*. Edited by Friedrich Giese. Vol. 1: *Text und Variantenverzeichnis*. Leipzig: Otto Harrassowitz, 1929.

Al-Bahkali, ʿAbd al-Rahman b. Hasan (1735–1809). *Quintessence de l'or du règne du Chérif Muhammad b. Ahmad*. Edited and translated by Michel Tuchscherer as *Imams, notables et bédouins du Yémen au XVIIIe siècle*. TAIE 30. Cairo: Institut Français d'Archéologie Orientale, 1992.

Al-Baji, Muhammad Efendi Hafiz al-Jarkasi, ed. *Kitāb qahar al-wujūh al-ʿābisa bi-dhikr nasab al-Jarākisa min Quraysh*. Cairo: Al-Matbaʿa al-Bahiyya al-Misriyya, 1316/1898–99.

Barkan, Ömer Lütfi, ed. "Mısır Kanunnâmesi." In *XV ve XVIıncı asırlarda Osmanlı İmparatorluğunda Ziraî Ekonominin Hukukî ve Malî Esasları*. Edited by Ömer Lütfi Barkan. Vol. 1: *Kanunlar*. Istanbul: İstanbul Üniversitesi Edebiyat Fakültesi Yayınları, 1943, chapter 105.

Başbakanlık Arşivi (Istanbul). Kamil Kepeci, Kahve Rusūmu 4519 (1129/1717).

———. Maliyeden Müdevver 4118 (1000/1591–92); 4442 (1010–14/1601–06); 7555 (1009/1600–01); 7069 (1150/1737–38); 16008 (1039/1629–30).

———. Mühimme Defteri 1 (961–62/1553–54).

———. Mühimme Defteri 2 (963–64/1555–56).

———. *3 Numaralı Mühimme Defteri (966–68/1558–60)*. 2 vols. Ankara: T. C. Başbakanlık Devlet Arşivi Genel Müdürlüğü, 1993.

———. *5 Numaralı Mühimme Defteri (973/1565–66)*. 2 vols. Ankara: T. C. Başbakanlık Devlet Arşivi Genel Müdürlüğü, 1994.

———. *6 Numaralı Mühimme Defteri (972/1564–65)*. 2 vols. Ankara: T. C. Başbakanlık Devlet Arşivi Genel Müdürlüğü, 1995.

———. Mühimme Defteri 7 (975–76/1567–68).

———. Mühimme Defteri 9 (977–78/1569–70).

———. Mühimme Defteri 10 (978–79/1570–71).

Bohas, Georges, and Jean-Patrick Guillaume, eds. *Le Roman de Baïbars*. 11 Vols. Paris: Actes Sud/Sindbad, 1985–98.

Celalzade Mustafa Çelebi (d. 1567). *Selîm-Nâme*. Edited by Ahmet Uğur and Mustafa Çuhadar. Ankara: Başbakanlık Basımevi, 1990.

Celalzade Salih Çelebi (d. 1566). *Tārīḫ-i Mıṣr-ı cedīd*. Istanbul: Süleymaniye Library, MS Çelebi Abdullah Efendi 248.

Al-Damurdashi, Ahmed Kâhya ʿAzeban. *Al-Durra al-muṣāna fī akhbār al-Kināna* (c. 1755). British Museum, MS Or. 1073–74.

Dasxuranci, Movses. *The History of the Caucasian Albanians*. Translated by C. J. F. Dowsett. London and New York: Oxford University Press, 1961.

Deflers, Albert. *Voyage au Yémen: Journal d'une excursion botanique faite en 1887 dans les montagnes de l'Arabie Heureuse*. Paris: Paul Klincksieck, 1889.

Evliya Çelebi (c. 1611–c. 1682). *Evliya Çelebi Seyahatnamesi*. Edited by Ahmed Cevdet. 10 Vols. Istanbul: Ikdâm Matbaası, 1314/1896–7—1938.

———. *Evliya Çelebi Seyahatnamesi*. Vol. 10: *Mısır ve Sudan*. Edited by Mehmed Zillîoğlu. Istanbul: Üçdal Neşriyat, 1966.

———. *The Intimate Life of an Ottoman Statesman: Melek Ahmed Pasha (1588–1662) as Portrayed in Evliya Çelebi's Book of Travels*. Translation and commentary by Robert Dankoff, with a historical introduction by Rhoads Murphey. Albany: State University of New York Press, 1991.

———. *Narrative of Travels in Europe, Asia, and Africa.* Translated by Josef von Hammer-Purgstall. 2 Vols. in 3. London: Parbury, Allen, 1834. Reprint, Johnson Reprint Corp., 1968.

Ferdowsi (c. 940–c. 1022). *The Epic of the Kings: Shāh-Nāma of Ferdowsi.* Abridged translation by Reuben Levy. Foreword by Ehsan Yarshater. Preface by Amin Banani. Introduction by Dick Davis. Costa Mesa, CA, and New York: Mazda Publishers, in association with Bibliotheca Persica, 1996.

Fulcher of Chartres. *Chronicle of the First Crusade (Fulcheri Carnotensis Historia Hierosolymitana).* Translated by Martha Evelyn McGinty. Philadelphia: University of Pennsylvania Press; London: Humphrey Milford, Oxford University Press, 1941.

Al-Ghitani, Jamal, ed. *Sīrat al-Ẓāhir Baybars.* 50 parts in 5 Vols. Cairo: Al-Ha᾽ya al-Misriyya al-ᶜAmma li'l-Kitab, 1996.

Gülşeni, Muhyi-yi (d. 1606). *Menâḳib-i İbrâhîm-i Gülşenî ve Şemleli-zâde Aḥmed Efendi, Şive-i Ṭarîḳat-i Gülşenîye.* Edited by Tahsin Yazıcı. Ankara: Türk Tarih Kurumu Basımevi, 1982.

Al-Hallaq, Mehmed b. Yusuf. *Tārīḫ-i Mıṣr-ı Ḳāhire* (to 1715). Istanbul: Istanbul University Library, T. Y. 628.

Al-Hamdani, al-Hasan b. Ahmad (c. 893–c. 945). *Al-Iklīl.* Rescension of Muhammad b. Nashwan b. Saᶜid al-Himyari (Berlin MS Or. Oct. 968). Vol. 1 in 2 books. Edited by Oscar Löfgren. Uppsala: Almqvist and Wiksells Boktryckeri AB, 1954–65.

Hertz, J. H., ed. and trans. *The Pentateuch and Haftorahs.* 2d ed. London: Soncino Press, 1981.

Ibn Battuta, ᶜAbdallah Muhammad b. Ibrahim (1304–77). *Riḥlat Ibn Baṭūṭa.* Introduction by Karam al-Bustani. Beirut: Dar Sadir, Dar Bayrut, 1964.

Ibn al-Daybaᶜ, ᶜAbd al-Rahman b. ᶜAli b. Muhammad (d. ca. 1537). *Bughyat al-mustafīd fī ta᾽rīkh madīnat Zabīd.* Edited by ᶜAbdallah al-Hibshi. Sanᶜa: Markaz al-Dirasat wa'l-Buhuth al-Yamani, 1979.

———. *Kitāb Qurrat al-ᶜuyūn bi-akhbār al-Yaman al-maymūn.* Edited by Muhammad b. ᶜAli al-Akwaᶜ al-Hiwali. 2 Vols. Cairo: Matbaᶜat al-Saᶜada, 1977.

———. *Tuḥfat al-zaman fī faḍā᾽il ahl al-Yaman.* Edited by Sayyid Kusrawi Hasan. Beirut: Dar al-Kutub al-ᶜIlmiyya, 1992.

Ibn Ishaq, Muhammad (d. ca. 768). *The Life of Muhammad.* Edited by ᶜAbd al-Malik b. Hisham (d. 834). Translated and with an introduction and notes by Alfred Guillaume. Lahore, Karachi, Dacca: Oxford University Press, Pakistan Branch, 1955, 1968, 1970.

Ibn Iyas, Muhammad b. Ahmad (1488–c. 1524). *An Account of the Ottoman Conquest of Egypt in the Year* A.H. *922 (*A.D. *1516).* Translated by W. H. Salmon. London: Royal Asiatic Society, 1921.

———. *Badā᾽iᶜ al-zuhūr fī waqā᾽iᶜ al-duhūr.* Edited by Muhammad Mustafa. Vol. 5 (922–28/1516–22). Cairo: Al-Ha᾽ya al-Misriyya al-ᶜAmma li'l-Kitab, 1404/1984.

———. *Histoire des Mamlouks circassiens.* Translated by Gaston Wiet. 2 Vols. Cairo: Institut Français d'Archéologie Orientale, 1945.

———. *Journal d'un bourgeois du Caire*. Translated by Gaston Wiet. 2 Vols. Paris: Armand Colin, 1955.

Ibn Khaldun, ʿAbd al-Rahman b. Muhammad (1332–1406). *The Muqaddimah: An Introduction to History*. Translated by Franz Rosenthal. Abridged and edited by N. J. Dawood. Princeton, NJ: Princeton University Press, 1967.

Ibn Maja, Muhammad b. Yazid (d. 887). *Sunan*. Edited by Muhammad Fuʾad ʿAbd al-Baqi. 2 Vols. Cairo: Halabi, 1372/1952.

Ibn al-Muqaffaʿ, Sawirus (fl. 955–87). *Taʾrīkh batārika al-kanīsa al-miṣriyya / History of the Patriarchs of the Egyptian Church*. Vol. 3, part 1. Edited and translated by Antoine Khater and O. H. E. KHS-Burmester. Cairo: Société d'Archéologie Copte, 1968.

Ibn Taghri Birdi, Abu'l-Mahasin Yusuf (1411–70). *History of Egypt, 1382–1469 A.D.* Translated by William Popper. 7 Vols. Berkeley: University of California Press, 1954–60.

Ibn Zunbul, Ahmad al-Rammal (d. 1553). *Wāqiʿat al-Sulṭān al-Ghawrī maʿ Salīm al-ʿUthmānī*. Edited by ʿAbd al-Munʿam ʿAmir. Cairo: Al-Haʾya al-Misriyya al-ʿAmma li'l-Kitab, 1997.

Al-Ishaqi, Muhammad ʿAbd al-Muʿti. *Kitāb akhbār al-uwal fī man taṣarrafa fī Miṣr min arbāb al-duwal* (1623). Bulaq: Al-Matbaʿa al-ʿUthmaniyya, 1304/1887.

Al-Jabarti, ʿAbd al-Rahman b. Hasan (1754–1825). *ʿAjāʾib al-āthār fī'l-tarājim wa'l-akhbār*. 7 Vols. Cairo: Lajnat al-Bayan al-ʿArabi, 1958–67. 3 Vols. Beirut: Dar al-Jil, 1983.

Jayyusi, Lena, trans. *The Adventures of Sayf Ben Dhi Yazan: An Arab Folk Epic*. Bloomington, IN: Indiana University Press, 1996.

Jewish Publication Society. *Hebrew-English Tanakh [Torah, Nevi'im, Kethuvim]: The Traditional Hebrew Text and the New JPS Translation*. 2d ed. Philadephia: Jewish Publication Society, 1999.

Kaeuper, Richard W., and Elspeth Kennedy, eds. and trans. *The Book of Chivalry of Geoffroi de Charny: Text, Context, and Translation*. Philadelphia: University of Pennsylvania Press, 1996.

Kâtib Çelebi (1609–57). *Tuḥfet ül-kibār fī esfār ül-biḥār*. Istanbul: Matbaʿat-i Bahriye, 1329/1911.

Keşfi Mehmed Çelebi (d. 1524). *Selimname*. Istanbul: Süleymaniye Library, MS Esad Efendi 2147.

Al-Khashshab, Ismail b. Saʿd (d. 1815). *Tadhkira li-ahl al-baṣāʾir wa'l-abṣār maʿ wajh al-ikhtiṣār*. Paris: Bibliothèque Nationale, MS Arabe 1858.

Al-Khazraji, ʿAli b. al-Hasan (d. 1410). *The Pearl-Strings: A History of the Resuliyy Dynasty of Yemen*. Translation, introduction, annotations, index, tables, and maps by Sir. J. W. Redhouse. Edited by E. G. Brown, R. A. Nicholson, and A. Rogers. E. J. W. Gibb Memorial Series. 2 Vols. Leiden: E. J. Brill; London: Luzac and Co., 1906.

Lane, Edward W. *An Account of the Manners and Customs of the Modern Egyptians*. 5th ed. Edited by Edward Stanley Poole. New introduction by John Manchip White. New York: Dover Publications, 1973.

Al-Majlisi, Muhammad Baqir (1627 or 1628–c. 1699). *Biḥār al-anwār*. 3d printing. Beirut: Dar Ihya᾽ al-Turath al-ᶜArabi, 1403/1983.

Marsigli, Luigi Ferdinando (1658–1730). *Stato militare dell' Imperio ottomanno/ L' état militaire de l'empire ottoman*. Graz: Akademische Druckerei und Verlagsanst, 1972.

Mathers, Powys, trans. *The Book of the Thousand Nights and One Night*. Translated into French by J. C. Mardrus. 4 Vols. New York: St. Martin's Press, 1972.

Mavrogordato, John, ed. and trans. *Digenes Akrites*. Oxford: Clarendon Press, 1956.

Al-Mawzaᶜi, Shams al-Din ᶜAbd al-Samad b. Ismail b. ᶜAbd al-Samad (fl. 1618–22). *Dukhūl al-Uthmāniyyīn al-awwal ilā al-Yaman*, a.k.a. *Al-Iḥsān fī dukhūl mamlakat al-Yaman taḥta ẓill ᶜadālat Āl ᶜUthmān*. Edited by ᶜAbdallah Muhammad al-Hibshi. Beirut: Dar al-Tanwir, 1986.

Membré, Michele. *Mission to the Lord Sophy of Persia (1539–1542)*. Edited and translated by A. H. Morton. London: School of Oriental and African Studies, University of London, 1993.

Mihalowicz, Konstantin. *Memoirs of a Janissary*. Translated by Benjamin Stolz. Historical commentary and notes by Svat Soucek. Ann Arbor, MI: Dept. of Slavic Languages and Literatures, University of Michigan, 1975.

Mishaqa, Mikhayil (1799–1888). *Murder, Mayhem, Pillage, and Plunder: The History of Lebanon in the Eighteenth and Nineteenth Centuries*. Translated by Wheeler M. Thackston, Jr. Albany: State University of New York Press, 1988.

Al-Munawi, ᶜAbd al-Rauf b. Taj al-Arifih (d. 1621). *Al-Tasyīr bi-sharḥ al-Jāmiᶜ al-ṣaghīr fī aḥādith al-bashīr al-naḍīr*. Commentary on Jalal al-Din ᶜAbd al-Rahman al-Suyuti (1445–1505), *Al-Jāmiᶜ al-ṣaghīr*. . . . Cairo: Al-Matbaᶜa al-Misriyya, 1286/1869-70.

Al-Muttaqi, ᶜAla al-Din ᶜAli b. Husam al-Din (1477–1567). *Kanz al-ᶜummāl*. 8 Parts. Hyderabad: Da᾽irat al-Maᶜarif, 1312/1894-95.

Al-Nahrawali al-Makki, Qutb al-Din Muhammad b. Ahmad (1511–82). *Al-Barq al-yamānī fī'l-fatḥ al-ᶜuthmānī*, a.k.a. *Ghazwāt al-Jarākisa wa'l-Atrāk fī janūb al-jazīra*. Edited by Jasir Hamad. Riyadh: Dar al-Yamama, 1968.

Al-Naqqash, Raja᾽. *Naguib Mahfouz: Ṣafaḥāt min mudhakkirātihi wa-aḍwā᾽ jadīda ᶜala adabihi wa-ḥayyātihi*. Cairo: Markaz al-Ahram li'l-Tarjama wa'l-Nashr, 1997.

Niebuhr, Carsten. *Travels through Arabia and Other Countries in the East*. Translated by Robert Heron. Edinburgh: R. Morrison and Son, Booksellers, Perth; G. Mudie, Edinburgh; and T. Vernor, London, 1792. Reprint Beirut: Librairie du Liban, n.d.

Ovid (Publius Ovidius Naso). *Selections from the Metamorphoses and Heroides of Publius Ovidius Naso, with a Literal and Interlinear Translation*. Translated by Hamilton. Edited by Thomas Clark and George William Heilig. New York: Charles De Silver and Sons; David McKay Co., Inc., 1889.

Playfair, Robert L. *A History of Arabia Felix or Yemen*. 1859. Reprint, Amsterdam: Philo Press; St. Leonards: Ad Orientem, Ltd., 1970.

Al-Qalqashandi, Ahmad b. ᶜAli (1365/6–1418). *Ṣubḥ al-aᶜsh᾽ā fī ṣināᶜat al-inshā*. 14 Vols. Cairo: Al-Mu᾽assasa al-Misriyya al-ᶜAmma li'l-Ta᾽lif wa'l-Tarjama wa'l-Tibaᶜa wa'l-Nashr, 1964.

Al-Qinali, Mustafa b. Ibrahim al-Maddah. *Majmūᶜ laṭīf* (to 1739). Vienna: Nationalbibliothek, MS Hist. Osm. 38.

Ridvan Paşazade, ᶜAbdullah Çelebi. *Tārīḫ-i Mıṣır* (c. 1646). Istanbul: Süleymaniye Library, MS Fatih 4362.

Rumuzi, [Mustafa Bey al-]. *Tārīḫ-i fetḥ-i Yemen* (to 1568). Istanbul: Topkapı Palace Library, MS Revan 1297.

Al-Sabiʾ, Hilal (970–1056). *Rusūm dār al-khilāfa: The Rules and Regulations of the ᶜAbbasid Court*. Translated with introduction and notes by Elie A. Salem. Beirut: American University in Beirut Press, 1977.

Scanlon, George F., ed. and trans. *A Muslim Manual of War*. Cairo: American University in Cairo Press, 1961.

Al-Shirbini, Yusuf b. Muhammad b. ᶜAbd al-Jawad b. Khidr (fl. late seventeenth century). *Hazz al-quḥūf fī sharḥ qaṣīd Abī Shādūf*. Edited by Shaykh Mahmud Musa. Bulaq: Al-Matbaᶜa al-Amiriyya, 1308 A.H.

Şiri ᶜAli. *Tārīḫ-i fetḥ-i Mıṣır* (to 1520). Istanbul: Topkapı Palace Library, MS Eminet Hazinesi 1433/2.

Süheyli Efendi. *Tevārīḫ-i Mıṣīr [sic] ül-ḳadīm* (c. 1630). Istanbul: Süleymaniye Library, MS Fatih 4229.

Sümer, Faruk, Ahmet E. Uysal, and Warren S. Walker, eds. and trans. *The Book of Dede Korkut: A Turkish Epic*. Austin: University of Texas Press, 1972, 1991.

Süreyya, Mehmed. *Sicill-i ᶜOsmānī*. 4 Vols. Istanbul: 1308–15/1890–97. Republished Westmead, Farnborough, Hants., England: Gregg International Publishers, Limited, 1971.

Al-Suwaydi, Abu'l-Fawz Muhammad Amin. *Sabāʾik al-dhahab fī maᶜrifat qabāʾil al-ᶜArab*. London: British Museum Library, MS Or. 1543.

Al-Tabari, Abu Jaᶜfar Muhammad b. Jarir (c. 838–923). *The Early ᶜAbbasi Empire*. Vol. 2: *The Sons and Gransdons of al-Mansur: The Reigns of al-Mahdi, al-Hadi, and Harun al-Rashid*. Translated by John Alden Williams. Cambridge: Cambridge University Press, 1989.

———. *The History of al-Tabari*. Vol. 9: *The Last Years of the Prophet*. Translated and annotated by Ismail K. Poonawala. Albany: State University of New York Press, 1990.

———. *The History of al-Tabari*. Vol. 11: *The Challenge to the Empires*. Translated and annotated by Khalid Yahya Blankinship. Albany: State University of New York Press, 1993.

———. *The History of al-Tabari*. Vol. 31: *The War between Brothers*. Translated and annotated by Michael Fishbein. Albany: State University of New York Press, 1992.

Tenniel, Sir John. Cartoon "Woodman, Spare that Tree!" *Punch* 1876. Reproduced in "The Eastern Question: Gladstone and Bulgaria." Exhibition, British Library, 21 February–10 May 1992.

Thackston, Wheeler M., ed., trans., and annotator. *The Baburnama: Memoirs of Babur, Prince and Emperor*. New York and Oxford: Oxford University Press, in association with the Freer Gallery of Art and the Arthur M. Sackler Gallery, Washington, DC, 1996.

Thévenot, Jean de. *Relation d'un voyage fait au Levant. . . .* Paris: T. Iolly, 1665.

Topkapı Palace Archives (Istanbul). D. 2520/3 (1166–67/1752–54), D. 7662 (1163/1750).

Al-Waqidi, Muhammad b. ᶜUmar (747 or 748–823). *Kitāb al-Maghāzi*. Edited by Marsden Jones. 3 Vols. London: Oxford University Press, 1966.

Winny, James, ed. and trans. *Sir Gawain and the Green Night*. Middle English text with facing translation. Peterborough, Ont.: Broadview Press, 1992.

Yahya b. al-Husayn b. al-Qasim (1625–89). *Ghāyat al-amānī fī akhbār al-quṭr al-yamānī*. Edited by Saᶜid ᶜAbd al-Fattah ᶜAshur. 2 Vols. Cairo: Dar al-Katib al-ᶜArabi, 1968.

Yusuf Efendi. *Tārīḫ-i Mıṣır* (1684). Istanbul: Süleymaniye Library, MS Esad Efendi 2148.

Secondary Sources

Aarne, Antti. *The Types of the Folktale*. Translated and enlarged by Stith Thompson. Helsinki: Academia Scientarum Fennica, 1961.

ᶜAbd al-Rahim, A. A. "Land Tenure in Egypt and Its Social Effects on Egyptian Society: 1798–1813." In *Land Tenure and Social Transformation in the Middle East*. Edited by Tarif Khalidi, 237–48. Beirut: American University in Beirut Press, 1984.

Abu-Husayn, Abdul-Rahim. "The *Iltizām* of Mansur Furaykh: A Case Study of *Iltizām* in Sixteenth-Century Syria." In *Land Tenure and Social Transformation in the Middle East*. Edited by Tarif Khalidi, 249–56. Beirut: American University in Beirut Press, 1984.

Akdağ, Mustafa. *Celali İsyanları (1550–1603)*. Ankara: Türk Tarih Kurumu, 1963.

Alvárez, Lourdes María. "Petrus Alfonsi." In *The Literature of al-Andalus*. Edited by María Rosa Menocal, Raymond P. Scheindlin, and Michael Sells. Cambridge: Cambridge University Press, 2000.

Amitai-Press, Reuven. *Mongols and Mamluks: The Mamluk-Ilkhanid War, 1260–1281*. Cambridge: Cambridge University Press, 1995.

And, Metin. *Ritüelden Drama: Karbelâ-Muharrem-Taᵓziye*. Istanbul: Yapıkredi Yayınları, 2002.

Anderson, Benedict. *Imagined Communities: Reflections on the Origins and Spread of Nationalism*. 1983. Revised and expanded ed. London and New York: Verso, 1991.

Artin, Yacoub. *Contribution à l'étude du blason en Orient*. London: B. Quaritch, 1902.

Ayalon, David. "Aspects of the Mamluk Phenomenon." Part 1: *Der Islam* 53 (1976): 196–225. Part 2: *Der Islam* 54 (1977): 1–32.

———. "The Circassians in the Mamluk Kingdom." *Journal of the American Oriental Society* 69, no. 3 (1949): 135–47.

———. *L'esclavage du mamelouk*. Jerusalem: Magnes Press, 1951.

———. *Gunpowder and Firearms in the Mamluk Kingdom: A Challenge to Medieval Society*. London: Vallentine, Mitchell, and Co., Ltd., 1956.

———. "The Historian al-Jabarti and His Background." *BSOAS* 23 (1960): 217–49.

———. "Notes on the *Furūsiyya* Exercises and Games in the Mamluk Sultanate," *Scripta Hierosolymitana* 9 (1961): 33–62.

———. "Studies in al-Jabarti I: Notes on the Transformation of Mamluk Society in Egypt under the Ottomans." *Journal of the Economic and Social History of the Orient* 3, no. 2 (1960): 148–74; 3, no. 3 (1960): 275–325.

———. "Studies on the Structure of the Mamluk Army." Part 1: *BSOAS* 15, no. 2 (1953): 203–28. Part 2: *BSOAS* 15, no. 3 (1953): 448–76. Part 3: *BSOAS* 16, no. 1 (1954): 57–90.

———. "The Wafidiyya in the Mamluk Kingdom." *Islamic Culture* 25 (1951): 81–104.

Bacqué-Grammont, Jean-Louis. *Les Ottomanes, les Safavides, et leurs voisins: Contribution à l'histoire des relations internationales dans l'Orient islamique de 1514 à 1524*. Istanbul: Nederlands Historisch-Archaeologisch Instituut, 1987.

Baer, Gabriel. "Shirbini's *Hazz al-quḥūf* and Its Significance." In *Fellah and Townsman in Ottoman Egypt: Studies in Social History*. By Gabriel Baer, 3–47. London: Frank Cass and Co., 1982.

Bafaqih, Muhammad ʿAbd al-Qadir. *L'Unification du Yémen antique: La lutte entre Sabaʾ, Himyar, et le Hadramawt du Ier au IIIème siècle de l'ère chrétienne*. Paris: Librairie Orientaliste Paul Geuthner, 1990.

Bannerth, Ernst. "La Khalwatiyya en Égypte: Quelques aspects de la vie d'une confrérie." *Mélange de l'Institut Dominicain d'Études Orientales* 8 (1960): 1–74.

Barbir, Karl K. *Ottoman Rule in Damascus, 1708–1758*. Princeton, NJ: Princeton University Press, 1980.

Barkan, Ömer Lütfi. "The Price Revolution of the Sixteenth Century: A Turning Point in the Economic History of the Near East." *International Journal of Middle East Studies* 6 (1975): 3–28.

Bayerle, Gustav. *Pashas, Begs, and Effendis: A Historical Dictionary of Titles and Terms in the Ottoman Empire*. Istanbul: Isis Press, 1997.

Behrens-Abouseif, Doris. *Azbakiyya and Its Environs: From Azbak to Ismail, 1476–1879*. Cairo: Institut Français d'Archéologie Orientale, 1985.

———. *Egypt's Adjustment to Ottoman Rule: Institutions,* Waqf, *and Architecture in Cairo (Sixteenth-Seventeenth Centuries)*. Leiden: Brill, 1994.

———. "Four Domes of the Late Mamluk Period." *Annales Islamologiques* 17 (1981): 191–201 and Plates 11–14.

———. "An Unlisted Monument of the Fifteenth Century: The Dome of Zawiyat al-Damirdaš," *Annales Islamologiques* 18 (1982): 105–21 and Plates 11–13.

———, and Leonor Fernandes. "Sufi Architecture in Early Ottoman Cairo." *Annales Islamologiques* 20 (1984): 103–14, and Plates 15–20.

Berkey, Jonathan. "Storytelling, Preaching, and Power in Mamluk Cairo." *Mamluk Studies Review* 4 (2000): 53–73.

Bidwell, R. L. "Western Accounts of San'a', 1510–1962." In *San'a': An Arabian Islamic City*. Edited by R. B. Serjeant and Ronald Lewcock, 108–21. London: World of Islam Festival Trust, 1983.

Bierman, Irene A. *Writing Signs: The Fatimid Public Text*. Berkeley: University of California Press, 1998.

Birge, John K. *The Bektashi Order of Dervishes*. London: Luzac and Co., 1937.

Blankinship, Khalid Yahya. *The End of the Jihad State: The Reign of Hisham Ibn 'Abd al-Malik and the Collapse of the Umayyads*. Albany: State University of New York Press, 1994.

Blukacz, François. "Le Yémen sous l'autorité des imams zaidites au XVIIe siècle: Une éphémère unité." In *Le Yémen, Passé et présent de l'unité. Revue du Monde Musulman et de la Méditerranée* no. 67. Edited by Michel Tuchscherer, 39–51. Paris: Édisud, 1994.

Bodman, Herbert L., Jr. *Political Factions in Aleppo, 1760–1826*. Chapel Hill, NC: University of North Carolina Press, 1963.

Çağman, Filiz. *Traditional Turkish Arts: Miniature*. Ankara: Turkish Republic, Ministry of Culture and Tourism, General Directorate of Fine Arts, n.d. [1987?].

———, and Zeren Tanındı. *The Topkapı Saray Museum: The Albums and Illuminated Manuscripts*. Translated, expanded, and edited by J. M. Rogers. London: Thames and Hudson, 1986.

Cameron, Alan. *Circus Factions: Blues and Greens at Rome and Byzantium*. Oxford: Clarendon Press, 1976.

Carter, J. R. L. *Tribes in Oman*. London: IMMEL Publishing, Ltd., 1982.

Chelkowski, Peter J. "*Ta'ziyeh*: Indigenous Avant-Garde Theatre of Iran." In *Ta'ziyeh: Ritual and Drama in Iran*. Edited by Peter J. Chelkowski, 1–11. New York: New York University Press and Soroush Press, 1979.

———. "When Time Is No Time and Space Is No Space: The Passion Plays of Husayn." In *Ta'ziyeh: Ritual and Popular Belief in Iran: Essays Prepared for a Drama Festival and Conference Held at Trinity College, Hartford Seminary, April 30–May 2, 1988*. Edited by Milla Cozart Riggio. Hartford, CT: Trinity College, 1988.

Cook, M. A. *Population Pressure in Rural Anatolia, 1450–1600*. New York and Oxford: Oxford University Press, 1972.

Coussonnet, Nahida. "Les assises du pouvoir zaydite au XIIIe siècle." In *Le Yémen, Passé et présent de l'unité. Revue du Monde Musulman et de la Méditerranée* no. 67. Edited by Michel Tuchscherer, 25–37. Paris: Édisud, 1994.

Crecelius, Daniel N. "Ahmad Shalabi ibn 'Abd al-Ghani and Ahmad Katkhuda 'Azaban al-Damurdashi: Two Sources for al-Jabarti's *'Ajā'ib al-āthār fī'l-tarājim wa'l-akhbār*." In *Eighteenth Century Egypt: The Arabic Manuscript Sources*. Edited by Daniel N. Crecelius, 89–102. Claremont, CA: Regina Books, 1990.

———. "Egypt in the Eighteenth Century." In *The Cambridge History of Egypt*. Vol. 2: *Modern Egypt from 1517 to the end of the Twentieth Century*. Edited by M. W. Daly, 59–86. Cambridge: Cambridge University Press, 1998.

———. *The Roots of Modern Egypt: A Study of the Regimes of ʿAli Bey al-Kabir and Muhammad Bey Abu al-Dhahab, 1760–1775*. Minneapolis and Chicago: Bibliotheca Islamica, 1981.

Crone, Patricia. "Were the Qays and Yemen of the Umayyad Period Political Parties?" *Der Islam* 71, no. 1 (1994): 1–57.

Daftary, Farhad. *The Ismailis: Their History and Doctrines*. 1990. Reprint, Cambridge: Cambridge University Press, 1995.

Dale, Stephen F. "The Legacy of the Timurids." *Journal of the Royal Asiatic Society* 8, no. 1 (April 1998): 45–58.

———. "The Poetry and Autobiography of the *Bâbur-nâma*." *Journal of Asian Studies* 55, no. 3 (August 1996): 635–64.

Daly, M. W., ed. *The Cambridge History of Egypt*. Vol. 2: *Modern Egypt from 1517 to the End of the Twentieth Century*. Cambridge: Cambridge University Press, 1998.

Darling, Linda T. *Revenue-Raising and Legitimacy: Tax Collection and Finance Administration in the Ottoman Empire, 1560–1660*. Leiden: Brill, 1996.

Dávid, Géza, and Pál Fodor, eds. *Hungarian-Ottoman Military and Diplomatic Relations in the Age of Süleyman the Magnificent*. Budapest: Loránd Eötvös University, Department of Turkish Studies, Hungarian Academy of Sciences, Institute of History, 1994.

———, eds. *Ottomans, Hungarians, and Hapsburgs in Central Europe: The Military Confines in the Era of Ottoman Conquest*. Leiden: Brill, 2000.

Davidson, H. R. Ellis. *Myths and Symbols in Pagan Europe: Early Scandinavian and Celtic Religions*. Manchester: Manchester University Press, 1988.

Davis, Robert C. *The War of the Fists: Popular Culture and Public Violence in Late Renaissance Venice*. New York and Oxford: Oxford University Press, 1994.

DeWeese, Devin. *Islamization and Native Religion in the Golden Horde: Baba Tükles and Conversion to Islam in Historical and Epic Tradition*. University Park, PA: Pennsylvania State University Press, 1990.

Diba, Layla S., ed., with Maryam Ekhtiar. *Royal Persian Paintings: The Qajar Epoch, 1785–1925*. Brooklyn: Brooklyn Museum of Art, in association with I. B. Tauris Publishers, 1998.

Dodge, Bayard. *Al-Azhar: A Millennium of Muslim Learning*. Memorial Ed. Washington, DC: Middle East Institute, 1974.

Downey, Fairfax D. *Soliman le Magnifique*. Translated by S. M. Guillemin. Paris: Payot, 1930.

Dozy, Reinhart. *Supplément aux dictionnaires arabes*. 2 Vols. Leiden: E. J. Brill, 1927.

Dresch, Paul. "Imams and Tribes: The Writing and Acting of History in Upper Yemen." In *Tribes and State Formation in the Middle East*. Edited by Philip S. Khoury and Joseph Kostiner, 252–87. Berkeley: University of California Press, 1990.

———. *Tribes, Government, and History in Yemen*. Oxford: Clarendon and Oxford University Press, 1989.

Dundas, Paul. *The Jains*. London and New York: Routledge, 1992.
Elbendary, Amina A. "The Sultan, the Tyrant, and the Hero: Changing Medieval Perceptions of al-Zahir Baybars." *Mamluk Studies Review* 5 (2001): 141–57.
El-Cheikh, Nadia M. "Constantinople through Arab Eyes: A Mythology." In *Myths, Historical Archetypes, and Symbolic Figures in Arabic Literature: Towards a New Hermeneutic Approach—Proceedings of the International Symposium in Beirut, June 25th–30th, 1996*. Edited by Angelika Neuwirth, Birgit Embaló, Sebastian Günther, and Maher Jarrar. Stuttgart: Franz Steiner Verlag, 1999.
EI[1], *s.v.* "Ghassān," by J. Schleifer.
———, *s.v.* "Hadramawt," by J. Schleifer.
———, *s.v.* "Ḥāshid and Bakīl," by J. Schleifer.
———, *s.v.* "Rasūlids," by A. S. Tritton.
EI[2], *s.v.*, "Badr," by W. Montgomery Watt.
———, *s.v.* "Bakr," by W. Caskel.
———, *s.v.* "al-Basūs," by J. W. Fück.
———, *s.v.* "Dhū'l-Faḳār," by E. Mittwoch.
———, *s.v.* "Ewliyā Çelebi," by J. H. Mordtmann [H. W. Duda].
———, *s.v.* "Ḥāshid wa-Bakīl," by G. Rentz.
———, *s.v.* "Hawwāra," by T. Lewicki.
———, *s.v.* "Hawwāra—Egypt and the Sudan," by P. M. Holt.
———, *s.v.* "Hilāl," by Richard Ettinghausen.
———, *s.v.* "Hilāl," by Hady Roger Idris.
———, *s.v.*, "Hilāl: The Saga of the Banū Hilāl," by J. Schleifer.
———, *s.v.* "Isfendiyār Oghlu," by J. H. Mordtmann.
———, *s.v.* "*Iskandarname*," by A. Abel.
———, *s.v.* "Kaᶜba," by A. J. Wensinck-J. Jomier.
———, *s.v.* "Kays ᶜAylān," by W. Montgomery Watt.
———, *s.v.* "Kays ᶜAylān: Kays and Yaman in the Ottoman Period," by Gabriel Baer and Miriam Hoexter.
———, *s.v.* "Khālid b. al-Walīd," by Patricia Crone.
———, *s.v.* "Ḳızıl Elma," by Pertev Naili Boratov.
———, *s.v.* "Kulayb b. Rabīᶜa," by Giorgio Levi Della Vida.
———, *s.v.* "Mamlūk," by David Ayalon.
———, *s.v.* "Mamlūks," by P. M. Holt.
———, *s.v.* "Ṣanᶜāᵓ," by R. Strothmann.
Faroqhi, Suraiya. "Crisis and Change, 1590–1699." In *An Economic and Social History of the Ottoman Empire*. Edited by Halil Inalcik with Donald Quataert. Part 2. Cambridge: Cambridge University Press, 1994.
———. *Pilgrims and Sultans: The Hajj under the Ottomans*. Cambridge: Cambridge University Press, 1994.
———. "Rural Society in Anatolia and the Balkans during the Sixteenth Century." *Turcica* 9 (1977): 161–96 and 11 (1979): 103–53.
———, with Leila Erder. "Population Rise and Fall in Anatolia, 1550–1620." *Middle Eastern Studies* 15 (1979): 322–45.

Finkel, Caroline. *The Administration of Warfare: The Ottoman Military Campaigns in Hungary, 1593–1606*. 2 Vols. Vienna: VWGÖ, 1988.

Fleischer, Cornell H. *Bureaucrat and Intellectual in the Ottoman Empire: The Historian Mustafa Âlî (1541–1600)*. Princeton, NJ: Princeton University Press, 1986.

———. "The Lawgiver as Messiah: The Making of the Imperial Image in the Reign of Süleymân." In *Soliman le Magnifique et son temps: Actes du Colloque de Paris Galeries Nationales du Grand Palais, 7–10 mars 1990*. Edited by Gilles Veinstein, 159–77. Paris: La Documentation Française, 1992.

Flemming, Barbara. "Public Opinion under Sultan Süleymân." In *Süleymân the Second [sic] and His Time*. Edited by Halil Inalcik and Cemal Kafadar, 49–57. Istanbul: Isis Press, 1993.

———. "Šerif, Sultan Gavrî, und die «Perser»." *Der Islam* 45 (1969): 81–93.

Freeman, John W. *Stories of the Great Operas*. New York and London: W. W. Norton and Co., 1984.

Frye, Richard N. *The Heritage of Central Asia*. Princeton, NJ: Markus Wiener Publishers, 1996.

Garcin, Jean-Claude. "Émirs Hawwâras et beys de Ğirğa aus XVIe et XVIIe siècles." *Annales Islamologiques* 12 (1984): 245–55.

Gibb, H. A. R. *Mohammedanism: An Historical Survey*. 2d ed. Oxford: Oxford University Press, 1970.

Giles, Herbert A. *Religions of Ancient China*. London: Archibald Constable and Co., Ltd., 1906.

Goitein, S. D. *A Mediterranean Society*. Vol. 1: *Economic Foundations*. Berkeley: University of California Press, 1967.

———. "Townsman and Fellah: A Geniza Text from the Seventeenth Century." *Asian and African Studies* 8, no. 3 (1972): 257–61.

Goldziher, Ignaz. *Muslim Studies*. Edited by S. M. Stern. Translated by C. R. Barber and S. M. Stern. 2 Vols. Chicago: Aldine Publishing Co., 1968.

Gordon, Matthew S. *The Breaking of a Thousand Swords: A History of the Turkish Community of Samarra, 200–275 A.H./815–889 C.E.* Albany: State University of New York Press, 2001.

Grabar, Oleg, and Sheila Blair. *Epic Images and Contemporary History: The Illustrations of the Great Mongol Shahname*. Chicago: University of Chicago Press, 1980.

Graves, Robert. *The Greek Myths*. Revised ed. 2 Vols. London: Penguin Books, 1960.

Gray, Basil. *Persian Painting*. 2d ed. 1961. New York: Rizzoli, 1977.

Gresham Carr, H. *Flags of the World*. Based on F. Edward Hulme, *The Flags of the World and Their History, Blazonry, and Associations*, 1897. London and New York: Frederick Warne and Co., Ltd., 1953.

Halm, Heinz. *Ägypten nach den mamlukischen Lehensregistern*. 2 Vols. Wiesbaden: Reichert, 1979.

———. *The Empire of the Mahdi: The Rise of the Fatimids*. Translated by Michael Bonner. Leiden: Brill, 1996.

Hanna, Nelly. *Making Big Money in 1600: The Life and Times of Ismail Abu Taqiyya, Egyptian Merchant*. Syracuse: Syracuse University Press, 1998.

Hathaway, Jane. "Çerkes Mehmed Bey: Rebel, Traitor, Hero?" *Turkish Studies Association Bulletin* 22, no. 1 (1998): 108–15.

———. "Egypt in the Seventeenth Century." In *The Cambridge History of Egypt*. Vol. 2: *Modern Egypt from 1517 to the end of the Twentieth Century*. Edited by M. W. Daly, 34–58. Cambridge: Cambridge University Press, 1998.

———. "The Household of Hasan Ağa Bilifya: An Assessment of Elite Politics in Seventeenth-Century Ottoman Egypt." *Turcica* 27 (1995): 135–51.

———. " 'Mamluk Households' and 'Mamluk Factions' in Ottoman Egypt: A Reconsideration." In *The Mamluks in Egyptian Politics and Society*. Edited by Thomas Philipp and Ulrich Haarmann, 107–17. Cambridge: Cambridge University Press, 1998.

———. "Mamluk 'Revivals' and Mamluk Nostalgia in Ottoman Egypt." In *The Mamluks in Egyptian and Syrian Politics and Society*. Edited by Amalia Levanoni and Michael Winter. Leiden: Brill, forthcoming.

———. "Marriage Alliances among the Military Households of Ottoman Egypt." *Annales Islamologiques* 29 (1995): 133–49.

———. "The Military Household in Ottoman Egypt." *International Journal of Middle East Studies* 27, no. 1 (1995): 39–52.

———. "Osmanlı Mısır'ında Yerli Askerî Unsurlar ve Yeniçeriler." In *Türkler*. Edited by Hasan Celâl Güzel, C. Cem Oğuz, and Osman Karatay, 10: 172–79. 20 Vols. Ankara: Yeni Türkiye Yayınları, 2002.

———. *The Politics of Households in Ottoman Egypt: The Rise of the Qazdağlıs*. Cambridge: Cambridge University Press, 1997.

———. "The Role of the Kızlar Ağası in 17th–18th Century Ottoman Egypt." *Studia Islamica* 75 (1992): 135–51.

———. "Sultans, Pashas, *Taqwīms*, and Mühimmes: A Reconsideration of Chronicle-Writing in Eighteenth-Century Ottoman Egypt." In *Eighteenth-Century Egypt: The Arabic Manuscript Sources*. Edited by Daniel N. Crecelius, 51–78. Claremont, CA: Regina Press, 1990.

———. "A Twelfth-Century Partnership in Silk-Trading in the Egyptian Delta: A Geniza Study." *Journal of the Middle East Studies Society at Columbia University* 2, no. 1 (1988): 23–37.

———. "The Wealth and Influence of an Ottoman Eunuch in Egypt: The *Waqf* Inventory of ᶜAbbas Agha." *Journal of the Economic and Social History of the Orient* 37 (1994): 295–317.

Hattox, Ralph. *Coffee and Coffeehouses: The Origins of a Social Beverage in the Medieval Near East*. Seattle, WA: University of Washington Press, 1985.

Haykel, Bernard. "Al-Shawkani and the Jurisprudential Unity of Yemen." In *Le Yémen, Passé et présent de l'unité. Revue du Monde Musulman et de la Méditerranée* no. 67. Edited by Michel Tuchscherer, 53–65. Paris: Édisud, 1994.

Hedges, Chris. "Satan's Alive and Well, but the Sect May be Dying." *New York Times*, 31 May 1993, p. A2.

Heyd, Uriel. *Studies in Old Ottoman Criminal Law*. Edited by V. L. Ménage. Oxford: Clarendon Press, 1973.

Heywood, Colin. "Filling the Black Hole: The Emergence of the Bithynian Atamanates." In *The Great Ottoman Turkish Civilisation*. Edited by Kemal Çiçek, Ercüment Kuran, Nejat Göyünç, and İlber Ortaylı, 1: 107–15. 4 Vols. Ankara: Yeni Türkiye Yayınevi, 2000.

Heyworth-Dunne, J. *An Introduction to the History of Education in Modern Egypt*. London: Luzac and Co., 1938.

Hickok, Michael R. *Ottoman Military Administration in Eighteenth-Century Bosnia*. Leiden: Brill, 1997.

Hinds, Martin. "The Banners and Battle Cries of the Arabs at Siffin (A.D. 657)." In *Studies in Early Islamic History*. By Martin Hinds. Edited by Jere Bacharach, Lawrence I. Conrad, and Patricia Crone, 97–142. With an introduction by G. R. Hawting. Princeton, NJ: The Darwin Press, 1996.

———, and Victor Ménage. *Qasr Ibrim in the Ottoman Period: Turkish and Further Arabic Documents*. London: Egypt Exploration Society, 1991.

Hobsbawm, Eric, and Terrence Ranger, eds. *The Invention of Tradition*. Cambridge: Cambridge University Press, 1983.

Hodgson, Marshall G. S. *The Venture of Islam: Continuity and Change in a World Civilization*. 3 Vols. Chicago: University of Chicago Press, 1974.

Hoexter, Miriam. "The Role of the Qays and Yaman Factions in Local Political Divisions: Jabal Nablus Compared with the Judean Hills in the First Half of the Nineteenth Century." *Asian and African Studies* 9 (1973): 249–311.

Holt, P. M. "The Beylicate in Ottoman Egypt during the Seventeenth Century." *BSOAS* 24, no. 2 (1961): 214–48.

———. *Egypt and the Fertile Crescent: A Political History, 1516–1922*. Ithaca and London: Cornell University Press, 1966.

———. "The Exalted Lineage of Ridwan Bey: Some Observations on a Seventeenth-Century Mamluk Genealogy." *BSOAS* 22, no. 2 (1959): 221–30.

———. "Al-Jabarti's Introduction to the History of Ottoman Egypt." *BSOAS* 25, no. 1 (1962): 38–51.

———. "Literary Offerings: A Genre of Courtly Literature." In *The Mamluks in Egyptian Politics and Society*. Edited by Thomas Philipp and Ulrich Haarmann, 3–16. Cambridge: Cambridge University Press, 1998.

———. "Ottoman Egypt (1517–1798): An Account of Arabic Historical Sources." In *Political and Social Change in Modern Egypt: Historical Studies from the Ottoman Conquest to the United Arab Republic*. Edited by P. M. Holt, 3–12. Oxford and London: Oxford University Press, 1968.

———. "Some Observations on the ʿAbbasid Caliphate of Cairo." *BSOAS* 47 (1984): 501–07.

Howe, Nicholas. *Migration and Mythmaking in Anglo-Saxon England*. New Haven, CT: Yale University Press, 1989. Paperback Notre Dame, IN: University of Notre Dame Press, 2001.

Inalcik, Halil. "Greeks in Ottoman Economy and Finances, 1453–1500." In *Essays in Ottoman History*. By Halil Inalcik, 377–89. Istanbul: Eren Yayıncılık, 1998.

———. "Military and Fiscal Transformation in the Ottoman Empire, 1600–1700." *Archivum Ottomanicum* 6 (1980): 283–337.

———. "The Ottoman State: Economy and Society, 1300–1600." In *An Economic and Social History of the Ottoman Empire*. Edited by Halil Inalcik with Donald Quataert. Part 1. Cambridge: Cambridge University Press, 1994.

———. "The Policy of Mehmed II toward the Greek Population of Istanbul and the Byzantine Buildings of the City." *Dumbarton Oaks Papers* 23–25 (1969–70): 231–49.

———. "The Rise of Ottoman Historiography." In *Historians of the Middle East*. Edited by Bernard Lewis and P. M. Holt, 152–67. London: Oxford University Press, 1962.

———. "The Socio-Political Effects of the Diffusion of Fire-Arms in the Middle East." In *War, Technology and Society in the Middle East*. Edited by V. J. Parry and Malcolm Yapp, 195–217. London and New York: Oxford University Press, 1975.

———. "State, Sovereignty, and Law during the Reign of Süleymân." In *Süleymân the Second [sic] and His Time*. Edited by Halil Inalcik and Cemal Kafadar, 59–92. Istanbul: Isis Press, 1993.

———. "Suleiman the Lawgiver and Ottoman Law." *Archivum Ottomanicum* 1 (1969): 105–38.

Irwin, Robert. "Factions in Medieval Egypt." *Journal of the Royal Asiatic Society* 1986, No. 2: 228–46.

———. *Islamic Art in Context: Art, Architecture, and the Literary World*. New York: Harry N. Abrams/Prenctice Hall, 1997.

———. *The Middle East in the Middle Ages: The Early Mamluk Sultanate, 1250–1382*. London and Sydney: Croom Helm, 1986.

Izady, Mehrdad R. *The Kurds: A Concise Handbook*. Washington, DC: Taylor and Francis, Inc., 1992.

Jaimoukha, Amjad. *The Circassians: A Handbook*. New York: Palgrave, 2001.

Jastrow, Marcus. *A Dictionary of the Targumim, the Talmud Babli and Yerushalmi, and the Midrashic Literature*. 2 Vols. New York: Traditional Press, Inc., 1903.

Kafadar, Cemal. *Between Two Worlds: The Origins of the Ottoman State*. Berkeley: University of California Press, 1995.

———. "The Myth of the Golden Age: Ottoman Historical Consciousness in the Post-Süleymânic Era." In *Süleymân the Second [sic] and His Time*. Edited by Halil Inalcik and Cemal Kafadar, 37–48. Istanbul: Isis Press, 1993.

Kaldy-Nágy, Gyula. "The 'Strangers' (*Ecnebiler*) in the Sixteenth-Century Ottoman Military Organization." In *Between the Danube and the Caucasus: Oriental Sources on the History of the Peoples of Central and South-Eastern Europe*. Edited by György Kara, 165–69. Budapest: Akadémiai Kiadó, 1987.

Khalid, Tarif, ed. *Land Tenure and Social Transformation in the Middle East*. Beirut: American University in Beirut Press, 1984.

Khoury, Dina Rizk. *State and Provincial Society in the Ottoman Empire: Mosul, 1540–1834*. Cambridge: Cambridge University Press, 1997.

Khuri, Fuad Ishaq. *Imams and Emirs: State, Religion, and Sects in Islam*. London: Saqi, 1990.

Kimmerling, Baruch, and Joel S. Migdal. *Palestinians: The Making of a People*. New York: The Free Press, 1993.

Knappert, Jan. *Islamic Legends: Stories of the Heroes, Saints, and Prophets of Islam*. 2 Vols. Leiden: E. J. Brill, 1985.

Köprülü, Mehmed Fuad. *The Seljuks of Anatolia: Their History and Culture according to Local Muslim Sources*. Translated by Gary Leiser. Salt Lake City: University of Utah Press, 1992.

Koram, Frank J., and Peter J. Chelkowski. "Community Process and the Performance of Muharram Observances in Trinidad." *The Drama Review* 38, no. 2 (1994): 150–75.

Kreyenbroek, Philip G. *Yezidism: Its Background, Observances and Textual Tradition*. Lewiston, NY: The Edwin Mellen Press, Ltd., 1995.

Kropp, Manfred. "The Realm of Evil: The Struggle of Ottomans and Zaidis in the 16th–17th Centuries as Reflected in Historiography." In *Yemen: Present and Past*. Edited by B. Knutsson, V. Mattsson, and M. Persson, 87–95. Lund, Sweden: Lund University Press, 1994.

Kunt, Metin. "Ethnic-Regional (*Cins*) Solidarity in the Seventeenth-Century Ottoman Establishment." *International Journal of Middle East Studies* 5 (1974): 233–39.

Kurtoğlu, Fevzi. *1877–1878 Türk-Rus Harbinde Deniz Hareketleri*. Istanbul: Deniz Matbaası, 1935.

———. *Türk Bayrağı ve Ay Yıldız*. Ankara: Türk Tarih Kurumu, 1938, 1987, 1992.

Lansing, Carol. *The Florentine Magnates: Lineage and Faction in a Medieval Commune*. Princeton, NJ: Princeton University Press, 1991.

Lellouch, Benjamin. "Le Douzième *ǧuzʾ* perdu des *Badāʾiʿ al-zuhūr* d'Ibn Iyas à la lumière d'une chronique turque d'Égypte." *Arabica* 45 (1998): 88–103.

Leonard, Irving A. *Books of the Brave: Being an Account of Books and of Men in the Spanish Conquest and Settlement of the Sixteenth-Century New World*. Cambridge, MA: Harvard University Press, 1949.

Levanoni, Amalia. *A Turning Point in Mamluk History: The Third Reign of al-Nasir Muhammad ibn Qalawun (1310–1341)*. Leiden: Brill, 1994.

Lewis, Bernard. *The Arabs in History*. Revised ed. New York: Harper and Row, 1966.

———, ed. and trans. *Islam from the Prophet Muhammad to the Capture of Constantinople*. Vol. 2: *Religion and Society*. Paperback ed. New York and Oxford: Oxford University Press, 1987 [1974].

Lewis, Geoffrey L. "The Utility of Ottoman *Fethnames*." In *Historians of the Middle East*. Edited by Bernard Lewis and P. M. Holt, 192–96. London: Oxford University Press, 1962.

Lindner, Rudi Paul. *Nomads and Ottomans in Medieval Anatolia*. Bloomington, IN: Research Institute for Inner Asian Studies, Indiana University, 1983.

Lopez, Robert S. "Silk Industry in the Byzantine Empire." *Speculum* 20 (1945): 1–42.

Lowry, Heath W. "The 'Sword of Roland' and the 'Sword of Abdal Murad': A Note on the History of Brusa (Bursa) in the Light of Six Centuries of Travellers' Accounts (1325–1925)." In *Aptullah Kuran için Yazılar/Essays in Honour of Aptullah Kuran*. Edited by Çiğdem Kafescioğlu and Lucienne Thys-Şenocak, 233–52. Istanbul: Yapı Kredi Yayınları, 1999.

Lyons, M. C. *The Arabian Epic: Heroic and Oral Story-Telling*. Vol. 1: *Introduction*. Vol. 2: *Analysis*. Vol. 3: *Texts*. Cambridge: Cambridge University Press, 1995.

Madelung, Wilferd. *Religious Trends in Early Islamic Iran*. New York: The Persian Heritage Foundation, Bibliotheca Persica, 1988.

Mahfouz, Naguib. *Fountain and Tomb* [*Ḥikāyāt ḥāratinā*]. Translated by Soad Sobhy, Essam Fattouh and James Kenneson. Washington, DC: Three Continents Press, 1988 [1975].

———. *Palace Walk* [*Bayn al-Qaṣrayn*]. Translated by William Maynard Hutchins and Olive E. Kenny. New York: Doubleday, 1990 [1956].

Mallette, Karla. "Poetries of the Norman Courts." In *The Literature of al-Andalus*. Edited by María Rosa Menocal, Raymond P. Scheindlin, and Michael Sells. Cambridge: Cambridge University Press, 2000.

Marcus, Abraham. *The Middle East on the Eve of Modernity: Aleppo in the Eighteenth Century*. New York: Columbia University Press, 1989.

Marmon, Shaun E. *Eunuchs and Sacred Boundaries in Islamic Society*. Oxford and New York: Oxford University Press, 1995.

Martin, B. G. "A Short History of the Khalwati Order of Dervishes." In *Scholars, Saints, and Sufis: Muslim Religious Institutions since 1500*. Edited by Nikki R. Keddie, 275–305. Berkeley: University of California Press, 1972.

Matthee, Rudolph P. *The Politics of Trade in Safavid Iran: Silk for Silver, 1600–1730*. Cambridge: Cambridge University Press, 1999.

Mayer, L. A. *Mamluk Costume: A Survey*. Geneva: A. Kundig, 1952.

———. *Saracenic Heraldry: A Survey*. Oxford: Clarendon Press, 1953.

McCabe, Ina Baghdiantz. *The Shah's Silk for Europe's Silver: The Eurasian Trade of the Julfa Armenians in Safavid Iran and India (1530–1750)*. University of Pennsylvania Armenian Texts and Studies. Atlanta: Scholars Press, 1999.

McNeill, William H. *Europe's Steppe Frontier, 1500–1800*. Chicago and London: University of Chicago Press, 1964.

Mélikoff, Irène. *Hadji Bektach: Une mythe et ses avatars—Genèse et évolution du soufisme populaire en Turquie*. Leiden: Brill, 1998.

Ménage, V. L. "The Beginnings of Ottoman Historiography." In *Historians of the Middle East*. Edited by Bernard Lewis and P. M. Holt, 168–79. London: Oxford University Press, 1962.

———. "Sidelights on the Devshirme from Idris and Saᶜduddin," *BSOAS* 18 (1956): 181–83.

Menocal, María Rosa, Raymond P. Scheindlin, and Michael Sells, eds. *The Literature of al-Andalus*. The Cambridge History of Arabic Literature. Cambridge: Cambridge University Press, 2000.

Mirjafari, Hossein. "The Haydari-Niʿmati Conflicts in Iran." Translated and adapted by J. R. Perry. *Iranian Studies* 12, no. 3–4 (1979): 135–62.

Morgan, David. *The Mongols*. Oxford and New York: Basil Blackwell, 1986.

Mottahedeh, Roy P. *Loyalty and Leadership in an Early Islamic Society*. Princeton, NJ: Princeton University Press, 1980.

Mughul, M. Yakub. "Portekizli'lerle Kızıldeniz'de Mücadele ve Hicaz'da Osmanlı Hâkimiyetinin Yerleşme hakkında bir Vesika." *Belleten* 2, no. 3–4 (1965): 37–48.

Murphey, Rhoads. *Ottoman Warfare, 1500–1700*. New Brunswick, NJ: Rutgers University Press, 1998.

Nakash, Yitzhak. "An Attempt to Trace the Origin of the Rituals of ʿĀshūrāʾ." *Die Welt des Islams* 33 (1993): 161–81.

Nicholson, Reynold A. *A Literary History of the Arabs*. Cambridge: Cambridge University Press, 1969.

Nicolle, David C. *Arms and Armour of the Crusading Era, 1050–1350*. Vol. 1: *Commentary*. Vol. 2: *Illustrations*. White Plains, New York: Kraus International Publications (Division of Kraus-Thomson Organization, Ltd.), 1988.

Nogmov, Shora Bekmursin (Schora Bekmursin Nogmow, 1794–1844). *Die Sagen und Lieder des Tscherkessen-Volks*. Translated by Adolf Bergé. Leipzig: Verlag von Otto Wigand, 1866.

Nour, Riza. "L'Histoire du croissant." *Revue de Turcologie* 1, no. 3 (February 1933): 3/233–181/410.

Nutku, Özdemir. *IV. Mehmed'in Edirne Şenliği (1675)*. Ankara: Türk Tarih Kurumu Basımevi, 1972, 1987.

Paksoy, H. B. "Two Altaic Games: 'Chelik-Chomak' and 'Jirid Oyunu.' " In *Aspects of Altaic Civilization III*. Edited by Denis Sinor, 187–96. Bloomington, IN: Indiana University Research Institute for Inner Asian Studies, 1990.

Palmer, J. A. B. "The Origin of the Janissaries." *Bulletin of the John Rylands Library* 35 (1952–53): 448–81.

Palmer, R. R., and Joel Coulton. *A History of the Modern World to 1815*. 5th ed. New York: Alfred A. Knopf, Inc., 1978.

Pankhurst, Richard. *Economic History of Ethiopia, 1800–1935*. Addis Ababa: Haile Sellassie I University Press, 1968.

Peirce, Leslie P. *The Imperial Harem: Women and Sovereignty in the Ottoman Empire*. New York and Oxford: Oxford University Press, 1993.

Pelikan, Jaroslav. *Mary through the Centuries: Her Place in the History of Culture*. New Haven, CT: Yale University Press, 1996.

Peterson, Samuel. "*Taʿziyeh*: Parts and Plays in Worship." In *Taʿziyeh: Ritual and Popular Belief in Iran: Essays Prepared for a Drama Festival and Conference Held at Trinity College, Hartford Seminary, April 30–May 2, 1988*. Edited by Milla Cozart Riggio. Hartford, CT: Trinity College, 1988.

Petrosyan, Yuri A., Marie Lukens Swietochowski, and Stefano Carboni. *Pages of Perfection: Islamic Paintings and Calligraphy from the Russian Academy of Sciences, St. Petersburg*. Lugano: Art Restoration for Cultural Heritage Foundation; Milan: Electa, 1995.

Phillips, Wendell. *Qataban and Sheba: Exploring the Ancient Kingdoms on the Biblical Spice Routes of Arabia*. New York: Harcourt, Brace and Co., 1955.

Piterberg, Gabriel. "The Alleged Rebellion of Abaza Mehmed Paşa: Historiography and the Ottoman State in the Seventeenth Century." In *Mutiny and Rebellion in the Ottoman Empire*. Edited by Jane Hathaway, 13–24. Madison, WI: University of Wisconsin Press, 2002.

———. "The Formation of an Ottoman Egyptian Elite in the Eighteenth Century." *International Journal of Middle East Studies* 22, no. 3 (1990): 275–89.

Popper, William. *Systematic Notes to Ibn Taghri Birdi's Chronicles of Egypt and Syria under the Circassian Sultans, 1382–1468 (Cont'd)*. Berkeley: University of California Press, 1957.

Rafeq, Abdul-Karim. *The Province of Damascus, 1723–1783*. Beirut: Khayats, 1966.

Raymond, André. *Le Caire des Janissaires: L'Apogée de la ville ottomane sous ʿAbd al-Rahman Katkhuda*. Paris: Éditions CNRS, 1995.

———. "Une 'Révolution' au Caire sous les Mamelouks: La Crise de 1123/1711." *Annales Islamologiques* 6 (1966): 95–120.

———. "Soldiers in Trade: The Case of Ottoman Cairo." *British Society for Middle Eastern Studies Bulletin* 18, no. 1 (1991): 16–37.

Renard, John. *Islam and the Heroic Image: Themes in Literature and the Visual Arts*. Columbia, SC: University of South Carolina Press, 1993.

Reynolds, Dwight F. *Heroic Poets, Poetic Heroes: The Ethnography of Performance in an Arabic Oral Epic Tradition*. Ithaca and London: Cornell University Press, 1995.

———. "Music." In *The Literature of al-Andalus*. Edited by María Rosa Menocal, Raymond P. Scheindlin, and Michael Sells. Cambridge: Cambridge University Press, 2000.

Rosen, Tovah. "The Muwashshah." In *The Literature of al-Andalus*. Edited by María Rosa Menocal, Raymond P. Scheindlin, and Michael Sells. Cambridge: Cambridge University Press, 2000.

Runciman, Stephen. *The First Crusade*. Abridged ed. Cambridge: Cambridge University Press, 1980.

Russell, Anna. "*The Ring of the Nibelungs* (An Analysis)." *Anna Russell Sings! Again?* Recorded at Town Hall, New York, 23 April 1953. Rereleased on *The Anna Russell Album?* Columbia Records, New York, 1972.

Russell, John Malcolm. *Sennacherib's Palace Without Rival at Nineveh*. Chicago: University of Chicago Press, 1991.

Salzmann, Ariel. "An Ancien Régime Revisited: 'Privatization' and Political Economy in the Eighteenth-Century Ottoman Empire." *Politics and Society* 21, no. 4 (1993): 393–423.

Sanders, Paula. *Ritual, Politics, and the City in Fatimid Cairo*. Albany: State University of New York Press, 1994.

Schacht, Joseph. *An Introduction to Islamic Law*. Oxford: Oxford University Press, 1964. Reprint 1995.

Schwarzlose, Friedrich Wilhelm. *Die Waffen der alten Araber aus ihren Dichtern dargestellt*. Hildesheim and New York: Georg Olms Verlag, 1982.

Scott, Hugh. *In the High Yemen*. London: John Murray, 1942.

Serjeant, R. B. "The Coastal Population of Socotra." In *Socotra: Island of Tranquility*. Compiled by Brian Doe, 133–80. London: IMMEL Publishing, Ltd., 1992.

———. "The Post-Medieval and Modern History of Sanʿaʾ and the Yemen, ca. 953–1382/1545–1962." In *Sanʿaʾ: An Arabian Islamic City*. Edited by R. B. Serjeant and Ronald Lewcock, 68–107. London: World of Islam Festival Trust, 1983.

———. *The South Arabian Hunt*. London: Luzac, 1976.

Serjeant, R. B., and Ronald Lewcock, eds. *Sanʿaʾ: An Arabian Islamic City*. London: World of Islam Festival Trust, 1983.

Şeşen, Ramazan. *Salâhaddin Eyyûbi ve Devri*. 2d printing. Foreword by Ekmeleddin İhsanoğlu. Istanbul: İslam Tarih, Sanat ve Kültürünü Araştırma Vakfı, 2000.

Shaban, M.A. *The ʿAbbasid Revolution*. Cambridge: Cambridge University Press, 1970.

Shahid, Irfan. *Byzantium and the Arabs in the Fifth Century*. Washington, DC: Dumbarton Oaks Research Library and Collection, 1989.

———. *Byzantium and the Arabs in the Fourth Century*. Washington, DC: Dumbarton Oaks Research Library and Collection, 1984.

———. *Byzantium and the Arabs in the Sixth Century*. Vol. 1. Washington, DC: Dumbarton Oaks Research Library and Collection, 1995.

———. "Ghassan Post Ghassan." In *The Islamic World from Classical to Modern Times: Essays in Honor of Bernard Lewis*. Edited by C. E. Bosworth, Charles Issawi, Roger Savory, and A. L. Udovitch, 323–36. Princeton: The Darwin Press, 1989.

Shaw, Stanford J. *The Financial and Administrative Organization and Development of Ottoman Egypt, 1517–1798*. Princeton, NJ: Princeton University Press, 1962.

Smith, Whitney. *Flags through the Ages and across the World*. New York: McGraw-Hill, 1975.

Soudan, Frédérique. *Le Yémen ottoman d'après la chronique d'al-Mawzaʿi*. Cairo: Institut Français d'Archéologie Orientale, 1999.

Southern, R. W. *Western Views of Islam in the Middle Ages*. Cambridge, MA: Harvard University Press, 1962.

Stanley, Peter. "Military Culture and Military Protest: The Bengal Europeans and the 'White Mutiny' of 1859." In *Rebellion, Repression, Reinvention: Mutiny in Comparative Perspective*. Edited by Jane Hathaway, 103–18. Westport, CT, and London: Praeger, 2001.

Steingass, F. *Persian-English Dictionary*. Beirut: Librarie du Liban, 1892, 1970.

Stetkevych, Jaroslav. *Muhammad and the Golden Bough: Reconstructing Arabian Myth*. Bloomington, IN: Indiana University Press, 1996.

Stewart, Devin J. "Ibn Zaydun." In *The Literature of al-Andalus*. Edited by María Rosa Menocal, Raymond P. Scheindlin, and Michael Sells. Cambridge: Cambridge University Press, 2000.

Stillman, Norman A. *The Jews of Arab Lands: A History and Source Book*. Philadelphia: Jewish Publication Society, 1979.

Subrahmanyam, Sanjay. "Du Tage au Gange au XVIe siècle: Une conjoncture millénariste à l'échelle eurasiatique," *Annales: Histoires, Sciences Sociales* 56, no. 1 (2001): 51–84.

Sulayman Gamal, Adel. "The Beginnings of Classical Arabic Poetry." In *Literary Heritage of Classical Islam: Arabic and Islamic Studies in Honor of James A. Bellamy*. Edited by Mustansir Mir, 45–54. Princeton, NJ: The Darwin Press, Inc., 1993.

Tamari, Salim. "Factionalism and Class Formation in Recent Palestinian History." In *Studies in the Economic and Social History of Palestine in the Nineteenth and Twentieth Centuries*. Edited by Roger Owen, 177–202. London: Macmillan; Oxford: St. Antony's, 1982.

Tezcan, Baki. "The 1622 Military Rebellion in Istanbul: A Historiographical Journey." In *Mutiny and Rebellion in the Ottoman Empire*. Edited by Jane Hathaway, 25–43. Madison, WI: University of Wisconsin Press, 2002.

Tezcan, Hülya, and Turgay Tezcan. *Türk Sancak Alemleri*. Ankara: Türk Tarih Kurumu Basımevi, 1992.

Toledano, Ehud R. "The Emergence of Ottoman-Local Elites in the Middle East and North Africa (1700–1900): A Framework for Research." In *Middle Eastern Politics and Ideas: A History from Within—Essays in Honour of Albert Hourani*. Edited by Ilan Pappé and Moshe Maʾoz, 145–62. London and New York: I. B. Tauris, 1997.

Trimingham, J. Spencer. *The Sufi Orders in Islam*. With a new foreword by John O. Voll. New York and Oxford: Oxford University Press, 1998 [1971, 1973].

Tritton, A. S. *The Rise of the Imams of Sanaa*. London: Oxford University Press, 1925. Reprint, Westport, CT: Hyperion Press, Inc., 1981.

Türk Ansiklopedisi, *s.v.* "Boncuk."

———, *s.v.* "Monçuk," by H. Eren.

———, *s.v.* "Tahtacılar," by E. R. Fiğlalı.

Uluhogian, Gabriella. *Un' antica mappa dell'Armenia: monasteri e santuari dal 1. al 17. secolo*. Ravenna: Longo, 2000.

Uzunçarşılı, İ. H. *Osmanlı Devleti Teşkilâtından Kapukulu Ocakları*. 2 Vols. Ankara: Türk Tarih Kurumu Basımevi, 1943.

Van Arendonk, C. *Les Débuts de l'imamat zaidite au Yémen*. Translated by Jacques Ryckmans. Leiden: E. J. Brill, 1960.

Vaughan, Dorothy M. *Europe and the Turk: A Pattern of Alliances, 1350–1700*. Liverpool: University of Liverpool Press, 1954. Reprint, New York: AMS Press, 1976.

Voll, John O. "Linking Groups in the Networks of Eighteenth-Century Revivalist Scholars: The Mizjaji Family in Yemen." In *Eighteenth-Century Renewal and Reform in Islam*. Edited by John O. Voll and Nehemiah Levtzion, 69–92. Syracuse: Syracuse University Press, 1987.

Vryonis, Speros, Jr. "Byzantine Circus Factions and Islamic *Futuwwa* Organizations (*Neaniai, Fityān, Aḥdāth*)." *Byzantinische Zeitschrift* 58 (1965): 46–59.

Waldman, Marilyn R. *Toward a Theory of Historical Narrative: A Case Study in Perso-Islamicate Historiography*. Columbus, OH: Ohio State University Press, 1980.

Walker, Bethany J. "Rethinking Mamluk Textiles." *Mamluk Studies Review* 4 (2000): 167–217.

Walker, Paul E. "Purloined Insignia: Stolen Symbols of Legitimacy in the ᶜAbbasid-Fatimid Rivalry." Paper delivered at the Middle East Studies Association conference, Providence, RI, November 1996.

Walker, Warren S., ed. *A Turkish Folktale: The Art of Behçet Mahir*. New York and London: Garland Publishing, Inc., 1996.

Wallace, David, dir. *In the Footsteps of Alexander the Great*. 2 Parts. Maya Vision production for the British Broadcasting Corporation and Maryland Public Television. Alexandria, VA: PBS Home Video, 1997.

Walls, Jan and Yvonne, eds. and trans. *Classical Chinese Myths*. Hong Kong: Joint Publishing Co., 1984.

Welch, Stuart Cary. *Imperial Mughal Painting*. New York: George Braziller, 1978.

Wellhausen, Julius. *The Arab Kingdom and Its Fall*. Translated by Margaret Graham Weir. Beirut: Khayats, 1927.

Werner, Edward T. C. *Ancient Tales and Folklore of China*. 2d ed. London: Bracken Books, 1986 [1922].

Wilford, John Noble. "Ruins in Yemeni Desert Mark Route of Frankincense Trade." *New York Times*, 28 January 1997, pp. B9–10.

Winter, Michael. *Egyptian Society under Ottoman Rule, 1517–1798*. London and New York: Routledge, 1992.

———. "Ottoman Egypt, 1525–1609." In *The Cambridge History of Egypt*. Vol. 2: *Modern Egypt from 1517 to the end of the Twentieth Century*. Edited by M. W. Daly, 1–33. Cambridge: Cambridge University Press, 1998.

Wirth, Andrzej. "Semiological Aspects of the *Taᶜziyeh*." In *Taᶜziyeh: Ritual and Drama in Iran*. Edited by Peter J. Chelkowski, 32–39. New York: New York University Press and Soroush Press, 1979.

Wittek, Paul. "Devshirme and Shariᶜa." *BSOAS* 17 (1955): 271–78.

Yavuz, Hulusi. *Kâbe ve Haremeyn için Yemen'de Osmanlı Hâkimiyeti (1517–1571)*. Istanbul: Marmara Üniversitesi İlâhiyat Fakültesi, 1984.

Yérasimos, Stephane. *Légendes d'empire: La formation de Constantinople et de Sainte-Sophie dans les traditions turques*. Paris: Institut Français d'Études Anatoliennes d'Istanbul and Jean Maisonneuve Successeur Librairie d'Amérique et d'Orient, 1990.

Zajaczkowski, Ananiasz. "La plus ancienne traduction turque en vers du *Šâh-nāme* de l'état mamelouk d'Égypte (XV–XVIe siècles)." Türk Dili Araştırmaları Yıllığı. *Belleten* 3 (1966): 51–63.

Zaki, Abdel Rahman. *Aᶜlām al-duwal al-ᶜarabiyya wa'l-islāmiyya*. Cairo: Matbaᶜat al-Tahrir, 1958.

———. *Al-Aᶜlām wa-shārāt al-mulk fī wādī al-Nīl*. Cairo: Dar al-Maᶜaref, 1948.

——— [Zaky, A. Rahman]. "On Islamic Swords." In *Studies in Islamic Art and Architecture in Honour of Professor K.A.C. Cresswell*, 270–91. Cairo: The

American University in Cairo Press, published for the Center for Arabic Studies, 1965.

Ze'evi, Dror. *An Ottoman Century: The District of Jerusalem in the 1600s.* Albany: State University of New York Press, 1996.

Zygulski, Zdzislaw, Jr. *Ottoman Art in the Service of the Empire.* New York: New York University Press, 1992.

Index